America's Election Handbook 2024

What to Know for the 2024 Election

By

Charles Patton

America's Election Handbook 2024.

Notice

Despite efforts to be factual and honest, errors and omissions are inevitable. I apologize for any inaccuracies, misinterpretations, exaggerations, or misremembered details. I encourage readers to point out significant flaws so that they can be corrected in future editions. I used the referential terminology (e.g., forefathers, congressman, and "he" when it was historically accurate, and more recent terminology such as congresspeople in later years when other genders began being recognized for serving in those roles.

When I refer to Democrats or Republicans, it means the political party as a policymaking and direction-setting body for their candidates and members or the majority of the party members as a group.

Additionally, I did not update punctuation to reflect current standards, nor did I correct words identified as spelling errors in historical documents (for example, "chuse [sic]") or party platforms, even when terms are used such as "Eskimo," which should be more accurately referred to as "Inuit." I relied on statistics from recent years, acknowledging that while not necessarily from this year due to data limitations, these figures are valid and reflective of trends that would extend into our current year. I also included information from political platforms going back up to 20 years (five presidential terms) to get a full picture of the parties' principles. Also, in discussing party positions, I have done so with the parties in alphabetical order: Democrats first, then Republicans, an arbitrary decision. I have tried to be thorough but undoubtedly there will be issues that I failed to cover, completely or in part. I offer my sincere apologies in advance for those omissions. If I misrepresented either party's position on anything, again, I apologize.

Short Mystery Press
ISBN: 979-8-9888054-8-9
Written for and sponsored by: Applied Market Solutions, LLC
Editing by Andrew Dawson through reedsy.com and Allesa Ciambriello
Book template and distribution by Amazon and PublishDrive.com.
Cover by artist: Diogo Leite of Book Design Company through 99Designs.com

Role of Artificial Intelligence (AI) in this book: I found OpenAI's ChatGPT and Google's Bard helpful, as I am dyslexic, in cleaning up, simplifying, organizing, and clarifying my writing and in finding or checking sources. I am responsible for the selection of subjects, outlines, ChatGPT prompts, opinions, intentions, proposals, and all the writing.

CONTENTS

Preface

The Genesis of This Book

In a rustic restaurant in Branson, Missouri, I regularly engaged in discussions with two friends: one an avid conservative, often referencing Fox TV, and the other, a neutral observer. My conservative friend was passionate in his beliefs, presenting viewpoints with a radical fervor that often conflicted with my rational thinking and intuition. In response, I would introduce alternative, more moderate perspectives, hoping to shift our discourse away from extremes. Our neutral observer helped keep our discussions from spiraling into rancor. My balancing act sometimes gave the impression that I leaned liberal, though this wasn't always my truth across various topics. Sometimes I was just playing devil's advocate. My intention was to encourage deeper reflection on the issues. Our conversations were always marked by mutual respect and a genuine desire to understand and subtly shape each other's views. Through these dialogues, I was inspired to delve deeper into various issues, seeking insights to enlighten my friends and other voters and find common ground between the contrasting political viewpoints.

My Diverse Background

My early political perspectives were shaped by growing up in a politically diverse household, with a Republican father and a Democratic mother, and my later education at the University of Illinois and the University of Chicago Graduate School of Business. For the most part, I hold conservative views on economic matters and the Constitution while favoring various liberal policies in other areas. These balanced views are shared by many Americans who prefer a stable, prosperous society with common goals despite having differing methods to achieve them.

My Political Beliefs: A Mixture of Ideologies

As a result of my upbringing, education, and the influence of my friends and associates, I do not align entirely with either Republicans or Democrats, reflecting a sentiment shared among many Americans. My voting history spans both parties based on prevalent issues at the time and candidate qualities. I value critical evaluation over unquestioning party loyalty. My stance is best described as an "American Principlest," with diverse beliefs rooted in American principles.

The Role of Political Parties: A Critique

I question the necessity of strict party allegiances, as political beliefs often transcend such narrow affiliations. The evolution of party ideologies and the lack of party-member consultation in decision-making contribute to the divisiveness of American politics. I advocate for a system where individuals are recognized for their stances on issues rather than party labels.

Qualification

My analysis of different political parties below is usually based on generalizations. It's essential to understand that not every opinion within a party is therefore covered. Each party contains a range of diverse perspectives, and there are always exceptions and contradictions. Furthermore, political views are not static; they change over time due to social, economic, and political shifts.

Initiating Constructive Debate

This book promotes informed and open-minded discussions on governance, encouraging an understanding democracy as envisioned by the Founding Fathers. It explores American politics to bridge divisions and foster unity among Americans.

Key facts and **proposals** are highlighted in distinct boxes for clarity and emphasis, aiming to educate new voters and stimulate constructive conversations among the electorate to lead us toward a more unified and consensus-driven America. The **proposals** reflect more of the author's independent and commonsense viewpoint.

Exploring the Founding Fathers' Perspectives

The Founding Fathers, including prominent figures like George Washington, Thomas Jefferson, and John Adams, held diverse views that shaped our nation. This book explores what the Founding Fathers intended while highlighting that we should rely on their combined wisdom and not just individual perspectives to understand their intentions.

A Maxim for Personal and National Integrity

Do NOT think what other people tell you to think. Look into your heart and mind, seek out the facts, and decide what is best for yourself, your family, friends, and our country.

If, upon reading the maxim above, you immediately thought, *I already know what's best for myself, my family, my friends, and my country*, then this book may not suit you. It is intended for readers who possess open minds and are willing to seek common ground and compromise while helping to guide our country back to a more stable, peaceful society. This does not mean you are expected to agree with everything in this book.

Initial Concerns

Here are some examples of aspects of our governance that should concern us all and which motivated the writing of this book. This is a sampling of issues that will be further discussed as we proceed.

A Lack of Critical Thinking

There is a rising concern among many Americans about the erosion of independent critical thinking skills, a trend closely linked with the escalating political polarization in the country and the speed at which word can now spread, good and bad. This issue is evident in how people engage with and understand media content, the growing influence of echo chambers in social media, and the increasingly divisive political discourse that discourages open-minded examination of opposing opinions or a diversity of viewpoints. These factors contribute to a polarized society where balanced, independent thought is overshadowed by partisan alignment, regardless of the truth.

This issue transcends the often superficial and polarizing rhetoric of prominent media figures across the political spectrum. Whether it's conservative or liberal commentators, there is a tendency to rely on sound bites, selective facts, fearmongering, and emotionally-charged rhetoric, including sarcasm, insinuations, name-calling, and even lies. Such methods, unfortunately, resonate mostly with audiences already holding extreme views, potentially discouraging critical analysis and reasoned debate.

The real problem lies in the way these communication tactics hinder constructive discourse and impede the development of balanced, well-informed perspectives.

Therefore, it's crucial to promote a nuanced, thoughtful approach in our political conversations. Prioritizing open-mindedness, encouraging critical thinking, and fostering debate beyond extreme ideologies is essential. Such efforts can mitigate polarization and cultivate a more informed, discerning, and peaceful citizenry, thereby laying the foundation for stability and economic progress in a harmonious society.

American Voter Apathy

According to the U.S. Census Bureau, the total voting-age population in the U.S. as of July 1, 2023, was 258,334,000 people. In the 2020 presidential election, 66.8% of eligible voters cast a ballot. This was the highest voter turnout rate since 1988 (George H.W. Bush vs. Michael Dukakis). But that means that 85,766,888 citizens who were eligible to vote, didn't. Is it that non-voting Americans trust those who do vote to choose the best candidate for their needs? Or do they not realize that an economy with steady growth, low crime, quality healthcare, secure retirement, and low inflation may depend on their participation? People often say one vote will not matter, so why waste my time? When a lot of people think that way, an election can swing from one candidate to the other, from one ideology to the opposite (more on this later). Collective apathy is a significant threat to the health of any democracy, as it can lead to unrepresentative governance and the erosion of citizen rights and freedoms.

Political campaigns commonly and intentionally employ strong, emotionally-charged language to mobilize their supporters and attract voters from other parties, which, while effective, can also lead to greater polarization.

Examples of Where a Single Vote Mattered

1. Virginia House of Delegates, 2017: This race for a single seat ended in a tie with more than 23,000 votes cast! Republican David Yancey and Democrat Shelly Simonds were neck and neck after multiple recounts, in the 94th District, resulting in the decision being made by a random drawing.
2. Vermont Democratic State Senate Primary, 2016: In this contest, in the Windham District, the outcome swung on just one vote out of more than 7,400 cast. Sarah Johnson emerged victorious by a hair's breadth over Becca Balint.

Note: It hasn't happened yet in the national election. The closest presidential election in U.S. history in terms of the popular vote was in 1960 between John F. Kennedy and Richard Nixon. Kennedy won with a slim margin, receiving only 0.17% more votes than Nixon. This equated to roughly 112,000 of more than 68 million votes cast. Of course, the more critical count was the electoral college votes, which were 303 for Kennedy and 219 for Nixon (a third candidate received 15). The large difference in the spreads between the popular votes and the electoral votes was caused by close wins in states with large numbers of electoral votes (e.g., Illinois, Texas, and Missouri). How electoral votes are awarded to candidates is up to the individual states to decide (only Maine and Nebraska assign electoral votes in proportion to the popular votes).

Conveying Party Positions Is Challenging

Explaining the positions of political parties is challenging. Their stances often change from what they promise during campaigns and can be complex, hard to simplify, and sometimes deliberately vague to ensure flexibility. They may also conceal hidden influences. Every effort was made to ensure an unbiased presentation here, avoiding manipulation, contextual misrepresentation, or distortion of party perspectives.

Parties Represent Only Some Citizens

Even when a party clearly states its intentions, its views may not reflect those of many citizens or even members of their own party. Party representatives can be out of touch or swayed by external influences. With only two parties, power is centralized in their leaders, limiting citizens to just two sets of candidate positions.

The two parties generally represent opposing views, often to the extremes. They focus on the issues that will stimulate and attract votes, and accordingly do not adequately reflect wider American public opinion, which to a large degree is closer to the middle on most issues.

Research shows that many Americans hold moderate political views, contrary to the polarized portrayal often seen in the media. A study led by Professor Anthony Fowler at the University of Chicago suggests that moderates are more prevalent and influential in the electorate than is commonly believed, as they are more influenced by candidate ideologies than strict party affiliations.[01-01] Additionally, an article in *The Politics Watcher* notes that the majority of Americans' views fall between the far left and far right, indicating that media emphasis on extreme viewpoints might not accurately reflect the general public's opinions .[01-02] Gallup's 2021 data supports this, showing that 37% of Americans identify as moderate, compared to 36% as conservative and 25% as liberal, highlighting the stable presence of moderates in the American political landscape and showing that the moderates are the ones who control the winning votes.[01-03]

When a political party wins the majority of votes and gains power, the policies and changes they implement often do not reflect the preferences or needs of the opposing voters. This situation can occur when one party controls the presidency and Congress and influences the Supreme Court, leading to the concerns and voices of nearly half the electorate being overlooked or overshadowed. Such scenarios highlight the need for a more equitable and balanced political system that considers the views and needs of the entire electorate rather than just the winning majority party once elections are over.

Parties Manipulate to Keep Control

Our government was founded based on preventing the same people from being in power all the time – namely kings, queens, or dictators. That is why term limits were included in our Constitution for some offices and why we later ended up with two parties. The overwhelming intention of our governmental structure as defined in our Constitution is "checks and balances." Unfortunately, sometimes when one party gets more control than the other, the checks and balances are negated.

In recent years, the two parties have also arranged rules and regulations to make it exceedingly difficult for independent thinkers or other political parties to vote into power anyone not sponsored by the Democrats or Republicans.

The 'Hanging Chad' incident during the 2000 U.S. Presidential election, in which George W. Bush competed against Al Gore, involved difficulty in determining voter intent due to incompletely punched paper ballots. This issue led to a prolonged and highly contested recount in Florida as it highlighted several issues in the voting process and led to significant changes in election laws and practices. While the primary focus was on improving the accuracy and reliability of voting systems, there were also indirect consequences that affected third-party candidates. Here are a couple of examples:

1. **Stricter Ballot Access Laws**: Following the 2000 election, several states revised their ballot access laws, making it more difficult for third-party and independent candidates to get on the ballot. These revisions often involved raising the number of required signatures and setting stricter submission deadlines, disproportionately impacting candidates with fewer resources and organizational support than those backed by the major parties.

2. **Heightened Focus on Major Party Candidates**: Media focus, campaign financing, and public discourse have increasingly favored Democratic and Republican candidates, hindering third-party and independent candidates' visibility and credibility. These candidates often face difficulties in securing media coverage, participating in debates, and fundraising, which further limits their electoral influence.

Contemporary electoral barriers echo the now-abolished Poll Tax of 1966, which hindered low-income and minority voters. Today, similar obstacles emerge through redistricting tactics favoring specific parties and the increasing financial and procedural challenges of running for office. For example:

Florida Requirements to Run for Offices (2024)

U.S. Senate

State	Office	Party	Signatures required	Filing fee	Filing deadline
Florida	U.S. Senate	Ballot-qualified party	144,419	$10,440	4/26/2024
Florida	U.S. Senate	Unaffiliated	144,419	$6,960	4/26/2024

U.S. House

State	Office	Party	Signatures required	Filing fee	Filing deadline
Florida	U.S. House	Ballot-qualified party	2,568	$10,440	4/26/2024
Florida	U.S. House	Unaffiliated	2,568	$6,960	4/26/2024

Note: Unaffiliated fees are less than those for party-affiliated candidates because unaffiliated candidates have other costs of running that parties fund for their affiliates. In 2024 in Florida, if you do not have $6,960 and 144,419 signatures from registered voters, which is exceedingly difficult to obtain without the help of an organized political party, you cannot run for the Senate. The two-party-system is designed to preclude, for the most part, other viewpoints from being brought into debates and forces people to choose between two imperfect options. Florida is just an example. Other states have similar structures.

Political parties continually vie for control of Congress, each aiming to secure the most seats. The aim of this power struggle is to implement their ideological agendas, which they believe are in the nation's best interests. However, a large portion of the electorate often disagree.

The enduring tenure of many congressional members, often spanning multiple terms, has entrenched a system where incumbents possess substantial advantages. These include widespread name recognition and significant financial and promotional support from their parties, supplemented by government-provided benefits like franking privileges for free mailings. Such privileges can tilt the electoral playing field in favor of incumbents over new challengers. This pattern of repeated reelection transforms congressional roles into near-permanent career positions, extending the influence of political parties over multiple presidential terms.

Parties wield significant control over their members by orchestrating campaign promotions and strategic campaign fundraising. Officeholders feel pressurized to toe the party line, aligning their votes with party stances to ensure continued support and a secured spot in future elections. Consequently, decision-making is centralized in the hands of **party leaders**, whose impact on legislative outcomes often surpasses their authority, as they are not democratically elected by the people to these influential positions.

Party Leader Selection Processes

The election process for a national political party chairperson in the United States varies. The president typically selects the national party chairperson when a party is in power. For other national political parties, the chairperson is elected through a vote by the national committee, which includes party officials from each state, such as state party chairs, vice chairs, and other leaders. The specific duties of a chairperson depend on each party's structure and bylaws, with common responsibilities including overseeing party operations, election strategy, candidate recruitment, and fundraising. The chairpersons of the Democratic National Committee and the Republican National Committee, for instance, are full-time, paid employees. This process can lead to the perception that party elites have significant influence, as the committee members are often seen as part of the party establishment. We will discuss later the influence of the party chairs on our representation.

Moreover, the current polarization between Democrats and Republicans has escalated to a point where bipartisan compromise borders on being unattainable. If this extremism exacerbates, our government could become entirely gridlocked. This entrenched division hinders effective governance and balanced legislative solutions.

Two Parties

In Part II of this book, we will contrast the views and ideologies of our two major political parties. These first-tier parties, the Democrats and Republicans, are presented alphabetically. The second-tier parties – the Libertarian Party, the Green Party, the Constitution Party, the Socialist Party USA, and others – are only included in a broad way and not the primary focus. Their coverage has been limited due to their small membership base, narrowly-defined party platforms, or perceived overlap of many of their positions with those of the major parties. We refer to these lesser parties as second-tier for convenience, not to diminish their significance, views, or aspirations to become significant national players.

The second-tier parties have played a crucial role in pushing the boundaries of political discourse and placing pressure on the major parties by advocating for their more extreme or different positions. However, by embracing such extreme stances, these second-tier parties have constrained their ability to gain widespread national recognition.

Readers are encouraged to "consider the source" when evaluating political commentary, including herein. While I have my convictions and biases, I have strived to be objective when commenting on the positions of the political parties.

I acknowledge that my analysis may have some imperfections, and I approach the critique of parties or viewpoints with a discerning eye. I provide insights where they are constructive. I will propose ideas when deemed appropriate. My intention is primarily to examine broader issues and avoid targeting specific party leaders, members, or current officeholders.

Must We Have Only Two Parties?

The dominance of two major parties in the American political landscape and the significant sway party leaders hold over their members raises serious concerns. Congressional incumbents often grapple with the dilemma of adhering to party directives, primarily driven by the necessity to secure support for reelection, such as funding and endorsements. This situation leads to a troubling scenario where representatives might prioritize party agendas over the interests of their constituents or their own convictions. As described above, the underlying dependence on party support for electoral success compels legislators to align closely with party leadership, raising questions about the true representation of citizen interests in governance.

A critical aspect of this dynamic is understanding who influences the party leadership. Often, it is wielded by large donors and lobbyists, especially those representing major business interests. The extent of this influence is a matter of ongoing debate, with concerns that it has led to governance skewed in favor of these powerful entities. This perception is further complicated by a lack of ethical oversight regarding interactions between lobbyists and non-elected party leaders. We will explore the issues surrounding party leaders and lobbyists as we proceed.

Is It Practical to Have More Than Two Parties?

While some argue that a multi-party system is impractical, it is a reality in many countries. There are valid arguments for a two-party system, such as avoiding prolonged elections and the complexity of run-off votes in the case of no clear majority (e.g., 33% of votes for each of three parties). Multi-round voting, coalition formation, and interim officeholders are necessary for such systems, which can lead to chaotic election processes and complicated dispute resolutions. However, it is possible to effectively overcome these challenges, as other countries across the globe have proved.

Another downside of introducing a third major party is that it might draw voters away from the dominant party on that side of the political spectrum, effectively "splitting the vote" of those on the right or left to the advantage of the other side. This could mean a right-leaning party winning an election despite there being more left-leaning voters, or vice versa.

Discrepancies Between Party Stances and Actions

We should be concerned about the disparity between what political parties claim to stand for and their actual deeds. This gap in performance versus promise is exacerbated by a lack of accountability among our elected officials between elections.

Furthermore, in our current political climate, the average citizen often lacks crucial information on key political issues and does not understand terms commonly tossed around in debates. What does left wing really mean? What does right wing really mean? How do conservatives differ from liberals? How do liberals differ from socialists? Where do progressives fit in? Are any of these communists? Is America a democracy or a republic? We will clarify these terms later.

Also, some voters do not know or understand what the major parties really want to accomplish. As we already mentioned, the parties will promise one thing during campaigning and then do something different once in power. So, what is their actual agenda? Some of their intentions may never be made public.

How can we tell what their real agenda is? Do they work for "big money" interests and the "major donors" to their party and campaigns? How many of us are aware of party manifestos for elections past, present, or future? How much can we tell about their true agenda by what they have and have not done? Are open government laws working? Is the Freedom of Information Act (FOIA) functioning effectively? How can we hold political parties accountable for their contradictions and shortcomings? These are questions to which many citizens would like answers. Fortunately, a deep understanding of civics isn't required for voting, but having some basic knowledge can be helpful. This book aims to equip the reader with essential information about our governance, making it accessible and relevant, regardless of your prior knowledge.

Parties Disguise Where They Really Stand

As voters, we need to understand where political parties stand on the ideological spectrum and how close or far they are from the extremes. Parties may have identical views on some issues, share the same objectives with different approaches on others, or be radically opposed on another. While parties declare their goals, they also focus on preventing the other party's actions or undoing their predecessors' policies. Voters must discern political parties' actual positions and objectives to make informed choices. What they truly stand for is muddy at best.

Politicians often use deceptive bill titles, both at state and federal levels, to mislead the public about the true intent of legislation, assuming citizens won't look at the details.

Examples of Deceptive Federal Bill Titles

1. **USA PATRIOT ACT** (Uniting and Strengthening America by Providing Appropriate Tools Required to Intercept and Obstruct Terrorism Act): Enacted shortly after the tragic events of September 11, 2001, the title invoked a sense of patriotism and determination to fight against terrorism. While it did contain measures to bolster national security, it also expanded the government's surveillance powers, sparking concerns about civil liberties and privacy.

2. **NO CHILD LEFT BEHIND ACT:** Signed into law in 2002, the title implied a commitment to ensuring every student received a high-quality education. Nonetheless, this law initiated a contentious framework of standardized testing and accountability that some critics contend had unintended consequences, such as narrowing educational curricula and excessively focusing on testing.

3. **THE INFLATION REDUCTION ACT**: This was passed by the House of Representatives and the Senate in July 2022 and signed into law by President Biden in August 2022. The title suggests a primary focus on reducing inflation, but it actually includes a wide range of provisions that go far beyond this, including:
    a. **Climate change**: Invests more than $369 billion in mitigation efforts.
    b. **Healthcare**: Allows Medicare to negotiate drug prices, extends subsidies for health insurance premiums, and caps out-of-pocket costs for prescription drugs.
    c. **Taxation**: Imposes a 15% minimum tax on the book income of corporations with profits of more than $1 billion, expands IRS's enforcement capabilities, and closes wealthy taxpayer loopholes.

    Critics of the bill argue that its title is misleading because it does not accurately reflect its wide-ranging scope and that it is tapping into public concerns about inflation to advance a much broader agenda.

Examples of Deceptive State Bill Titles FLORIDA

1. **PARENTAL RIGHTS IN EDUCATION ACT**: In 2021, Florida passed this bill with the intention of banning discussions on sexual orientation and gender identity in K-3 classrooms. Supporters see it as protecting parental rights and age-appropriate curricula, but critics consider it potentially discriminatory against LGBTQ+ students, that it restricts diversity and inclusion conversations, and that it infringes on parental rights.

2. **FLORIDA - STUDENT SUCCESS ACT**: Historically, the Florida Legislature uses titles like this for bills about education. Although the name suggests a dedication to enhancing student outcomes, the actual content can be multifaceted and has in the past included controversial provisions related to standardized testing, school choice, rules to restrict teachers, or other education policies that have the potential to create divisions among stakeholders.

3. **ARIZONA - THE PROTECT THE ELDERLY ACT**: This bill, introduced in 2017, would have made it more difficult for seniors to access affordable healthcare had it passed, having the opposite effect to what the name suggests.

4. **MISSOURI - THE RIGHT TO FARM ACT**: This bill, passed by the Missouri Legislature in 2022, made it more difficult to sue agribusinesses for environmental damage. The title suggests that it is designed to protect farmers' rights, but its actual provisions could have the opposite effect by allowing agribusinesses to pollute the environment with impunity.

5. **CONNECTICUT - AN ACT CONCERNING VARIOUS PAY EQUITY AND FAIRNESS MATTERS (HB5386)**: The bill was presented as addressing pay equity and the gender pay gap, focusing on equal pay for equal work. However, it had a specific scope: prohibiting employers from asking about wage history unless disclosed by the employee, with exceptions for legal requirements. It did not prevent inquiries into other types of compensation elements as long as their value was not discussed.

Shifting Party Allegiances

Constituents from a certain region tend to align with one or other of the two main parties (e.g., red and blue states), although this has shifted over time. For instance, the South was solidly pro-Democrat until the mid-1960s, when it turned Republican after the civil rights laws passed. The reasons for this shift, whether bigotry, state rights, or religious influences, are unclear. What is evident is that political support should not be taken for granted, and parties should change to adapt to voter's wants and needs.

What Parties Pitch vs. What They Deliver

Political commentators often use strong, sometimes extreme, rhetoric to engage their audience, frequently tapping into emotions like fear and anger. It's important for voters (True Patriots) to critically evaluate these messages, distinguishing between political strategies and the actual intentions of government and politics. In today's media landscape, fostering such critical thinking and objective analysis is more important than ever.

Many citizens are weary of the lies, innuendos, dirty tricks, name-calling, and distortions. Conversely, others merely echo the catchphrases, buzzwords, and derogatory nicknames (e.g., Small Trump, Sleepy Joe, Ron DeSanctimonious) used by their favorite pundits. Thus, we must ask ourselves: What principles do we believe in? Are we patriots or parrots?

For these reasons and all those above, this book will attempt to explore the party positions and provide enough information to motivate all citizens to vote in every election and to help them decide rationally who or which party to vote for.

PART I: OUR GOVERNANCE HISTORY

In the first of this book's three parts, we will revisit some of our historical foundations. While not providing an exhaustive history lesson, we will examine vital principles enshrined in our foundational documents, which were subjects of intense debate among our nation's Founding Fathers.

Their roles, such as Jefferson's drafting of the Declaration of Independence and Adams' involvement in early diplomatic missions, offer significant insight into their principles. Moreover, historical records and documents from the era confirm their beliefs, and their influence on their contemporaries cannot be denied. However, it must be acknowledged that the Founding Fathers, who thought deeply before shaping our country, exhibited a wide array of complex and multifaceted opinions.

Chapter 1: What Life Was Like in 1775-1787

Colonial Society

The American colonies were predominantly agrarian societies with a population that included settlers of various ethnic backgrounds, including English, Dutch, German, and others. People lived in small, tightly-knit communities. Life was hard – most families were engaged in labor-intensive farming activities and onerous household chores. Shipping was also a major industry.

Limited Technology

Technology and infrastructure were rudimentary compared to today. Transportation took time, relying as it did on horses, carriages, and boats. Communication was also slow, with news and information spreading primarily through word of mouth, newspapers, and printed pamphlets.

Social Structure

Colonial society was hierarchical, with a class system that included wealthy landowners, merchants, and professionals at the top, followed by a larger middle class of skilled craftsmen and small landholders, and a lower class of laborers, indentured servants, and enslaved individuals. Social mobility was limited, and one's social status often depended on birth and wealth.[01-05]

Religion

Religion played a significant role in daily life, and many colonists were devout Christians, with various other denominations present, including Puritans, Anglicans, Quakers, Jews, and Baptists.[01-05] Religious values influenced everything from education to moral behavior. Amid this diverse religious and cultural melting pot, Thomas Jefferson and John Adams emerged as prominent figures.

Thomas Jefferson

Thomas Jefferson fulfilled many roles during his lifetime, including the author of the Declaration of Independence, representing Virginia in the Continental Congress, Virginia's governor in 1779, the first secretary of state under George Washington, Minister to France in 1785, John Adams' vice president from 1797 to 1801, and ultimately becoming the third president of the United States from 1801 to 1809.

Jefferson is often described as a Deist, meaning he held religious naturalism beliefs. Deism is a philosophical position that rejects traditional religious teachings and supernatural aspects of religion in favor of a belief in a creator or God who set the universe in motion but does not intervene in human affairs.

Jefferson's religious views were unconventional for his time, when Christianity was the predominant religion in the United States. He was critical of organized religion, particularly institutionalized Christianity. He is quoted as saying, "Christianity neither is nor ever was a part of the common law."[19-01]

He believed in the separation of church and state yet strongly advocated religious freedom. He is best known for his writings on this topic, including the Virginia Statute for Religious Freedom, which he authored in 1777 as a precursor to the First Amendment to the United States Constitution.

While Jefferson had a complex and unorthodox relationship with religion, he is often associated with promoting secularism, religious tolerance, and the idea that an individual's religious beliefs are a private matter that should not be subject to state interference.[06]

John Adams

Another influential figure, John Adams, represented Massachusetts in the Continental Congress and served as a diplomat in France, the Netherlands, and Great Britain. He was crucial in negotiating the Treaty of Paris in 1783, formally ending the Revolutionary War. Adams also held the position of vice president under George Washington from 1789 to 1797, before becoming the second president of the United States from 1797 to 1801. The election of 1800, when he lost to Thomas Jefferson, marked a significant milestone in American history as it represented the peaceful transfer of power from one political party to another, a tradition we have maintained for 235 years and counting.

Adams also left a lasting impact on the U.S. Constitution. He played a pivotal role in crafting the Massachusetts Constitution of 1780, which served as a model for numerous state constitutions and significantly influenced the development of the U.S. Constitution.

Additionally, Adams authored a three-part essay titled "Thoughts on Government," in which he articulated his perspectives on government and contributed to shaping America's republican principles.

Overview of John Adam's Essay

Part I - John Adams' Object of Government:

In this section, Adams discussed the fundamental purpose of government. He argued that government exists to promote and protect the "general happiness" and well-being of society. He believed that government should be designed to serve the common good and secure the rights and liberties of its citizens. Adams also emphasized the importance of a government that is responsive to the will of the people.

Part II - The Form of Government Suitable to the United States:

Adams explored the idea of a balanced government, which he believed was essential for the stability and effectiveness of a republic. He advocated for separate executive, legislative, and judicial branches of government, each with its own distinct powers and responsibilities. Adams argued that this separation of powers would prevent any one branch from becoming too powerful and would provide a system of checks and balances.

Part III - The True Principles of Government Examined and Applied:

In the final part of the essay, Adams delved into the principles of republicanism and the importance of a written constitution. He argued that a republican government should be based on the rule of law and a constitution that clearly defines the powers and limitations of government. Adams also stressed the need for a system of representation in which elected officials are accountable to the people. He favored a bicameral legislature, with one house representing the people directly and the other representing the interests of the states.

In his essay, Adams consistently emphasized the importance of virtue and public morality in sustaining a republican government. He believed that a virtuous citizenry was essential for the success of a self-governing society. The standards of virtue and morality have evolved significantly since Adams' day, but the need for these qualities in America remains as relevant as ever.

Significantly, Adams' "Thoughts on Government" helped shape the prevailing thought of his era. His ideas contributed substantially to the development of the U.S. Constitution and the structure of the American government. Adams' notions regarding the separation of powers and the necessity of written constitutions remain foundational principles in American governance and political thought.

John Adams was a Unitarian. Unitarianism is a Christian theological movement that rejects the traditional Christian doctrine of the Trinity, which holds that God is three persons in one: the Father, the Son (Jesus Christ), and the Holy Spirit. Instead, Unitarians believe in the unity or singularity of God and the humanity of Jesus Christ, as do Islam and Judaism, viewing Jesus as a great moral teacher and prophet but not as divine.

It is important to note that during the American revolutionary period, there was a diversity of religious beliefs, which was reflected in the eclectic and unorthodox views of the Founding Fathers. They did not share the same uniform Christian beliefs.[06]

Adams' religious beliefs evolved, and he became more aligned with Unitarianism as he aged. Unitarian ministers and writings influenced him, and he attended Unitarian churches during his later years. However, he is quoted as saying, "The government of the United States is not, in any sense, founded on the Christian religion."[18] Adams was also known for his commitment to religious freedom and the separation of church and state, as reflected in his support for the Massachusetts Constitution's provision that protected religious liberty.

Other Founders on Church and State

Other prominent figures of the day supported the constitutional principle of separating church and state. James Madison, the fourth president, said, "The purpose of the separation of church and state is to keep forever from these shores the ceaseless strife that has soaked the soil of Europe with blood for so many centuries."[19-02] Thomas Paine also said about the separation of church and state, "All national institutions of churches, whether Jewish, Christian, or Turkish, appear to me no other than human inventions set up to terrify and enslave mankind and monopolize power and profit."[19-03]

It is accurate to say that America is not officially a Christian country, nor is it a theocracy. The United States was founded on the principles of religious freedom, as enshrined in the First Amendment to the Constitution, which prohibits the establishment of a state religion while protecting the free exercise of all religions. While some of the Founding Fathers were Christians and the nation has historically had a strong Christian influence, the Constitution and the Bill of Rights do not explicitly establish Christianity as the official religion of our country or bestow any privileges to Christian organizations, any more so than to other religions.

How These Two Founders Might Align with Today's Parties

We might characterize Jefferson as having conservative tendencies due to his preference for limited government and emphasis on self-sufficiency. On issues of religious freedom and freedom of expression, he could be viewed as having more liberal positions. Therefore, he might be considered independent in today's political landscape.

Conversely, Adams could be seen as having liberal inclinations because he supported a strong central government, had an unwavering commitment to the rule of law, and underscored the importance of a just legal system. Yet he aligned with conservative positions on security and having a robust national defense. Similarly, in contemporary terms, he might be classified as an independent.

These two major examples demonstrate how we did not need political parties back then. Simply addressing each issue on its own merits was sufficient.

Given the significance of such issues in our nation's history, we will examine many of the pressing concerns that remain pertinent today in chapters to follow.

Political Climate

The year 1775 was marked by growing tension between the American colonies and the British Crown. The colonies were increasingly asserting their desire for greater self-governance and resistance to British policies such as taxation without representation. Committees of Correspondence and other grassroots organizations were formed to coordinate opposition to British rule, and the Continental Congress was convened to address these issues.

It is crucial to recognize that the United States was founded on principles that emerged from thoughtful deliberation and organized rebellion against British rule rather than from unstructured mob violence. While the American Revolution involved acts of defiance, such as the Boston Tea Party, which could be seen as mob action, the overall movement was marked by strategic planning and coordination. The Founding Fathers engaged in intelligent deliberation, laying the groundwork for a new nation based on representative government and democratic ideals. This process included the formation of individual state governments that eventually united to create a federal system. This history underscores the importance of organized, rational efforts in establishing new governments.

Challenges and Hardships

Life in the colonies came with many challenges. Epidemics were common, and medical knowledge was limited. Healthcare insurance did not exist. Families produced their own food, clothing, and household goods. The threat of conflicts with Native American tribes was ever-present on the frontier. Citizens were independent; they had to be self-sufficient and rely on their own initiatives or the kindness of friends and neighbors, such as with barn-raisings. Education was only for the well-to-do. There were no governmental "safety nets," such as healthcare, education, or welfare, back then. So much has changed since our founding.

Chapter 2: History of Our Founding

Thomas Jefferson and John Adams were intimately engaged with all our Founding Fathers, and their writings reasonably reflect the collective intentions of our founders. Fifty-six Patriots signed the Declaration of Independence, including both Jefferson and Adams. Thirty-nine state representatives signed the Constitution. Interestingly, neither Jefferson nor Adams were among them, as Jefferson was the United States minister to France then, and John Adams was also in Europe, serving as the United States minister to Great Britain. Only eight men signed both: George Clymer, Benjamin Franklin, Robert Morris, George Read, Roger Sherman, James Wilson, George Wythe, and Thomas Fitzsimons.

What Is a Patriot?

Patriots are so loyal to their country that they will defend it with their lives. Being loyal requires that you think often and deeply about our country's leadership, the rules by which we are governed, and our current state of governance. This requires independent thought, not merely adopting what is seen on TV, heard on the radio, seen on social media, preached in church, or read in a newspaper. We are constantly bombarded by attempts to shape our opinions. But we must come to our own conclusions through our personal observations and experiences and reading, researching, and studying philosophies, beliefs, and ideas, not from the sound bites and rhetoric of extreme political pundits or politicians trying to force their own agendas upon you. Simply agreeing with something someone says without reflection is different from formulating an opinion based on your thoughts.

If we are patriots by this definition, then we must talk among ourselves and come to a consensus on how to make the changes that America needs. If we are not open to discussion and compromise, then we are doomed to continual deterioration of our liberty and freedom.

And as we consider our future, we should remember our founders' visions.

What Jefferson Wanted for America

Jefferson, as one of our Founding Fathers and our third president (1801-1809), had a vision for America that was shaped by his Enlightenment-era beliefs and political philosophy. Below are some key aspects of what he wanted for America:

Jefferson's Vision

Democracy and Republic: Jefferson believed in a democratic form of government where power ultimately resided with the people. He saw America as a republic, where citizens would have the right to elect their leaders and participate in government decision-making.

Limited Government: Jefferson was a strong advocate for limited government intervention in the lives of citizens. He believed that the government should protect individual rights and liberties, but otherwise should have a minimal role in people's affairs.

Individual Rights: Jefferson emphasized the importance of individual rights, including freedom of speech, religion, and the press. He is best known for drafting the Declaration of Independence in 1776, which declared that "all men are created equal" and have the unalienable rights of "life, liberty, and the pursuit of happiness."

Agrarian Society: Jefferson had a vision of America as an agrarian society, where most citizens were independent farmers. He believed that this way of life would promote self-sufficiency and reduce the potential for corruption associated with concentrated wealth.

Westward Expansion: Jefferson was a strong proponent of westward expansion, and, as president, he oversaw the Louisiana Purchase in 1803, which doubled the size of the United States. He believed that this expansion would provide opportunities for American citizens to own land and achieve economic independence.

Education: Jefferson was a strong advocate for public education, believing that an educated citizenry was essential for the success of a democratic republic. He founded the University of Virginia and advocated for public education at the state level.

Religious Freedom: Jefferson championed the idea of religious freedom and the separation of church and state. He is credited with coining the phrase "a wall of separation between church and state" in a letter to the Danbury Baptist Association in 1802.

Jefferson's vision for America was not without controversy, and his views and actions, particularly regarding issues like slavery and his relationship with Native American tribes, have been subjects of debate and criticism. However, his ideas and principles played a significant role in shaping the early American republic and continue to influence American political thought to this day.

Jefferson on Revising the Constitution

Jefferson believed that the Constitution should be revised over time. He said, "Whatever be the Constitution, great care must be taken to provide a mode of amendment when experience or change of circumstances shall have manifested that any part of it is unadapted to the good of the nation."[04]

Jefferson wrote, "Let us provide in our Constitution for its revision at stated periods. What these periods should be nature herself indicates. By the European tables of mortality, of the adults living at any one moment of time, a majority will be dead in about nineteen years. At the end of that period, then, a new majority is come into place; or, in other words, a new generation. Each generation is as independent as the one preceding, as that was of all which had gone before. It has then, like them, a right to choose for itself the form of government it believes most promotive of its own happiness; consequently, to accommodate to the circumstances in which it finds itself that received from its predecessors; and it is for the peace and good of mankind that a solemn opportunity of doing this every nineteen or twenty years should be provided by the Constitution, so that it may be handed on with periodical repairs from generation to generation to the end of time, if anything human can so long endure."[05]

What Adams Wanted for America

Adams, one of the Founding Fathers and the second president of the United States (1797-1801), had a vision for America shaped by his beliefs and principles.

Adams' Vision for America

Independence and Self-Governance: Like many of his contemporaries, Adams wanted an America independent from British rule. He played a crucial role in advocating for independence and was one of the drafters of the Declaration of Independence.

Republican Government: Adams was a staunch supporter of republican government, which meant a government where power was vested in elected representatives who served the people's interests. He believed in a system of checks and balances to prevent the concentration of power.

Strong Central Government: Adams also recognized the need for a strong central government to maintain order and protect the nation's interests, especially in foreign affairs. He played a role in drafting the Massachusetts Constitution of 1780, which served as a model for the U.S. Constitution.

Respect for the Rule of Law: Adams emphasized the importance of a society governed by the rule of law. He believed that laws should be applied impartially and that a just legal system was essential to protect individual rights and liberties.

A Strong Defense: As a diplomat and statesman, Adams recognized the importance of a strong national defense. He played a role in negotiations with European powers during the Revolutionary War and later as a diplomat in Europe.

Diplomacy and Foreign Relations: Adams advocated for diplomacy in resolving international conflicts. He is best known for his role in negotiating the Treaty of Paris in 1783, which officially ended the Revolutionary War and recognized American independence.

Civic Virtue and Education: Adams believed that civic virtue, or the commitment of citizens to the common good, was essential for the republic's success. He also supported education to promote civic knowledge and civic participation.

Adams' vision for America, like those of other Founding Fathers, was not without controversy, and there were differing opinions and debates among the Founders about the specifics of how the new nation should be structured and governed. Nonetheless, his ideas and contributions played a significant role in the early development of the United States.

Adams on the Constitution

About the need for future revisions to the Constitution, Adams said, in his book *A Defence [sic] of the Constitutions of Government of the United States of America* (1787), "No government can be perfect, and every government will require revision and amendment from time to time, as circumstances shall change or as the opinions of men shall vary."

Adams also had some thoughts about how long the Constitution might last. In a letter to David Humphreys in 1819, he wrote: "I do not think that our Republic will last forever. It will last for a long time, but it will not last forever. No government has ever lasted forever."

Comparing the Views of Adams and Jefferson

Jefferson's views were aligned more so with current-day Republicans while Adam's views were more akin to those of the Democrats, but it is not that simple. While lifelong friends, they often debated their opposing views:

1. **Foreign Aid**: Foreign aid includes a wide range of programs and initiatives to promote U.S. interests abroad, support international development, and address global government and federalism:
   a. Adams favored a strong central government and believed in a more centralized federal system. He supported a strong executive branch and was one of the architects of the Massachusetts Constitution, which had a two-chamber legislature and a governor with significant powers.
   b. Jefferson was a proponent of limited government and a strict interpretation of the Constitution. He believed in states' rights and a weaker federal government, favoring agrarian democracy and a decentralized system.

2. **Political Parties**:
   a. Adams was a Federalist and believed that political parties were a necessary and legitimate part of the political process. He saw them as necessary to maintain order and stability in government.
   b. Jefferson was a Democratic-Republican (later known as a Jeffersonian Republican) and believed that political parties were a potential threat to

democracy and should be minimized. He favored a more participatory and populist form of government.

3. **Economy and Finance**:
   a. Adams supported a strong national economy and the establishment of a national bank. He believed in a protective tariff system to promote domestic industries and economic growth.
   b. Jefferson was more wary of the financial system and believed in a limited role for the federal government in economic matters. He was a proponent of agrarianism and favored a more laissez-faire economic approach.

4. **Foreign Policy**:
   a. Adams, during his presidency, faced challenges like the Quasi-War with France and signed the Alien and Sedition Acts, which limited immigration and restricted freedom of speech. He prioritized maintaining peace with foreign powers.
   b. Jefferson, in contrast, pursued a policy of territorial expansion, most notably with the Louisiana Purchase. He was more focused on westward expansion and the growth of the United States' territory.

5. **Slavery**:
   a. Adams was against expanding slavery into new territories, but he did not take a strong stance against slavery itself, especially early in his political career.
   b. Jefferson, while he expressed concerns about slavery, owned enslaved people and did not take significant steps to end the institution during his lifetime.

How These Founders Felt about the Constitution

Americans have disagreed about our governance ever since our founding. Differences of opinion began with the drafting of our Constitution, and many are still being debated today.

In his letter to Adams on January 21, 1812, Jefferson made clear that he and Adams agreed on the Constitution and the structure of our government even though they held opposing viewpoints on certain administrative issues. Some areas where they disagreed were:

- Adams was for a strong federal government, including wanting a strong navy; Jefferson was against it.

- Adams wanted more federal authority; Jefferson preferred that states retain the authority.
- Adams was for a national bank; Jefferson was against it.
- Adams supported growth of manufacturing while Jefferson supported agriculture.[11,12]

They both considered the union of states to be important. Adams, responding on February 3, 1812, to a letter from Jefferson, expressed his concern about keeping the union together, saying (in Latin), "Small communities grow great through harmony, great ones fall to pieces through discord."[03] Our Founding Fathers believed in our Constitution and in the unity of the country. We should all be concerned that our "great one" could fall to pieces under the weight of political wrangling and squabbling parties more pre-occupied with their own self-interests than representing the genuine needs or desires of those they are meant to represent.

The Early Parties

The parties that arose following the time of Jefferson and Adams (early to mid-1800s) were the Whig Party, the early Democrats, and the Jeffersonians.

The Whig Party

The Whig Party was formed in the winter of 1833–1834 by former National Republicans such as Henry Clay and John Quincy Adams, and by Southern States' Rights supporters such as W. P. Mangum. Opponents ridiculed the party as a reconstitution of the old Federalist Party. The Federalist Party believed in a strong federal Government, favored commerce, manufacturing, and financial stability, close relations with Britain, central banks, and rule by a well-educated, elite class of leaders.

In its early form, the Whig Party was united only by opposition to the policies of President Andrew Jackson, especially his removal of the deposits from the Bank of the United States without the consent of Congress. The Whigs pledged themselves to congressional supremacy, as opposed to "King Andrew's" executive actions. The Whigs saw President Jackson as "a dangerous maverick on horseback with a reactionary opposition to the forces of social, economic, and moral modernization."[41]

As Jackson purged his opponents, vetoed internal improvements, and vetoed the renewal of the Bank of the United States, alarmed local elites fought back. They argued that Congress, not the president, reflected the will of the people. During their control of the Senate, Jackson's enemies passed a censure motion denouncing his arrogant assumption of executive power in the face of the true will of the people as represented by Congress. The censure was later expunged.[41] Does that remind you of any recent governmental conflicts?

The central issue of the early 1830s was the Second Bank of the United States. Backing various regional candidates in 1836, the opposition finally coalesced in 1840 behind a popular general, William Henry Harrison, who proved the national Whig Party could win.[41]

The Whigs came to unite around economic policy, celebrating Clay's vision of the "American System" which favored government support for a more modern, industrial economy in which education and commerce would equal physical labor or land ownership as a means of productive wealth. Whigs sought to promote domestic manufacturing through protective tariffs, a growth-oriented monetary policy with a new Bank of the United States, and a vigorous program of "internal improvements" – especially to roads, canal systems, and railroads – funded by the proceeds of public land sales. The Whigs also promoted public schools, private colleges, charities, and cultural institutions.[41] Again, does this sound familiar to more recent political battles?

The Early Democrats

By contrast, the Democrats hearkened to the Jeffersonian political philosophy ideal of an egalitarian agricultural society, advising that "traditional farm life bred republican simplicity, while modernization threatened to create a politically powerful caste of rich aristocrats who threatened to subvert democracy."[41-01] The Democrats wanted America to expand westward across the continent. Whigs had quite a different vision: They wanted to deepen the socio-economic system by adding increased layers of complexity, such as banks, factories, and railroads. In general, the Democrats were more successful at enacting their policies on the national level, while the Whigs were more successful in passing modernization projects, such as canals and railroads, at the state level, but not the federal – that only started to be fully realized during Abraham Lincoln's presidency.[41-01]

Jeffersonians

Jeffersonians, obviously named after Thomas Jefferson, supported a federal government with constrained powers, and a strict interpretation of the U.S. Constitution. Jefferson expressed that each generation should have the right to update or amend the Constitution. As mentioned above, he suggested a time frame of about 19 years for revisiting the Constitution, aligning with his belief in the "consent of the governed" and that one generation should not be able to impose its laws indefinitely on future generations.

Contrary to the Jeffersonians, he did not believe that the Constitution should be strictly interpreted. Jefferson's approach was more flexible and pragmatic, often contrasting with some of his contemporaries like Alexander Hamilton. Jefferson leaned more towards a living Constitution that could adapt to changing times rather than a rigid interpretation.

Jefferson himself followed and exhibited these principles. Jeffersonian philosophy also called for state and local governments to safeguard the rights and property of citizens. Jeffersonians recognized both private and common property. During his early public career, Jefferson hoped that each state and county would be smaller examples of the national American Republic. He believed that republican governments established at these levels would best keep the federal government in check. The Jeffersonian philosophy held that all men had the right to be informed, and thus, to have a say in the government. The protection and expansion of human liberty was one of the chief goals of the Jeffersonians. They also reformed their respective state systems of education, believing that citizens had the right to be educated no matter their circumstance or status in life.[42]

Jefferson said in his inaugural address, and the Jeffersonians believed, that America was "the world's best hope."[43] They believed that the United States would be an example to the rest of the world in establishing its own sovereign constitutional republics. When the French Revolution broke out, American supporters and allies of France had hopes that the monarchy would fall, and the people would form a government themselves. Domestically, original Jeffersonians believed that the farmer should be the backbone of any nation, supplying it with a strong work ethic and virtue. And criticizing leaders was considered fully legitimate and expected.[42]

Chapter 3: Our Constitution's Foundation

The political principles embedded in the U.S. Constitution and the structure of our government had been the subject of much debate long before the Founding Fathers came along. John Adams, Thomas Jefferson, George Washington, James Madison, Alexander Hamilton, and others were well educated in the classics and history. They attended the College of William and Mary, King's College (now Columbia University), College of New Jersey (now Princeton), or private academies that required learning Latin and Greek grammar, the classic writings of Cicero and Virgil, and Greek and Latin histories.[34-02] They considered all the governing systems that were known at the time in choosing America's form of government. Reminding ourselves of the principles our Founding Fathers considered is necessary to truly understand and judge our government today.

Roman Law

According to the Romans, who believed in the concept of natural justice, certain basic legal principles are so obvious that they should be applied universally without needing to be enacted into law. The phrase in the United States' Declaration of Independence, "We hold these truths to be self-evident," expresses a comparable sentiment. Centuries before the United States of America was formed, natural justice was part of the common law. Natural justice is based on the principles that most people are good, that good people should not be harmed, and that one should treat others as one would like to be treated.[21]

Natural justice includes the idea of procedural fairness and may include the following rules:

Natural Justice Rules[26]

- A right to advanced warning [of legal charges]
- Contractual obligations depriving individuals of their rights cannot be imposed retrospectively.
- A person accused of a crime or placed at risk of loss should be given adequate notice about the proceedings, including any charges.
- The decision-maker, judge, or jury should declare any personal interest they may have in the proceedings.
- The deciding person should be unbiased and act in good faith.
- The deciding person cannot be one of the parties in the case nor have an interest in the outcome.
- Proceedings should be conducted so they are fair to all those involved.
- Each party is entitled to ask questions and contradict the opposing party's evidence.
- The decision-maker should take into account relevant considerations and extenuating circumstances and ignore irrelevant considerations.
- A community's faith in their courts depends on justice being done.

In the evolution of legal principles, the significance of Roman Law and Natural Justice is undeniable. Still, it's also critical to recognize the transformative contributions from various cultural and religious texts that have guided society's ethical and legal progress. Among these, the Bible plays a pivotal role, particularly in its departure from the principle of exact retaliation, often summarized as the "eye for an eye" philosophy. By advocating for forgiveness and promoting principles of restorative justice over retributive justice, the teachings found in the New Testament, especially those of Jesus, signify a profound shift in legal and moral thought. This transition highlights a broader move towards understanding justice not merely as a means of punishment but as a pathway to reconciliation and healing, marking a significant evolution in the conception of justice itself. Similarly, the Magna Carta stands as a landmark document, recognizing the rights of fiefs and effectively limiting the power of monarchies. The creation of this document was a pivotal moment in the history of law, establishing the foundation for constitutional governance by asserting the principle that everyone, including the king, is subject to the law.

The establishment of the United States brought further advancements with documents like the Declaration of Independence, the Bill of Rights, and the U.S. Constitution. These texts collectively laid the groundwork for one of the most democratic republics in history, setting a global precedent for the balance of powers, the rule of law, and the protection of individual liberties.

Moreover, the Emancipation Proclamation was another critical milestone, signaling the end of slavery in the United States. This historic decree not only transformed American society but also resonated globally, highlighting every individual's inherent rights and dignity.

Each of these documents contributed significantly to advancing legal principles and societal progress, echoing the foundational themes of natural justice and Roman law. Together, they represent pivotal moments in the journey towards a more just and equitable world.

The Social Contract

English philosopher John Locke was one of the most prominent figures of the Enlightenment and is often referred to as the "Father of Liberalism." His ideas greatly influenced fellow philosopher Jean-Jacques Rousseau, who, in 1762, authored *The Social Contract*, theorizing about the ideal structure of a political community. Like Locke, Rousseau believed in the inherent goodness of individuals within a societal framework. Locke's theory suggested that people could collectively appoint a neutral arbiter and establish a government to safeguard their rights. Contrastingly, Rousseau contended that a government's legitimacy stems from the people's sanction, underscoring the significance of the general will and advocating for direct democracy. **Rousseau claimed that a perfect society would be controlled by the "general will" of its populace, suggesting assemblies in which every citizen assists in determining the general will**. Without this contribution from the people, there can be no legitimate government. Most notably, the input must come from the people, not from representatives. According to Rousseau, the citizens must ratify every law directly.[27] We will discuss later how this principle is broken in our present times.

Rousseau's social contract was a progressive idea that helped inspire political reforms, and even revolutions in Europe. It argued that monarchs were not divinely empowered to legislate and that only the people have that all-powerful right.

The core idea of the social contract is this: Each of us places his or her person and authority under the supreme direction of the general will, and the group sees each individual as an indivisible part of the whole. In America, application of this idea means the majority cannot deny the minority of any natural rights.[27]

Socrates on Politics

Jefferson and Adams, being educated in the classics and history, considered past philosophies when helping to shape our founding principles. Some of these originated with Socrates and Plato. The *New World Encyclopedia* reports that Socrates believed "ideals belong in a world only the wise man can understand, meaning only the philosopher is suited to govern others."[28] In Plato's dialogue, *The Republic*, Socrates openly objected to the democracy in Athens during his adult life. He not only placed Athenian democracy under the spotlight; he objected to any form of government that did not conform to his ideal of a perfect republic led by philosophers. During the last years of Socrates' life, Athens was in continual flux from political upheaval. Democracy was at last overthrown by a junta known as the Thirty Tyrants, led by Plato's relative Critias, who had been a student of Socrates. The Tyrants ruled for about a year before the Athenian democracy was reinstated.[28]

According to Plato's *Apology of Socrates*, Socrates refused to pursue conventional politics; he often stated that **he could not look into another's matters or tell people how to live their lives when he did not yet understand how to live his own**. He believed he was a philosopher engaged in the pursuit of truth and did not claim to know it fully. Socrates thought the rule of the Thirty Tyrants was at least as objectionable as democracy. When called before them to assist in the arrest of a fellow Athenian, Socrates refused and narrowly escaped death before the Tyrants were overthrown. He maintained an uncompromising attitude, being one of those who **refused to proceed in a manner not supported by the laws,** despite intense pressure. Judging by his actions, he considered the rule of the Thirty Tyrants less legitimate than the democratic senate that sentenced him to death, but at the same time he abhorred Athenian democracy.[28]

Athenian democracy developed around 500 BC in the Greek city-state of Athens, which included the surrounding territory of Attica. It was governed by the first well-known and well-documented direct democracy – an experiment where people did not elect representatives to vote on their behalf but voted on legislation and executive bills. Participation was open only to an in-group of participants, constituted without reference to economic class. **Direct democracies seem to work best where the number of citizens is small**.[28]

Direct democracy may also be called pure democracy because it encompasses the assembly of all citizens who choose to participate. Depending on the system, this assembly might pass executive motions, enact laws, elect and dismiss officials, and conduct trials. **When the number of citizens becomes large, another level of democracy may be considered – representative democracy**.[29]

"In Representative Democracy, sovereignty (i.e., Power) is exercised by a subset of the people, usually based on election. Countries that are representative democracies allow for three forms of political action that provide limited direct democracy: initiative, referendum (an expression of will that may or may not be binding), and recall. Referendums can include voting on whether a given law should be scrapped, granting citizens with a veto on government legislation. Recall gives citizens the right to remove elected officials from office before their term ends."[29]

Types of Governments and Economic Systems

Socialism

Socialism is often confused with democracy, but they are different. Democracy is about how citizens are represented in the formation of laws. Socialism means the good of the whole takes precedence over the good of the individual.[30] At the extreme of socialism, a concept close to Communism, everyone collectively owns the means of production and work towards a common goal, share their products, and contribute their labor without wages or on an equal-wage basis.[22]

The collectivism of the Internet is real. Millions of people create things and give them away for free, share things of value for free, use things for free, belong to collective software farms, work on projects that require communal decisions, and otherwise enjoy the benefits of decentralized socialism. Over the last decades, communities founded on collective principles have both emerged and dissolved, ranging from small communes in the U.S. to large-scale examples like the U.S.S.R. While many such initiatives have faced challenges, a number continue to operate, often characterized by their smaller scale and the dedication of their participants who are willing to navigate compromises.

The motivation to live this way is often rooted in personal fulfillment – developing oneself, winning praise, avoiding stress, making friends, etc. Some seek a commune for solitude – pursuing a form of quiet "bliss" or a place for intense concentration. Such societies demonstrate collective effort, charitable acts, and not "keeping book" on who does what for whom. Karl Marx preached "from each according to his ability, to each according to his needs."[39-02] Such communities depend on having at least half the people being willing to give more than they receive in return (assuming their basic needs are met). When the takers exceed the givers, on balance, that society will begin to break down. Of course, even in socialist communities, a politician usually surfaces as the leader. The leader assumes control for credit, status, reputation, enjoyment, power, satisfaction, control, and/or the experience. In large-scale socialist societies, the challenge becomes establishing a "fair" distribution of what society produces. Significant imbalances resulted – recall the empty grocery store shelves in the U.S.S.R. in the 1960s. Undoubtedly, the Kremlin was eating well; remember corpulent Khrushchev? An interesting difference between socialism and democracy is that "fairness," other than in the voting process for representatives, has little formal place in the latter but is central to the former.

Property ownership is another difference between a socialist society and a democracy. In a democracy, property ownership is an individual right. In socialism, no one or everyone owns the property. Even in China, before communism was adopted as the official doctrine (1853), the government owned the soil and 60% of all production from the soil had to be paid over to it.[31] Ownership implies the fruits of the property or profits and the right to sell it. Work implies wages, and wages may be paid under both a democracy and a socialist regime. Accumulation of wealth by citizens not in political office or favored by the leaders, however, is unique to a democracy.

One drawback of community effort is that it can result in a lack of responsibility by some individuals. Socialism only rewards extraordinary performance with intangibles such as praise and respect. If personal responsibility is a foundation of society and its government, then a socialist regime makes no sense. Without personal responsibility, setting priorities becomes homogenized by committee decisions and the decision-making process slows down, which is only helpful when "gradualness" is a goal. Some people are self-directed, while others are followers. The adage, "Lead, follow, or get out of the way," applies to society. However, danger exists in democracy as well: Behind every government, there is an "old-boy" network that really wields the power.

Animals form societies that tend to gravitate toward dictatorships, with the dominant male having a harem of females and children. But the groups never increase beyond their "tribe." Humans often form societies that resemble tribal structures, with social hierarchies similar to those observed in animal kingdoms, where a dominant individual controls a group. From familial units to larger communal entities, these human groups reflect our ancestral tendencies toward forming tribes. Cultures, social behaviors, and organizational structures today mirror these tribal origins. Within societies, diverse groups exist, such as castes, regional distinctions, ethnic tribes, clans, religious congregations, and various associations, each with its unique identity and internal hierarchy. Leadership dynamics are evident in every group, where individuals may assume control, displacing predecessors to lead the collective.

Democracies can have components that are socialist in nature and vice versa. For example, free market democracies have socialized education, while socialized societies may allow some private property ownership. The picture is not always clear and simple.

Totalitarianism

Totalitarian governments are those where absolute control is exercised by the state or a governing branch of a highly-centralized institution. Autocracies and authoritarian governments are by nature totalitarian.[64]

Marxism

At the other extreme is Marxism, a doctrine expounded by the German philosophers Karl Marx and Friedrich Engels in the mid-1800s and published in *The Communist Manifesto* in 1848. In the first chapter of the manifesto, according to Dictionary.com, the doctrine espoused that "the State throughout history has been a device for the exploitation of the masses by a dominant class, that class struggle has been the main agency of historical change, and that the capitalist system, containing from its inception the seeds of its own decay, will inevitably, after the period of dictatorship of the proletariat, be superseded by a socialist order and a classless society." This doctrine became highly popular just after Marx's death in 1883 during the upsurge of communism.[65]

Capitalism

According to Wikipedia, "Capitalism is an economic and social system in which capital, the non-labor elements of production (also known as the means of production), is privately controlled; labor, goods and capital are traded in markets; profits distributed to owners or invested in technologies and industries; and wages are paid to labor."[44] Capitalism is criticized for reputedly exploiting the masses – wealthy capitalists making profits from the labors of others.[66]

Capitalism is an economic system characterized by private ownership of the means of production and the pursuit of profit through market competition. It can coexist with various government systems, as explained below, and the relationship can vary significantly depending on the degree of government intervention in the economy.[45]

How Capitalism relates to Government Systems
Laissez-Faire Capitalism: In a pure laissez-faire capitalist system, the government's role is minimal. It provides a legal framework to protect property rights and enforce contracts but does not interfere in economic activities. This

minimal government intervention is often associated with a "free-market" or "hands-off" approach.

Mixed Economy: Most modern economies are mixed, combining elements of capitalism and government intervention. In these systems, governments regulate certain industries, provide public goods and services (such as education and healthcare), and implement social safety nets. The extent of government intervention can vary widely from one country to another.

Social Democracy: Some countries adopt a social democratic approach, which combines a market-based capitalist economy with an extensive welfare state. Governments in social democracies regulate markets, provide social services, and redistribute wealth to reduce economic inequality.

State Capitalism: In some countries, the government plays a more direct role in the economy by owning or controlling key industries and resources. This approach is often associated with authoritarian governments and is sometimes called "state capitalism."

Planned Economy: In planned or command economies, such as those seen in communist or socialist systems, the government exercises significant control over the means of production and economic planning. Capitalism, in the sense of private ownership and market competition, is limited or absent in these systems.

In summary, capitalism is often viewed as an economic framework, while the government system determines how capitalism is regulated, managed, or supplemented with social programs and services.

Democracy

What is democracy? A democracy can denote either direct or indirect rule by the people but does not necessarily include socialism. Principles of democracy include:[32]

- All citizens, not invested with the power to govern, have equal access to power.
- Citizens are governed based on majority rule, through either direct or representative voting.
- All citizens enjoy freedoms and liberties, either because they are considered natural rights or because they have been defined by law.

Essential Processes in Democracies [32]

1. **Competitive and fair elections** – to prevent rule by birthright or force and vote for issues of personal interest.

2. **Freedom of political expression** – to put forth individual ideas, needs, and desires to lawmakers.

3. **Freedom of speech** – to feel able to express one's opinions without reproach from the state and promote personal interests.

4. **Freedom of the press** – to inform citizens without censorship or dictated propaganda.

Democracy is not a homogeneous concept; it is not the same everywhere and has changed over time. In some countries, democracy includes the philosophical principle of equal rights.

Liberal democracy may include elements such as political pluralism (see below), equality before the law, the right to petition elected officials for redress of grievances, due process, civil liberties, human rights, and elements of civil society outside the government. [32]

In the United States, the separation of powers is a key principle, ensuring that the legislative, executive, and judicial branches operate independently. Contrastingly, the United Kingdom follows the doctrine of parliamentary sovereignty, where Parliament holds supreme legal authority, complemented by an independent judiciary. This difference underscores the diversity in governance structures globally. Over the last century, the successes attributed to various democratic systems have encouraged their adoption and adaptation worldwide, reflecting a global trend towards embracing democratic principles in governance. [30-01]

Pluralism

Classical pluralism is a belief that politics and decision-making is largely confined within the governmental framework, while non-governmental groups use their resources to exert influence. As groups of individuals attempt to maximize their interests, the lines of conflict are shifting. Under this governmental tug-of-war, change can be slow and incremental, as these various interest groups use the power of veto to defeat or terminate legislation. The existence of diverse and competing interests can create a democratic equilibrium and is crucial for the obtaining of goals by individuals. Benjamin Franklin said about pluralism: "In free governments the rulers are the servants and the people their superiors and sovereigns."[33]

Pluralists stress civil rights, such as the freedom of expression and organization, and an electoral system with at least two parties. On the other hand, since the participants in governments with this structure constitute only a tiny fraction of the populace, the citizens become bystanders after voting for their representatives. Some people (including those in power, and some philosophers) believe that relegating the populace in this way is not necessarily undesirable: because political issues require continuous and expert attention, which the average citizen may in general lack.[23]

Nationalization

As described above, the first American political parties emerged in the late 1700s and, by 1824, the Federalist party faded away.[24]

In 1901, when comparing Germany under an emperor to America's republican democracy, prominent psychologist Hugo Münsterberg said, "First, that the achievements of democratic America are not the achievements of American Democracy; secondly, that democracy in itself has as many bad tendencies as good ones, and is thus not better than aristocracy; thirdly, that the question whether democracy or aristocracy is better does not exist today; fourthly, that Germany daily becomes more democratic, while America steadily grows aristocratic; fifthly, that there is no difference between the two nations anyway. My friend insisted that my argument stood on the same level with the oath of the woman who was accused before the court of breaking a pot which she had borrowed from her neighbor, and who swore, first, that the pot was not broken when she returned it; secondly, that the pot was broken when she borrowed it; and, thirdly, that she had not borrowed the pot. Well, that may be, but my haste alone was to blame, as I could not explain, in the few words that I had time for, that democracy can cover very different tendencies." [25]

Our Founding Fathers had a range of options to choose from in forming our government, from an aristocracy to a dictatorship, from conservatism to liberalism, from a republic to a representative democracy, from pure democracy to socialism, and from totalitarianism to communalism (communism had not yet been conceived, emerging around 1829[39-01]). In the end, they chose a republic with representative democracy flexible enough to fluctuate between conservatism and liberalism as needed to meet the changing needs of our citizens. They incorporated many of these essential, but not necessarily unique, American principles in our governmental structure.

So, to summarize this chapter, democracy, as a system of government, can coexist with various ideologies, such as liberalism and conservatism, which emphasize individual freedoms and traditional values, respectively, while socialism and communism, with their focus on collective ownership and societal equality, can either complement or challenge democratic principles and pluralism serves as a framework within which these diverse ideologies interact and coexist, shaping the governance and societal structure.[29-03]

Chapter 4: The Purposes of Government

The Purposes of Government

The fundamental purpose of any government is to control and regulate human behavior, with our Constitution designed to "protect the minority from the tyranny of the majority," a concept articulated by Alexis de Tocqueville in 1835. In its rawest form, unchecked human behavior tends to be self-serving and self-centered, leading to a survival-of-the-fittest scenario. To avoid chaos, most individuals must cede some degree of liberty and freedom.

The founders of America aimed to minimize the loss of personal liberty and freedom required for a peaceful coexistence. They structured our government to safeguard our liberties and ensure a balance of power among different branches. However, over time, our federal government has assumed roles not originally outlined in the Constitution, such as operating a central bank, instituting a permanent income tax, running huge administrative departments, and overseeing large businesses and industries.

While these institutions may have their merits, corporations are often better suited to managing large businesses, and local governments are often more effective at regulating individual behavior. Therefore, we might be at the point where we should reevaluate the additional roles the government has taken on considering our founding principles and the changing landscape of our society since the Constitution's signing.

The primary purposes of our federal government, as outlined in the Constitution, include:

- maintaining order;
- protecting citizens from internal and external threats;
- defending borders;
- safeguarding citizens' rights;
- facilitating commerce through currency regulation; and
- establishing treaties and trade relationships with other nations.

Post-World War II, the U.S. government expanded its role to include defending critical external resources, promoting democracy through foreign aid, and occasionally intervening in the affairs of other nations. Similar expansion has been seen in other global powers like Japan, Russia, Germany, and China, increasing competition for vital resources.

> **Proposal: America must find a bilateral balance between having a limited federal government with minimal intrusion into individual lives and activities and the broader role of "promoting the general welfare." We also must balance the cost and administrative size of our safety nets, such as military defense, social security, Medicare/Medicaid, and other departments (FAA, DHS, DOE, DOT, DOI, USDA, HUD, DOC, DOL, HHS, DoED, VA, etc.)**

Our country's challenge is that power has become too concentrated – within the consortium of large businesses, special interest groups, and the two major political parties. For example, the political parties should not dictate the thinking of senators and congresspeople, who in turn should not dictate the behavior of individual states and their citizens. Power also has become too concentrated in the chairmanships of House committees, Party leaderships, and the role of Leader of the House.

> **Proposal: We need to devise constitutional revisions to how we are governed to defuse this increasing concentration of power. (More on this later.)**

The General Responsibility of Government

In establishing a new government, a central challenge lies in appointing wise leaders while constraining their authority to prevent misuse of power. It is a common phenomenon that individuals who occupy positions of authority for extended periods succumb to the allure of power. Instances abound where initially popular candidates, upon assuming leadership roles, manipulate laws to prolong their terms, censor the media, and suppress dissenting voices.

Our Founding Fathers, including eminent figures like John Adams and Thomas Jefferson, grappled with this issue. Drawing from a wealth of historical knowledge, they weighed various forms of government, ranging from English aristocracies to early Athenian democracies. Even after the Constitution's signing, they continued to debate the merits of monarchies versus representative bodies, the balance between manufacturing and agriculture, and the impact of taxation on individual motivation. At the core of these discussions was the fundamental question of a government's purpose.

Role of Local Government

Amendment X of the Constitutions says, "The powers not delegated to the United States by the Constitution, nor prohibited by it to the states, are reserved to the states respectively, or to the people."

This clause defines for local government a role in controlling harmful behavior, maintaining order, and protecting liberty. Murder, manslaughter, robbery, rape, aggravated assault, arson, fraud, weapons violations, vandalism, prostitution, drug possession, vagrancy, and theft are just some of the crimes perpetrated in local communities. Controlling such harmful behaviors requires laws and enforcement. According to the original principles of our forefathers, such crimes are and should be handled by local government.

Other crimes that go beyond local community boundaries (towns and cities) require the oversight of higher government levels, such as counties or states. Crimes that fall under the auspices of county or state include corporate fraud, drug trafficking, driving on state roads while intoxicated, gambling, and kidnapping. Higher-level crimes, such as treason, sedition, forgery, and secession, and those that cross state boundaries, fall under the jurisdiction of the federal government and are handled by the FBI. We should reconsider whether the inclusion of counties has relevance for a function like policing.

The closer our governance is to home, the more likely we are to feel that we have control over our lives and the ability to direct our leadership.

> **Proposal: To widen the role of local governments, we need to consider improving efficiency by consolidating: state and county police departments for efficiency where distances are great; and counties and their main city, such as Indianapolis and Marion county did, especially where the city has grown to encompass most of the county. Chicago and Cook County, IL, are candidates, as are Orange County and Orlando, and Miami and Dade County, FL. Their administrations, school districts, policing, health services, fire departments, and other government functions should be considered for consolidation.**

It's becoming increasingly apparent that there's a trend toward more centralized governance, with control shifting upwards to the state and from there to the federal level.

> **Proposal**: **The autonomy of local governments to pass laws appropriate to their own local citizens must be preserved. States should not interfere with the governance of counties and cities (or county if consolidated). If Harrison, AR, wants to remain a dry county, they should be able to do so. If California wants to legalize marijuana, even though science shows the drug suppresses initiative and drive, it should have the right to do so. If Orange County, FL, wants to ban further commercial development or limit building densities, that right should not be overridden by state edict.**

Ensuring Domestic Tranquility

A guiding principle should be that the individual's welfare takes priority over the state's needs, except in national defense or situations endangering many citizens. Most Americans believe the government should not interfere in personal choices, which should be left to individual conscience. Yet, attitudes often shift regarding legally permissible actions considered immoral by some religions. While religious institutions may seek to influence individual conscience, this role is questionable for the government, which should persuade rather than dictate.

Despite some political groups' desire to regulate personal behavior, it's crucial to affirm that individual needs and rights outweigh those of society or any political party. A government at any given time may claim to represent society, but, in reality, it only represents a segment. Accepting the supremacy of individual rights over societal ones leads to certain implications: For instance, we shouldn't mandate helmet use for motorcyclists or deny women the right to choose abortion. (More on this later.)

The Union of States

We have drawn valuable lessons from the early days of our nation and the leadership of figures like Abraham Lincoln. These lessons underscore the imperative that when the actions of individual states undermine the greater good of the Union, the Union's interests must take precedence. It follows therefore that states should refrain from taking steps that obstruct national defense or essential national services.

Conversely, it is equally essential for the federal government to respect the principle that actions falling outside its core mission should be left to the states' discretion. As defined by our Constitution, **the federal government's primary mission encompasses conducting foreign relations, safeguarding its citizens from external threats, defending our rights and national resources, promoting a foundational level of health and welfare, and facilitating interstate commerce, communication, and trade.** Beyond these fundamental duties, the federal government's involvement with states and citizens should remain limited and reserved for instances of extraordinary necessity – or we should amend our Constitution.

> **Proposal**: **The federal government should make every effort to limit its activities to its primary mission (see bold text in paragraph above).**

Fairness

Citizens often mix up the concept of equal rights with the idea of fairness. It is important to note that our Constitution does not guarantee a specific right to "fairness." Life is inherently unpredictable and sometimes unfair, resulting in inequality in our society, legal system, governance, and daily lives.

As a nation, the United States recognizes the importance of compassion for individuals who cannot provide for their own well-being through no fault of their own. While not formally codified, there is a widely held belief that no one should suffer from hunger, extreme cold, or lack of primary healthcare. This support extends to all, including productive members of society and those who, due to physical or mental challenges, cannot fully support themselves. However, implementing these principles varies and is often subject to political, economic, and social debates and policies.

Here are other examples where our country's policies are incomplete or lacking:

1. **Children Starving in America**: The existence of extensive food assistance programs like the Supplemental Nutrition Assistance Program (SNAP) and the National School Lunch Program Food means food insecurity remains an issue in the U.S. According to Feeding America, millions of children in our country lack consistent access to enough food for an active, healthy life. This suggests that the policies in place to prevent child hunger do not always work.
2. **Bankruptcy Due to Medical Bills**: Medical expenses are a significant issue in the U.S. Despite healthcare programs like Medicaid and the Affordable Care Act, medical bankruptcy remains a concern. A study published in the *American Journal of Public Health* in 2019 found that medical issues contributed to 66.5% of all bankruptcies in the U.S. This indicates that medical costs can and do lead to financial ruin for some Americans.

> **Proposal**: **We need to define finally what our minimum threshold is for when government assistance should come into play. Children should not be starving in America and people should not be bankrupted by hospital bills. How these goals are achieved needs to be determined through bipartisan negotiation.**

Our Founding Principles

The concept of freedom of opportunity is inherent to America. As Elizabeth Dole stated in 1997 when she spoke at the College of the Ozarks, "America is about dreams." It is a place where dreams can be realized. Our forefathers came to this continent seeking their dreams – land, means of sustenance, religious freedom, and the liberty to enjoy the fruits of their labor. They came here driven by the promise of prosperity and the opportunity for full self-expression. America has a long history of rewarding creativity and fostering a spirit of neighborly assistance to those in need.[45]

Our nation was founded upon diverse principles, extending beyond the pursuit of wealth. Over time, there has been a noticeable shift in America's focus, with an increasing emphasis on financial matters such as economic growth, the stock market, the Federal Reserve System, military spending, budget deficits, foreign financial transactions like Chinese bond sales, and other monetary concerns. This financial-centric perspective has come to dominate the workings of our Congress, even though America stands for so much more.

It is essential to recognize that our Founding Fathers were not primarily motivated by financial interests when they created our government. Quite the opposite: They often jeopardized their financial security to establish a new government that prioritized the ideals of liberty, justice, and democratic representation.

In summary, America's rich history is marked by noble principles and economic pursuits, shifting over time toward a more pronounced focus on financial matters within a messy political landscape. This transformation has brought with it a greater emphasis on fundraising in modern campaigns, altering the nature of power and influence in our political system.

> **Proposal**: **Congress needs to shift their focus away from doling out money to one or more of the following higher principles – world peace, getting unemployed Americans back to work so they can feel good about themselves, and stimulating creativity - the driving force behind our robust economy.**

Once a candidate is elected to Congress, their responsibilities often include allocating funds and crafting legislation to support business interests in generating greater profits. Simultaneously, lobbyists spring into action, aiming to influence decisions by investing money in securing favorable rule changes or funding allocations for their clients. The authority to enact these changes primarily rests with members of Congress. Recognizing this, they vigorously pursue reelection while lobbyists seek to ensure their interests are represented.

The Founding Fathers viewed government service as a duty to citizens, not a means to personal gain or power. They didn't focus on using their positions for personal enrichment, distributing money to constituents or donors, or trading votes for financial benefits, as has been alleged in discussions surrounding political practices. Furthermore, they were not preoccupied with potential economic benefits they might accrue after leaving office from contacts made while in office. These practices starkly contrast with the original principles of the Founding Fathers, highlighting the significant deviation of Congress from these ideals.

Chapter 5: A Republic and a Democracy

America was formed from ideas that evolved over many hundreds of years, which coalesced between 1776 and 1787 in our Constitution. The consolidation of many grand ideas required the unique education and intellect of people like John Adams, Thomas Jefferson, and the members of the Constitutional Convention, which included most of the signers and framers of the Declaration of Independence (but not Adams or Jefferson, both of whom were in Europe).

The U.S. Is a Republic and a Democracy

America is first a republic – a government run by an elected or appointed leader, not a hereditary one. Our Constitution also guarantees that states are republics. So, we are a republic of republics as well – because citizens have a role in the control of state governments as well as federal governments, although more directly at the state level. Our Founding Fathers recognized that the separate states had their own personalities, peculiarities, and priorities and that those should be preserved.

Civil and Political Rights of a Republic[35]

1. Ensuring people's physical integrity and safety.
2. Natural justice (procedural fairness) in law (such as the rights of the accused, including the right to a fair trial; due process; the right to seek redress – a legal remedy).
3. Protection from discrimination.
4. Individual political freedoms, including freedom of:
    a.   thought;
    b.   speech and expression;
    c.   religion;
    d.   press;
    e.   movement;
    f. participation in civil society and politics, including:
        i) freedom of association;
        ii) right to assemble;
        iii) right to petition; and
        iv) right to vote.

America is also a democracy, meaning that the right to govern is bestowed by the people and exercised through the vote and majority rule, except for inalienable rights.

Democracy is said to have two conditions: "All citizens, not invested with the power to govern, have equal access to power and the second that all citizens enjoy legitimized freedoms and liberties."[36]

Republics Support Individual Independence

Republics stress independence and self-reliance. Individualists promote their own goals and desires, while opposing external interference with their choices, whether by society or any other individual, group, or institution. Individualism is opposed to collectivism, which stresses that communal, community, group, societal, or national goals should take priority over individual goals.[37]

In political philosophy, the individualist theory of government holds that the state should protect the liberty of individuals to act as they wish so long as they do not infringe upon the liberties of others. This contrasts with collectivist political theories, where rather than leaving individuals to pursue their own ends, the state ensures that the individual serves the whole society, even by force if necessary.

Individual independence includes the concept of "laissez faire," which means in French "let [the people] do" [for themselves what they know how to do]. This term is commonly associated with a free market system in economics, where individuals and businesses own and control most factors of production. Government interferences are kept to a minimum.[37]

Individualists are chiefly concerned with protecting their civil and economic autonomy against obligations, like taxes and regulations imposed by social institutions such as the state. For example, they oppose any concentration of commercial and industrial enterprise in the hands of the state and the municipality.

Individualism Beliefs[37]

1. Popularly-elected representatives are unlikely to have the qualifications for managing numerous enterprises and the large sums of public money involved in civic administration.

2. The "health of the state" depends upon the exertions of individuals for their personal benefit.

For some political individualists, the word "society" can never refer to anything more than a large collection of individuals. Society does not have an existence above or beyond these individuals, and thus cannot be properly said to carry out actions, since actions require intentionality, intentionality requires an agent, and society as a whole cannot be properly said to possess agency; only individuals can be agents. The same holds for the government. Government does not have existence beyond the individuals it represents.[37]

In one view of individualism, the government is seen to be composed of individuals. Despite democratic governments being elected by popular vote, the fact remains that all activities of government are carried out by the intentions and actions of individuals, not always constrained by the written laws and regulations. Actions approved or taken may not be consistent with what the majority of voters intended. The individualist wishes to highlight the importance of the individual and prevent absorption into a collective.[37]

Adapting comments made by Chris Anderson in the July 2009 *Wired* magazine article "Waste is Good," laws can be oriented either of two ways. **In totalitarian regimes, everything is forbidden unless it is permitted. In democracies, everything is permitted unless it is forbidden. In totalitarian regimes, dictates come from the top-down. In democracies, dictates come from the bottom-up.**

Laws provide the basis for command and control and keep citizens from getting out of control. Totalitarian regimes are characterized by strict, often repressive control over many aspects of life, including political, economic, and personal freedoms, with little to no tolerance for dissent.[59-08]

Rule by the majority depends on the honesty of the competitive election process. Many supposed democracies maintain power through election fraud, which invalidates their status as a true democracy. The rights of the people to establish or disassemble their government are inviolable.[37] However, this concept of dissemble stems from democratic principles and philosophies like those of John Locke, who advocated for the right of people to change their government should it fail to protect their rights and liberties. However, exercising this right through violent means or outside the framework of the law typically falls into the realm of rebellion or insurrection. **So, we have the right, even the obligation, to dissemble our government if it fails to protect our rights, but only if we do so peacefully. Otherwise, it is treason.**

Balance of Power

Being a democracy is insufficient in and of itself, if power can gravitate to any portion of the government. Separation of powers is one way America tries to maintain a balanced political system. Like in a sound accounting process, checks and balances are essential to keep power from becoming absolute. As Lord Acton, a British historian and politician, said, "Power tends to corrupt, and absolute power corrupts absolutely. Great men are almost always bad men." [39-03]

Unlike the U.S., the judicial system in the UK is entirely independent of the other branches of the government and from the prime minister, who as their executive is also a member of their legislature. [38]

Legislative power must belong to the people directly or through elected representatives. The elite or biased should not be allowed to make the law. [38]

> **Proposal**: **People should be given the ability to ratify or veto every law. This requirement will restrict the number of laws, force them to be clearer and well communicated, and promote tranquility through broader acceptance. However, the ratification (or veto) cannot be done by simple majority – as mentioned earlier, it must be overwhelmingly approved or overwhelmingly rejected, like 80%.**

There also needs to be a role for wise people in our government and in the creation of our laws. However, wisdom can be trumped and buried by power.

Our government structure is not perfect, but none are. It is nothing short of a miracle that our forefathers considered all the above options and others to arrive at the form of government they defined for us.

Our Constitution, Bill of Rights, and Subsequent Amendments

All Americans, especially American voters, advocates of constitutional principles, and students of constitutional governments, should be familiar with:

• our Constitution, signed September 17, 1787;

• the Bill of Rights, which consists of the first 10 Amendments and was introduced by James Madison, supported by Thomas Jefferson, and passed at the first U.S. Congress in 1789;

• the subsequent 17 amendments, signed from 1795 to 1992.

These visionary documents set forth the basic American principles, clearly spell out our rights, natural and conveyed, and define our governmental processes. You are encouraged to read the summary of these documents in the Appendix at the end of this book.

Our Constitution significantly influenced the United Nations' Universal Declaration of Human Rights as well as the constitutions of many countries around the world. According to the democracy index by the Economist Intelligence Unit, a research and analysis division of The Economist Group, as of 2022, the world had about 75 "full" and "flawed" democracies combined out of 167 countries and territories.[59-23]

Free and Honest Elections

Free and honest elections are non-existent in a dictatorship and essential for representative democracies. Where elections are not free and honest, representative democracy cannot exist. **To be free, every qualified voter must have full access to polling places and not face any intimidation related to their electoral choices**. To be honest, the integrity of the votes must be protected throughout the counting process and no manipulation of the results takes place during or after the counts. Bipartisan or multi-partisan supervision at every step of the counting process is necessary to ensure objective outcomes. Of course, the voting process also depends on clear identification of votes (i.e., no "Hanging Chads").

While recognized as fundamental in many global declarations and national constitutions, not all governments across the world recognize and defend basic human rights. The United States, with its historical commitment to individual liberties and democratic values, has the potential to be a role model in this regard. However, this requires the U.S. to continually refine and improve its governance, ensuring it upholds and evolves its foundational principles and rights. By doing so, America can better adhere to its constitutional commitments and inspire other nations to enhance their respect for and protection of human rights.

U.N.'s Universal Declaration of Human Rights

For the most part, the freedoms and rights embodied in the U.S. Constitution are also included in the U.N.'s Declaration of Human Rights.[63]

Overview of U.N.'s Declaration of Human Rights

1. The "first generation" rights include freedom of speech, the right to assemble, and freedom of religion.

2. The "second generation" rights are economic, social, and cultural, such as the right to food, housing, and good health.

3. The "third generation" rights include the natural law. Natural law is how a rational human being, seeking to survive and prosper, would act, protecting life, liberty, and property. Under natural law, civil and political right include:

  a. ensuring people's physical integrity and safety;

  b. natural justice (procedural fairness) in law, such as the rights of the accused, including the right to a fair trial; due process; the right to seek redress or a legal remedy;

  c. protection from discrimination based on gender, religion, race, sexual orientation, etc.; and

  d. participation in civil society and politics (as described above).

According to the United Nations:[63]

1. Article 1 declares all human beings are born free and equal in dignity and rights. They are endowed with reason and conscience and should act towards one another in a spirit of brotherhood.

2. Article 2 sets out the basic principle of equality and non-discrimination and the enjoyment of human rights and fundamental freedoms. It also forbids "distinction of any kind, such as race, color, sex, language, religion, political or other opinion, national or social origin, property, birth or other status."

3. Article 3, a cornerstone of the declaration, proclaims the right to life, liberty, and security of person – a right essential to the enjoyment of all other rights.

4. Later articles spell out other civil and political rights, including:

- freedom from slavery and servitude;

- freedom from torture and cruel, inhuman, or degrading treatment or punishment;
- the right to recognition everywhere as a person before the law;
- the right to an effective judicial remedy;
- freedom from arbitrary arrest, detention, or exile;
- the right to a fair trial and public hearing by an independent and impartial tribunal;
- the right to be presumed innocent until proved guilty;
- freedom from arbitrary interference with privacy, family, home, or correspondence;
- freedom of movement and residence;
- the right of asylum;
- the right to a nationality;
- the right to marry and to found a family;
- the right to own property;
- freedom of thought, conscience, and religion;
- freedom of opinion and expression;
- the right to peaceful assembly and association;
- the right to take part in the government of one's country; and
- the right to equal access to public service in one's country.

Later articles further set out economic, social, and cultural rights to which everyone is entitled "as a member of society." These rights are as indispensable for human dignity and the free development of personality and can only be realized "through national effort and international cooperation."[63] At the same time, it points out the limitations of some states due to the scarcity of their resources. Other articles include the right to:

- social security;
- work;
- equal pay for equal work;
- rest and leisure;
- a standard of living adequate for health and well-being;
- education; and
- participate in the cultural life of the community.

The final sections of the declaration affirm that everyone has the right to live within a social and international framework where human rights and fundamental freedoms can be fully realized. They emphasize the responsibilities each individual holds towards their community. One specific article further elaborates that exercising one's rights and freedoms is subject to legal limitations necessary to ensure the respect and recognition of others' rights and to uphold morality, public order, and the general welfare in a democratic society. This same article underscores that no state, group, or person has the right to undertake actions that would destroy the rights and freedoms outlined in the declaration. Additionally, it mentions a particular provision stating that the right not to be executed may be considered optional. These principles highlight the balance between individual liberties and the collective good, underlining the importance of respecting and protecting human rights within legal and ethical boundaries.[63]

Human Rights on a Global Scale

While the U.S. has had its Constitution for more than 200 years, the world as a whole has no such guiding cornerstone until the United Nations was formed. The United Nations established a Commission on Human Rights in 1946 that worked until December 10, 1948, when the general assembly adopted a Universal Declaration of Human Rights. The broadest legally binding human rights agreements negotiated under U.N. auspices are the International Covenant on Civil and Political Rights and the International Covenant on Economic, Social and Cultural Rights, which were adopted in 1966 and put into force in 1976. Even though many of the principles in the U.S. Constitution were not original, the way they were gathered together was unique and formed one of the longest stable governments in history.

At the international level, the U.N. Charter reflects ideals embodied in the U.S. Constitution, such as the promotion of peace, respect for human rights, and encouraging social progress. The U.S. pioneered constitutional democracy, and our Constitution has had an enduring impact on the global discourse on governance and human rights.

The principles of the U.S. Constitution, noted for promoting democracy, individual rights, and the rule of law, have a widespread, albeit varied, influence globally. These principles often intersect with religious doctrines and practices, particularly in regions where religion significantly influences governance and social norms. In some instances, this has led to resistance from religious leaders who perceive these principles as undermining their traditional authority.[59-24] Additionally, in 2023, the international efforts of organizations like the United Nations to uphold human rights and foster world peace are being challenged by conflicts involving "bad actors." These actors often flout international laws and human rights standards, contributing to humanitarian crises and setting back decades of progress toward world peace.

Why should Americans care about international human rights? In an increasingly interconnected world, human rights violations anywhere can lead to instability and conflict, compromising global security, including that of the United States.

Upholding human rights aligns with America's foundational values of freedom and justice, and promoting these rights abroad is both a moral and ethical responsibility. Furthermore, respecting human rights contributes to global stability and prosperity, directly affecting U.S. national security and economic interests.[59-09,10]

Promoting and respecting human rights contributes to prosperity by creating stable, law-abiding societies that foster educational and economic opportunities, attract investments, and facilitate inclusive growth. Healthy, educated, and empowered populations are key drivers of productivity and sustainable economic development nationally and globally.

By championing human rights, the U.S. supports democratic governance worldwide, creating more stable and cooperative international partners. This stance enhances America's global reputation and influence, which is crucial for broader foreign policy objectives. Beyond these pragmatic reasons, there is a fundamental human aspect – empathy and solidarity with those who suffer rights abuses, which everyone, including Americans, should care about.

Diversity vs. Homogenization

Society faces an inherent contradiction: It wants to embrace and preserve diversity of cultures, identities, and perspectives while steadily moving toward equal and consistent treatment for all. Homogenization seeks to standardize and unify, often at the cost of unique identities and practices. Think of how McDonalds has spread across the world. Everyone eating the same type of food instead of eating their local specialties: German, Japanese, Chinese, Mexican, etc. Equal treatment can mean homogenizing everyone – pushing everyone into wanting to be the same.

In a broader context, should we prioritize preserving diversity in cultures, viewpoints, and identities? Despite our varying appearances, languages, and culinary preferences, we share common aspirations – the pursuit of freedom, safety, nourishment, shelter, warmth, and, most importantly, meaningful connections with family and friends. As humans, we are not naturally inclined to solitude; instead, our intrinsic purpose is to support one another in various ways. To act otherwise would mean resigning ourselves to isolation, which contradicts our inherent nature. And, given current trends in technology and culture, the eventual homogenization of the entire world is inevitable – some day in the distant future. It is only a matter of how gradually or quickly it happens.[59-11,12]

However, in the meantime we must be concerned about the next election in America to keep our country on the course set forth by our Founders,

PART II: OUR REPRESENTATION NOW

In Part II, on our current governance, we explore the American character and the diverse traits and values that define the United States as a nation. Americans are often characterized by their resilience, adaptability, and pioneering spirit, which have shaped the country's history and continue to influence its present. A spirit of innovation and a relentless pursuit of progress define the American mindset, while a deep-rooted sense of individualism underscores a culture that celebrates personal freedom and responsibility. This blend of characteristics not only shapes the daily lives of its people but also profoundly impacts the nation's governance. As we delve into the intricacies of American political and social structures, we see how these traits are reflected in the policies, leadership, and civic engagement that form the backbone of the country's democracy.

Chapter 6: How We Have Changed Since 1787

The United States of America has changed vastly as a country and as a people since our Founding Fathers signed our Constitution on September 17, 1787. Over the years that followed, our Constitution has been amended 27 times. The most recent amendment (the 27th, about congressional compensation) was ratified on May 7, 1992. The one before that, the 26th, allowed 18-year-olds to vote and was ratified on July 1, 1971.

Because so much has changed in our lives over the last 236 years, and even since 1992, it is reasonable to conclude that Americans are overdue in considering whether our governance should be updated to keep pace. Many of these changes should be of concern if they continue to outstrip our government's ability to govern. Let us begin with our governmental representation and the qualifications of our leaders.

The reality is that, as citizens, our representation in Congress has become gradually but thoroughly diluted and diminished over the years. Without representation and changes in how we are governed, we risk us losing our founding principles as we continue to move away from doing what most America's citizens want and need.

Here are some further illustrative examples of the many changes America has gone through since our Constitution was written. Political parties came into power years after our Constitution was written. It was not until our eighth president, Martin Van Buren, ran for office that political parties began dictating the platform and picking the candidates, which eventually led to the political machinations we know today. In our formative years as a country, independent organizations did not decide who would run for office, what they would say, or what rewards would be doled out to the faithful. Giving political parties the power to select the candidates for whom America's citizens will get to vote to represent them in our government was neither contemplated nor provided for in the design of our Constitution. The same is true for lobbying. The growth in political party power and the increasing influence of lobbyists should give us pause for thought as to whether our governance today continues to work as our Founding Fathers intended.

What Makes Americans Different?

What makes Americans different from citizens in other countries? Here are some candidates:

Traits Often Cited as Distinctively American

- **Cultural Diversity**: The United States is known for its cultural diversity, shaped by centuries of immigration. This "melting pot" or "salad bowl" has created a unique blend of cultures, languages, and traditions.
- **Emphasis on Individualism**: Individualism, personal freedom, and self-reliance are hallmarks of American culture. These traits are reflected in social norms, economic practices, and political ideologies.
- **Innovative Spirit**: The U.S. has a reputation for innovation and entrepreneurship, as seen in the country's leading role in technological advancements, business practices, and scientific research.
- **Political System and Values**: The U.S. has a distinct political system focusing on democratic governance, the rule of law, and a system of checks and balances. The country's political culture is deeply influenced by the principles in the Constitution and the Bill of Rights.
- **Patriotism and National Identity**: Americans often have a strong sense of patriotism and national identity tied to historical narratives like the American Revolution and symbols like the stars-and-stripes flag. Millennials and subsequent generations are reshaping American patriotism, blending critical perspectives on historical narratives with a desire for national improvement and global responsibility.[59-25]
- **Optimism and Forward-Looking Attitude**: Americans are often characterized by a belief in the possibility of positive change and improvement.
- **Consumer Culture**: The U.S. has high consumption levels and a significant focus on consumer goods and services.
- **Diverse Geographical and Natural Landscapes**: The vast and varied natural landscapes of the U.S., from its coasts to its mountain ranges and plains, contribute to a wide range of lifestyles and regional cultures within the country.
- **Global Influence**: The United States has significant international influence, culturally, politically, and economically, shaping how Americans are perceived and how they perceive themselves in the world context.

These American traits reflect our founding principles. We are passionate about our liberty, our freedom of speech, our pursuit of happiness, our right to change our government when it isn't doing well for our citizens, and our right to practice our religion. Different societies have varying approaches to governance and social control. Some, like the Taliban, use religious principles to enforce authority, while others, such as Venezuela, manipulate their laws.[69-07] In nations like Cuba, China, and Russia, the leadership might adopt forms of communism or socialism, leading to centralized control over national resources and decision-making.

Comparatively, the United States is often viewed as a country with significant freedoms stemming from its historical origins, diverse population, and a collective commitment to defending these liberties. Democracies worldwide strive to promote human rights but face challenges in achieving global unity, partly due to certain countries' diverse political systems and power dynamics. Ethnic differences and historical conflicts also contribute to international tensions, underscoring the ongoing challenges in attaining worldwide peace.

The U.S. has historically been cautious in engaging in conflicts but has shown decisiveness and strength when directly attacked, as seen in responses to Pearl Harbor and 9/11. The country's approach to international conflicts is often influenced by congressional debate and decision-making, reflecting a balance between restraint and action.

The governance style of countries like China, Russia, Venezuela, Cuba, Iran, and North Korea, often characterized as authoritarian, typically concentrates power within a small elite. These regimes may limit freedoms like speech, press, and assembly, and their economic policies can be seen as serving the interests of those in power. However, the relationship between the state and the economy in these countries is complex and varies significantly from one to another.

American culture is noted for its creativity, work ethic, and emphasis on keeping commitments, such as honoring international treaties. While the U.S. is known for its generosity and military prowess, it is essential to recognize that these traits are not uniquely American. The perception of Americans as arrogant in some global contexts can be attributed to various factors, including the country's prominent role in international diplomacy, brash, outspoken behavior by some tourists, and certain public personas in sports and entertainment. Like other nations, America has its strengths and weaknesses, and its culture has influenced and been influenced by global trends in various fields.

In her article in *American Consumer*, Cheryl Russell, editorial director of New Strategist Publications, denoted the following American traits (note: author of this book added the last six): [69-08]

American Traits

1. **Struggle with Crime**: America imprisons a higher proportion of its population than any other country, yet it has one of the highest crime rates in the world.[53] Our media plays up crime, stoking irrational fear at times, leading to our fascination and dependency with guns.

2. **Not Knowing What We Want from Our Government but Not Liking What We Get**: We say we want government spending cuts and smaller government, but we do not want to cut spending on major programs. To illustrate, below is the percentage of Americans who want to cut spending in key areas)
   a. Education: 4%
   b. Healthcare: 6%
   c. Retirement benefits: 7%
   d. Law enforcement: 8%
   e. Environment: 13%
   f. Natural disasters: 14%
   g. Military: 26%
   h. Arts: 30%

3. **Careless about Our Rights**: Americans are forever thumping their chests with pride, and the one thing we boast about the most is our freedom. Yet many Americans are willing to give up that freedom without much of a fight: 56% think, or probably think, the government should have the right to jail people without a trial.

4. **Religious Freedom but a History of Intolerance**: We are religious but not as religious as most Americans think. Among the world's developed countries, the United States stands alone in its religiosity: 59% pray at least once a day and only 50% believe in evolution. Skeptical about this statistic? Further research (a 2007 Gallup survey) showed that 57% of Democrats, 30% of Republicans, and 61% of independents believe in evolution; 40% of Democrats, 37% of independents and 68% of Republicans do not.[71-02]

5. **Hard Working and Hard Playing**: In fact, we are workaholics. This may explain why American workers take so little vacation time compared to their European counterparts and why we do not demand more time off: 70% would continue to work even if rich. Of course, other countries may be as hard-working or even more so.

6. **Becoming More Diverse**: The Census Bureau continually tells us how diverse we are. Survey results suggest that the racial divide is not so big: 74% of black people have trusted white friends and 52% of whites have trusted black friends. Also, 54% of black people have white family members and 20% of whites have black family members.

7. **Lack of Trust in Others**: Americans do not have warm and fuzzy feelings toward public officials or their fellow citizens: Only 35% say politicians are interested in the problems of the average person. Also, only 32% believe most people can be trusted and 80% believe others will take advantage of you if you are not careful.

8. **Uptight**: Americans have a well-deserved reputation for being prudish about sex: Only 46% believe premarital sex is not wrong at all and only 32% believe homosexuality is not wrong at all. But we are also practical: 89% support sex education in the public schools, while 54% think teens should have access to birth control.

9. **Immobile**: We like to stay put. Americans live in the third largest country in the world, but they restrict themselves to a small portion of it: 38% still live in the same city and 62% live in the same state as when they were 16.

10. **Dreamers**: The single defining characteristic of Americans in both good times and bad is our steadfast belief in the American Dream: 69% say hard work, rather than luck or connections, determines success and 70% say the United States gives people like them the opportunity to improve their standard of living.

11. **Adventurous**: Americans are known for their adventurous spirit, though the realms of adventure have evolved over the centuries. The vast oceans, the mysterious inner core of our planet, and outer space — famously referred to as "the final frontier" by Star Trek — remain vast fields for exploration and discovery.

12. **Competitive**: Americans are competitive – part of our being fighters. It stimulates us when we compete to win.

13. **Materialistic**: Americans appear materialistic – because our standard of living allows us to be. This is the understandable source of global jealousy.[72-01]

14. **Direct**: Americans tend to be blunt and outspoken, sometimes tactless. We are viewed by some as crude, ungentlemanly, and uncultured. "Greedy and brutal; vulgar and corrupt," according to Hugo Münsterberg in 1901.[61]

15. **Yes to Religious Freedom, but Tolerance?** Americans have successfully separated religion from state without outlawing any particular faiths, but we have not always been religiously tolerant. The Irish were stoned in New England for being Catholic in the early 1900s. Likewise, women's suffrage and a belief in racial equality have not always been part of the American fabric. These changes prove that our constitutional system does evolve and eventually gets around to trying to protect the people it should protect.

16. **Private Property Ownership**: Americans value their private property. We have wars over zoning, what neighbors keep in their front yard or on their front porch, fences, and eminent domain. Our passion for our private property is rooted in the American belief that it is sacrosanct from government intrusion. A man should be able to do whatever he wants to do on his own property – even when he owes a bank more that the property is worth.

17. **Value of Education**: Americans are generally well educated and are willing to support even the poorest children's education through taxation. This is an area where redistribution of wealth seems acceptable because education is believed to encourage working for a living, thereby protecting our citizens from crime and poverty.

Hugo Münsterberg was a German-American psychologist, a pioneer in the field of applied, industrial, and forensic psychology, and a professor at Harvard University, where he carried on his research and writing until his death in 1916. He wrote: "But the American man is of course very well known. He is a haggard creature, with vulgar tastes and brutal manners, who drinks whiskey and chews tobacco, spits, fights, puts his feet on the table, and habitually rushes along in wild haste, absorbed by a greedy desire for the dollars of his neighbors. He does not care for education or art, for the public's welfare or for justice, except so far as they mean money to him. Corrupt from top to toe, he buys legislation and courts and government; and when he wants fun, he gambles. He has his family home usually in a skyscraper of twenty-four stories; his business is founded on misleading advertisements; his newspapers are filled with accounts of murders, and his churches swarm with hypocrites."

His statement was written in 1901, and the view of Americans by the rest of the world has changed much since even though we do not hear it as often – we have just become less relevant to the rest of the world except as a marketplace for their goods and services.[62]

How many of these traits are a result of our Constitution cannot be determined, but prescribing freedom and liberty for all our citizens may certainly have encouraged them.

Keeping the Constitution Up to Date

Our Constitution does not appear to be keeping up with the rapidly changing world, which has undergone numerous changes that the Founding Fathers could not have foreseen; not in the alteration or removal of inalienable rights but rather in administrative facets such as representation in Congress, the role of lobbyists, and term limits. These changes reflect a significant shift in the political and administrative landscape, diverging in various ways from the original vision laid out by the Founding Fathers. Even though our early presidents, especially John Adams and Thomas Jefferson, debated many of the same issues that still face us today, some of the conditions are very different, such as having 335 million American citizens in 2023 compared to the 2.5 million we had in 1776, according to the latest census.[01] We also have a much greater role in the world. In fact, the entire world is much larger, in terms of population, and much closer, in terms of communications. In 2023, we are much more involved in international law and wide-ranging economic interests than our forefathers were in 1777, when our Constitution was signed. There are now more than eight billion people in the world, and many are vying for America's attention. Also, some concepts have crept into our governmental fabric, which were not incorporated into our Constitution by our Founding Fathers, like term limits.

Term Limits

One practical approach to curbing the concentration of power is to impose term limits on elected officials. It is imperative to encourage ordinary citizens with the requisite qualifications to engage in public service rather than perpetuating the dominance of professional politicians, where perhaps too many of whom are lawyers. In doing so, we uphold an important principle of government – to strike a balance between capable leadership and accountability.

The Pros and Cons of Changing Term Limits

Pros:

Increased Turnover: Shorter term limits for senators and congresspeople leads to more frequent turnover, reducing the influence of incumbency and encouraging fresh perspectives.

Preventing Career Politicians: Limiting senators to a single term and congresspeople to a specific number of terms can help prevent individuals from becoming career politicians and promote greater diversity in elected officials.

Balancing Power: Term limits can prevent the accumulation of excessive power and influence by long-serving individuals, which aligns with principles of democratic representation.

Accountability: Frequent elections ensure that elected officials remain accountable to their constituents and responsive to changing public needs and sentiments.

Cons:

Loss of Experience: Shorter term limits may lead to a loss of experienced lawmakers who have a deep understanding of legislative processes and the intricacies of governance, making it challenging to navigate complex issues and maintain consistency in policymaking.

Disruption: Frequent turnover can disrupt the continuity and effectiveness of legislative bodies, potentially impeding long-term policy goals.

Limited Accountability: Elected officials in their final terms might not be as accountable to their constituents, as they are not seeking reelection.

Potential for Political Polarization: Frequent elections could incentivize politicians to focus on short-term, populist policies rather than addressing more complex, long-term issues.

Judicial Independence: Imposing term limits on Supreme Court justices may risk undermining the independence of the judiciary and the principle of lifetime appointments, which were designed to insulate them from political pressures.

Our forefathers did not envision membership of Congress to even be a full-time commitment, let alone a lifelong job. The early congressmen all had professions and returned to their "day jobs" when they were not in session. We should return to this approach.

With shorter sessions and limited terms, the opportunities for the creation of more restrictive laws will be limited. We have enough laws – all we need now are the necessary updates to adapt to new developments. Term limits are essential for breaking the control of power.

> **Proposal: The length of terms for senators (six years with one-third each two years) and congresspeople (two years) seem appropriate. However, the number of times they can be reelected should be no more than twice for senators (12 years total) and no more than three times for congresspeople (six years). Otherwise, we will be led by a cabal of professional politicians.**

With these restrictions in place, the potential for special interests to influence legislators is lessened, allowing for a greater focus on the needs and concerns of regular citizens.

In 2002, law professors Paul Carrington (Duke University) and Roger Cramton (Cornell University) proposed a plan for reforming the Supreme Court that included term limits for justices. Their proposal, which called for staggered, 18-year terms, helped to spark a modern debate on the topic. More recently, academics and politicians have been proposing 20-year terms for Supreme Court justices.

> **Proposal: Establish staggered 20-year term limits on Supreme Court justices. Establish term limits for ALL lower-level federal judges that are partisan-appointed.**

How We Got to Where We Are?

The Declaration of Independence describes our responsibilities as American citizens:

> **"We hold these truths to be self-evident, that all men are created equal, that they are endowed by their Creator with certain unalienable Rights, that among these are Life, Liberty and the pursuit of Happiness. — That to secure these rights, Governments are instituted among Men, deriving their just powers from the consent of the governed, — That whenever any Form of Government becomes destructive of these ends, it is the Right of the People to alter or to abolish it, and to institute new Government, laying its foundation on such principles and organizing its powers in such form, as to them shall seem most likely to effect [sic] their Safety and Happiness. <u>Prudence, indeed, will dictate that Governments long established should not be changed for light and transient causes</u>; and accordingly, all experience hath shewn that mankind are more disposed to suffer, while evils are sufferable than to right themselves by abolishing the forms to which they are accustomed. But when a long train of abuses and usurpations, pursuing invariably the same Object evinces a design to reduce them under absolute Despotism, it is their right, it is their duty, to throw off such Government, and to provide new Guards for their future security."**

With the above commitment to ourselves, we announced our separation from Great Britain and their despotic taxes without representation on July 4, 1776. Now, currently, we suffer under a wide range of taxes laid upon us by a Congress over which we have little direct control. We may be approaching the time when we need to "alter or abolish" our current form of government. To use a car analogy, we do not need a completely new model, but we may need to overhaul the engine. Congress energizes the government to move in the direction its citizens really care about.

Political parties' platforms usually reflect much of what Americans want, such as a simpler income tax structure, smaller government, and less waste. But this is not the case for many issues, which need to be resolved by compromise and agreement (not by dictatorship).

> **Proposal: The U.S. should conduct an unbiased national "referendum" that polls the nation's voters to specify and rank their preferences for potential revisions to our Constitution.**

Representation Dilution

Since the days of our founders, the voice of the people is being heard less and less.

Change in Ratio of Citizens to Representatives

For example, the number of representatives has not kept up with the growth of our population. When our government was founded, one house member was elected for every 20,000 citizens. This number was later amended to 30,000, and then to 40,000, after which Congress stopped amending the rule. If we still had one representative for every 40,000 citizens today, the number of representatives in Congress would be 8,298. Instead, each of the 345 representatives represents on average nearly a million people. There is no way that they can adequately represent us while understanding and reflecting the needs of a million diverse people. One might argue that representing a valid illustrative sample of a million people is as good as representing each of them, but that makes each of us feel like a number not a citizen, and we all know how unreliable polls are.

Congress only nominally represents America's citizens in the creation and passage of laws. The best we can do is to vote for a political party that represents as much of our viewpoint as possible. Unfortunately, most of us do not know what all our viewpoints need to be or do not know enough about the positions of our preferred political party. So, we vote for the party closest to our opinions based on what we hear from friends or those who influence our lives, TV, news sources, or social media, most of which is slanted toward a specific political agenda (i.e., propaganda) or badly biased. Or we vote against the party whose positions we perceive as unfavorable, often influenced by that party's pundits, negative propaganda, and media buzzwords. As a result, we may find ourselves choosing the lesser of two evils and in doing so we go against our own values.

Change in Ratio of Senators to Citizens

The House of Representatives is not the only instance of our representation being diluted. The number of states in America has grown from 13 to 50 since the founding of our country, and the number of senators has grown from 26 to 100. This is appropriate because according to John Adams, senators are intended to represent the interests of the states. However, each senator who had to represent about 25,000 people in 1787, on average, now must represent more than **six million** citizens. We would need 12,220 senators to have the same level of representation as we had originally. Or, alternatively, the states would need to develop some system to accurately inform their senators of the needs of their citizens.

Members of Congress are already so distant from the people they represent that they are now highly susceptible to the influence of the limited few who do have access to them – lobbyists and wealthy donors. Kristina Karamo, Michigan's Republican party chairwoman, said of their party's top donors, "You are required to do their bidding to get their funds, and so we just simply wind up destroying the country slower than the Democrats."[69-01] And, of course, the needs of different parts of the country differ widely (urban Chicago versus downstate agricultural Illinois, for example).

In politics, voters sometimes reevaluate their principles and beliefs. Just as Catholics may reconsider their positions on issues such as priestly celibacy or the role of women in the clergy, voters may contemplate their stances on matters such as population control versus birth control, the importance of stem cell research for medical advancements, or the equal treatment of LGBTQ individuals. Reevaluating one's political principles and evolving perspectives can be a natural part of personal growth. Similarly, as voters, we are forced to compromise our standards when we pick one of just two political parties who have a realistic chance of winning. In considering the issues of the day and trying to sort out the genuine concerns from the hype, we should be mindful of our basic American principles: We need a better form of representation – a new way of representation.

Proposal: Create regional committees to advise Congress. The committees will connect with citizens online and through mail surveys and town hall meetings. Every issue will be addressed via national referendums. To address American citizens being so poorly represented in our government, there should be two levels of intermediate representatives. The first level would be regional – one person for every 50,000 people. The geographic areas would not follow state, county, or any other political boundaries but would be designed to include a wide variety of people and interests radiating from large and small population centers. Each region would be assigned to one of 13 districts – a west, mid-west, mid-east, and east for each of the north, central, and south (4x3=12) and another for the U.S. possessions, Hawaii, Alaska, and D.C.

That way, the districts represent every part of the country. A representative elected by each district would form a committee reporting directly to Congress to present the concerns, issues, needs, and requirements rolled up from the regions and consolidated at the district level.

The idea is to shift the debate to the level closest to the public to encourage multiple viewpoints and approaches from different districts. A committee of district representatives would provide advice and counsel to the House of Representatives on a non-binding but strongly recommended basis. This way, the existing structure of our government remains intact but there would be an efficient mechanism in place to understand and communicate the will of the people from across the country at every level of society. The regional and

> **district representatives would be in part-time, minimally-paid positions. They would meet no more than once per quarter.**

Another example of questionable citizen representation is that the speaker of the House, third in line for the presidency, is not elected directly by the people but by members of the House of Representatives. This contrasts with the election of the vice president of the United States, who, as part of the presidential ticket, is voted in by the public and serves as the president of the Senate. Citizens should have more direct influence over the presidential line of succession.

> **Proposal: Consider modifying the system to include the speaker of the House on the party's national ticket, alongside the candidates for president and vice president. Such a change would require significant amendments to the U.S. political process and Constitution.**

With these changes, people would be more engaged, and legislating would be easier.

Who Picks the Party's Candidates?

As mentioned earlier, the party leadership has too much power in determining who runs, the rules around running and participating in debates, who gets funding from the party, and ultimately the outcome of elections. The approach outlined below would ensure a more democratic and representative selection process, giving every member a voice in choosing the leadership that reflects the collective will and values of the entire party membership.

> **Proposal: The national chairperson of each party should be elected by the vote of all registered members of the party, not hand-picked by state party officials, who often are also not elected to their roles. Party committee members should also be elected not appointed. This approach would enhance democratic participation within the party, ensuring that leadership reflects the preferences of its broader membership base.**

Evolution of Job Qualifications

Jefferson's Job Qualifications

Our Founding Fathers were highly intelligent and educated but most had little experience leading large organizations. Government departments were much smaller when Jefferson and Adams served as presidents.

Jefferson received a comprehensive education. He was tutored in various subjects, including mathematics, Latin, Greek, and the classics. His formal education continued at the College of William and Mary, where he studied philosophy, science, and literature and further honed his classical knowledge. Additionally, he studied law under George Wythe, a prominent Virginia attorney and judge.

Jefferson's commitment to learning extended beyond formal education. He was an avid reader and self-learner, amassing a vast personal library that covered history, science, literature, and politics. He was interested in languages and was proficient in Latin, Greek, French, Italian, Spanish, and Anglo-Saxon. His library of 6,500 books was sold to the new Library of Congress in 1815, after the British burned down the original library in 1814. Furthermore, his management skills were honed on his 5,000-acre property, where he conducted agricultural experiments, cultivating crops like tobacco, wheat, corn, and various fruits and vegetables. He also maintained livestock, gardens, orchards, and vineyards on his estate, Monticello.

Adams' Job Qualifications

Adams' qualifications were different but equally impressive. He began his education at a local common school and received guidance from his father and uncle, who were farmers and deacons. Adams pursued a liberal arts education at Harvard, obtaining a bachelor's and a master's degree. His legal career began as an apprentice under James Putnam, a prominent lawyer, where he gained practical experience in the legal profession.

Besides his legal expertise, Adams was known for his avid writing and intellectual contributions. He developed a successful law firm, lived on a small 14-acre farm, Peacefield, and served as a diplomat before entering government. He authored numerous essays, pamphlets, and letters on a wide range of topics, including politics, government, and philosophy.

The point of the above comparison is to emphasize that our Founding Fathers were highly educated, and mostly self-taught, before entering government service. They did not have extensive experience managing large global businesses anywhere near the size of our current government, but then our government was small. They led by their contributions to the structure of the government and by the principles they established.

Current Job Qualifications

Today, our government needs experienced leaders because the population of our country grows exponentially, as does the size and complexity of our government. We need leaders with greater qualifications than spelled out in the Constitution.

Constitutional Requirements for Top Three Roles

1. **Qualifications for President** (Article II, Section 1, Clause 5 of the Constitution):
   a. Natural-born Citizen: The candidate must be a natural-born citizen of the United States, meaning they must have been born on U.S. soil or be born to U.S. citizen parents, even if born abroad.
   b. Age Requirement: The candidate must be at least 35 years old.
   c. Residency: The candidate must have been a resident of the United States for at least 14 years.
2. **Qualifications for the Senate** (Article I, Section 3, Clause 3 of the Constitution):
   a. Must be at least 30 years old.
   b. Must be a U.S. citizen for at least nine years.
   c. Must be an inhabitant of the state they wish to represent at the time of their election.
3. **Qualifications for the House of Representatives** (Article I, Section 2, Clause 2 of the Constitution):
   a. Must be at least 25 years old.
   b. Must be a U.S. citizen for at least seven years.
   c. Must be an inhabitant of the state they wish to represent at the time of their election.

These qualifications are specified in the original text of the Constitution and have not been amended since the founding of the United States. It is important to note that states may have additional requirements so long as they do not conflict with the constitutional qualifications.

The essential point is that these qualifications need to adequately encompass the skills requisite for the present size and scope of these offices, specifying the extent and nature of prior relevant experience candidates should possess, and the educational backgrounds they should ideally have. The business of our government is also international in scope. Individuals with no more than these minimum qualifications should never be considered for leadership positions. The president supervises 2.1 million federal civilian employees, as of 2023. The staffs of Congress, including the congressional and senatorial staffs, Capitol Police, Library of Congress, Government Accountability Office (GAO), architect of the Capitol, and maintenance staff number more than 40,000.

Some parties believe that our government should be radically reduced, even torn down and rebuilt, because it requires a lot of tax dollars. Have they considered how large and complicated America has become? Maybe they have. But, clearly, the required qualifications to run our large country need to be more comprehensive.

All government offices have a pressing need for true statespersons, not just politicians. It is essential that, during their campaigns, candidates be thoroughly evaluated for their capability to effectively lead a complex entity like the United States. While campaigning, their focus may naturally be on addressing the immediate concerns of their constituents to secure votes. However, once elected, it is imperative that senators and congresspeople exercise their voting power in consideration of the entire nation's welfare. This embodiment of statecraft (gender neutral term replacing old term of statesmanship) requires them to diligently attend to their constituents' needs while also considering the interests of those who did not vote for them. Their commitment should extend beyond just a portion of their electorate, lobbyists, or political party affiliations, ensuring they represent the broader interests of all citizens.

Complexity Drives Today's Qualifications

Our government has expanded substantially over the years. In 1787, we had only four government departments: state, treasury, defense, and justice. Today, we have 16: interior, agriculture, commerce, labor, health and human services, housing and urban development, transportation, energy, education, veteran affairs, environmental protection, and homeland security.

During the early years of our nation, the federal workforce, excluding the military, numbered only in the hundreds. While it is true that the number of federal employees declined from 5,354,000 in 1962 to 4,206,000 in 2008, it is important to note that many jobs may have been outsourced or automated out of existence during this period. Presently, in 2023, there are 2.1 million civilian employees and 2.3 million military members.

Over this time, the federal budget has grown significantly, from $886.3 billion in 1962 (adjusted for inflation) to $4.79 trillion in 2020. While the number of employees decreased by 21%, government spending increased by 552%.

> **Proposal: The number of people employed or contracted by the government should be made more transparent.**

The trend of increasing federal expenditures per citizen in the United States is marked by significant growth over several decades. Adjusted for inflation, the spending per citizen rose from **$2,000** in 1947 to **$8,000** in 2004, representing a **400%** increase over 57 years. By 2022, the latest data indicates a further boost to **$19,432** per citizen. When adjusted for inflation, this is equivalent to **$12,800**, signifying a **160%** rise in the last 18 years. This increase translates to an annual growth rate of 8.7%, with inflation removed. This substantial growth in federal spending reflects the rising U.S. population, the addition of new programs like Medicare, and the escalating complexity of managing one of the world's largest organizations.

> **Proposal: Set a cap on federal expenditures that cannot exceed 27.3% of the prior year's average per capita personal income of its citizens (in 2022 this was $74,580)." Such a limitation could be considered the equivalent of a "Gold" standard for government spending.**

Managing this colossal organization and budget now involves addressing increasingly intricate issues, such as a growing federal deficit, international financial dependencies, and reliance on foreign trade, oil, and loans. The skills and experience required to oversee the 16 administrative departments in the early days of our nation have evolved significantly. Consequently, merely being a friend of the president is no longer sufficient to qualify someone for a position as the head of an executive office department. Nor should anyone be elected to a government office without the necessary qualifications just because they have a lot of money.

> **Proposal: Define in more detail the qualifications and experience required for all senior level positions in our government, including elected officials, and ensure they receive commensurate compensation.**

Proposal: Enhance our school curriculums by incorporating broader lessons on morals, manners, ethics, values, laws, civics, and financial studies, thereby equipping students with the understanding of how and why to support our form of government.

In summary, we need to reconsider all aspects of how we are governed in light of the rapid growth of our population and the huge advancements that have been made in areas like technology and communications. We need more representation, better leadership, stricter rules surrounding campaign financing, curbs on the growing influence of lobbyists, and a clearer resolve to better understand and support the needs of our citizens as well as businesses.

Lobbyists and Other Undue Influence on Our Leaders

The intricate web of lobbying has become an integral yet controversial aspect of modern governance, raising questions about the balance of power and the integrity of decision-making processes. The dynamics between elected officials and various interest groups reflect the complexities of how influence is exerted when formulating policies and representing the public interest. It is crucial to examine how lobbying has shaped today's political landscape. It all started with the constitutional right to petition.

While Congress has developed laws to enforce ethical behavior, they haven't been all that effective. The adage of the "fox guarding the henhouse" springs to mind. Recent ethical controversies, including those involving Supreme Court justices in 2023, underline the need for more stringent ethical standards across all government branches, reform of political finance and lobbying practices, and a more transparent and accountable political process.

Right to Petition

In representative and liberal democracies, the right to petition the government is typically considered an individual freedom that may be extended to groups and corporations.

Per the first amendment to the Constitution, individuals can petition the government to address injustices without fearing punishment. Civil liberties can sometimes only be upheld against the government by exercising this fundamental right, which encompasses both state and federal courts and legislatures. In many democracies, including the United States, individuals already have the legal right to engage in grassroots lobbying, which involves ordinary citizens or advocacy groups mobilizing and advocating for specific policy changes. This right often includes contacting legislators, organizing public demonstrations, and engaging in advocacy campaigns. Although, recently, the UK has enacted ultra-conservative laws making some forms of public demonstrations illegal.

Report from the UK[39-03]

In the UK, a series of strict laws targeting protest activities has led to a contentious debate, balancing concerns about public order and civil liberties. The Conservative government has introduced these laws, arguing they are necessary to prevent extremist activists from disrupting the economy and daily life. Notable legal changes include the 2022 statute creating a "public nuisance" offense, punishable by up to 10 years in prison, and the 2023 Public Order Act, which broadens the definition of "serious disruption" and imposes prison sentences for blocking key infrastructure.

Critics, including civil rights advocates and environmental activists, argue these laws erode civil liberties, with some peaceful demonstrators being arrested and labeled as extremists. They assert that such sweeping actions and labeling by the government mark a worrying shift for a liberal democracy. The parliamentary cross-party Joint Committee on Human Rights warned that these changes could have a chilling effect on the right to protest. Meanwhile, figures like Jonathon Porritt, an ecologist and former director of Friends of the Earth, emphasize that legitimate protest is vital for a civilized society.

The right to petition is the foundation for justifying or explaining lobbying activities. However, the specific rules and regulations surrounding individual (grassroots) lobbying can vary from one jurisdiction to another and may be subject to campaign finance laws, disclosure requirements, and other legal considerations. Therefore, there have been efforts in some cases to clarify or modify the legal framework governing grassroots lobbying or advocacy activities to ensure transparency and accountability. It is essential to recognize that some sizable organizations, such as the National Rifle Association (NRA) and the American Civil Liberties Union (ACLU), both dedicated to lobbying, have reportedly opposed such a bill. While any American has the direct right to petition their government representatives, lobbyists, including those representing large interest groups, can exploit this privilege to much greater effect because they have more money and better connections with those in power. This situation appears inconsistent with the intentions of our Founding Fathers.

Number, Organization, and Influence of Special Interests

Large corporations and labor unions wield a level of influence and representation in Congress that greatly surpasses that of the average citizen. But it has not always been that way. Lobbying in the United States' early years was informal and less organized than it is today. Individuals and interest groups would approach lawmakers directly to advocate for their interests. It was often characterized by personal relationships and informal gatherings.

In the 1800s and 1900s, lobbying became more organized as businesses and interest groups hired professional lobbyists to influence legislation. This era saw the emergence of the first lobbying firms. By the 1940s and 1950s, lobbying had grown rapidly in influence and sophistication, a trend that continued throughout the 20th century. The passage of lobbying disclosure laws and regulations in the 1940s and 1950s aimed to make the industry more transparent and professional. In the late 1990s, lobbying became highly specialized, with firms and groups employing well-connected experts in policy, law, and government affairs. They use many tactics, including direct lobbying, grassroots campaigns, and public relations, to influence lawmakers and public opinion.

In recent decades, the Internet and digital communications have transformed the lobbying landscape further. Lobbyists now use technology to mobilize supporters, target messages, and track legislative developments in real time. Social media and online advocacy campaigns have become powerful tools for influencing policy decisions. The amount of money spent on lobbying has grown significantly over the years and now has expanded to be international in scope – with foreign powers trying to influence our government and U.S. lobbyists trying to influence governments abroad.

According to Statistica, a research company, in 2022, there were a staggering 12,644 registered lobbyists in Washington, D.C., along with an additional 21,750 individuals employed within their firms.[69-15] These lobbyists typically command starting salaries of approximately $300,000 per year. Multiplying these figures indicates that special interests invest at least $5 billion annually in persuading 535 legislators to align with their objectives, which often do not take into account the needs of the general populace.

Money Spent on Lobbying (2022)				
	Starting Pay	#	Total Expended	Per Lobbied
Lobbyists	$ 300,000	12,644.00	$3,793,200,000	
Staff	$ 60,000	21,750.00	$1,305,000,000	
		34,394.00	$5,098,200,000	$9,529,346
			# Lobbyed:	535

The sheer magnitude of this financial power inevitably raises concerns about distracting our representatives in Washington and the potential for corruption within the political process, affecting it in myriad ways.

And 427 former members of Congress have passed through the revolving door by moving to K Street as lobbyists or senior advisers performing similar work, according to data from the Center for Responsive Politics.

Of the 75 members who left the 113th Congress, 42 have found new employment. Of those, 45.2% went to work for lobbying firms, while another 19%went to a lobbying client, meaning that 64.2% have found post-congressional work in the lobbying sector.[69-03] Does that constitute a conflict of interest while in power?

Having highlighted various concerns and challenges within our governance system, it is now essential to revisit and reaffirm our fundamental governing principles. These principles serve as the bedrock of our society and guide us in addressing the issues we have identified and many others, hopefully leading toward a more effective and equitable governing framework that aligns with our core values and ideals.

> **Proposal: Create an independent counsel as watchdog over lobbying and require all lobbying meetings to be documented and a matter of public record.**

> **Proposal: Alternatively, eliminate group lobbying and create a government body that accepts petitions from individual citizens as part of the regional structure previously proposed to improve representation.**

> **Proposal: We need stronger ethics regulations and independent, non-partisan enforcement of ethics violations.**

> **Proposal: We also need to limit the amount of time lobbyists have access to party leaders and legislators, say just for one day of the week. And all such meetings need to be documented/recorded and available as public records.**

> **Proposal: Strengthen lobbying disclosure laws to provide more comprehensive and real-time reporting of lobbying activities, including contacts with government officials, campaign contributions, and grassroots efforts.**

> **Proposal: Alternatively, eliminate all organized lobbying and replace it with the councils recommended above so that the main influence on Congress comes directly from America's citizens.**

Chapter 7: The Importance of Power Balance

To fully understand the distinctions between political parties, it is essential to explore the intricate relationships among five key areas: the division of power within the government, the array of political issues prioritized by Congress, the influential role of the Supreme Court, the operational intricacies of the executive branch, and the overarching dynamics within the judiciary. These areas are interconnected, each influencing and being influenced by the others. For example, the division of power in government often dictates the legislative agenda in Congress, which in turn can be impacted by Supreme Court rulings. Decisions and policies from the executive branch not only respond to but also shape the legislative and judicial landscapes, while the judiciary's interpretations of law can redefine power dynamics and influence political debates. How the different political parties view this interdependent relationship gives us valuable insight into' their contrasting philosophies and strategies, revealing how they collectively mold the political and governmental framework.

Limits on Executive Power

In the past, concern has arisen about the power of the president to issue "executive orders" and act without congressional authorization. Here is a summary:

Limits on Executive Orders

Executive orders, which are directives issued by the president of the United States to manage operations within the federal government, have limits. Some key constraints:

1. **Constitutional Boundaries**: Executive orders cannot violate the U.S. Constitution (e.g., an order cannot override constitutional rights or amendments.) Only Congress can create laws or appropriate funds.
2. **Legislative Limitations**:
   Executive orders must be grounded in a constitutional power vested in the president or a power delegated by Congress. They cannot contravene federal laws. If Congress disagrees with an executive order, it can pass legislation to render the order ineffective, assuming it can override a presidential veto.
3. **Judicial Review**: The courts have the authority to overturn an executive order if it is found to be unconstitutional or not properly based on legislative authority, which has been done over the years. The Supreme Court acted by invalidating President Harry Truman's (Democrat) Executive Order in

---

> Youngstown Sheet & Tube Co. v. Sawyer regarding the seizure of steel mills, and reviewed Executive Orders issued by President Ronald Reagan (Republican) related to freezing Iranian assets and lifting sanctions in Dames & Moore v. Reagan, though in this latter case, the Court showed deference to the executive power.[79-05,06]
>
> 4. **Scope and Implementation**: Executive orders are limited to the executive branch of the government and cannot dictate actions to the legislative or judicial branches, nor directly affect state governments, other than indirect effects through federal funding and regulatory powers.
> 5. **Duration and Reversibility**: An Executive order remains in effect until it is rescinded by the sitting president, overridden by legislation from Congress, or invalidated by the courts. Future presidents can also revoke, modify, or supersede executive orders issued by their predecessors.

While the president has significant authority to manage federal operations and enforce laws, this power is balanced by the other branches of government and the principles of the Constitution.

Division of Powers

There are growing concerns regarding the division of powers within the U.S. government, particularly the expanded role of the president in shaping laws through executive orders and policy directives. This worrying shift, which has accelerated in recent decades, contravenes the original intent behind the separation of powers envisioned by the nation's founders. It diverts power away from Congress, the primary legislative body that effectively represents the people's will, to the executive branch. Partisanship compounds the challenges in rectifying this imbalance; when one party holds the executive office and Congress, there's little incentive to alter the status quo. Conversely, a divided government struggles to enact significant changes. Ultimately, restoring the balance of power may hinge on enhancing the representativeness and effectiveness of Congress, reaffirming its role as a cornerstone of governance by the people.

Concerns about Congress

Voters' focus should be on Congress, including the Senate and the House of Representatives. As we described earlier, the effectiveness of Congress as being truly representative of the American people has been declining ever since our democratic republic was formed and our population mushroomed. Given the significant role of Congress in lawmaking, budgeting, and national direction – a role often more impactful than that of the president – its structure, processes, and actions need thorough scrutiny. While acknowledging the president's essential roles in military leadership, foreign relations, and setting national priorities, concerns arise over the executive branch's extensive administrative reach. This includes departments issuing regulations akin to laws, bypassing the essential democratic step of elected representatives' approval.

Most current issues plaguing our government, such as the insufficient funding of social security, inefficiencies in Medicare, and economic problems, can be traced back to the decisions, or lack thereof, made by Congress. This situation is further compounded by the predominance of lawyers in the legislative process and the self-preserving systems they have established, favoring the interests of legal professionals, legislators, and prospective private-sector employers. This concentration of lawyers creates the perception that Congress is more focused on serving its own agendas than the well-being of American citizens. They appear to be working for the benefit of their financial backers, potential future employers, their colleagues in the legal profession, and for themselves. Examples include the debate over Tort Reform, which some critics argue reflects a conflict of interest, suggesting that lawmakers may avoid passing reforms to protect personal interests, such as their medical and retirement benefits, as well as potential career opportunities post-congressional service.

The party not in control blames the party in control and vice versa. Although many current challenges have roots in decisions made by Congress in the past, it is also true that Congress has been instrumental in positive developments, like enacting anti-discrimination laws, aiding disabled people, and establishing national parks. Yet, over the last two centuries, the evolving political and social landscape appears to have caused some confusion among members of Congress about their roles and duties.

The continuous creation of new laws has led to an overly extensive and burdensome legal system that many believe is increasingly encroaching on individual freedoms. There is a concern that Congress has strayed from the foundational principles set by the Founding Fathers, instead becoming overly influenced by big business, greed, and special interests. This situation demands that Congress be realigned to adhere more to the foundational values established by the nation's founders and is dedicated to representing a broader cross-section of the citizenry, not just the limited groups mentioned above.

> **Proposal: Reduce the number and frequency of new laws, perhaps using national referendums as previously proposed to ratify any proposed legislation.**

Supreme Court

The Supreme Court of the United States (SCOTUS) has faced criticism for appointing judges with perceived political biases. This politicization has led to contentious decisions, including the reversal of Roe v. Wade, a case previously upheld by the court. Concerns have also been raised about justices receiving financial benefits deemed unethical for elected officials. Additionally, at various levels of the federal courts, there are issues with prolonged delays of months or even years in administering justice.

The way a person is elected to the Supreme Court attempts to limit political influence through the process that has not changed since Jefferson's and Adams' day.

The Process for Appointing Federal Judges, as Outlined in the U.S. Constitution

1. **Nomination**: Federal judges, including Supreme Court justices, are nominated by the president of the United States. These nominations are typically based on the judge's qualifications, legal expertise, and other relevant factors. Candidates most often come from the ranks of state courts and may have been elected in a partisan or non-partisan election or appointed by a state governor.
2. **Senate Confirmation**: After being nominated, the prospective federal judge must go through a confirmation process in the U.S. Senate. The Senate Judiciary Committee holds hearings to examine the nominee's qualifications and ask questions about their judicial philosophy and legal views.
3. **Senate Vote**: Following the committee hearings, the full Senate votes on whether to confirm the nominee. A simple majority vote is usually required for confirmation. If confirmed, the nominee becomes a federal judge.
4. **Lifetime Tenure**: Federal judges, including those on the U.S. Supreme Court, serve lifetime appointments, which means they hold their positions for the rest of their lives or until they choose to retire or are impeached and removed by Congress for "high crimes and misdemeanors." This lifetime tenure is designed to insulate federal judges from political pressure and ensure their independence.

This process is designed to allow federal judges to make impartial and fair decisions based on the law. However, it is essential to note that this ideal is not always realized. Cases with political overtones have occurred throughout the Supreme Court's history.

These politically charged cases have included instances when the court ruled that it had the authority to declare acts of Congress unconstitutional, denied citizenship to African Americans, and declared the Missouri Compromise unconstitutional, exacerbating tensions leading up to the Civil War. Other examples include when the court upheld racial segregation, endorsing the "separate but equal" doctrine, and declared state laws establishing as unconstitutional separate public schools for black and white students. The court's involvement in the 2000 presidential election, ending the recount in Florida and resulting in George W. Bush becoming president, was another highly politically case.

The Supreme Court has not always been perfect in providing "checks and balances" against the executive and congressional branches of government. This is why more must be done to ensure the absence of political bias and the presence of the purest rule of law.

Rather than being appointed for life, term limits of 20 years have been suggested as one way to balance the political influence of SCOTUS justices and thereby their findings. However, a certain stability and consistency of rulings supports the concept of lifetime appointment. An age limit does not make sense because it reflects the wisdom that comes with age. However, some non-political mechanism should be created.

Proposal: These three mechanisms could be put in place for ensuring the fitness of serving justices:

1. **Regular Health Assessments: Conducted by medical professionals, including cognitive evaluations, on all federal judges to help identify any decline in mental capacity.**
2. **Peer Review: Establish a peer review process within the judiciary. Colleagues of a justice, including other justices, could confidentially report concerns about mental fitness to an independent panel of experts.**
3. **Independent Medical Evaluation: If concerns are raised about a justice's mental capacity, an independent medical evaluation could be ordered by a consensus of four jurists and conducted by medical experts to determine if the justice is fit to continue serving.**

Concerns about the Executive Branch

First, our forefathers intended our government to be balanced – to have an inherent, built-in balance of power. No one branch of the government was meant to exercise its powers without the control of the other two branches. The president is the head of the administration and the military – commander in chief. His job is to handle treaty negotiations, propose the annual budget, and manage the military. **The president's position is NOT intended to wield power like the CEO of a company. He is NOT the sole person in charge! Neither is Congress nor the Supreme Court.**

Second, the branches of the government were not intended to be controlled by any outside "faction," especially religions. The Constitution establishes a separation of church and state, as reflected in the First Amendment, to ensure that government does not favor or establish any religion. This separation acknowledges the diverse religious beliefs of America's population and aims to prevent any single group's religious morality from dominating government policy. While many of America's early settlers sought religious freedom, the Founding Fathers designed these constitutional protections to safeguard individual liberty and prevent the government from becoming entangled with or endorsing religious institutions and doctrines.

States Rights

Democrats view states and territories as collaborative partners with the federal government and are committed to providing financial assistance when necessary. They advocate for granting voting rights to the 600,000 residents of the District of Columbia and support the right to self-determination for U.S. territories.

On the other hand, Republicans emphasize adherence to the 10th Amendment, which states that powers not delegated to the federal government nor prohibited to the states are reserved for the states or the people. They advocate for shifting more programs back to state control. While they do not support the idea of D.C. statehood, they are in favor of specific measures such as providing assistance to D.C. schools and offering homebuyer credits to improve housing in the district.

Based on the principles of our Constitution, matters that do not impact other states should be left to the discretion of individual states. Conversely, it follows that the federal government should uniformly regulate issues that affect all states to ensure consistency across the nation. There is a need for greater standardization and simplification of laws among states. Laws that are nearly identical in various states should be unified, though not necessarily enforced by the federal government. Standardization should occur for state laws on subjects that could impact neighboring states. However, in cases where state laws on a particular topic (such as California's stance on marijuana or state-specific gambling regulations) do not affect other states, federal intervention should be minimized.

Chapter 8: Party Positions

In the upcoming chapters, we will examine the promises made by the parties, aiming to discern their genuine intentions and commitments. We'll look at the alignment between their stated goals and past actions, identify core principles that reflect the true values of each party, and highlight the issues that are of genuine concern to our citizens. This analysis seeks to provide a clear and objective understanding of what each party stands for and intends to achieve.

Introduction

To get Americans to rally behind them, political parties cast out hot emotional issues like fishing lures, and too often some Americans take their bait. What Americans were not even thinking about one day suddenly become a passionate issue for them the next because a political pundit has railed against it. And, now with social media, issues pass around the country and the world in seconds or minutes. Social media platforms often serve as a battleground for conflicting perspectives, where the rapid dissemination of information, true or not, is commonplace. Amidst this digital chaos, fake news and propaganda are frequently encountered, some of which may be orchestrated by external entities aiming to sow discord. These rogue agents, possibly backed by foreign interests, strategically use inflammatory content to aggravate societal tensions, with an underlying objective that could be as extreme as inciting civil unrest. While not every piece of content on social media is designed to provoke outrage, the prevalence of such material raises concerns about its potential impact on social harmony and public discourse.

Party extremists on social media similarly amplify this polarization by rallying their base with emotionally-charged content. They focus on divisive issues to forge group cohesion, spur supporters into action, and shape narratives that idealize their candidates or causes. While effective in mobilizing support, this strategy often exacerbates extremism and division in online discourse.

Both political parties share responsibility for inciting citizens, and excessive incitement by either or both could cross the line to threatening public order and national stability, i.e., insurrection.

In trying to sort out the genuine issues of the day from the hype, we should all reflect on our basic American principles.

Individual Opinions

American voters mostly vote *against* what they think is wrong rather than voting *for* something they think is good. Politicians run on fixing something that is broken, stopping something the other party did that they do not like, or saving voters from something fearful. In a more cynical view, they also often exploit voters' fears and insecurities, make unrealistic promises of rapid improvement, use their personal stories to emotionally manipulate, exaggerate their track record and experience for self-promotion, adopt moral and ethical stances more for votes than for genuine belief, claim bipartisanship while engaging in partisan tactics, give the illusion of grassroots support while being influenced by special interests, promise innovation and modernization without clear plans, use global issues as tools for political positioning, and overstate their crisis management abilities to appear more competent and authoritative.

So, the political parties pick things the opponents are doing that make voters so mad they are prompted to vote against it. People often say they voted for the lesser of two evils.

Politicians might run on messages of hope and progress, promoting equitable and sustainable policies, sharing authentic personal journeys that resonate with voters, leveraging a solid track record of effective governance, upholding strong moral and ethical principles, fostering bipartisanship and unity, genuinely engaging with and empowering grassroots movements, committing to practical and innovative solutions, adopting a well-informed and cooperative approach to global issues, and demonstrating a clear, responsible strategy for crisis management and leadership. But that will not spur people to go out and vote as much as anger, fear, threats of increasing taxes or losing benefits, and the potential loss of civil liberties.

We should be voting for independent thinkers who cannot be bought by special interests. We should be voting for the positive promises that are achievable.

Media Involvement

The media influences many Americans' opinions on politics and current affairs. Rather than a reflection of diverse viewpoints, there is a tendency to echo extreme pundits on television.

Simultaneously, Americans' fascination with sensational news, akin to the appeal of tabloids, has transitioned to television and social media. This shift is driven by the pursuit of high ratings and advertising revenue (not necessarily an objective truth). The shift from broadcast to cable TV and the rise of social media has reduced government oversight, leading to an increase in distorted, extremist news coverage. This change poses risks to

American free thought, replacing honest debate with propaganda. However, it is essential to recognize the diversity in media and the presence of individuals and groups striving for informed and independent perspectives in political discourse.

There are ways to increase responsibility and accountability, and improve communication, in identifying misinformation. See the following proposals.

Proposal: Ways to Enhance Accountability on Social Media

1. Fact-checking Mechanisms: Social media platforms should implement robust fact-checking mechanisms to identify and flag potentially false or misleading content. This objective can be achieved through partnerships with independent fact-checking organizations and utilizing artificial intelligence algorithms trained to detect patterns of misinformation.

2. Content Transparency: Social media platforms should provide users with more transparency regarding the origins and distribution of content. This includes labeling content as sponsored, identifying bots and fake accounts, and disclosing the algorithms determining content visibility. Require watermarking of all information distributed by, affiliated with, or for the benefit of major political parties.

3. User Ratings: Require media companies to allow users to vote (rate or rank) every posting or news article as to whether it is valid and truthful, suspicious, clearly biased, patently false, or blatantly wrong. The results will reflect the will of the people and remove the obligation from the media owner.

Similarly, there are ways for our country to improve media literacy and critical thinking:

Proposal to Promote Media Literacy and Critical Thinking:

1. Media Literacy Education: Integrate media literacy education into school curricula, equipping students with the critical thinking skills to analyze information, assess credibility, and identify biases critically. This includes understanding the nature of propaganda, recognizing manipulative techniques, and evaluating the trustworthiness of sources.

2. Public Awareness Campaigns: Launch public service announcements (PSAs) to educate the public about the dangers of fake news, propaganda, and blatant lies. These PSAs can be run on various media channels to reach a broad audience, including television, radio, social media, news releases, and community events.

Likewise, strengthening legal frameworks and enforcement are essential to ensuring those responsible for misinformation are held accountable.

Proposal to Strengthen Legal Frameworks and Enforcement:

1. Review Existing Laws: Review and update laws related to defamation, disinformation, and hate speech to ensure they adequately address the online environment. Such updates may involve adapting legal definitions, establishing more precise liability standards, and streamlining enforcement mechanisms. It might also include blocking certain range of Internet protocol (IP) addresses from known bad actor countries (e.g., Russia, North Korea, maybe China).

2. International Cooperation: Foster international cooperation among governments and regulatory bodies to address the cross-border nature of online misinformation. This effort includes sharing best practices, harmonizing legal frameworks, and coordinating enforcement efforts.

3. Hold Platforms Accountable: Establish clear accountability mechanisms for social media platforms in addressing misinformation and harmful content. Such steps would involve introducing financial penalties for persistent violations, imposing the changes described herein, and establishing an independent oversight body.

Educating the public to be more discerning and adept at recognizing deceptive information is crucial, as it empowers individuals to become responsible consumers of online content and plays a vital role in mitigating the spread of misinformation.

Proposals:

1. **Encourage Skepticism and Critical Thinking: Publicize examples of misinformation to encourage individuals to adopt a skeptical mindset when encountering online information; show how to question the source, evaluate evidence, and seek corroboration. Promote the available fact-checking tools and publicly show how to use them. Create and promote a truth-checking AI tool.**

2. **Avoid Sharing Unverified Information: Discourage sharing unverified or misleading information, emphasizing the importance of responsible sharing and the potential consequences of spreading misinformation.**

3. **Traceable Sources: Provide clear trackable information on the source of all publicly available information.**

The Main Issues

Here are the main issues culled from the party positions of the Democrats and Republicans in 2023-2024:

Section	Issue Area
1	Anti-corruption
2	Campaign contributions reforms
3	Civil rights and liberties
4	Domestic affairs and criminal justice
5	Economy
6	Education
7	Energy and environmental stewardship
8	Foreign relations, trade, multilateralism, security
9	Government regulations
10	Gun control, Second Amendment
11	Healthcare and wellness
12	Citizenship, immigration, and enforcement
13	Individual freedoms
14	Judiciary
15	Military
16	Privacy
17	Racial and ethnic equity
18	The rule of law
19	Size of government
20	Cultural issues and human rights

This list reflects each party's core concerns, although others may arise at any time. We'll explore these in relation to party stances and foundational principles. Each section concludes with a recap, summarizing key points for quick reference.

1. Anti-Corruption

Trust in government institutions is pivotal for the stability and advancement of societies, particularly in democracies. Corruption, manifesting in various forms, not only undermines democratic foundations but also erodes public trust and impedes economic development. Addressing corruption requires transparency, accountability, and ethical leadership. It is vital to understand the strategies of political parties in combating this challenge.

Both major parties in the United States recognize the importance of addressing corruption, albeit with approaches shaped by their core principles. Democrats prioritize strong ethics and anti-corruption measures, advocating for rigorous laws and regulations. These measures include preventing conflicts of interest, regulating lobbying activities, and reforming campaign finance to reduce money's influence in politics.

The Supreme Court Ethics, Recusal, and Transparency Act of 2022 is a recent illustration of this approach. This legislation, which aims to establish a code of conduct for Supreme Court justices and enhance disclosure standards, advanced through the House committee with support from Democrats. However, it faced significant opposition from Republicans, who criticized it as intimidation and a personal attack targeting Justice Clarence Thomas.

Despite their commitment to ethics and anti-corruption efforts, the Democratic approach is not immune to criticism. Concerns about perceived partisanship and the practical challenges of implementing reforms have been raised. Additionally, the use of ethics investigations and their potential political implications remain contentious topics. Moreover, despite the party's stance on campaign finance reform, worries persist regarding the influence of corporate interests. Instances of questionable accountability within the party have also emerged, although they may not reflect the party's overarching ethics stance.

Republicans also endorse ethics laws and regulations mandating public officials to disclose financial interests, avoid conflicts of interest, and refrain from corrupt practices. They advocate for principles such as integrity, transparency, and accountability. One criticism often levied against Republicans in their approach to ethics and corruption legislation is their perceived reluctance to enact comprehensive and stringent reforms.

Critics argue that the party tends to prioritize deregulation and limited government intervention, which can sometimes create an environment where opportunities for unethical behavior or corruption may flourish. This criticism is particularly prominent when it comes to campaign finance reform. Some Republicans have been accused of resisting efforts to impose stricter regulations on campaign contributions, arguing for the protection of free speech and limited government interference in the electoral process. Additionally, Republican lawmakers have been accused of resisting calls for greater transparency and accountability in government operations, such as not supporting measures to release presidential tax returns or fully cooperating with ethics investigations. This perceived resistance to robust ethics and corruption legislation has led to concerns among some observers about the party's commitment to addressing these critical issues. Of course, not all Republicans share the same stance on ethics and corruption legislation.

> **Proposal: The law on ethics bill needs to be expanded to include all "meaningful contact" by a private individual and passed into law. The Executive Branch Reform Act, H.R. 984, of 2007, proposed that more than 8,000 executive branch officials report into a public database any "significant contact" from any "private party," defined as all persons other than government officials. The bill defines "significant contact" to be any "oral or written communication (including electronic communication) . . . in which the private party seeks to [garner support for or] influence official action by any officer or employee of the executive branch of the United States."[183] This bill should be revisited and passed.**

Recap - Anti-Corruption

2023-2024 Positions on Anti-Corruption		
Area of Concern	**Democrats**	**Republicans**
Ethics	For robust laws and regulations	Supporting ethics laws and regulations that require public officials to disclose financial interests, avoid conflicts of interest, and refrain from engaging in corrupt practices. Advocate for principles such as integrity, transparency, and accountability.
Transparency	Advocates for policies that ensure government operates transparently.	
Accountability	For accountability across all aspects of government	
Special Interests Influence	Against undue influence	

2. Campaign Contributions Reform

Campaign Contributions Issues

The considerable impact of money in politics extends beyond campaign contributions. In the 1952 presidential election featuring Dwight D. Eisenhower and Adlai Stevenson, the combined spending of both major party candidates amounted to an estimated $19 million (approximately $191 million when adjusted for inflation to 2020 dollars). In the 2020 United States presidential election, including spending by presidential candidates, political parties, various political action committees (PACs), and interest groups, the total expenditure soared to more than $14 billion, marking a staggering 7,130% increase, adjusted for inflation.[89-03]

The pivotal Citizens United case, decided by the Supreme Court in 2010, granted corporations, unions, and specific nonprofit organizations the ability to make unlimited independent expenditures in support of or in opposition to candidates. Notably, this ruling did not alter the ban on direct corporate contributions to candidates but opened the door to heightened spending by external groups. Consequently, this affords organizations a disproportionate level of influence over Congress when compared to individual citizens.

The Federal Election Campaign Act imposes limits to regulate campaign finance, restricting individual contributions to no more than $2,400 for a specific federal election candidate and $30,400 per year for a political party. The act also prohibits corporations and labor unions from directly contributing to candidates. However, corporations and unions can establish political action committees (PACs), and, as per the 2010 Supreme Court decisions, they can finance advertisements advocating for or against presidential or congressional candidates, provided these ads are produced independently from the candidate's campaign.

Additionally, per the Supreme Court ruling, corporations and unions can fund issue-oriented advertisements within 30 days of a primary election and 60 days before a general election. These campaign regulations are designed to prevent individuals and organizations from influencing candidates by making substantial contributions and seeking favors when the candidate is in office.

On the other hand, "soft money" donations represent a workaround to these rules. These are given to political parties, ostensibly for "party building" activities not directly related to the election of specific candidates. In the 2000 presidential election, soft money contributions were estimated at $500 million. However, in 2002, Congress banned them with the passage of the Bipartisan Campaign Reform Act (the McCain-Feingold Act). This law was initially ruled unconstitutional by federal courts but was eventually upheld by the Supreme Court in December 2003.

As a result of these dynamics, the representation of the average citizen in the political process has been overshadowed by the financial influence wielded by large corporations and unions.

Proposals to Address the Continued Use of "Soft Money":

1. **Strengthening and Clarifying Existing Laws: Amend the Bipartisan Campaign Reform Act to close loopholes that allow for the indirect use of soft money in federal campaigns. This would involve clearer definitions and stricter limits on funds raised and spent by state committees and other entities indirectly involved in federal campaigns.**
2. **Enhanced Enforcement Mechanisms: Empower the Federal Election Commission (FEC) with greater resources and authority to enforce campaign finance laws. This includes implementing stricter penalties for violations and establishing a more efficient process for investigating and prosecuting cases of illegal soft money usage.**
3. **Transparency and Reporting Requirements: Mandate comprehensive disclosure of all political contributions and expenditures, including those made to and by super PACs. Implement real-time reporting systems to ensure prompt public access to campaign finance data.**
4. **Public Financing of Campaigns: Introduce a system of public financing for federal campaigns to reduce candidates' reliance on private donations. This system could offer matching funds for small contributions, incentivizing candidates to seek support from a broader base of small donors.**
5. **Educational and Advocacy Campaigns: Launch public awareness campaigns to educate both politicians and the public about the importance of campaign finance laws and the negative impact of soft money on democratic processes. Encourage civic organizations to advocate for stronger campaign finance regulations.**
6. **Investigate illegal donations: Empower the IRS to look for donations passed by corporations to specific candidates by paying its managers to make those donations.**

Campaign Contribution Limits

The following table shows the existing Contribution limits per calendar year:[94]

Campaign Donation Limits Overview

The following information represents the donation limits applicable for various donor categories to different recipient entities. The limits are established to regulate the flow of money and ensure transparency and fairness in political funding.

Donor Types

Individual: An individual person donating.
Candidate Committee: A committee set up by a candidate for the purpose of financing their election campaign.
PAC (Political Action Committee): Classified into two types - Multicandidate and No multicandidate.
Party Committee: This can refer to different levels including State, District, Local, or National committees.

Recipients and Donation Limits by Donor Type

Additional National Party Committee (Non-federal account):

> Individual: $123,300 per year.
> Candidate Committee: Unlimited.
> PAC, Multicandidate: Unlimited.
> PAC, Non-multicandidate: Unlimited.
> Party Committee (State/District/Local): Unlimited transfers.
> Party Committee (National): Unlimited transfers.

Party Committee (State/District/Local):
> Individual: $10,000 per year (combined).
> Candidate Committee: Unlimited transfers.
> PAC, Multicandidate: $5,000 per year.
> PAC, Non-multicandidate: $5,000 per year.
> Party Committee (National): Unlimited transfers.

PAC (Separate Segregated and Nonconnected):
> Individual: $5,000 per year.
> Candidate Committee: Unlimited transfers.
> PAC, Multicandidate: $5,000 per year.
> PAC, Non-multicandidate: $5,000 per year.
> Party Committee (State/District/Local): Unlimited transfers.
> Party Committee (National): Unlimited transfers.

Candidate Committee:
    Individual: $3,300 per election.
    Candidate Committee: $2,000 per election.
    PAC, Multicandidate: $5,000 per election.
    PAC, Non-multicandidate: $5,000 per election.
    Party Committee (State/District/Local): $5,000 per election (combined).
    Party Committee (National): $5,000 per election.

Note: The donation limits are designed to maintain a balance between freedom of expression and the potential for undue influence. These limits are subject to change based on legislation and regulatory guidance. The specifics can vary by jurisdiction and the type of election (e.g., primary, general, special, or runoff elections).

Political Reform

Political parties advocating for political reform present an interesting paradox. The same parties, which have been instrumental in shaping our current political landscape, are now the ones pushing for changes and reforms. The Democrats have said they will:[81-85]

- "… make government more transparent, accountable, and inclusive.

- "… rather than obstruct people's use of the Freedom of Information Act, agencies [will be required to] conduct significant business in public and release all relevant information unless an agency reasonably foresees harm to a protected interest.

- "… lift the veil of secret deals in Washington by publishing searchable, online information about federal grants, contracts, earmarks, loans, and lobbyist contacts with government officials.

- "… make government data available online and have an online video archive of significant agency meetings.

- "… put all non-emergency bills that Congress has passed online for five days, to allow the American public to review and comment on them before they are signed into law.

- "… require cabinet officials to have periodic national online town hall meetings to discuss issues before their agencies.

> • "… not privatize public services for the sake of privatizing but use carefully crafted guidelines when determining whether to contract out any government service and whether a function is "inherently governmental."
>
> • "… provide improved accountability, oversight, and management in the contracting process to protect the public."

Republicans acknowledged in their platform that, "Short-term politics [in Washington] overshadow the long-term interests of the nation. Our national legislature uses a budget process devised long before the Internet and seems unable to deal in realistic ways with the most pressing problems of families, businesses, and communities. Members of Congress have been indicted for violating public trust. Public disgust with Washington is entirely warranted."

Of course, one might ask why this was not corrected when the Republicans (or Democrats) had control of Congress.

Republicans also said they would, "Constrain the federal government to its legitimate Constitutional functions. Let it empower people, while limiting its reach into their lives. Spend only what is necessary, and tax only to raise revenue for essential government functions. Unleash the power of enterprise, innovation, civic energy, and the American spirit – and never pretend that government is a substitute for family or community."[89-01]

> **Proposal: Redesign election campaign financing so that all donations must come through individual citizens, or at least limit donations from large organizations so they do not exceed those from individual citizen donations in aggregate.**

> **Proposal: Set a strict maximum limit from a single source or related sources so that no donation buys influence from the candidate.**

*Recap - **Campaign Contributions Reform***

2023-2024 Positions on Campaign Contributions Reform		
Area of Concern	**Democrats**	**Republicans**
Campaign Finance	For reforming campaign finance laws to reduce the influence of large donors and increase the role of small donors in the political process. Support measures like public financing of elections and stricter disclosure requirements.	Emphasize the importance of protecting free speech rights in the context of campaign finance regulations. Argue against restrictions on political donations and spending, viewing them as potential infringing on First Amendment rights.

3. Civil Rights and Liberties

According to the principles in our Constitution, a just and equitable society needs political parties that address civil rights and liberties for the benefit of ALL American citizens, not just for the benefit of their own supporters. Civil rights and liberties are the bedrock of democracy, ensuring that all citizens enjoy equal protection under the law and are free to express themselves, participate in the political process, and live without discrimination. As the nation grapples with complex issues surrounding racial and gender equality, LGBTQ+ rights, voting rights, and more, it is imperative to examine how political parties envision addressing these concerns while safeguarding and advancing our nation's fundamental principles.

Democrats have long positioned themselves as champions of civil rights and liberties, emphasizing a commitment to ensuring equal opportunities and protection for all Americans. Their approach often includes advocating for policies that address systemic racism, gender inequality, and discrimination. Democrats have pushed for voting rights reforms, seeking to expand access to the ballot box and combat voter suppression. They have also been at the forefront of advocating for LGBTQ+ rights, women's reproductive rights, and immigration reform. Additionally, Democrats have supported criminal justice reform initiatives aimed at reducing mass incarceration and addressing racial disparities within the criminal justice system. Their vision centers on a more inclusive and equitable society where every individual can exercise their rights and liberties without fear of discrimination or infringement.

Common criticisms of the Democrats' approach to civil rights and liberties often revolve around the party's commitment to individual freedoms and the potential overreach of government authority. Critics argue that Democrats' support for expanding the role of government in areas such as healthcare, education, and economic regulation can lead to excessive bureaucracy, increased costs, and reduced personal liberties. Some also express apprehension about the potential curbing of religious freedoms and free speech rights in the name of combating discrimination and hate speech. Furthermore, there is concern in some quarters that the Democrats' emphasis on identity politics may contribute to division and polarization, undermining the goal of achieving a more inclusive and united society.

Republicans have a different approach to civil rights and liberties, often emphasizing limited government intervention and individual liberties as core principles. They tend to prioritize the protection of religious freedoms and gun rights as essential civil liberties. Republicans argue that economic policies promoting small government and deregulation can lead to greater personal freedom and prosperity, which they see as integral to civil liberties.

While they may support criminal justice reform efforts, they often place a greater emphasis on law and order as a means of ensuring civil rights and safety and privatizing prison management. Republicans have also voiced concerns about what they view as excessive government regulations that they believe can encroach on individual liberties and free-market capitalism. Their vision centers on safeguarding individual freedoms to protect civil rights and liberties, with a belief that these goals are best achieved with limited government intervention.

Critics of the Republican approach to civil rights and liberties often contend that the party's emphasis on limited government can undermine protections for marginalized groups, potentially perpetuating discrimination and inequality. Key areas of concern include voting rights, with critics arguing that stricter voter ID laws and voting restrictions disproportionately affect minority communities and are thinly-veiled voter suppression tactics. Additionally, the Republican stance on LGBTQ+ rights and opposition to same-sex marriage has been criticized for being discriminatory. Even though in 2015, more than 300 Republicans asked the Supreme Court to back Gay Marriage.[39-15] There is also concern that the party's support for limited government can result in inadequate social safety nets and limited access to healthcare, posing challenges to achieving greater social and economic equality.

Here are some dimensions to these issues.

Liberty

Life, liberty, and the pursuit of happiness are fundamental principles Americans hold dear, with liberty occupying a central role. Liberty is not only vital for the pursuit of happiness but also integral to our way of life. Therefore, many consider liberty the paramount American principle. The primary function of our government is to protect liberty and prevent any undue influence or factions from undermining the rights of our citizens.[51]

In the government's role of preserving our liberty, all three branches – executive, legislature, and judiciary – operate with the shared objective of maintaining a system of checks and balances.

The American principles of freedom of speech, the right to assemble, and freedom of religion emerged in response to the oppression of monarchial governments and the founders' unwavering commitment to liberty. Our federal government plays a crucial role in safeguarding these freedoms. Although these rights are not as absolute as liberty, they are intricately connected to and reliant upon it. For instance, freedom of speech has limitations, including the prohibition of causing harm to others or inciting imminent lawless action, as defined by the Supreme Court. Additionally, certain forms of commercial speech are not protected.

The government usually grants corporations similar legal rights as individual citizens, treating them as distinct legal entities with some similarities but not complete equivalence to individuals. However, there are instances where the government intervenes to protect citizens from corporate actions.

Corporate vs. Individual Treatment: Case Studies

1. Establishing the federal do-not-call (DNC) list, which restricts corporate telemarketing.

2. The Environmental Protection Agency (EPA) enforces laws that limit pollution and ensure clean air and water, including regulations like the Clean Air Act and the Clean Water Act, which impose restrictions on industries to prevent environmental degradation and protect public health.

3. The Consumer Financial Protection Bureau (CFPB) aims to ensure fair, transparent, and competitive practices in the financial industry. The CFPB oversees mortgage lending, credit card offers, and payday loans to protect consumers from predatory practices and financial fraud.

It is essential to recognize that protecting citizens' rights is a delicate balancing act, and the more exceptions the government introduces, the greater the potential for erosion of those rights. Power begets the desire for more power. And, as John Dalberg-Acton, 1st Baron Acton, said in April 1887 in a letter to ecclesiastic scholar Mandell Creighton about why monarchs and popes are not above judgment by their subjects, "Power tends to corrupt, and absolute power corrupts absolutely." What many seldom hear is the comments that follow that statement, "Great men are almost always bad men, even when they exercise influence and not authority: still more when you superadd the tendency or certainty of corruption by full authority. There is no worse heresy than the fact that the office sanctifies the holder of it."[55]

Proposal: We need to better define which parts of our Constitution should never change and which parts should be reconsidered from time to time. Some sections are clearly out of date and others are so fundamental that they must endure.

What rousing debates the country would experience if we undertook such an endeavor, and what a message we would send to the rest of the world.

Just as Jefferson had hoped, our Constitution has set an example for the rest of the world and has, along with principles from other countries, influenced the United Nations to define for the entire world a set of human rights.

Media

The current media landscape is often perceived as being biased. Major cable news channels are sometimes accused of sensationalizing news, with some perceived as leaning significantly towards either the left or the right politically. Various factors influence this perception of bias.

As background, the nature of journalism often involves highlighting social injustices and giving a voice to the marginalized, which can lead to a focus on "underdog" narratives. This focus is sometimes interpreted as a left-leaning bias, as stories about disadvantaged groups' challenges tend to receive more attention. Additionally, negative stories are often seen as more newsworthy or engaging than positive ones, also influencing the type of content that is more frequently broadcast or published.

That said, it is essential to acknowledge that media outlets have diverse editorial policies and perspectives, and the perception of bias can vary among audiences, depending on the "the view of the viewer."

Some believe that the perceived leanings of various media reflect the views of the owners of those media. This is a topic often discussed in media studies and political communication. It is generally accepted that the owners of media outlets can influence the editorial stance and content of their publications or broadcasts, although the degree of this influence varies.

For example, consider Rupert Murdoch's News Corporation, which owns various media outlets worldwide, including Fox News in the United States. Murdoch's conservative political views are often seen as reflected in the editorial stance of Fox News, particularly in its opinion programming, which has a reputation for leaning conservative.

Since Jeff Bezos, known for founding Amazon, acquired *The Washington Post*, there have been discussions about how his business interests and personal views might influence the newspaper's reporting. However, it is worth noting that *The Washington Post* maintains editorial independence, and there has been no clear evidence of Bezos directly influencing its news coverage.

It is essential to recognize that many news organizations have editorial policies and journalistic standards designed to maintain a degree of independence from their owners' personal views. So, accusing the media of "owner bias" may not stand up as a generalization.

While there is a growing perception among some viewers that television news media often lack balance and objectivity, this view is not universally held. Many people still seek and value news sources that provide balanced views, honesty, and truth.

Our goal should be to eliminate or at least "call out" propaganda – information, especially of a biased or misleading nature, used to promote a political cause or point of view. It often involves the dissemination of selected facts, arguments, rumors, half-truths, or lies to influence public opinion or obscure the truth. Propaganda is typically used to persuade or manipulate the audience to align with a particular agenda, and it can be found in various forms such as TV and Cable broadcasts, social media, online blogs and articles, public statements, educational materials, and even entertainment. The key characteristic of propaganda is its intent to persuade or influence, often by using emotional or irrational appeals, rather than purely providing information.[39-05]

Oxford Reference Dictionary Definition of "Propaganda"

Persuasive mass communication that filters and frames the issues of the day in a way that strongly favors particular interests; usually those of a government or corporation. Also, the intentional manipulation of public opinion through lies, half-truths, and the selective re-telling of history.[39-04]

Proposal: Introduce a robust media transparency system requiring all media outlets, including digital and social platforms, to adhere to several key disclosures:

1. **Create an independent regulatory body that would assign an overall 'political leanings label'—ranging from blue (Democrat) to red (Republican)—to networks, individual media sources, or their articles, similar to the ratings given to movies by the Motion Picture Association (MPA). This labeling system would signal to readers the media's degree of leaning and objectivity.**
2. **Media owners must disclose their relationships with lobbyists and political entities to highlight potential biases.**
3. **The political positions and affiliations of major media advertisers/sponsors and their owners would be made transparent. This comprehensive system will also include strict enforcement and compliance measures, with clear penalties for non-adherence. It would be universally applicable and adaptable to regional or national contexts while maintaining its core principles.**

This information would be easily accessible to the public, and educational initiatives would help people interpret and effectively use this information, thus fostering a more informed and critical audience.

The concentration or consolidation of media ownership is also an issue, where fewer individuals or organizations control increasingly larger shares of the mass media outlets. This can lead to a lack of diversity in perspectives and a single narrative dominating public discourse. Ensuring the independence of the press is crucial for safeguarding all our freedoms.

Such centralization can be seen in companies like Comcast, which owns NBCUniversal, or Disney, which owns ABC, ESPN, and several other media entities, or Paramount Global, which owns TV stations, production companies, and streaming services.

Critics argue that when a few entities control a substantial portion of the media landscape, it can negatively impact democratic processes by limiting the range of viewpoints and information accessible to the public. This concentration can be seen as a threat to freedom of expression and a well-informed citizenry, which are crucial for a healthy democracy.

However, the rise of digital media and the Internet has introduced new platforms and voices, countering the effects of traditional media concentration. Recently, though, the acquisition and control of online media by entities like Meta (Facebook), X (Twitter), Instagram, and others is becoming a new area of consolidation and concern.

> **Proposal: Limit the size of communications channels to a maximum like 15% or 20% of market share.**

Antitrust

While the United States has been actively pursuing antitrust cases against various industries, including technology, since the Sherman Act of 1890 and the Clayton Act of 1914, some politicians think the U.S. has not done enough, especially against large companies. The European Union has also been notable for its stringent regulatory actions against some of America's largest companies, particularly in the tech sector. The goal of antitrust actions is to ensure competition and address monopolistic practices in the market. Another motive is to constrain big tech companies from gaining overwhelming control of global communications and commerce. Once more, this objective is about averting excessive concentration of power.

The EU's rigorous antitrust investigations and regulations, including implementing the Digital Markets Act, reflect a concerted effort to ensure fair competition, protect consumer interests, and maintain a balanced digital market. This approach is driven by concerns over the potential for tech giants to dominate critical aspects of the digital economy and influence societal and economic activities. The EU's measures are aimed at curbing the market power of these large firms and ensuring that the digital marketplace remains open and competitive.[39-09]

Here are examples of the EU taking the lead in antitrust actions compared to the U.S.

Major EU Antitrust Actions against U.S. Tech Companies[39-05]

1. **Google**: The European Commission has levied multiple fines against Google for alleged anti-competitive practices, including abusing its market dominance in online searches and advertising.
2. **Apple**: The EU has investigated Apple for issues related to tax practices and the operation of its App Store, with concerns about how the company allegedly stifles competition.
3. **Facebook (now Meta Platforms)**: The EU has also scrutinized Facebook for its data practices and potential anti-competitive behavior, particularly regarding its acquisitions and market dominance.
4. **Microsoft**: In the past, Microsoft faced significant scrutiny and fines from the EU, particularly related to its Windows operating system and bundling practices.

These cases underscore the differing regulatory philosophies and approaches between the U.S. and the EU. The latter's actions often prioritize market structure and long-term competition, while the former traditionally places greater emphasis on consumer welfare and prices. The EU's proactive stance has influenced international discussions about digital markets, competition, and consumer protection. At the same time, U.S. actions need to strike a balance between corporate interests and the necessity of fostering fair global competition, particularly in the context of digital markets and antitrust laws. Additionally, it is crucial to consider the impact on consumers, innovation, and broader market dynamics, all of which should be aligned with diplomatic and trade relations to ensure that transatlantic cooperation remains unaffected.

That said, the U.S. is pursuing some of its own actions.

U.S. Antitrust Issues and Cases to Watch in 2024

1. **Live Nation and Ticketmaster:** The Department of Justice (DOJ) is scrutinizing the dominant role of Live Nation in the live music industry, a merger that dates to 2010. This case is a top priority for the DOJ.
2. **Apple:** The DOJ's ongoing investigation focuses on Apple's control over its mobile operating system and App Store, examining potential harm to developers and customers through higher prices.
3. **RealPage:** The subject of a DOJ investigation for allegedly conspiring with landlords and property managers to fix apartment listing prices.
4. **Visa:** Under DOJ investigation for potentially illegal actions to exclude competing payment processing networks.
5. **UnitedHealthcare and Amedisys:** DOJ is investigating UnitedHealthcare's acquisitions in the health sector, notably its purchase of home health company Amedisys.
6. **Amazon and iRobot:** The Federal Trade Commission (FTC) is reviewing Amazon's $1.4 billion purchase of Roomba-maker iRobot, concerned about potential favoritism towards Roomba products over competitors.
7. **Kroger and Albertsons:** The FTC is deciding whether to intervene in this mega-merger, which could create the nation's largest chain of grocery stores.
8. **Oil Mergers:** The FTC is reviewing significant mergers in the oil sector, like Exxon Mobil's deal for Pioneer Natural Resources and Chevron's takeover of Hess Corp.
9. **Subway:** Under FTC investigation for its takeover by Roark Capital, which already owns competing chains.
10. **Qualcomm and Autotalks:** The FTC is scrutinizing Qualcomm's acquisition of Autotalks, a company specializing in assisted and autonomous vehicle technology.

The Republican position on antitrust heading into the 2024 elections reflects a mix of traditional and evolving views. Traditionally, many Republicans favor a free-market approach, emphasizing minimal government intervention in the market. However, a growing faction within the party is calling for stricter antitrust enforcement against large technology companies, driven by concerns over market dominance, especially in social media and e-commerce. This shift has led to various legislative proposals to update antitrust laws to address digital market challenges, indicating a divergence within the party between those advocating for robust enforcement and those adhering to conventional laissez-faire principles. Additionally,

Republicans are mindful of international competition, particularly Chinese tech firms, and balancing the need to regulate domestically while ensuring American companies remain globally competitive.

The Democrats' stance on antitrust going into the 2024 elections is oriented towards more vigorous enforcement, particularly against the market dominance of big technology companies. This position highlights the need to protect consumers and small businesses from monopolistic practices and calls for legislative and regulatory reforms to update antitrust laws for the digital age. Democrats link robust antitrust enforcement with broader issues such as labor rights and economic inequality, emphasizing that unchecked corporate power can negatively impact wages and worker conditions. Their focus extends beyond the tech sector to concerns about consolidation in industries like pharmaceuticals and agriculture. Some members are pushing for radical changes, while others are supporting more moderate updates. The Democrats' approach also considers the global economic landscape, emphasizing the need for American companies to be competitive internationally while maintaining fair market practices domestically.

> **Proposal: The U.S. should take stronger measures to counter the heavy restrictions imposed by the EU on American companies, prioritizing the protection of creativity and economic growth.**

Our antitrust laws could benefit from improvements.

Proposals for Improving U.S. Antitrust Laws:

1. **Modernizing Antitrust Laws**: Update antitrust laws to better address the realities of today's digital economy. This would involve refining definitions and standards for anti-competitive practices to accommodate the nuances of digital markets and platforms.
2. **Bipartisan Commission on Antitrust**: Establish a bipartisan commission or task force to study current market dynamics and make recommendations. This commission would include economics, law, technology, and consumer rights experts, ensuring a balanced perspective.
3. **Enhanced Merger Guidelines**: Update merger guidelines to more effectively assess the long-term competitive impacts of corporate mergers and acquisitions, especially in rapidly evolving sectors like technology and pharmaceuticals.
4. **Balanced Enforcement**: Advocate for consistent and balanced enforcement of existing antitrust laws, avoiding overreach and under-enforcement. This would ensure that the antitrust divisions of the DOJ and the FTC are adequately resourced.
5. **Promoting Competition and Innovation**: Introduce policies that support small businesses and startups, reduce barriers to market entry, and encourage open markets.
6. **Consumer Welfare Focus**: Maintain a focus on consumer welfare, not just in terms of prices but also quality, choice, and innovation. This approach recognizes that consumer interests may not always align with those of competitors in the market.
7. **Global Coordination**: Coordinate with international regulatory bodies to address global antitrust concerns, especially with the rise of multinational corporations and digital platforms that operate across borders.
8. **Regular Review and Adaptation**: Implement a mechanism for regularly reviewing antitrust policies and their effectiveness, allowing for adaptations as market conditions and technologies evolve.

On a smaller scale, fostering competition remains vital within the framework of American capitalism. Competition plays a pivotal role in improving efficiency and driving down prices. One key issue lies in the unfair advantage bestowed upon larger corporations through volume discounts. For instance, small businesses encounter significant challenges in terms of pricing when competing with giants like Walmart, primarily because these large companies can leverage their massive purchasing power to secure more substantial volume discounts and concessions from suppliers. This enables manufacturers to operate more efficiently and offer lower wholesale prices that ultimately benefit consumers. Consequently, this dynamic often confers monopolistic advantages to retail giants like Walmart, contributing to the decline of many local small businesses.

> **Proposal: Wholesale pricing should be the same for all retailers regardless of order size. Let competition be based on a company's own efficiencies, not the efficiencies of their suppliers. If all companies paid the same wholesale rate (including all promotional co-op advertising and other marketing assistance), then Walmart and other retail giants would not as readily put all the smaller stores out of business.**

Equal Rights and Equity

According to our Constitution, Americans are born with equal rights, but their opportunities in life may not always be equal due to innate differences in capabilities, family resources, and societal circumstances. This has been termed "equal opportunity but not necessarily equal results."[39-15] It is important to clarify that we are not talking about equality for minority groups here, which is another topic. Everyone is born with uniquely different innate capacities for thinking, learning, and prospering. These differences manifest in varying levels of intelligence, accomplishments, and rewards resulting from individual efforts. If society does not erect artificial barriers preventing individuals from reaching their maximum potential, that should be considered an adequate level of equality. Our government should equally protect our right to be different.

This perspective underscores the significance of individual initiative, taking personal responsibility, and safeguarding the fruits of one's labor, all while recognizing the imperative of helping those confronted with dire circumstances they cannot control.

> **Proposal: Our taxes should support those who are genuinely struggling through no fault of their own without redistributing wealth beyond what is necessary to assist those in need. That said, the poor should not go hungry, the children of the poor should not suffer their parents' inadequacies, and everyone should be afforded opportunities to learn, work, grow, and prosper.**

Redistribution of Wealth and Taxes

The principle of "equal opportunity but not necessarily equal results" acknowledges that individuals will achieve varying levels of success. This principle does not imply that the rewards of the more successful should be arbitrarily redistributed to the less successful.

In debates on government wealth redistribution, many argue that those who have failed to take advantage of the opportunities afforded them due to a lack of hard work, preparation, or responsibility should not automatically be entitled to the rewards earned by those who have achieved success. Critics of this viewpoint believe redistribution demotivates hardworking individuals and encourages others to rely on financial support without effort. However, support should be given to those who are in dire need due to circumstances beyond their control.

Individuals are encouraged to practice "self-propelled generosity," meaning the more successful one is, the more generous one should be. However, this does not always hold true.

"Self-propelled generosity" differs from government-aided wealth redistribution in its consistency and fairness. In challenging economic times, such generosity may wane, and its distribution can be uneven. Government assistance, on the other hand, is viewed as more reliable and equitable.

Philanthropists face challenges in effectively allocating funds and navigating legal, ethical, and cultural considerations. Philanthropy aims to create sustainable, positive change but requires careful planning and coordination.

The redistribution of wealth by the central government was considered unacceptable by America's Founding Fathers. However, the complexities of today's federal government and the increased need for revenue have changed perspectives.

America's tax systems often result in double or triple taxation, as seen in thrift shops collecting sales tax on already taxed items and the taxation of pensions in states where they were not earned.

As stated in Wikipedia, Samuel Adams criticized the concept of wealth leveling and communal goods as impractical and contrary to American principles. The notion of wealth redistribution can disincentivize risk-taking and success, which is central to the American dream. While the intention of redistribution is to protect the helpless, taxation does not always serve this purpose. The focus should be on enabling the less fortunate through means like job training, with government support providing a safety net.

Capitalism, the foundation of America's economy, involves private control of production, free market trade, profit distribution, and wage payment. However, the assumption that everyone has an equal chance to become rich or poor is not always valid, particularly for those born into poverty. Ensuring equal opportunity without enforcing uniformity in wealth is crucial for maintaining the incentive to excel.

Thomas Jefferson wrote about the taxation system, emphasizing the importance of selecting a basis for taxation that reaches every member of society and draws an equal proportion of public contributions from them. He warned against double taxation, where the same income is taxed multiple times, and stressed the duty of the government to provide equal and impartial justice to all citizens. He also mentioned the possibility of using laws of equal inheritance as a corrective measure if overgrown wealth threatens the state.

Jefferson wrote,

"The taxes with which we are familiar, class themselves readily according to the basis on which they rest. 1. Capital. 2. Income. 3. Consumption. These may be considered as commensurate; Consumption being generally equal to Income, and Income the annual profit of Capital. A government may select any one of these bases for the establishment of its system of taxation, and so frame it as to reach the faculties of every member of the society and to draw from him his equal proportion of the public contributions; and, if this be correctly obtained, it is the perfection of the function of taxation. But, when once a government has assumed its basis, to select and tax special articles from either of the other classes, is double taxation. For example, if the system be established on the basis of Income, and his just proportion on that scale has been already drawn from every one, to step into the field of Consumption, and tax special articles in that, as broadcloth or homespun, wine or whiskey, a coach or a wagon, is doubly taxing the same article. For that portion of Income with which these articles are purchased, having already paid its tax as Income, to pay another tax on the thing it purchased, is paying twice for the same thing, it is an aggrievance [sic] on the citizens who use these articles in exoneration of those who do not, contrary to the most sacred of the duties of a government, to do equal and impartial justice to all its citizens. How far it may be the interest and the duty of all to submit to this sacrifice on other grounds; for instance, to pay for a time an impost on the importation of certain articles, in order to encourage their manufacture at home, or an excise on others injurious to the morals or health of the citizens, will depend on a series of considerations of another order, and beyond the proper limits of this note. … To this a single observation shall yet be added. Whether property alone, and the whole of what each citizen possesses, shall be subject to contribution, or only its surplus after satisfying his first wants, or whether the faculties of body and mind shall contribute also from their annual earnings, is a question to be decided. But, when decided, and the principle settled, it is to be equally and fairly applied to all. To take from one, because it is thought that his own industry and that of his fathers' has acquired too much, in order to spare to others, who, or whose fathers have not exercised equal industry and skill, is to violate arbitrarily the first principle of association, 'the guarantee to every one of a free

> exercise of his industry, and the fruits acquired by it.' If the overgrown wealth of an individual be deemed dangerous to the State, the best corrective is the law of equal inheritance to all in equal degree; and the better, as this enforces a law of nature, while extra-taxation violates it."[02-c]

Jefferson, in his autobiography in 1821, expressed dislike of wealth-driven aristocracy, writing, "An aristocracy of wealth [is] of more harm and danger than benefit to society."[180-02-b]

He added later, in a letter to John Adams, "Enough wealthy men will find their way into every branch of the legislature to protect themselves."[181-02]

> **Proposal: Corporate dividends should not be taxed at the federal level as part of personal income, because they were already taxed at the corporate level, which violates the standard of no double taxation, especially, when corporations are treated as individuals.**

> **Proposal: A substantial overhaul of the current tax system, such as:**
>
> **A Simplified Income Tax Structure: Simplify the tax structure to one with a few fixed tiers based on income (indexed after 2023) with no deductions – to minimize government bureaucracy and associated costs, thereby potentially reducing the overall tax burden.**
>
> **Or, alternatively, phase out all income taxes and institute a national tax on consumption, such as a Federal Sales Tax (or VAT).**

Protection of Rights, Liberty, and Individual Freedoms

In America, the government exists, according to our Constitution, to "promote the general welfare" of its citizens. This means the government exists to protect its citizens' well-being – sheltering them from evil, calamity, and other disturbances to their common blessings of life, which means personal prosperity and happiness. These protections are constitutionally-guaranteed human rights.

Maintaining constitutionally-guaranteed human rights is an essential role of America's government and includes, as Tocqueville described, **"protecting the inalienable rights of minorities against oppression by the majority."**[39-14] If this government role did not exist, America's minorities might still be enslaved and unable to vote, let alone run for and hold office. However, the American definition of human rights does not include all rights; for example, our protected rights do not preclude the death penalty (i.e., even though it includes the protections of **life**, liberty, and the pursuit of happiness), which is the case in other democracies. A constitution defines what the government is bound to defend and protect and, therefore, we must ensure that our Constitution reflects our beliefs and defends the rights we believe should be inviolable.

The Democratic Party's position on civil rights and liberties focuses on ending discrimination based on race, ethnicity, national origin, language, religion, gender, age, sexual orientation, gender identity, or disability. They are committed to protecting voting rights, freedom of religion, women's healthcare decisions, and equal federal rights for LGBT couples. Their platform also includes striving for criminal justice reform and "common-sense" approaches to reduce and prevent gun violence.

The Republican Party take a socially conservative position on civil rights and liberties. It advocates for traditional family values, often rooted in Christianity, and includes opposition to abortion, same-sex marriage, transgender rights, and comprehensive sex education. The party also tends to oppose gun control, affirmative action, and illegal immigration. Within the party, there are diverse views on some of these issues, but, overall, the Republican platform tends to emphasize traditional social values and individual liberties.

> **Proposal: We should develop a timeline for harmonizing our human rights policies with the other democracies in the world. The plan would include launching a worldwide information campaign that focuses on the positive attributes of democracy. This campaign would aim to shift the narrative from "death to America" to "why not govern like America."**

Discrimination

While Republicans and Democrats may have differing viewpoints on the significance and nature of discrimination, it is recognized by both parties as an issue of concern that merits attention and discussion in American politics.

Democrats often prioritize addressing systemic discrimination and promoting social justice through policies such as affirmative action and anti-discrimination laws. They advocate for government intervention and social programs to reduce economic disparities and emphasize diversity, equity, and inclusion.

Republicans, on the other hand, emphasize individual liberties and limited government intervention, leading to skepticism about government-enforced anti-discrimination policies. They prioritize individual responsibility and market-driven solutions to address inequalities and may argue that some policies, like affirmative action, equate to reverse discrimination. Republicans also stress traditional values and may have varying views on LGBTQ+ rights and immigration policies.

> **Proposal: Discrimination laws should continue to evolve and be enforced as elimination of discrimination is the essence of our Constitution. Age discrimination in hiring warrants special attention. Hiring must be in proportion to the number of applicants for all age groups – and verified, as is the case for race and gender.**

Recap – Civil Rights and Liberties

2023-2024 Positions on Civil Rights and Liberties		
Area of Concern	**Democrats**	**Republicans**
Protections of Constitutional Rights	Advocate for protection of individuals' rights to free speech, freedom of religion, LGBTQ+ rights, and other constitutional rights. Oppose hate speech, advocate for online speech moderation.	Some Republicans advocate for religious exemptions in cases involving civil rights issues, protecting individual rights, including free speech, religious freedom, and the Second Amendment (guns), but some do not recognize LGBTQ+ rights.
Antitrust	Their overarching goals are to promote competition, regulate corporate power, and address economic disparities.	Their stance is evolving, blending traditional free-market beliefs with a newer push for targeted antitrust action in specific sectors.
Redistribution of wealth	Support progressive taxation and government policies aimed at reducing income and wealth disparities by increasing taxes on higher income earners and corporations to fund social programs and support for those in need.	Emphasize limited government intervention in the economy, favoring policies that encourage economic growth, job creation, and individual prosperity through lower taxes, reduced regulations. They believe that individuals should have greater control over their wealth and financial decisions.
Protection of Liberty and Individual Rights	Focus on government intervention and regulation to ensure equal access, opportunity, and protection of civil liberties, often advocating for policies that address social and economic inequalities while upholding individual freedoms.	Prioritize limited government intervention, emphasizing personal responsibility, individual liberties, and free-market principles, often advocating for reduced government regulations and taxation to safeguard individual freedoms.

| Discrimination | Emphasize the importance of addressing systemic inequalities and promoting policies that combat discrimination based on race, gender, sexual orientation, and other factors. They encourage government intervention, equal protection under the law, and social justice initiatives. | Emphasize individual liberties, personal responsibility, and limited government intervention, often advocating for market-driven solutions and opposing certain government-mandated measures designed to address discrimination, while also acknowledging the importance of individual rights and equal treatment under the law. |

4. Domestic Affairs and Criminal Justice

Domestic Affairs

"Domestic affairs" refers to the management and governance of activities, policies, and issues that occur within a nation's borders, directly affecting a country's citizens. This encompasses many areas, such as internal politics, law and order, public health, education, infrastructure development, economic policy, and social welfare.

Democrats advocate for a more active role of the government in society and the economy. They support policies like expanded access to healthcare, increased funding for public education, progressive taxation to reduce income inequality, and stronger regulations to address climate change.

In contrast, Republicans prioritize limited government intervention, individual liberties, and free-market principles. They often advocate for lower taxes, particularly for businesses and high-income individuals, reducing government expenditure on social programs, and minimizing business regulations. Republicans consistently back policies aimed at fostering economic growth and encouraging personal responsibility. In education, they commonly endorse school choice and voucher programs. Environmental policy positions also differ, with Republicans favoring fewer business regulations to stimulate economic growth and achieve energy independence. These positions underscore a fundamental divergence in perspectives regarding the role and scope of government when it comes to the economy and social welfare.

Domestic Aid and General Welfare

This refers to policies aimed at improving citizens' living conditions and well-being and can include diverse programs and services in the fields of healthcare, education, social security, public safety, infrastructure development, housing assistance, and disaster relief. These efforts are designed to support various segments of the population, particularly those in need or at risk, to ensure a basic living standard and promote overall societal welfare.

Democrats believe that investing in the nation's infrastructure is not only a means of improving physical assets but also a way to stimulate economic growth, create jobs, and address critical societal challenges. They advocate for substantial investments in repairing and modernizing the nation's roads, bridges, public transportation systems, and utilities, arguing that this not only enhances safety and efficiency but also contributes to long-term economic competitiveness. Additionally, Democrats prioritize addressing climate change through green infrastructure projects, like renewable energy initiatives and electric vehicle charging networks.

Their approach extends to expanding broadband in underserved areas and strengthening healthcare and education infrastructure. While some critics question the cost of these plans and the focus on reducing oil and gas use to combat global warming, Democrats argue that these investments are crucial for a sustainable and prosperous future for all Americans.

Democrats lean heavily toward "addressing catastrophe recovery (e.g., Gulf Coast, New Orleans, Maui, etc.), improved preparedness for national emergencies, repair of infrastructure, and the creation of jobs to help reduce poverty."[123] They do not ignore the importance of appropriate foreign aid, but they lean more toward prioritizing domestic rather than foreign spending.

Common concerns of the Democrats' position on domestic infrastructure spending often revolve around the potential cost and funding mechanisms of such ambitious plans. Critiques of the Democratic approach to domestic infrastructure investment typically highlight concerns over the costs and financial strategies for implementing such comprehensive initiatives. They raise questions about the feasibility of financing these projects and whether they would stimulate economic growth as promised. Some also express concerns about government inefficiency and waste in managing large-scale infrastructure programs. Additionally, some believe that the emphasis on green infrastructure may neglect other critical needs, such as immediate repairs and maintenance. The challenge of achieving bipartisan support for these infrastructure plans in a divided political landscape is also a point of contention. While infrastructure investment is seen as a necessary endeavor, the specific details and funding mechanisms remain a subject of debate and negotiation.[122]

Republicans have expressed concern about the devastation in New Orleans, the Gulf Coast, and Maui. Their approach favors partnering with large corporations to enhance the operational efficiency of the Federal Emergency Management Agency (FEMA). They advocate for "restoring our infrastructure," aiming to provide Americans with safer roads, bridges, better airports, and more efficient harbors by reevaluating government spending priorities. They criticize the impact of "pork-barrel politics" (i.e., Government spending in and to benefit a politicians' district) on resource allocation for modernizing the nation's infrastructure, which leaves communities vulnerable to natural disasters and hampers necessary economic growth and job creation. Republicans commit to a business-like, cost-effective approach to infrastructure spending, attentive to the specific needs of both rural and urban communities. They support an investment level in the nation's transportation system that promotes a healthy economy, sustains jobs, and maintains global competitiveness. Their goals include improving system performance and capacity to address congestion, freight movement, traffic fatalities, and ensuring mobility in rural and urban areas. They emphasize the urgent need to preserve and maintain existing highways, transit, and air facilities to serve future generations. At the same time, they are committed to minimizing transportation's impact on climate change, local environments, and the nation's energy reserves. They advocate for carefully reforming environmental reviews and the permission process to speed projects to completion. Safeguarding transportation infrastructure is critical to homeland security, in their view. They believe an integrated, flexible system – developed and sustained in partnership between state, local, federal government – must also share responsibilities with the private sector. They call for more prudent stewardship of the nation's Highway Trust Fund to restore the program's purchasing power and ensure that it will meet the changing needs of a mobile nation.[125]

Some would take the Republicans to task on their position above on infrastructure, given their track record on repairing the damage caused by Hurricane Katrina, lack of domestic infrastructure spending, and their loosening of environmental protections. This is another example of a political party telling voters what they think they want to hear while doing something different.[122]

> **Proposal: In general, Americans should collectively fight against homelessness, child hunger, and extreme poverty. The law cannot keep a person from being "somewhere." If they are not wanted "here", then the law must give them "somewhere" to be. It is vital to advocate for human dignity and stand against oppressive regimes, promoting human rights. Providing necessities such as adequate food, healthcare, and housing is crucial and should be guaranteed at some basic level. Linking these essential services to government-sponsored work could be a way to maintain individual dignity. Furthermore, support systems must be in place to ensure that no one feels isolated or without help. Providing a listening ear and compassionate assistance is vital to fostering a community where everyone feels heard and supported.**

Policing, Crime, and Punishment

Policing, crime, and punishment are pressing concerns at the heart of contemporary political discourse. As our society grapples with the complexities of law enforcement, criminal justice reform, and community safety, political parties have outlined their distinct visions and strategies to address these challenges. From proposals for comprehensive police reform and community policing initiatives to debates over sentencing and incarceration, the approaches and priorities of political parties vary significantly. Consider the diverse and often polarizing perspectives of the different parties as they strive to shape the future of policing, crime prevention, and the justice system in our ever-evolving society.

In 1950 there were approximately 151,300,000 people in the U.S. and about 190,000 police, or one policeperson for every 796 people. In 1970 there were 203.1 million people in the U.S. and 388,000 full-time policepersons, which is 523 people per policeperson. And, in 2021, there were 331,400,000 people in the U.S. and about 697,195 police, or one policeperson for every 475 people. These figures may be a reflection of higher crime rates or a desire for improved safety.[122]

FBI Crime Rate History from 1950 through 2021[47]			
Year	Violent Crime	Property Crime	Total Crime
1950	14.2	28.6	42.8
1955	16.3	32.7	49.0
1960	18.3	36.4	54.7
1965	20.5	39.7	60.2
1970	32.3	44.1	76.4
1975	37.2	50.8	88.0
1980	38.5	53.3	91.8
1985	34.9	52.1	87.0
1990	29.8	50.9	80.7
1995	27.0	49.7	76.7
2000	24.8	45.0	69.8
2005	26.8	45.9	72.7
2010	25.6	41.2	66.8
2015	28.5	41.3	69.8
2020	30.7	42.2	72.9
2021	31.1	43.0	74.1

Note: 2021 was the latest year available (and pre-Covid)

You will note that there was a jump in rates starting in 1970, possibly from more accurate reporting with the introduction of computers, and that the crime rates since 1970 have not changed dramatically, while the number of police per person has increased. Of course, more people mean more density in areas that were not inhabited in the early years, so some increase may be due just to geographic coverage.

Online media's expansive and swift coverage of tragedies from a much broader geographical scope than before can create the impression of increased crime, employing a tactic historically used by tabloids to draw readers with the allure of tragedy.

Democrats' approach to fighting crime is to target the **root causes** – lack of jobs, drugs, and domestic violence – through better schools, rehabilitation programs, and social justice initiatives, combined with community policing equipped with the best technology, equipment, and innovative strategies to prevent and fight crimes. They also are for policy reviews, increased accountability, and civilian oversight. They advocate for measures such as body cameras, de-escalation training, and increased oversight to address instances of police misconduct and brutality.

Democrats prioritize **social justice initiatives**, aiming to address root causes of crime by investing in education, healthcare, and affordable housing to create opportunities and reduce inequality. Additionally, the party supports efforts to reform sentencing laws, reduce mandatory minimums, and expand alternatives to incarceration, emphasizing rehabilitation and restorative justice. Overall, this approach seeks to balance public safety with the pursuit of equitable and humane solutions to the complex issues of policing, crime, and punishment.

Critics of the Democrats' approach to policing, crime, and punishment often perceive their emphasis on police reform and reduced incarceration as a lack of support for law enforcement, potentially impacting public safety. Some also contend that the focus on social justice initiatives, while crucial, may not directly address the immediate concerns of rising crime rates in specific communities.

The Republican Party's approach to policing, crime, and punishment tends to prioritize law and order, emphasizing **a tough-on-crime stance**. Republicans often advocate for increasing law enforcement resources, including **additional funding** for police departments and support for **a more robust police presence in communities**. They argue for stricter sentencing policies, such as **mandatory minimums**, and are less inclined towards criminal justice reform measures that reduce penalties or focus on rehabilitation. Republicans also emphasize the importance of the Second Amendment and **citizens' rights to bear arms** for self-defense. While their approach emphasizes maintaining public safety, critics argue it may not adequately address the root causes of crime or issues related to police accountability and social justice. Republicans also focus on **gang violence**, including the growing prevalence of **illegal alien gangs**, **mandatory sentencing**, **life sentences for gang rape**, **child rape,** and **rapes in the course of committing another felony**, and **removal of unreasonable delays with death penalties**.[122]

Republican Proposals on Crime and Punishment[125]

- Prisons need to be reformed.
- The government needs to work with faith-based institutions that have proven track records in diverting young and first offenders from criminal careers through Second Chance and similar programs.
- Prison time should be mandatory for all assaults involving bodily injury to law enforcement officers.
- Criminals should be barred from seeking monetary damages for injuries they incur while committing a crime.
- Our government needs to continue the fight against illegal drugs.
- A constitutional amendment is needed to secure the formal rights of crime victims. Innocent victims – battered women, abused children, the loved ones of the murdered – still may not be told when their case is being heard. They can be excluded from the courtroom even when the defendant and his friends may be present.
- Because our Constitution is based on the principles of individual liberty and limited government, we must always ensure that law enforcement respects the civil and constitutional rights of the people. While we wage war on terrorism in foreign lands, it is sometimes necessary for intelligence agencies and law enforcement officials to pursue terrorist threats at home. However, no expansion of governmental powers should occur at the expense of our constitutional liberties.

Critics argue that the Republican emphasis on stricter sentencing policies and increased police presence can result in over-policing, leading to a disproportionate impact on communities of color and exacerbating issues of racial profiling and police brutality. Detractors also argue that the Republican "tough-on-crime" stance, including mandatory minimum sentences, may lead to unnecessarily harsh punishments, overcrowded prisons, and the potential for non-violent offenders to receive disproportionately lengthy sentences.

Some opponents contend that the Republican approach may not effectively address the root causes of crime, such as poverty, lack of access to education, and systemic inequalities, potentially perpetuating a cycle of criminal behavior without providing meaningful opportunities for rehabilitation and social reintegration. Critics also argue that the emphasis on increased police presence without adequate oversight and accountability measures could exacerbate instances of police misconduct and undermine community trust in law enforcement, particularly in marginalized communities where interactions with the police can be fraught with tension.[122]

There have been concerns by both parties about the implementation of the Patriot Act and possibly inappropriate Executive Letters authorizing wiretaps of Americans.

Law and Punishment

We have a lot of laws; we do not need to keep creating more except in areas where entirely new ideas require new regulations. This would mean we need fewer lawyers in Congress, making way for more regular citizens. According to the American Bar Association, the U.S. has about 1,150,000 lawyers.[181-08] That is one for about every 300 Americans, which hints that every American would need an attorney at least one day every year; clearly demonstrating there may be too many. However, the primary concern may lie in Congress, specifically in that 77% of the Senate and 71% of the House consist of lawyers. Additionally, numerous senior positions within the government are held by individuals with legal backgrounds, although specific statistics on this matter are not readily accessible.

Criminal Punishment

Punishing criminals is an essential role of government too. As much as we would rather not think about it, evil exists in this world. Whether through genes, physical chemistry, upbringing, influence of drugs, or unbalanced psyches causing uncontrolled anger, greed, or lust, there will always be people who harm others. The government's role is to enact and enforce laws to protect its citizens against evil and to remove the perpetrators of evil from society and appropriately punish them.

Totalitarian governments control human behavior through dominance and intimidation. Democracies control behavior through laws, enforcement, and defined punishment, i.e., the Rule of Law. In America, if you really want to ruin your life with drugs, you are free to do so. In Singapore, if their police catch you with drugs, you might be jailed, caned (i.e., flogged), or even hanged if you are deemed to be dealing. Singapore also has severe punishments prescribed in their laws for "failing to flush toilets after use, littering, jaywalking, possession of pornography, sale of chewing gum, and homosexual activity."[10] With these strict laws, they have exceptionally low crime rates, and remain one of the least corrupt countries in the world. This could result in a more restrictive society; however, the fact that that one-third of crimes are solved with help from their citizens suggests most favor the stricter laws.[13] Strict control of society is a trade-off against your freedom of movement, speech, and activity. It is a choice: The U.S. prefers to be lenient, and Singapore prefers to be extremely strict.

> **Proposal: Our laws need to be more consistent and fairer. Artificial intelligence should be used to ensure fair, just, and balanced sentencing.**

Death Penalty

In taking an objective look at the death penalty and whether it should continue to exist in the United States, the following may be considered:

Revenge

One of the underlying premises of having a death penalty appears to be the concept of "an eye for an eye" – payback equal to the crime or, as some might put it, as close to revenge that we can get without appearing to be as barbaric as the criminal. In the United States, we do not take "eye for an eye" literally. We do not take an eye when someone puts out another's eye. We do not torture someone because they tortured someone else, usually. We do not use rape as a punishment for rapists. Therefore, justifying the death penalty as punishment for murder based on the "eye for an eye" premise does not follow – it is illogical.

Expense

Then why do we have the death penalty? Is it to remove that person from society? Prison already does that. Is it to save money? Nope!

Imprisonment Is Cheaper than Execution[49]

Much to the surprise of many, it turns out that it is cheaper to imprison someone for life than to execute them. In fact, it is almost ten times cheaper! One might ask, "How can that be?"

Every state that has a death penalty also has an intricate system and basis for appeals. These appeals relate to everything from due process claims to equal protection (minorities are convicted at far higher rates than whites) and, most famously, to the cruel and unusual punishment prohibition of the Eighth Amendment to the U.S. Constitution. The result? In California, the slowest state in the Union, the average wait time between conviction and execution for someone sentenced to death is 20 years. The national average is just under nine years.

And, while all this waiting is going on, the process has not ground to a halt. Quite the opposite, in fact. The appeals process consumes hours of labor, not only by court staff, but also by the often court-appointed, taxpayer-funded, and constitutionally-guaranteed public defenders. As a result, some estimate that it costs U.S. taxpayers between \$50 million and \$90 million dollars more per year (depending on the jurisdiction) to prosecute death penalty cases than life sentences.[49-01]

Of course, the normal response to this fact during a death penalty debate is that we should simply get rid of the appeals. While this would eliminate some of the expenses involved (increased trial and security would still need to be paid for), it would also eliminate fundamental civil rights granted every American. Considering the significant number of individuals exonerated due to DNA evidence unavailable during their initial trials, the provision for multiple appeals seems essential in allowing the development of evidence that could prove the innocence of the accused.

While cost is not the only factor to be considered, the argument that it is cheaper to execute someone than keep them alive in prison for the rest of their lives is utterly wrong.

Different Approaches Across the World

Sentencing guidelines for premeditated murder vary significantly across the world. Some countries, such as the UK, Australia, and Canada, have abolished the death penalty and rely on long-term imprisonment. Others may impose life sentences or have the death penalty on their books. Out of approximately 193 countries worldwide, about 111 have entirely abolished the death penalty for all crimes, while 54 still retain it. The remaining countries have it, but only for special circumstances (like war crimes).

Necessary for Victim Closure?

Seeking retribution in the form of revenge is an emotional response that should have no place in criminal punishment. There is a premise that the death penalty brings "closure" to the family and friends of the victim. One cannot deny that emotional closure for the family or friends is important. However, sentencing the perpetrator to life in prison should provide for the necessary closure without indulging people's primitive urges for revenge.

The death penalty is certainly not the only way to resolve the emotional distress of the victim's families and friends or satisfy an incensed public. Which would be better retribution? Suffering a long, uncomfortable life, reflecting daily on the deed that placed them there, ending in an ignoble death without friend or family present, or dying a quick and painless death?

The Fallacy that Prisoners Live a Life of Ease

Living a life in prison is generally a profoundly harsh experience, marked by a rigid daily routine and limited personal freedoms. Inmates typically reside in small, austere cells with basic amenities, sharing confined spaces in overcrowded facilities. Access to outdoor activities, educational programs, and work opportunities vary, often dependent on the security level of the institution and the inmate's behavior. Social interactions are mostly restricted to fellow inmates and prison staff, with occasional visits from outside, subject to strict regulations. Healthcare can be inconsistent, and the mental strain of facing a lifetime behind bars weighs heavily, affecting mental and emotional well-being. The environment is frequently tense, with the constant presence of strict security measures and the potential for conflict. Overall, life in prison for those serving life sentences is defined by its limitations, monotony, and the ongoing challenge of coping with the reality of a life spent in confinement.

> **Proposal: Federal standards for life incarcerations should be established making it clear to the public that prisoners are not living a life of comfort and ease, nor a life of undue physical discomfort or mental torment.**

Thou Shall Not Kill?

If someone tries to kill you, you have a right and even an obligation to kill him or her to defend yourself, unless you can incapacitate the attacker in some non-lethal way. Society also has the right and obligation to kill someone who is in the act of attempting to kill one of its members, but it does not NEED to kill that person after the crime has happened and the perpetrator captured. A person defending against attack cannot avoid being emotionally involved, but society should not run on emotion because that is when mistakes are made.

Deterrent

Another justification for the death penalty is it being an important deterrent to criminals. One might argue that the true deterrent for crime is the potential of getting caught (more than the punishment that follows). When the potential for getting caught is removed as a deterrent, criminals do come out in force (witness looting during disasters such as Hurricane Katrina in New Orleans). However, it is less clear that the severity of the penalty creates a proportionally greater deterrent.

Evidence suggests that the strict penalties in Singapore, such as caning or execution for drug offenses and fines and community service for littering, act as a deterrent. The high probability of being caught and punished contributes to this deterrent effect. To effectively address the powerful root causes of crime, such as poverty, drug abuse, and economic inequity, through enforcement, there must be a significantly high probability of apprehension. This comprehensive approach to law enforcement is essential to overcoming the various factors that lead to criminal behavior.

Considering the possibility of decades on death row, is life in prison any less of a deterrent—especially if the criminal believes they won't be caught in the first place? It is rare that a death row inmate tries to kill his or her guards even though, in theory, they could not receive any harsher punishment than that they already face. Maybe they fear more the solitary confinement that would follow? Perhaps the death penalty is not the most feared punishment after all.

Considering the typical circumstances surrounding capital crimes, the notion of the death penalty as an effective deterrent becomes less convincing. Police detectives often observe that such crimes are frequently committed by those who are mentally unstable, under the influence of substances like drugs and alcohol, or driven by intense emotions like jealousy and uncontrolled anger. Notably, crimes committed in the throes of such extreme emotional states seldom result in the death penalty. A portion of murders are done by truly incorrigibly evil people, but those are unlikely to be deterred by threat of the death penalty. Furthermore, capital crimes committed in a premeditated, calculated fashion are relatively rare. Even in these cases, perpetrators sometimes evade the ultimate punishment due to unsolved investigations, legal technicalities, or by hiring expensive defense attorneys. The infrequency of executions and the extensive delays in their implementation further diminish their intended deterrent effect. Challenging the assumption that the fear of death is paramount, it is essential to recognize that some fates may be perceived as worse than death. Given that rational thinking is often absent in the minds of those committing capital crimes, the argument that the death penalty effectively deters most potential killers holds little weight.

Unequal Application

Our Declaration of Independence, Constitution and Bill of Rights established the basis for all laws being applied equally to all citizens. Yet, it is also true that the death penalty is not equally applied. The worst offenders are often not executed (e.g., Ted Kozinski, Terry Nichols, and Andrea Yates). Facts show that those who cannot afford to pay for an experienced attorney and require a common public defender are more likely to be sentenced to death than those who can.[161] A public attorney does not have the time or funds to fully investigate the circumstances around their defendant's alleged crimes nor prepare a full and effective defense. For example, an examination of 461 capital cases by *The Dallas Morning News* found that one in four condemned inmates has been represented at trial or on appeal by court-appointed attorneys who have been disciplined for professional misconduct at some point in their careers. [161]

Severity of Consequences of a Mistake

It is not just that the poor are misrepresented, but also that the justice system is prone to human error, whether from the investigating detectives and the labs that support them, the defense and prosecution attorneys, or the judges and juries – all are prone to emotions, mistakes, misinterpretations, and misperceptions, and even potentially tampering.

Once a death penalty sentence has been imposed, a series of appeals, delays, and technicalities ensue that are prone to more errors. This can lead to retrials. When retried, statistics show 7% of defendants are acquitted – proof of the human error we mentioned. Some of those reversals may even be errors on top of errors (i.e., they really were guilty). The application of the death penalty is inconsistent, sometimes unfair, and irreversible. According to an entry in Wikipedia, as many as 39 people have been executed "in face of compelling evidence of innocence or serious doubt about guilt." Life is not fair, so despite our best efforts we cannot ensure fairness within our justice system. It is not fair to an innocent person who has been found guilty and will be executed. How many times have people serving long sentences or in prison under the threat of execution had those sentences overturned because DNA testing became available which shows that they were never guilty in the first place? (At least 15 since 1992)[162]

To some religions, life is sacred. If so, then no lives should ever be taken. But most religions recognize that there are times when it is necessary for the protection of society. We take the lives of our enemies in wars and stop violent criminals in the act of committing an offence. But should we take lives once the threat to our safety has been neutralized?

Some argue, "The existence of some systematic problems is no reason to abandon the whole death penalty system."[163] If you were the one innocent person about to be executed, would you agree with this argument? Problems with the judicial system, technicalities that free the guilty, and errors that sometimes convict the innocent are all good reasons why the death penalty should be eliminated. Would it not be better to put all capital criminals in prison for life so we could avoid the risk of taking the life of even one innocent person?

Religious Viewpoints

Other reasons for and against the death penalty are grounded in religion. One consideration might be that executing a criminal may deprive that person of their opportunity to repent for their sins before their death. Some on death row find religion and seek forgiveness, but many do not. Some would argue that it is appropriate that criminals deserving of the death penalty should not get the chance to repent; that they deserve to spend eternity in hell. However, religions also teach that we are not the judge, God is. So, it is not for us to decide who should have a chance to repent or whether their request for repentance should be granted.

Also, one could argue that, with the death penalty, the victim's family and friends may lose their opportunity to forgive. One could argue further that if a perpetrator did come to realize the wrongs they committed, then living with that for the rest of their lives could be a punishment worse than death. And, of course, with a death sentence, any chance of correcting a mistake of an innocent person wrongly sentenced, and apologizing for that error, would be long gone as well.

Inconsistency with Religious Principles

Is there a sanctity of life contradiction? Many religions emphasize the sanctity of life. In the context of abortion, this principle is often interpreted as protecting the unborn, whom religious adherents may believe to possess full human dignity and rights from conception. However, the application of the sanctity of life principle to the death penalty can vary. Some religious traditions may see it as a just punishment for the most heinous crimes, while others view it as incompatible with the sanctity of life.

Rush to Judgment

Criminals used to be hanged or summarily executed for common crimes, like cattle rustling, shooting a man in the back, and many times for no crime at all. Sometimes, the perpetrator was subjected to a "kangaroo court" – a hastily gathered court that trades expediency for due process. The worst cases were to justify lynchings during the late 1800s and early 1900s in America – for reasons such as a black man looking at a white woman, fabricated "crimes," enforcing white supremacy, for asserting independence, to intimidate, for wanting to vote, and so on. Lynchings were always perpetrated by hastily assembled groups of white men driven by emotions and mob mentality. In rare cases, mob action might have been excused because it needed to protect remote society from a mad killer, for example, but the actions against black men were far too often completely unjustified and the consequence of unfettered racial discrimination. Mob action ran on irrational emotion, lacking any system of justice or fair trial to validate the actions taken. As time has progressed, we have become more aware of how fair trials should be managed – and we still get it wrong too often.

> **Proposal: We should no longer execute people, but we should, at the same time, make prison time for capital criminals "not comfortable." The principle would be "no pain, but no joy." We need to agree on a set of standards for premeditated capital crimes. These should include providing no forms of 'entertainment' other than books for reading, offering only basic food and medical treatment, allowing limited exercise, permitting minimal interaction with other inmates, and restricting visitations to immediate family only.**

On a related note, at the time of writing federal prosecutors are seeking the death penalty for a kidnapping, molestation, and murder case in Vermont where the state has no death penalty law. The federal government is imposing its own penalty at the state level, which appears to be a violation of states' rights and our Constitution.[163-02]

Criminal Justice

Democrats advocate for criminal justice reform, emphasizing the need to address systemic inequalities, reduce mass incarceration, and reform policing practices. They often support measures such as ending mandatory minimum sentences for non-violent crimes, decriminalizing or legalizing marijuana, and investing in community-based solutions to prevent crime. Democrats also tend to favor policies aimed at rehabilitating offenders and reducing recidivism, such as job training and education programs for inmates. On the other hand, Republicans traditionally emphasize law and order, advocating for tough-on-crime policies. These include support for strict sentencing guidelines, the death penalty, and an increased focus on law enforcement and prosecutorial discretion. While there is some bipartisan agreement on specific issues like the need to address opioid addiction and some aspects of sentencing reform, Republicans view a more stringent criminal justice system as essential for maintaining public safety and order.

These contrasting views highlight fundamental differences in how each party perceives the causes of crime and the criminal justice system's role in society.

Law Enforcement

Laws are created on the assumption they will be enforced – because there are always individuals who believe the rules do not apply to them or exhibit antisocial behavior. Ideally, laws should originate from the governmental level responsible for their primary enforcement. Furthermore, the federal government should refrain from passing laws that require enforcement by national law enforcement agencies unless there is no viable alternative at the state level.

The primary law enforcement responsibilities of the federal government include safeguarding our borders, protecting our society and economy from external threats beyond our borders, and maintaining law and order across states. They do not include law enforcement at local levels.

In practical terms, this means that laws concerning localized matters like gambling, alcohol, firearms, or drugs – despite their potential as sources of taxation – should not fall under the purview of the federal government unless intervention is necessary to ensure consistent application across states. Conversely, issues such as antitrust laws, securities and investment regulations, telecommunications, racketeering, and other national or international matters affecting citizens in multiple states are, and should remain, federal concerns.

So, when addressing illegal activities within their borders, it is more appropriate for states and local governments to take the lead. Their proximity and familiarity with local conditions and needs make them better suited for this role. And this is a requirement of our Constitution.

Recap – Domestic Affairs and Criminal Justice

2023-2024 Positions on Domestic Affairs and Criminal Justice		
Area of Concern	**Democrats**	**Republicans**
Domestic Affairs	Focuses on advancing social justice, strengthening the social safety net, addressing climate change, and promoting economic policies that favor middle- and lower-income groups.	Focuses on reducing government spending, implementing tax cuts, deregulating industries, prioritizing traditional values, and law-and-order policies.
Criminal Justice	Advocates for comprehensive reform focused on reducing incarceration rates, addressing systemic racial disparities, promoting community policing, and greater rehabilitation and reintegration.	Emphasizes strict law enforcement, tougher sentencing for crimes, maintaining order and public safety, and limited reforms primarily focused on cost efficiency and effectiveness.
Racial disparities in policing and sentencing	For providing police with stricter guidelines, training (de-escalation), and body-worn cameras.	For providing police with the resources and tools they need to maintain public safety.
Ending cash bail	For.	Up to local governments.
Reducing mandatory minimum sentences	For.	Up to local governments.
Police reform	For policy reviews, increased accountability, and civilian oversight.	In favor of tough-on-crime policies; oppose efforts to defund the police.

5. The Economy

The economy and the government's budget, income (taxes and tariffs), expenses, and debt continue to grow. The political parties' positions on these subject areas begin to give us a picture of how fiscally responsible and capable they are or should be.

Bank Control

The debate about having a central bank or not has raged since the beginning of our country but most seriously since Andrew Jackson.

The Second Bank of the United States was chartered for twenty years during James Madison's presidency in 1816. It was given responsibilities similar to those of the First Bank, serving as a central repository for federal funds and the government's fiscal agent. The Bank was also responsible for regulating state banks and promoting a stable currency.[59-30] When Andrew Jackson became president, he worked to rescind the bank's federal charter. In Jackson's veto message, the bank needed to be abolished because it:

- concentrated the nation's financial strength in a single institution;
- exposed the government to control by foreign interests;
- served mainly to make the rich richer;
- exercised too much control over members of Congress; and
- favored northeastern states over southern and western states.

"As did Jefferson, Jackson supported an 'agricultural republic' and felt the bank improved the fortunes of an 'elite circle' of commercial and industrial entrepreneurs at the expense of farmers and laborers. After a titanic struggle, Jackson succeeded in destroying the bank by vetoing its 1832 re-charter by Congress and by withdrawing U.S. funds in 1833."[181-03] In closing the Second National Bank of the United States, Jackson moved the government's money and the role of lending to small banks that supported agriculture. This stimulated an expansion of credit and speculation, which led first to inflation (banknotes were not backed by "specie" – gold or silver) and then economic instability. Then Jackson required banknotes to become backed by "specie," but it was too limited in supply. This instability led to the collapse of the banks, the Panic of 1837, and a deep economic depression.[181-03]

The concept of a national bank continued to be debated and ebbed and flowed through the succeeding presidents until the Independent Treasury Act of 1846 was passed. This put government money into the treasury, reducing hard money circulation and therefore tightening credit, which restricted trade.[181-05] In the ensuing years, a variety of national banks were tried until 1913, when the Federal Reserve System, known as the Fed, was created.

Ron Paul, the libertarian Republican congressman, published a book, *End the Fed*,[181-04] that makes a case for doing away with the Fed and returning to the gold standard. His arguments fall short, according to his critics, because the existence of a gold standard in the past did not prevent the total collapse of the stock market and runs on banks which cause many to lose their life savings – not once but at least twice.

The Fed exists to create and regulate the money supply, safeguard against banking crises, and manage monetary policy through instruments like interest rates and reserve requirements. Its decisions do not have to be ratified by the president or anyone else in the executive or legislative branches of government. However, it is subject to oversight by Congress, which can amend the Federal Reserve Act of 1913.

Democrats tend to support more active government involvement in the economy, particularly in situations where jobs and broader economic stability are at risk. They argue that strategic government interventions, such as bailouts during financial crises, can preserve jobs, protect the economy, and maintain critical industries. Democrats might view the failure of a large company like General Motors (GM) not just as a market outcome but as a situation with significant repercussions for workers, communities, and the overall economy, meriting government action to prevent collapse. This reflects a fundamental ideological divide with Republicans, who prioritize market freedom, self-regulation, and minimal interference in business operations. They are against government bailouts, which they believe distort market dynamics and can lead to inefficiencies. They emphasize that businesses should succeed or fail based on their competitiveness and market forces. Republicans would argue that if a company like GM becomes unviable due to high labor costs or other issues, it should not be artificially sustained by government intervention, as more efficient competitors will fill market gaps. Of course, the saving of jobs in the case of GM was a consideration.

Bank Control might be considered a necessary evil. Ironically, Americans often tolerate more controls imposed by their neighborhood homeowners' association than they would from their federal government. They may also yield to government pressure to relinquish more liberty in response to a crisis (e.g., the enactment of the Patriot Act following 9/11) than they would under normal circumstances. A real or perceived crisis becomes a catalyst for consolidating more power and authority in the executive branch, potentially with just a single individual, a situation otherwise viewed as a significant danger. Concentration of control is something to watch out for.

The SEC

The Securities Exchange Commission (SEC), while primarily tasked with upholding investor protection and market integrity, has sometimes faced criticism regarding its effectiveness and internal practices. Despite its significant role and resources, particularly the enforcement division, questions have been asked about its approach to Wall Street regulation, especially in high-profile cases like the Bernard Madoff scandal. Concerns have also been raised about the agency's internal culture, including handling of whistleblowers and document management. However, the SEC's establishment of a whistleblower rewards program demonstrates its ongoing efforts to strengthen market oversight and regulatory compliance.

The Democratic Party's position on the SEC aligns with its broader commitment to stringent financial regulation and consumer protection. Democrats typically support the SEC's role in enforcing transparency, accountability, and fairness in the financial markets. They often advocate for strong regulatory measures to prevent fraud, insider trading, and other malpractices that could harm investors and the integrity of financial markets. Additionally, Democrats may push for the SEC to play a significant role in addressing contemporary matters such as environmental, social, and governance (ESG), which ensures that corporations are responsive to climate change and social justice issues. This stance reflects the party's broader goals of ensuring financial stability and protecting the interests of average Americans in the financial system.

The Republican Party's position on the SEC emphasizes a balance between effective financial regulation and promoting market efficiency and growth. Republicans typically advocate for a regulatory approach that prevents fraud and protects investors while avoiding overly burdensome bureaucracy for businesses. They often support measures that foster capital formation and economic growth, arguing that excessive regulation can hinder these objectives.

Republicans tend to favor a more limited government role in financial regulation, as they do with the economy at large. They may call for more streamlined regulatory processes, reduced red tape, and a focus on compliance rather than punitive measures. This approach reflects the party's broader principles of free-market capitalism.

Furthermore, in recent years, there has been a focus within the Republican Party on reviewing and potentially rolling back certain financial regulations implemented in the wake of the 2008 financial crisis. This includes reassessing provisions of the Dodd-Frank Act, which significantly increased financial regulation, with the aim of easing restrictions on smaller banks and fostering a more conducive environment for business and economic growth.

Wall Street

Wall Street is a pivotal marketplace for capital investment and plays a crucial role in the global financial system. While it facilitates essential services like raising capital and trading securities, it also faces ethical challenges related to speculative activities. Charlie Munger, the vice chairman of Berkshire Hathaway once said that Wall Street is "like a denizen of thieves, and they'll sell you what they can sell you."[59-26]

Managing investments on behalf of clients is a standard and legitimate practice, but there is huge scope for abuse depending on the methods used. This prompts discussions about the need for oversight and potential reform, particularly regarding practices perceived as speculative or not adding value.

The Democratic Party's stance on Wall Street encompasses several key aspects:

Firstly, Democrats have been actively defending free-market capitalism, primarily environmental, social, and governance (ESG investing. This defense arises in response to criticisms from Republicans directed at major financial institutions and their investment strategies. High-profile Democrats, such as Representative Maxine Waters and Minnesota Attorney General Keith Ellison, support ESG investing as crucial for addressing risks associated with climate change.

Secondly, the party has been critical of Republican efforts that seem aimed at protecting the fossil fuel industry. Democrats argue that opposition to sustainable investing by Republicans is an attempt to safeguard the interests of the fossil fuel sector. They express concerns that legislation against ESG practices could prevent public companies from receiving necessary shareholder input and limit investors' access to essential information.

Internally, the Democratic Party wrangles over the extent and form of financial regulation. While President Joe Biden has pledged to enhance financial oversight, the party has encountered challenges confirming nominees for vital regulatory roles. This has slowed progress on reversing deregulatory measures implemented during the Trump administration and delayed the advancement of progressive goals, such as stricter rules governing banking mergers and addressing financial risks from climate change.

Furthermore, Democrats emphasize the need for regulators to focus on contemporary challenges, again including the climate crisis but also the risks posed by cryptocurrency. This reflects a broader concern for addressing emerging financial risks and ensuring stability and equity in the financial system.

Finally, the Democratic Party officially commits to reversing the over-financialization of the economy and curbing Wall Street speculation. Their policy includes maintaining and expanding safeguards to separate retail banking from investment operations, ensuring fair tax contributions from Wall Street investors, and enforcing financial reform laws like Dodd-Frank and the Volcker Rule, a provision of the Dodd-Frank Act, that restricts banks from engaging in speculative trading activities such as proprietary trading and investing in hedge funds or private equity funds. They also support criminal penalties for executives who engage in reckless financial practices and advocate for expanded access to credit and stronger banking regulations to ensure equitable financial services for all Americans.

The Republican Party's stance on Wall Street represents a departure from its traditional pro-big business position, with growing criticism of perceived "woke" business practices, particularly in the House majority, pushing back against major financial firms for aligning with ESG initiatives deemed harmful to the fossil fuel industry. This shift contrasts sharply with historical alignment with Wall Street's interests, with frustration now expressed over the perceived politicization of capital allocation, including distancing from firearms financing and embracing climate change mitigation efforts. Republican representatives call for prioritizing investor interests and traditional business activities over ESG initiatives, accusing banks of weaponizing financial regulation against American energy companies. Additionally, Republicans advocate for a free-market approach, arguing banks should conduct lawful business freely without breaching anti-discrimination laws to maintain a robust financial system, criticizing banks for yielding to pressures on non-banking issues and embracing a liberal ESG agenda outside traditional democratic processes, reflecting broader concerns about increasing politicization of financial decision-making and its economic impacts.

Any significant reforms would need careful consideration of their impacts on the financial system and the broader economy. Large banks play a crucial role in managing international financial transactions and relationships. However, the risks posed by the size and power of large banks is a growing concern, particularly considering the "too big to fail" phenomenon.

> **Proposal: Congress should restructure large banks into more specialized entities, each focusing on distinct aspects such as retail banking, investment banking, or international finance. This aims to enhance their efficiency and expertise in specific financial sectors. At the same time, reducing their overall size would mitigate the risks associated with large financial institutions. This restructuring would require careful regulatory planning and consultation with banking and financial experts to determine the most effective way forward while ensuring stability in the financial system.**

Proposals for Better Control of Wall Street[58]

1. **Stricter Regulation of High-Frequency Trading (HFT):** High-frequency trading uses complex algorithms to execute a large number of orders at extremely high speeds. Critics argue that HFT can lead to market instability and provide an unfair advantage to firms with the resources to use these technologies. Tighter regulation or imposing a "transaction tax" on each trade could mitigate these issues.

2. **Enhanced Transparency in Derivatives Trading:** Derivatives, like futures and options, are crucial financial instruments but can pose significant risks if not adequately managed and regulated. Requiring more transparency in these markets through centralized clearinghouses or increased reporting requirements could reduce systemic risks.

3. **Reforming the Credit Rating System:** The financial crisis of 2007-2008 exposed significant flaws in the credit rating system. Overhauls could involve creating more independent and accountable rating agencies supported by a public or a mixed public-private framework. Doing so would avoid conflicts of interest and enhance the reliability of credit ratings.

4. **Reinforcing the Separation between Investment and Commercial Banking:** Strengthening regulations akin to the Glass-Steagall Act of 1933, which separated commercial banking from investment banking activities in the United States, can prevent conflicts of interest, speculative trading, and protect depositors' funds from being risked in the stock market. This measure could help prevent banks from taking excessive risks with depositors' money. separation can reduce the likelihood of financial crises where speculative investment activities put consumer deposits at risk.

The Mint and Currency

The future of U.S. currency faces multifaceted challenges, particularly in counterfeiting perpetrated by various countries, with notable culprits including China, Russia, and North Korea. These nations have sophisticated counterfeiting operations that pose a significant threat to the integrity of U.S. currency. Despite ongoing efforts to implement advanced security features, counterfeiters continue adapting and innovating, necessitating constant vigilance and technological advancements to combat illicit activities. Additionally, the rise of electronic currencies, such as credit cards, digital payment platforms like Venmo, and cryptocurrencies like Bitcoin, presents a compelling alternative to traditional paper currency. With the convenience, security, and efficiency offered by electronic transactions, coupled with the global trend towards digitization, it is increasingly likely that paper currency will be gradually phased out in favor of electronic forms of payment. While challenges persist, including privacy, cybersecurity, and regulatory frameworks, the shift towards electronic currencies represents a transformative evolution in how financial transactions are conducted, shaping the future landscape of U.S. currency and global monetary systems.

> **Proposal: Formulate a plan to eliminate U.S. paper currency entirely.**

Taxation Today

The government runs on money; taxpayer money. The economy runs on taxpayer money too, specifically what citizens have left over for spending after the government taxes them. A larger government requires more funding from taxpayers, which means withdrawing more money from the economy. Conversely, downsizing the government and lowering taxes would result in more money being retained in the economy. Stimulus payments are like tax cuts, putting money into the economy, but they are rare. Even though our country began with no income tax, this was anticipated – Jefferson spoke against it, believing a consumption tax would be better. **Jefferson also advocated for not changing taxes very often so the economy can adjust to them** (see the Jefferson on Taxation section later). Over the years, two dominant economic theories have emerged about America's economy, which have significantly influenced understanding and policymaking – yet neither could explain what happened during the financial crisis of 2007-2008.

The Two Dominant Theories in Government Economics

1. **Keynesian Economics**: Developed by John Maynard Keynes, this theory emphasizes the role of government policies in stabilizing the economy. According to Keynesian economics, during economic downturns, government intervention in the form of increased public spending and lower taxes can stimulate demand and pull the economy out of a recession.
2. **Neoclassical Economics**: This theory, rooted in the ideas of economists like Adam Smith and David Ricardo, focuses on the belief that free markets are the most efficient way to allocate resources. It suggests minimal government intervention allows for the most efficient operation of markets, driven by supply and demand.

During the financial crisis of 2007-2008, both theories faced criticism. Keynesianism was questioned as massive government interventions and stimulus packages seemed unable to quickly resolve the crisis or restore economic stability. Neoclassical economics was also criticized, particularly regarding its emphasis on deregulation, which some argued had contributed to the financial system's vulnerabilities.

The Chicago School

This set of economic principles is developed, studied, tested, and endorsed by members of the Department of Economics of the University of Chicago over the last century. They have often been implemented by several administrations through the Council of Economic Advisors to the president, and many of the economists ensconced in the financial departments of the federal government and on Wall Street were schooled in these principles. This illustrious group of economists has collectively been awarded more Nobel prizes (25) and John Bates Clark awards (17) than any other university or group of economists in the world.

The "Chicago school" adheres strictly to neoclassical price theory and believes in laissez-faire, i.e., "free markets," radically lower taxation, private sector regulation, and government-regulated monetary policy. Their work is based on highly empirical studies. This approach aligns more with economic views of the Republicans than the Democrats.

However, experience has demonstrated that sometimes a modified approach, incorporating elements of Keynesian economics that advocate for government intervention, can be more effective in certain situations.

Keynesian Economics

According to Investopedia.com, Keynesian economic theory states that active government intervention in the marketplace and monetary policy is the best method of ensuring economic growth and stability. A supporter of Keynesian economics believes it is the government's job to smooth out the bumps in business cycles. Intervention would come in the form of increased government spending and tax breaks to stimulate the economy in bad times; and government spending cuts and tax hikes in good times, to curb inflation. In 2007-2008, the government did intervene but did not cut taxes. They adopted a mixed strategy. This approach to the economy is more consistent with Democrat philosophies than Republican.

The Chicago school's approach to economics is well proven and, while claimed as a principle of the Republican Party, it is not in itself contradictory to Democratic Party politics. Rebates and stimulus checks can work the same as temporary tax cuts.

Recent Global Trends

Our economy has been shaped in recent years by a complex interplay of global economic trends, technological advancements, shifts in trade policies, the impact of the COVID-19 pandemic, geopolitical tensions, environmental challenges, and socio-political changes. While some aspects of the economy may have self-corrected in line with the Chicago school of thought, other areas have continued to require careful monitoring and, in some cases, further intervention to address persistent challenges and emerging new issues such as the wars in Ukraine and Palestine. The economy is complicated, to say the least.

The Role of Greed

The assertion has been made that American economics are fundamentally driven by greed. This debatable perspective was notably echoed by Ivan Boesky, a Wall Street trader convicted of insider trading in 1986, who allegedly stated in the 1980s that the economy and market would recover with the resurgence of greed.[55] The argument posits that greed is intrinsically linked to economic growth, including higher salaries and more jobs. The idea is that growth provides avenues for satisfying greed; and, conversely, greed can stimulate growth through the reinvestment of profits. This view acknowledges greed as a human trait but raises ethical concerns about achieving excessive profits through what some might consider gambling with or manipulating others' finances. From this perspective, while greed can be a driver of economic activity, regulatory scrutiny and potentially higher taxation might be warranted to discourage its more questionable manifestations, especially those bordering on immorality.

Greed, in the context of self-interest, is not immoral and should not be illegal or penalized so long as it is not satisfied on the backs of hard-working people through fraud, trickery, speculation, markets manipulation, or unconscionable fees.

> **Proposal: The taxation framework for those on higher incomes should continue to align with the principles of prioritizing economic growth and innovation while addressing social responsibilities: A modestly progressive tax structure ensures high earners contribute a fair share without being subjected to excessively burdensome rates. This approach ensures that successful individuals are not disincentivized from further wealth creation and investment, which are vital for economic dynamism and job creation. Simultaneously, this taxation model supports essential public services and social welfare programs, helping to bridge income inequality gaps. The objective is to strike a balance between rewarding success and ensuring social equity, fostering an environment where individual ambition and collective well-being can thrive.**

Jefferson on Taxation

Jefferson said in a letter to General Washington in 1787, "Wealth acquired by speculation and plunder is fugacious in its nature and fills society with the spirit of gambling."[02-a]

About taxation, Thomas Jefferson wrote to James Madison in December 1784, "The simplest system of taxation yet adopted is that of levying on the land and the laborer. But it would be better to levy the same sums on the produce of that labor when collected in the barn of the farmer; because then if through the badness of the year he made little, he would pay little. It would be better yet to levy only on the surplus of this product above his own wants. It would be better, too, to levy it not in his hands, but in those of the merchant purchaser; because though the farmer would in fact pay it, as the merchant purchaser would deduct it from the original price of his produce, yet the farmer would not be sensible that he paid it. This idea would no doubt meet its difficulties and objections when it should be reduced to practice; yet I suspect it would be practical and expedient. ... What a comfort to the farmer to be allowed to supply his own wants before he should."

In a letter to James Madison in 1789, Jefferson wrote, "Let taxes be few, non-enumerate, and variable only with the indispensable necessities of government." He advocated for a tax system that was predictable and reliable, allowing individuals to plan their finances effectively. A stable tax rate is generally optimal for economic equilibrium, allowing for consistent pricing adjustments. However, exceptions should be allowed when deemed necessary by the government, even though altering tax rates can disrupt economic stability and predictability.

Individual Rights Applied to Businesses and Taxation

In law, corporations are being treated like individuals and, in theory, therefore deserve the same rights; but, in practice, the application of individual rights to corporations is inexact and inconsistent. For example, when it comes to a constitutional right such freedom of speech, corporations have more restrictions than individuals, such as the federal do not call (DNC) list. This is unfair on its face, not just because it violates the principle of commercial free speech, but because it is not equally applied: The DNC law excludes charities and political organizations. If corporations should not be deemed the same as individuals, then they should certainly not have more favorable treatment, as they do when it comes to being allowed to make large political contributions. Corporations are taxed differently and have substantially greater resources than individuals, giving them undue influence with political donations. The law is not consistent in the treatment of corporations as individuals.

Proposal: Congress should better define the rights of corporations to ensure they are distinct and more limited than those of individuals. Equating corporate rights with those of individuals raises legal and ethical concerns, often leading to imbalances and gaps in the legal and economic systems. A thorough legal review by experts will be necessary to identify areas where corporate rights differ significantly from individual rights. This review would aim to establish clear legal distinctions, particularly in corporate speech, political contributions, and liability. The goal is to craft a legal framework that appropriately limits corporate rights, recognizing their unique role while protecting the rights and interests of individuals. The objective would be to align current law with the original intention of the Constitution, which did not anticipate extending citizen-like rights to corporate entities.

Proposal: Set a maximum limit on all forms of taxes (excluding charges imposed by a government for accessing specific services or facilities, such as issuing a passport) separately for federal, state and local government. This will establish stability in tax structures.

Use of Taxes to Control or Direct Behavior

The original principles of America, as laid out by the Founding Fathers, did not precisely anticipate or make provisions for manipulating behavior through taxes. There was significant debate in the nation's early years about the imposition of taxes, with a consensus that they should be limited to funding common defense and the administration of the government. Some argue that the Founding Fathers did not intend for taxes to be used to steer citizen behaviors in specific directions.

However, these days, the federal government extensively utilizes tax deductions, tax credits, and excise taxes to encourage or discourage various behaviors among citizens. Whether it's incentivizing home ownership, funding education, or encouraging energy efficiency, these practices are part of broader fiscal policies aimed at achieving various social, economic, and environmental goals. While setting the foundation for American governance, the Constitution also does not explicitly preclude using taxes as a tool for social and economic engineering. Its evolving nature has allowed the government to adapt tax policies to suit contemporary challenges and goals. Excise taxes are one of the most common ways this has been achieved.

Excise taxes are explicitly levied on certain goods (such as gasoline, alcohol, and tobacco), services, or activities. Unlike the broader income or sales taxes, this distinct form of taxation is imposed directly at the point of manufacture or import and is often charged per unit (e.g., cents per gallon) rather than as a percentage of value. Its purpose often extends beyond revenue generation, aiming to influence consumer behavior and discourage using certain products due to health or environmental concerns. Additionally, the revenue from excise taxes is frequently ringfenced for related public expenditures, such as using tobacco taxes for healthcare initiatives or gasoline taxes for road maintenance, creating a direct link between the tax and its intended use in public policy.

Three main criticisms have been raised about excise taxes:

- **Regressive Nature**: Excise taxes can be regressive, disproportionately affecting lower-income individuals. Since these taxes are a fixed amount per unit and not based on the buyer's income or ability to pay, they take up a larger percentage of income for lower-income groups. For instance, a tobacco or fuel tax will represent a more significant expense for a low earner than someone with a higher income.
- **Economic Distortion**: Excise taxes can distort market economics. Making certain goods more expensive can reduce demand for these goods, which may lead to less production and potentially impact jobs in those industries. While this can be beneficial in the case of harmful products like tobacco, it can be problematic if the tax affects essential goods or services.

- **Possible Unintended Consequences**: Excise taxes might lead to the development of a black market for the taxed goods, especially if the tax rate is very high. This can lead to a loss of tax revenue and increased criminal activity. Additionally, if the tax is on a commodity like gasoline, it might disproportionately affect industries reliant on transportation, creating a ripple effect on the wider economy.

Often, the justification for excise taxes is the health of our citizens (e.g. reduce pollution, prevent cancer, etc.).

Common Products with Federal Excise Taxes[59-07]

1. **Alcoholic Beverages**: Including beer, wine, and distilled spirits. The tax rate can vary based on the type and alcohol content. Federal beer taxes range from $0.11 to $0.581 per gallon, depending on production, location, and quantity. The tax rate for most wines is $1.07 per gallon, and for distilled spirits is $13.50. State taxes on distilled spirits are up to $36.55 per proof gallon at volume (Washington). State-level beer taxes vary from $0.02 per gallon (Wyoming) to $1.29 (Tennessee).
2. **Tobacco Products**: Such as cigarettes, cigars, snuff, chewing tobacco, and pipe tobacco. From $1.01 per pack plus state excise tax of $0.17 (Missouri) to $4.35 (Connecticut and New York) per pack.
3. **Fuel**: This includes gasoline, diesel, and other types of motor fuels. Aviation fuel is also taxed (from $0.184 to $0.244 per gallon).
4. **Firearms and Ammunition**: Generally, these are taxed at the point of manufacture (10% on handguns and 11% on other firearms and ammunition).
5. **Air Transportation**: Taxes on passenger tickets (7.54%), freight, and aviation fuel.
6. **Health-Related Products**: This includes taxes on certain types of medical devices and pharmaceuticals (was 2.3% but was repealed.)
7. **Communication Services**: Excise taxes can be levied on telephone and other communication services (3% as part of the overall 30% taxes).
8. **Tanning Services**: A tax on services provided by indoor tanning salons (10%).
9. **Gambling**: This includes wagers, certain types of betting, and gaming (0.25% plus $50 for each involved employee).
10. **Insurance Policies**: Certain types are subject to an excise tax (~1%). Excise taxes on insurance can apply to high-cost health plans, various premium insurances like life and automobile, and surplus lines, varying by jurisdiction.
11. **Heavy Trucks and Trailers**: The sale of certain trucks, trailers, and tractors, like vehicles over 55,000 pounds and 75,000 pounds, can be subject to an excise tax (12%).
12. **Environmental Taxes**: Including taxes related to the sale or use of ozone-depleting chemicals, coal, and other chemicals (For example, petroleum Superfund tax rate was $0.164 per barrel in 2023).

In 2019, the latest data available, the federal government in the United States collected nearly $100 billion in excise tax revenues. These taxes primarily came from motor fuel sales, airline tickets, tobacco, alcohol, and health-related goods and services, representing about 2.9% of the $3.5 trillion total of federal tax receipts for that year (of which excise tax on alcohol was $10 billion or 10% of the total, and taxes on tobacco was $12.5 billion or 12.5%).[59]

Sugar

The U.S. taxes legally-available addictive substances such as alcohol and cigarettes, and, no doubt, marijuana upon national legalization, but not one of the most addictive of all: sugar. Excessive sugar consumption is linked to various health problems, including obesity, type 2 diabetes, heart disease, and dental issues. High sugar intake can lead to obesity and elevated insulin levels, both of which may influence the development of certain cancers. And yet it has escaped the taxman.

What the Medical Community Says about Sugar and Cancer

- "Understanding the Link between Sugar and Cancer: An Examination of the Preclinical and Clinical Evidence": This 2016 article published in the National Institutes of Health's database reviews preclinical and clinical studies suggesting a potential link between sugar intake and cancer development. The authors highlight that although existing evidence is not conclusive, some studies show associations between sugar consumption and specific cancer types, even after controlling for weight and BMI.[59-02]
- "Does Sugar Cause Cancer?": This article from the MD Anderson Cancer Center acknowledges that while sugar doesn't directly cause cancer, it can contribute to obesity, which is a major risk factor for several cancers. It also mentions studies suggesting that high blood sugar levels might promote cancer growth.[59-03]
- "Sugar and Cancer – What You Need to Know": This 2023 article from Cancer Research UK clarifies that sugar itself is not a known carcinogen but emphasizes the strong link between high sugar intake and weight gain, which is a major risk factor for 13 different types of cancer.[59-04]
- "Does Sugar Cause Cancer?": This article from Australia's Cancer Council emphasizes that while sugar does fuel cancer cells, it's not a direct cause of cancer. They cite the National Health and Medical Research Council's review finding no evidence of a direct association between sugar and specific cancers like pancreatic, bowel, breast, and bladder.[59-05]

U.S. sugar production (cane and beet) expanded from an average of 6 million short tons raw value (STRV) in the early 1980s, which is 12 billion pounds, to an average of 8.6 million STRV (17.2 billion pounds) since 2005/06. This increase in production is due to demand and investments in new processing equipment, improved crop varieties, and expanded acreage.[59-01] It basically means that sugar consumption has increased 43% in the last 40 to 50 years.

Perspective on Sugar as a Tax Target

General Sales Tax: Sugar is already subject to state and local sales taxes, which vary by region. Some states exempt basic food items, including sugar, from sales tax. Despite not being essential, sugar is treated similarly to foods that are deemed as such when it comes to sales tax.

Complexity: Implementing a federal tax on sugar would be complex, requiring the establishment of definitions, tax rates, and a collection system. As these exist for alcohol, gasoline, and nicotine, managing such complexity should be feasible.

Public Health Considerations: The issue of taxing sugar to reduce obesity and diabetes is primarily addressed by state and local governments through soda taxes, rather than a federal tax on sugar. That approach focuses on local solutions rather than adopting a uniform federal strategy.

Lobbying Congress: The sugar industry, which includes sugar cane and beet producers, processors, and refiners, is a powerful lobbying influence in Congress. It has a long history of protecting its interests when it comes to issues like sugar subsidies, import quotas, price supports, and other policies that can affect its profitability and competitiveness.

Proposal: Implement an excise tax on all sweeteners, including natural and sugar equivalents such as high-fructose corn syrup (HFCS), corn syrup, dextrose, fructose, glucose, sucrose, maltose, lactose, cane juice, evaporated cane juice, sugar alcohols, sugar polyols and fruit juice concentrate. A flat rate per ounce for all forms of added sweeteners could raise billions in federal revenue and have a positive impact on the health of all Americans.

Federal Taxes on Addictive Substances

Taxing addictive substances, such as alcohol, tobacco, and, increasingly, cannabis, is an issue that governments worldwide grapple with. These substances are often subject to special taxes, sometimes referred to as "sin taxes"(included in the excise taxes above) due to the potentially negative impact of their consumption on individuals and society at large. The primary objectives of taxing addictive substances are to generate revenue, discourage consumption, and offset some of the societal costs which arise from their use.

Higher taxes can act as a deterrent by increasing the price of these products and making them less affordable. For example, research has shown that a 10% increase in the price of cigarettes led to a 4% reduction in cigarette consumption in the United States.[59-13]. Similarly, in Canada, studies have found that a 10% increase in the price of alcohol leads to a 5.7% reduction in alcohol consumption.[59-14]

Additionally, these taxes provide governments with a dedicated revenue stream that can be earmarked for specific purposes. For instance, in the United States, federal and state excise taxes on alcohol and tobacco generated in 2019 approximately $12.5 billion and $10.0 billion in revenue respectively.[59-15,16] These funds can be used to treat addiction and for prevention programs, which are essential for mitigating the public health impacts of substance misuse.

However, the taxation of addictive substances is not without its challenges. The existence of an illegal market or illicit production of addictive substances can undermine the effectiveness of taxation efforts. In the case of cannabis, for example, states in the U.S. which have legalized recreational use have implemented taxes ranging from 10% to 37%, aiming to strike a balance between generating revenue and competing with illicit markets (Tax Foundation, 2021).[131-135]

> **Proposal: We need to do more to discourage "institutionalized addictions." Currently, substances like alcohol, caffeine, and nicotine are taxed to curb excessive consumption. Increasing excise taxes to further discourage the use of unhealthy substances seems rational considering the extensive presence of sugar-laden products, alcohol, caffeine, and cigarettes on grocery store shelves, indicating that current taxation levels may not sufficiently deter consumption. However, there is an inherent conflict of interest in governments relying on taxes derived from addictive substances. To mitigate our complicity in this, 40% of these "sin" taxes should not flow into the general fund as the Tax Policy Center's briefing book suggests. Instead, this money should be set aside for specific uses like infrastructure or other non-recurring expenses. This way, the government's budget will not rely on such revenues, preventing economic shock when public consumption habits significantly change.**

As far as marijuana is concerned, its sale is indirectly taxed at the federal level. Under section 280E of the Internal Revenue Code, businesses involved in controlled substances, a category that includes marijuana, are barred from deducting typical business expenses when calculating federal income tax. This results in marijuana businesses, even in states where they operate legally, facing higher federal tax burdens due to the inability to deduct expenses like rent, utilities, and wages. This could all be simplified by legalizing the substance and placing a clear excise tax on the sales. Furthermore, states and local governments where marijuana is legal often levy taxes on its sale, significantly boosting their revenues. If legalized, jobs will be created, the taxation approach would be simplified, and there will be no need to police its production, distribution, and use.

> **Proposal: We should consider the federal legalization of marijuana. By cultivating it domestically and imposing heavy but not overly burdensome taxes on its sale, the resulting funds could be directed toward educating our youth about the risks of drug use. This approach offers a potential revenue stream and aligns with responsible public health and fiscal policy. More importantly it upholds the premise of individual responsibility.**

Business Taxation

Advocates for minimal taxation on businesses believe this enables companies to reinvest more of their earnings into creating new products, purchasing new equipment, creating jobs, profit-sharing, and overall expansion. The underlying logic is that when businesses thrive, they fuel broader economic growth, potentially leading to more job opportunities and technological advancements.

On the other hand, personal taxation should be calibrated to sufficiently fund government operations. The rationale here is that government services – from infrastructure to social programs – benefit the populace, and, thus, it is fair for individuals to contribute towards these costs through taxes.

Implementing a scaled tax system for businesses could help address disparities in earning capacity. Under this approach, which some would call a progressive tax system, larger corporations might pay higher taxes relative to their earnings, while smaller businesses receive tax relief or incentives to foster entrepreneurship.

A balanced government budget, with contingencies for unforeseen events, is a cornerstone of fiscal responsibility. This approach advocates for prudent financial planning, ensuring government expenditures align with revenues, barring exceptional circumstances. Setting aside funds during prosperous times for major future expenses, such as wartime spending, reflects a proactive and sustainable approach to fiscal management.

The target of an annual inflation rate of around 3% aligns with some economic theories that suggest moderate inflation can be beneficial. 3% is also the average over the last 75 years.[59-31] It reflects the natural growth in economic productivity and efficiency and can help avoid the pitfalls of deflation. Monetary authorities must manage this target carefully to maintain economic stability and consumer confidence.

Thomas Jefferson wrote in a letter to J. W. Eppes in Sep. 1813, "The public contributions should be as uniform as practicable from year to year, that our habits of industry and of expense may become adapted to them; and that they may be duly digested and incorporated with our annual economy."[02]

Resources are limited on earth, and they need to be shepherded by everyone – but especially big consumers like America. If possible, we should preserve our domestic resources – first for our country and then for others. Resources should be renewed where they can be, recycled where they cannot, and limited in use where neither is possible. The debate will be whether such use of resources should be voluntary, government encouraged, or government mandated.

Completely exempting small family-operated farms, under some size limit, from taxation can align with a broader goal of supporting rural communities and sustainable agriculture.

> **Proposal: We need to protect the quality and quantity of our food production sources. Agriculture was one of our founding industries, and we remain heavily dependent on having enough families with the specialized skills needed to operate farms. We also must protect the condition of the ground in which our food is grown. Small farms (up to 1,200 acres or so) that are family operated should be permitted to operate tax free, so that small-scale farming is attractively lucrative. We need farms to produce our food for our rapidly growing population, so we must stop them from being eaten up by encroaching suburbs. Any further conversion of open land to residential or commercial should cease.**

Inflation

Inflation is universally disliked due to its multifaceted negative impacts. Not only does it diminish the purchasing power of currency, but it also fosters uncertainty in the economy, disproportionately affects fixed-income earners, distorts relative prices, leads to higher interest rates, undermines the value of savings and investments, and reduces international competitiveness. Furthermore, inflation creates ripe conditions for price gouging, a practice where businesses exploit inflationary pressures to unfairly raise prices. This can take various forms, including manipulating packaging sizes (known as "shrinkflation"), accelerating price hikes beyond the inflation rate, maintaining elevated prices even after inflation recedes, imposing additional fees, and disguising profiteering through hidden charges.

In response to inflation, political parties often propose contrasting approaches. Republicans typically advocate for tighter monetary policies aimed at controlling inflation, such as raising interest rates and reducing the money supply. In contrast, Democrats tend to favor fiscal stimulus measures, which involve government spending and tax policies designed to stimulate economic activity and mitigate the negative effects of inflation, particularly on lower-income individuals and vulnerable communities.

Society of the Future and Economics

We can predict the future: It is one of disappearing borders – not physical borders but our conceptual ones. Our physical borders must be strengthened but not in traditional ways.

Our physical borders are already very porous. It is impossible to protect more than 8,000 miles of borders (2,000 by sea on two coasts and 6,000 by land, lakes, and rivers), even if we walled ourselves in. If we were to surround our country with guards placed six feet apart, it would require eight million guards per shift. With 21 shifts per week plus vacation time, we would need more than 24 million guards to protect us 24/7 – one out of every eight Americans would be on patrol. And, at $25,000 per guard, the cost would be $600 billion per year. Obviously, this is not a practical solution.

Illegal immigration is best dealt with at the source. For example, if we could do more to help Mexico, Central America, South America, and other countries around the world retain their citizens by offering the same economic opportunities as the U.S., then perhaps their citizens would not need or want to seek a better life here. They come to America because Americans will pay them more than they can earn in their country, even though living costs are proportionally much higher here.

The border that is disappearing is that of concepts and ideas. This idea is radical: Governance could go global through the Internet if people everywhere believed in the same principles and pulled together to run the world like a single country. Everyone recognizes that "the world is getting smaller" every day. Communications are faster, ideas travel at light speed, and human nature, being mostly the same the world over, might begin to endorse the idea of global, citizen-run self-government. However, this radical idea might face resistance from established power structures and various belief systems, such as those of radical Muslims and American Christians.

What about the rule of law and law enforcement in this new world without physical borders? Addressing these issues is essential if global governance is to be a reality. The primary obstacle would be religious groups in control of their governments. Should people have the right to determine who governs them and how they are governed, regardless of geographic borders?

Rule of Law - Future

How might the rule of law apply with no borders? It requires having laws on which everyone in the world agrees. If there are laws, then there need to be lawmakers and there will be lawbreakers. The lawmakers would need to be global in distribution, perspective, and representation. This doesn't work so well when tackling lawbreakers. The larger the geographical scope of the law, the more difficult, expensive, and complicated it becomes to enforce it. So there needs to be some localization: Laws based on international principles should be encoded so they can apply as much as possible to the areas in which they are being enforced. Punishments need to be the same and applied consistently everywhere. The more consistently international principles are encoded in laws around the world, the more peaceful the world will become. The internationalization of governance begins at the highest levels – like with the U.N.'s Human Rights declaration. Once the world has consistency and all countries stick to those principles, they can then filter through to the populace at ground level.

The major impediments to this approach include the role of religion in governing, maintaining freedom of speech, assembly, suffrage, and election fairness. The U.S., with its globalization policies, seems to be trying to "level the economic playing field" as one way to help take democracy global – even though that is not necessarily the priority for the rest of the world. However, the missing piece is that citizens elsewhere in the world have too little real say in how they are governed. So, is this radical idea practical? Not at the moment, or in the near future, but perhaps one day. Is the idea intriguing as a long-term possibility? The sooner we reach a unified government without borders (which is different from illegal immigrants being free to enter our country as they do now), the sooner the world can find peace.

Foreign Policy

We should help our strategic partners and our allies, of course. We should help poor countries to develop as much as we can afford. We should consider economic protectionism only when defending against unfair trade practices (i.e., monopolies) and preserving critical natural resources. When other governments help their manufacturing companies, which then bid against American firms, our firms are at a disadvantage unless we help them to the same degree.

For example, Germany, France, Spain, and the UK were known for subsidizing Airbus. The World Trade Organization (WTO) found that these EU member states provided subsidized loans for developing new aircraft, such as the Airbus A380 and A350. These subsidies were part of a longstanding dispute between the EU and the U.S. regarding unfair advantages in the aerospace industry.[59-06]

When to help our own citizens and when to be altruistic to the world is an ongoing challenge.

The Budget

While every political party expresses a commitment to balancing the budget, reducing debt, and fiscal responsibility, these noble intentions often face substantial challenges in practice. The constant change of power between parties and long-term financial commitments, such as wars and entitlement programs, make it difficult to realize these goals fully. The dynamic and enduring nature of these commitments can complicate the pursuit of fiscal restraint, stability, and sustainability, as the Republicans admit:

"Since enactment of the Budget Act of 1974 by a Democrat-controlled Congress, the federal government has operated within a rigged system notable for its lack of transparency. The earlier approach – annual passage of the appropriation bills, amended and voted up or down, with the numbers there for all to see – had its flaws and generated much red ink. But its replacement, the current budget process, only worsened the money flow and came to rely on monstrous omnibus spending bills. The results are averse to all seeking to limit government's growth."[124]

This admission by the Heritage Foundation (frequent critic of the Democrats) was made after the Republicans were unable to change the fiscal situation or the surrounding processes despite having complete control of Congress for eight years. The fact that the ruling party is hamstrung in this way means that Congress has been unable to make the process more transparent and more controlled.

Every new administration inherits the successes and the mistakes of the prior administrations, and the Democrats inherited an economy in severe trouble in 2008. The priority they set forth in their platform was to stimulate the economy through various "investments." However, their philosophy is better described in their own words:

"Our free market was never meant to be a free license to take whatever you can get; however you can get it. That is why we have put in place rules of the road to make competition fair, open, and honest"[127]; and

"Since the time of our founders, we have struggled to balance the same forces that confronted Alexander Hamilton and Thomas Jefferson – self-interest and community; markets and democracy; the concentration of wealth and power; and the necessity of transparency and opportunity for each and every American."[127]

No references have been found in documents authored by the Founding Fathers that address the issue of wealth concentration; their concerns primarily centered around the concentration of political power – though the former may lead to the latter. However, if the Constitution's structure is adhered to, it should safeguard against wealth completely overpowering our governance.

The Democrats state, "We will maintain fiscal responsibility, so that we do not mortgage our children's future on a mountain of debt. We can do this while we invest in our future. We will restore fairness and responsibility to our tax code. We will bring balance back to the housing markets, so that people do not have to lose their homes. And we will encourage personal savings, so that our economy remains strong, and Americans can live well in their retirements."[127]

The Republicans "…support a tax code that encourages personal savings. High tax rates discourage thrift by penalizing the return on savings and should be replaced with incentives to save."[126]

They say, "America is … an engine of charity, empowering everything from Sabbath collection plates to great endowments. It creates opportunity, rewards self-reliance and hard work, and unleashes productive energies that other societies can only imagine."[126]

Republicans ascribe a purpose to economics: "Economic freedom – and the prosperity it makes possible – are not ends in themselves. They are [the] means by which families and individuals can maintain their independence from government, raise their children by their own values, and build communities of self-reliant neighbors."[126]

Income (Taxes and Tariffs)

Like any company or family, the country has its sources of income and its expenses.

The primary sources of government revenue include income taxes (both personal and corporate), tariffs (which are taxes imposed on imported goods to create a level competitive field for American producers against foreign monopolies), and service fees (such as the cost of issuing a passport).

Another major source of income for the government is the sums remitted by individuals and corporations for social security, Medicare, Medicaid, and other public healthcare programs. The expenses, covered in more detail below, primarily fall into the broad categories of operating expenses (overhead), the military, entitlements (social security, Medicare, Medicaid, and, if Democrats have their way, soon more comprehensive healthcare), and aid (foreign and domestic)

Since at least 2008, Democrats have believed they must reform our tax code, saying: "It is thousands of pages long, a monstrosity that high-priced lobbyists have rigged with page after page of special interest loopholes and tax shelters. We will shut down the corporate loopholes, tax havens, and use the money to provide an immediate middle-class tax cut that will offer relief to workers [retirees] and their families."

Notice how Democrats talk about tax cuts, as do Republicans. Republicans would cut taxes at all levels while the Democrats would lower taxes on lower- to middle-income ranges and increase them for those on higher income levels and corporations. The problem of Tax forms and reporting processes being too complex and cumbersome is another subject that all the parties seem to agree on but never fix.

Republicans believe "government should tax only to raise money for its essential functions" and not use taxes as a tool for social engineering or wealth redistribution. However, the reality is that Republicans have used the tax code for all kinds of commercial engineering. The Republican Party says they will put a stop to both social engineering and corporate handouts by "simplifying tax policy, eliminating special deals, and putting those saved dollars back into the taxpayers' pockets." In a nutshell, Republicans believe in lower taxes and smaller government, but they made little progress on simplifying taxes when they were in power. This criticism is not to be cynical but rather to show that the power of lobbying can prevent things from happening upon which both parties agree.

Taxes and the Individual

Thomas Jefferson felt that too much tax takes away from production. He said, "To equalize and moderate the public contributions, that while the requisite services are invited by due remuneration, nothing beyond this may exist to attract the attention of our citizens from the pursuits of useful industry, nor unjustly to burthen those who continue in those pursuits … [is one of the] functions of the General Government on which you have a right to call."[172-02]

He went on to say, "I thought at first that the power of taxation [given in the new federal Constitution] might have been limited. A little reflection soon convinced me it ought not to be."[173-02]

Jefferson also believed that taxation should reflect the will of the people as much as possible. He said, "Taxation is the most difficult function of government, and that against which their citizens are most apt to be refractory. The general aim is, therefore, to adopt the mode most consonant with the circumstances and sentiments of the country."[174-02]

He also did not believe we should tax citizens for wars until needed. He said, "Sound principles will not justify our taxing the industry of our fellow citizens for wars to happen we know not when, and which might not perhaps happen but from temptations offered by that treasure."[175-02]

Jefferson also made an especially crucial point about the consistency of taxes, "Taxes on consumption like those on capital or income, to be just, must be uniform."[176-02]

He also made clear that taxes should not exceed necessities, "No tax should ever be yielded for a longer term than that of the Congress wanting it, except when pledged for the reimbursement of a loan."[177-02]

He also did not think taxes should place a burden on our citizens, "To impose on our citizens no unnecessary burden … [is one of] the landmarks by which we are to guide ourselves in all our proceedings."[178-02]

Work could be distinguished as either honorable or parasitic. Parasitic work needs to be treated differently, taxed more heavily, and controlled by the government. How often do opposing attorneys exacerbate issues to drive up their combined fees? A lawyer's work is parasitic – feeding off people's problems. How is it that they all raise their rates by about the same amount every year too? Securities manipulators and market manipulators are parasitic – siphoning off other people's money.

Diverse types of work make different contributions to society. A person's labors are "work of the first order." Putting your own money to work as an investment is the second order of work. The third order of work is earning money by siphoning money from other people. This third category should be taxed most heavily.

In 2020, according to the most recent available IRS data, those earning below $42,184 paid an average income tax rate of 3.1% while the top 1% of earners paid an average of 26% and accounted for 42.3% of all federal income taxes paid.[50] Rates have been stable since 1988, which is a good policy as changes can impact the economy.

Historical Tax Rates – 1862 to 2023[56]		
Era	Top Rate	Bottom Rate
Early Days (1862-1913)	7%	No income tax
World Wars (1914-1964)	94%	1% to 14%
Great Society (1965-1987)	70%	11% to 14%
Modern (1988-present)	37%	12%

Here are some proposals to make taxes simpler, fairer, and more effective.

Proposal: Restrict the use of tax credits for social engineering, except in health-related cases. This would adhere to certain interpretations of constitutional principles that limit government intervention in personal activities except in public health matters, a recognized area of government responsibility.

Proposal: When tax credits are considered necessary, direct them towards capital investments rather than affecting citizens' behavior in order to stimulate job creation and economic growth through business expansion, technological upgrades, and infrastructure development.

Proposal: Undertake a comprehensive review of federal excise taxes to simplify them and reduce rates where possible. Then, maintain these taxes at a stable rate.

Proposal: Reevaluate the tax exemption on unrealized capital gains for non-profit organizations, particularly those holding appreciable assets that are not actively used to further their charitable mission. Consider taxing such assets if they remain unsold and inactive for an extended period, ensuring that non-profits continue to fulfill their intended public service roles effectively and efficiently.

Imports and Tariffs

Tariffs are meant to protect skilled jobs from leaving the country and to maintain competitiveness against subsidized industries in other countries. When foreign corporations receive aid, tax breaks, and other protective or financial help from their local governments that constitute unfair trade tactics, then it stands to reason that their products should be equally taxed through tariffs or offset by matching subsidies by our government to our companies. Most would agree that the idea of raising the living standards of the lower and middle classes of other countries at the expense of our own middle class is bad business for Americans, especially when done too quickly, which has happened with certain trade agreements. Also, placing tariffs on essential imports has the dangerous upside of fueling inflation. As examples, In 2009, tariffs of up to 35% on Chinese tire imports intended to protect U.S. jobs increased tire prices for American consumers, contributing to inflationary pressures.[59-27] In 2017-2018, 25% tariffs on imported steel and 10% on aluminum, intended to support domestic production, led to increased manufacturing costs and higher prices for various consumer goods, contributing to inflation.[59-28] Additionally, tariffs of up to 24% on Canadian softwood lumber escalated construction expenses, raising new housing costs in the U.S.[59-29]

Proposal: Tariffs should be reserved for where American jobs need to be protected from unfair competition, and avoided on consumer products in high demand or otherwise inflation may result.

Proposal: Imports to the U.S. should only be accepted from countries whose water and air pollution laws are comparable to ours and equally enforced – to put us on the same economic playing field.

Test Your Knowledge about Government Expenses

How many of the top 10 government budgetary expenditures can you name? If you think government spending should be reduced, which of these budgets would you cut and what would be the impact on your fellow Americans if you did?

Here they are:

Top Ten U.S. Government Expenditures

1. **Social Security**: This is the largest expenditure in the U.S. federal budget. It covers retirement, disability, and survivor benefits to eligible workers and their families. People have been contributing, as have their employers, since 1937. It was enacted by Democratic President Franklin D. Roosevelt during the Depression.
2. **Medicare**: Medicare is a federal healthcare program primarily for seniors aged 65 and older. It also covers some individuals with disabilities. People and their employers have been contributing since 1966. Democratic President Lyndon B. Johnson enacted this program.
3. **Medicaid**: Medicaid is a joint federal and state program that provides healthcare coverage to low-income individuals and families. The federal government shares the cost of Medicaid with the states, making it a substantial budgetary expense. This program began with Medicare above, enacted by President Johnson.
4. **Defense**: The Department of Defense (DoD) budget includes funding for the military branches (Army, Navy, Air Force, Marines), as well as defense-related research, development, and procurement. National defense is a longstanding priority, and defense spending is a sizable portion of the budget. Our Army and Navy began in 1775 when George Washington was president. President Washington had no party affiliation and, in fact, was known for his strong aversion to the formation of political parties and factions, which he warned against in his Farewell Address in 1796. Washington believed that political parties could lead to division and discord within the young nation.
5. **Interest on the National Debt**: The U.S. government borrows money by issuing Treasury securities and must pay interest on this debt. Interest payments on the national debt make up a substantial part of the federal budget. Our country began accumulating debt in the 1790s when it assumed the states' debts from the Revolutionary War. This was signed into law by President Washington.
6. **Supplemental Nutrition Assistance Program (SNAP)**: SNAP, formerly known as food stamps, assists low-income individuals and families in purchasing food. It is an essential part of the safety net for those in need. This program was enacted in 1964 by Democratic President John F. Kennedy and completed by President Johnson.

7. **Income Security Programs**: This category In the United States, the social safety net comprises several key programs developed over the years to aid individuals and families during economic challenges. Unemployment Insurance, established in 1935 by President Franklin D. Roosevelt, offers temporary financial support to unemployed workers. Supplemental Security Income (SSI), initiated in 1972 under Republican President Richard Nixon and operational from January 1974, provides assistance to elderly, blind, and disabled individuals with little to no income, helping cover basic needs. In 1996, Democratic President Bill Clinton introduced Temporary Assistance for Needy Families (TANF), replacing the previous Aid to Families with Dependent Children (AFDC) program, to support needy families while promoting work, job preparation, and marriage. These programs, reflecting contributions from both Republican and Democratic administrations, showcase the evolving efforts to address the socio-economic needs of Americans through various periods of the nation's history.

8. **Veterans Benefits and Services**: This category covers benefits and services provided to veterans of the U.S. military. It includes healthcare, disability compensation, education benefits, and more. These benefits began in 1775 but were expanded with the GI Bill in 1944, started by President Roosevelt and finished by Democratic President Harry S. Truman, and these programs have been expanded with every war or "conflict" ever since.

9. **Transportation**: Maintaining and improving the country's transportation infrastructure, including highways, transit systems, and aviation, is a significant budgetary expenditure. This began with the Bankhead Act of 1916 and was expanded by Republican President Dwight D. Eisenhower in 1956.

10. **Education**: The federal government allocates funds for education programs, including student grants, support for K-12 education, and higher education assistance such as Federal Pell Grants. The Elementary and Secondary Education Act (ESEA) and the Higher Education Act (HEA) were established in 1965 by President Johnson.

Further down the list is foreign aid, which only amounts to about 1% of the federal budget. This includes a wide range of programs and initiatives to promote U.S. interests abroad, support international development, and address global challenges such as poverty, health crises, and humanitarian emergencies. These programs include economic help, humanitarian aid, security assistance, and contributions to international organizations. Some expenditure helps to protect our importing of certain critical raw materials, such as oil, platinum, and palladium.

Should governmental expenditure be cut? How, and who will be affected? Your grandmother who lives on your grandfather's social security? Those receiving social security who have been contributing along with their employers their whole working lives. Where would be the justice in that? Would you end pensions for future generations so that the many people who fail to save and live hand to mouth become a burden on society when they reach old age? (This is surely kicking the proverbial can down the road) We must think about both the intended and possible unintended consequences when proposing changes. Many highly intelligent senators and congresspersons were involved in crafting these programs; hopefully, any subsequent changes will be carefully thought through.

Debt

The difference between income and expenditure for the U.S. government results in a surplus or deficit, with deficits being more common historically. In the 232 years since our Constitution was signed, our government only ran a surplus budget in 14 years.

Budget Surplus Years by Party[56]				
Year	President	Party	House	Senate	Surplus
1791	Washington	Federalist	Federalist	Federalist	$ 1,949,926
1836	Jackson	Democratic	Whig	Whig	$ 39,430,255
1837	Van Buren	Democratic	Whig	Whig	$ 6,492,969
1846	Polk	Democratic	Whig	Whig	$ 5,546,619
1880	Hayes	Republican	Democratic	Democratic	$ 47,335,653
1881	Garfield	Republican	Republican	Republican	$ 81,690,473
1882	Arthur	Republican	Republican	Republican	$ 145,723,269
1907	T. Roosevelt	Republican	Republican	Republican	$ 89,015,565
1947	Truman	Democratic	Republican	Republican	$ 31,797,512,449
1948	Truman	Democratic	Republican	Republican	$ 11,705,000,000
1998	Clinton	Democratic	Republican	Republican	$ 69,000,000,000
1999	Clinton	Democratic	Republican	Republican	$124,000,000,000
2000	Clinton	Democratic	Republican	Republican	$230,000,000,000
2001	G. W. Bush	Republican	Republican	Republican	$128,000,000,000

The largest deficit so far was approximately $3.1 trillion in 2020, a year marked by extraordinary pandemic-related spending. In 2021, the deficit decreased to $2.8 trillion, followed by a further reduction to $1.375 trillion in 2022, both lower than the 2020 figures. The Congressional Budget Office projects the 2023 deficit to be around $1.5 trillion, potentially higher due to military aid to Ukraine and Israel.[59-17-20]

You will notice in the above table that neither political party can claim better fiscal responsibility than the other. It appears that the ability to control the budget has little to do with political party agendas and more to do with the circumstances of the time – namely, economic conditions and external events, which play the dominant role in fiscal management. Of course, deficits pile up to form our country's total debt.

Our national debt, as of October 6, 2023, was more than $33.5 trillion. Our history of federal debt is shown in the following table (the dollar amounts are not adjusted for inflation, but this does not affect the ratio).

Federal Debt 1970-2022[57]			
END OF FISCAL YEAR	DEBT (IN BILLIONS, ROUNDED)	DEBT-TO-GDP RATIO	MAJOR EVENTS BY PRESIDENTIAL TERM
1970	$371	35%	Recession
1971	$398	35%	Wage-price controls
1972	$427	34%	Stagflation
1973	$458	33%	Gold standard ended and OPEC oil embargo
1974	$475	31%	Watergate and budget process created
1975	$533	32%	Vietnam War ended
1976	$620	33%	Stagflation
1977	$699	34%	Stagflation
1978	$772	33%	Recession
1979	$827	32%	
1980	$908	32%	Fed rate raised to 20%
1981	$998	31%	Tax cut
1982	$1,142	34%	Spending increase
1983	$1,377	37%	Jobless rate 10.8%
1984	$1,572	38%	Increased defense spending
1985	$1,823	41%	
1986	$2,125	46%	Lowered taxes
1987	$2,350	48%	Market crash
1988	$2,602	50%	Fed raised rates
1989	$2,857	51%	S&L Crisis
1990	$3,233	54%	First Iraq War
1991	$3,665	58%	Recession
1992	$4,065	61%	
1993	$4,411	63%	Omnibus Budget Act
1994	$4,693	64%	
1995	$4,974	64%	
1996	$5,225	64%	Welfare reform
1997	$5,413	63%	
1998	$5,526	60%	LTCM crisis and recession
1999	$5,656	58%	Glass-Steagall repealed
2000	$5,674	55%	Budget surplus
2001	$5,807	55%	9/11 attacks and EGTRRA
2002	$6,228	57%	War on Terror
2003	$6,783	59%	JGTRRA and Iraq War
2004	$7,379	60%	Iraq War
2005	$7,933	61%	Bankruptcy Act and Hurricane Katrina.
2006	$8,507	61%	Fed
2007	$9,008	62%	Bank crisis
2008	$10,025	68%	Bank bailout and QE
2009	$11,910	82%	Bailout cost $250B ARRA added $242B
2010	$13,562	90%	Payroll tax holiday ended, Tax cuts, ACA
2011	$14,790	95%	Debt crisis, recession and tax cuts
2012	$16,066	99%	Fiscal cliff
2013	$16,738	99%	Sequester, government shutdown
2014	$17,824	101%	QE ended, debt ceiling crisis
2015	$18,151	100%	Oil prices fell
2016	$19,573	105%	Brexit
2017	$20,245	104%	Congress raised the debt ceiling
2018	$21,516	105%	Tax cuts
2019	$22,719	107%	Trade wars
2020	$27,748	129%	COVID-19 and 2020 recession
2021	$29,617	124%	COVID-19 and American Rescue Plan Act
2022	$30,824	123%	Inflation Reduction Act and student loan forgiveness
2023 (p)	$33,500	tbd	Ukraine, Isreal Conflicts

Note: (p) = Projected

Can our country continue to afford this mounting debt? The critical concern is not so much the size of the debt but its sustainability over the long term. An important metric is the ratio of gross domestic product (GDP) to debt. When the ratio exceeds 100%, that means that the U.S. owes more money than it generates in a year through economic activities. This can become a concern for its lenders (bond buyers). If a country consistently runs large deficits without a credible plan to address them, it can lead to problems like inflation, decreased investor confidence, and higher interest rates. Of course, higher interest rates exacerbate the problem as more needs to be paid to service the debt, which becomes an increasing drain on the economy and restricts our ability to support domestic projects.[101]

In January 2009, at the onset of President Barack Obama's term, the United States faced an unprecedented fiscal challenge, with the fiscal year 2009 deficit soaring to $1.4 trillion. This spike primarily resulted from the global financial crisis, necessitating significant government interventions such as stimulus spending and financial sector bailouts. This period marked a historical high for the deficit in relation to the economy, not seen since World War II, reflecting bipartisan efforts to stabilize and recover from a global economic downturn. To address this, they said they would enforce "pay-as-you-go budgeting rules." In honoring these rules, they promised to "end the Iraq war responsibly, eliminate waste in existing government programs, generate revenue by charging polluters for the greenhouse gases they are releasing, and put an end to the reckless, special interest driven corporate loopholes and tax cuts for the wealthy."

Political parties have said for many years that they will "eliminate waste in government programs." This always turns out to be the controlling party ending a program of the previous party, yet starting up new programs that end up costing the same or more. Looking at the steadily increasing debt supports this conclusion.

Below is a statement by the Republicans (edited for readability), who have repeatedly said they would "attack wasteful Washington spending immediately."

Examples of Republican Proposals (2020)

• Adoption of the Balanced Budget Amendment to require a balanced federal budget except in time of war.

• Earmarking must stop – to eliminate wasteful projects and pay-offs to special interests. Tax dollars must be distributed on the basis of clear national priorities, not a politician's seniority or party position.

• Government waste must be taken off autopilot, including a one-year pause in nondefense, non-veterans discretionary spending to force a critical cost-benefit review of all current programs.

• A constitutionally sound presidential line-item veto.

• The billions worth spending should be spent in the light of day, including presenting every spending bill in advance to the taxpayers on the Internet before either the House or Senate considers it.

• Because the problem is too much spending, not too few taxes, we support a supermajority requirement in both the House and Senate to guard against tax hikes.

• New authorizations should be offset by reducing another program, and no appropriation permitted without a current authorization.

• Congressional ethics rules governing special interests should apply across the board, without the special exemptions now granted to favored institutions.

• Passage of the Government Shutdown Protection Act to ensure the continuance of essential federal functions when advocates of pork barrel spending [government spending on local projects] threaten to shut down the government unless their wasteful spending is accepted.

• Establish a budget that reasonably plans for the long-term costs of pension and healthcare programs and convert them to defined contribution programs.

The reality is that unless one party is in control of the White House, the House, and the Senate, radical restructuring of the budget is very difficult to accomplish. And, even when they are, neither party takes the actions necessary to shrink the budget. Both parties claim they want transparency and efficient government departments, but getting there may be challenging because the two parties have opposing agendas.

Having reviewed the party positions on economics, budgeting, taxes, income redistribution, and national debt, it becomes evident that these interrelated elements can significantly impact social programs, citizen prosperity, and governance. But it also becomes evident that the budget is impacted more from external events affecting our security, economy, and priorities. These complex issues lie at the core of political discourse, shaping the social contract between our citizens and government. The pursuit of sound fiscal policies, equitable tax systems, and responsible budgeting should be paramount, along with tackling the ongoing challenge of addressing income inequality and managing national debt. Striking a balance between economic growth, fiscal responsibility, and social equity is an ever-evolving endeavor that hinges on our politicians' commitment to our foundational principles.

The last aspect of government economics to mention is the push-pull known as the "Guns versus Butter" model:

Guns versus Butter Model

This is a classic economic concept that illustrates the trade-off between a nation's investment in defense and civilian goods. In this model, "guns" represent military spending, while "butter" symbolizes civilian goods and services such as food, education, and healthcare. The core idea is that a country's national budget is limited, and the government must decide on allocating resources between defense and civilian needs.

When a government spends more on the military (guns), fewer resources are available for civilian goods (butter), and vice versa. This trade-off is often used to discuss and analyze the priorities of a nation's economic policy, especially in times of war or high military tension.

Globalization

A significant global phenomenon of recent times is certain countries exhibiting a unique blend of characteristics in their governance. While promoting capitalism in their business sectors, these nations maintain tight political control under the pretext of socialism or communism. Notable examples of such mixed governments include China, Russia, Venezuela, Iran, and North Korea.

These governments often claim to be democratic, and, in some cases, elections may occur; but they frequently lack transparency and genuine choice. Furthermore, they employ practices such as detaining non-combatant individuals without formal charges or a fair hearing, holding numerous individuals as "political prisoners," and carrying out executions with minimal or no proper judicial processes. Secret police forces play a pivotal role in their governance, and they exert control over their citizens through tactics that induce fear and lead to "disappearances." Additionally, these governments suppress the media, subjecting it to harsh scrutiny and censorship. Despite these concerning practices, the United States continues to engage in business and diplomacy with these countries.

The Democratic Party supports the concept of globalization but emphasizes the importance of fair trade, which integrates strong labor and environmental protections into international trade agreements. This approach aims to avoid a "race to the bottom" in global standards and wages, prioritizing equitable and sustainable economic practices.

A central focus of the Democratic perspective on globalization is protecting American workers. The party advocates for policies that aid workers in adapting to the global economy, such as enhanced job training and education programs. This approach is coupled with efforts to safeguard domestic industries from unfair international competition, particularly from countries with lower labor and environmental standards.

Moreover, Democrats underscore the importance of the United States' proactive engagement in international bodies and agreements, considering this essential for guiding globalization in directions congruent with American values and priorities. This includes a strong commitment to global climate accords and playing a significant role in organizations such as the United Nations.

Addressing the inequalities exacerbated by globalization is another critical concern for Democrats. They propose domestic measures like progressive taxation, robust social safety nets, and international efforts to assist developing nations. The party supports fostering innovation and the digital economy, balanced with concerns for privacy and cybersecurity in an increasingly interconnected world.

The Democrats view immigration as a positive facet of globalization contributing to cultural diversity and economic vitality. Some Democrats lean towards protectionist stances, while others favor free trade more. Overall, the Democrats are committed to shaping a global economy that is fair, sustainable, and beneficial to a wide range of stakeholders.

The Republican Party has historically favored free trade policies, emphasizing the importance of reducing trade barriers to promote economic growth and job creation. They often advocate for deregulation and increased economic freedom, aiming to enhance the competitiveness of American businesses in the global market. However, some Republicans express concerns about national security and fair trade, particularly in industries vital to national interests. While supportive of free trade in principle, there is skepticism toward certain multilateral trade agreements that are seen as potentially detrimental to American workers.

Additionally, Republicans stress the need to protect American intellectual property rights and may tie globalization to immigration and border security issues. There is also an emphasis on American sovereignty, with some Republicans wary of international organizations and agreements that they believe could encroach upon U.S. autonomy. It is important to note that Republican positions on globalization, just as with the Democrats, can vary among individual party members and are subject to evolution over time.

The stark contrast between the governance styles of the countries mentioned and the principles upheld in the United States underscores the complexities inherent in international relations and trade. As the U.S. navigates these choppy waters, there is a domestic focus on preserving democratic values and ensuring stringent financial oversight. In this landscape, the Securities and Exchange Commission (SEC) plays a significant role in promoting transparency, fairness, and stability within financial markets. This is essential for safeguarding the integrity of the U.S. financial system, but it can also be significant in interactions with nations that may have less rigorous governance standards.

From a global perspective, it is becoming increasingly apparent that existing legal structures may be outdated. There is a pressing need to determine how to engage in the governance of the world at large. Questions arise about whether to collaborate with the United Nations or the World Court or join other countries more equitably to promote world peace, as opposed to attempting to dominate the global stage independently. Many believe that maintaining a presence in the world to defend national interests is crucial; otherwise, there is a risk of losing access to essential natural resources to other nations. Additionally, there is a viewpoint that more should be demanded in return for overseas contributions. For instance, financial support is provided to Israel, yet there are concerns about espionage activities against their supporting nation.

Expenses

The largest expenses of our government, beyond administrative costs, are the "entitlements" – social security, Medicare, Medicaid, and healthcare. It was originally intended to cover these annual costs with money collected during that year, but in recent years and projected for the years ahead, costs exceed income.

This is because of a bulge in the population curve caused by the large number of "baby-boomers" approaching retirement age. These programs never anticipated such a huge increase in demand. Of course, our Congress did not take preemptive action even though the situation has been obvious since the late 1940s. Also, life expectancy has increased by 11 years since 1950, from 68 years to 79 years in 2024 after recovering from a drop due to Covid.[59-21,22] At this point, if you are a proponent of a balanced budget, action is needed – whether that's reducing benefits, changing the qualifying criteria, or increasing the population (i.e., number of people contributing) through increased immigration or absorption of illegal immigrants.

> **Proposal: We need to consolidate all the separate benefits provided to those who work for the government, including health plans, retirement packages, franking privileges, etc. into the general population programs of social security, IRAs, the Affordable Care Act (ACA), and such. The same providers should be used for government and non-governmental workers for greater efficiency.**

Social Security Outlook[59-16, 17, 18]

The Social Security Board of Trustees projects that the Social Security Trust Fund will be depleted in 2035 unless changes are made to the program. This projection means that the government will begin to pay out more in benefits than it collects in taxes and interest in 2035.

The projected social security costs for the next 40 years are as follows:
- 2023: $1.2 trillion
- 2033: $2.2 trillion
- 2043: $3.2 trillion
- 2053: $4.2 trillion
- 2063: $5.2 trillion

These projections are based on the following assumptions:
- The economy will grow at an average rate of 2.1% per year.
- Unemployment will average 4.7% per year.
- Inflation will average 2.3% per year. (Note: Average over last 75 years is 3%)
- The average life expectancy will continue to increase.

Note: These are projections, and the actual costs of social security could be higher or lower depending on economic and demographic conditions.

Ways to address the projected shortfall in the Social Security Trust Fund include:
- raising taxes;
- cutting benefits;
- raising the retirement age;
- means-testing benefits;
- investing in the stock market; and
- increasing the population through immigration.

The number of social security recipients is expected to decline after 2035. The decline in the Social Security Trust Fund is attributable to the retirement of the baby boomer generation, which increases withdrawals from the fund. This occurs at a rate that exceeds the number of new entrants into the workforce contributing to it.

According to the Social Security Administration, the number of social security beneficiaries will peak at 100 million in 2035 and then decline to 80 million by 2060. This decline in beneficiaries will help to offset the projected shortfall in the Social Security Trust Fund. However, it is essential to note that the decline in beneficiaries will only partially offset the shortfall. The trustees of the fund predict it will still be depleted in 2035, even with the decrease in beneficiaries.

Democrats created the entitlement programs but now both parties recognize the problems faced and are focused on strengthening personal pension programs. The Democrats have no plans to privatize it, as the Republicans might. As far as Medicare/Medicaid is concerned, the Democrats say they would reduce its cost by trimming waste, negotiating drug prices, and forcing more competition. The Democrats are implementing a comprehensive overhaul of healthcare, the full implications of which will unfold over the next decade. This overhaul includes expanding and adjusting the Affordable Care Act, introducing a public option or expanding Medicare, reforming prescription drug pricing, enhancing access to mental health and substance use disorder treatments, and improving healthcare infrastructure and pandemic preparedness. Democrats would argue that the government should provide basic protections.

The Republicans reported that America faces "a profound demographic shift over the next twenty-five years, from today's ratio of 3.3 workers for every retiree to only 2.1 workers by 2034." Of course, they have known this was coming for 50 years. Their plan proposes substantially reducing the program from its existing scope, except for individuals already retired or close to retirement age. For younger workers, the option of personal investment accounts is introduced. This effectively privatizes the program, potentially leading to increased profits for Wall Street. The proposal assumes that young people have the discipline to save, the knowledge to manage investment accounts, and the financial capability to handle these investments independently or afford fees for private financial advisors.

Republicans propose reviving Medicare/Medicaid "by incentivizing high-quality care, fostering competition, eliminating waste, fraud, and abuse, and empowering both patients and healthcare providers with treatment choices." They also envision forging a "fresh Medicaid partnership with the states to enhance public health through increased flexibility and innovation." Republicans prefer a state- or private company-centered approach rather than a federal government one. And Republicans would argue that individuals should be responsible for their own basic protections – retirement, health, food, etc. and receive no help from the government at all.

Proposal: There needs to be more equal access to schooling, basic healthcare, food, and shelter. For example, everyone should be provided with basic health insurance and every child between five and 18 should have a constitutional right to a free education. Given these privileges, people then need to take more responsibility for their own financial situation. The rich should not be punished for being rich. Anyone who slips through this safety net or does not have the physical ability to work, should have their basic needs met through government programs. Students should be offered the opportunity of either a traditional academic education or going to a trade school. High schools need to have a well-rounded curriculum to include art, wood and metal shop, PE, music, theatre, civics, classical readings, Latin, other foreign languages, and geography. More variety in education in the early years will help students find their favored interests before specializing after high school.

Recap - Economy

2023-2024 Positions on the Economy		
Area of Concern	**Democrats**	**Republicans**
The Economy	Advocate for a mixed economy where both the private sector and government play significant roles. They tend to support government intervention in the economy to address issues like income inequality, climate change, and consumer protection. Commonly support policies promoting economic equality and job creation through government investment in infrastructure, education, and green technology.	Advocate for free-market capitalism, believing that less government intervention in the economy leads to more efficient outcomes. They often support policies that encourage entrepreneurship and private enterprise, arguing that this stimulates economic growth and job creation.
Taxes and Tariffs	Generally, favor a progressive tax system where higher income earners are taxed at a higher rate. This approach is seen to address income inequality and fund social welfare programs. On tariffs, Democrats have historically supported fair trade policies that protect American workers and industries, though views on specific trade agreements and tariffs can vary within the party.	Usually favor lower taxes for individuals and businesses, arguing that this spurs economic growth by increasing disposable income and encouraging investment. They often support simplifying the tax code and reducing regulations. Regarding tariffs, positions can vary, but many Republicans traditionally support free trade and are cautious about imposing tariffs that could lead to trade wars.

Society of the Future	Emphasize diversity, equality, and inclusivity. They typically support civil rights, gender equality, LGBTQ+ rights, and immigration reform. There is also a focus on addressing climate change and transitioning to sustainable energy sources.	Emphasize traditional values, personal responsibility, and a limited government role in social affairs. They may prioritize issues like national security, law and order, and policies that they believe support family and community stability.
Entitlements	Advocate for the protection and expansion of entitlement programs like social security, Medicare, and Medicaid. They argue that these programs are essential for the well-being of vulnerable populations and should be strengthened to ensure long-term viability.	Advocates for reforming entitlement programs like social security, Medicare, and Medicaid, to reduce government spending and increase efficiency, including like raising the retirement age, introducing means-testing, or encouraging private savings alternatives.
Globalization	Usually support globalization policies that include both the promotion of international trade and the protection of workers' rights and environmental standards. The party tends to favor engagement in international institutions and agreements to address global challenges.	Some support it to expand markets and encourage free trade, while others are more cautious, concerned about its impact on domestic industries and jobs. The party has seen a range of perspectives, from advocating for global engagement to supporting more nationalist policies.

Wall Street	Support stricter regulation of the financial industry to prevent practices that could lead to economic crises. This includes advocating for measures like the Dodd-Frank Wall Street Reform and the Consumer Protection Act, designed to increase transparency and accountability in the financial Sector.	Support deregulation of the financial industry, arguing that it fosters a more dynamic and efficient financial sector. They often oppose stringent regulations, believing that they can stifle economic growth and innovation.

6. Education

Public Education

Public education is one of the longest standing American "rights" that is not spelled out in the Constitution or the Bill of Rights. It is a big topic and one that has helped America stand out against the rest of the world. Public education provides one of the greatest opportunities for the equalization of classes.

Public education, being limited to the primary and secondary levels – grade school and high school – is usually directed locally or by the state, as opposed to the federal level. States may also certify private schools and set standards for home schooling. Governments may also sponsor (subsidize and oversee) college education. The concept of public education originated in medieval times as schools for the poor and first came to America through the churches (Puritans and Quakers), later becoming institutionalized in the mid-1800s.

Jefferson tried to get Virginia to open free public schools, but the legislature did not want to levy a school tax, so it failed. The first public schools in America as we know them today were in Massachusetts in the 1850s. That is not to say there was not a high level of literacy in many places in the colonies. Connecticut had modern levels of literacy before the Revolutionary War. New Orleans' public schools date back to the 1830s and remained independent until the 20th century, even after the reconstruction government decided to open state-wide public schools in the late 1860s.[116]

The Democrats state, "In the 21st century, where the most valuable skill is knowledge, countries that out-educate us today will out-compete us tomorrow. In the platform hearings, Americans made it clear that it is morally and economically unacceptable that our high-schoolers continue to score lower on math and science tests than most other students in the world and continue to drop-out at higher rates than their peers in other industrialized nations. We cannot accept the persistent achievement gap between minority and white students or the harmful disparities that exist between different schools within a state or even a district."[128]

Some Democratic Party Platform Statements

- "... [We believe] that graduation from a quality public school and the opportunity to succeed in college must be the birthright of every child – not the privilege of the few."
- "... [We would] make quality, affordable early childhood care and education available to every American child from the day he or she is born. Our Children's First Agenda, including increases in Head Start and Early Head Start, and investments in high-quality Pre-K, will improve quality and provide learning and support to families with children ages zero to five. Our Presidential Early Learning Council will coordinate these efforts."
- "... [We favor] recruiting a new generation of teachers and principals by making this pledge – if you commit your life to teaching, America will commit to paying for your college education. We'll provide better preparation, mentoring, and career ladders. Where there are teachers who are still struggling and underperforming, we should provide them with individual help and support. And if they're still underperforming after that, we should find a quick and fair way – consistent with due process – to put another teacher in that classroom."
- "... We will also meet our commitment to special education and to students who are English Language Learners."
- "... We support full funding of the Individuals with Disabilities Education Act."
- "... We support transitional bilingual education and will help Limited English Proficient students get ahead by supporting and funding English Language Learner classes."
- "... We support teaching students second languages, as well as contributing through education to the revitalization of American Indian languages."
- "... We believe responsibility for our children's education has to start at home."
- "... We will invest in short-term accelerated training and technical certifications for the unemployed and under-employed to speed their transition to careers in high-demand occupations and emerging industries."
- "... We will reward successful community colleges with grants so they can continue their good work."
- "... We support education delivery that makes it possible for non-traditional students to receive support and encouragement to obtain a college education, including Internet, distance education, and night and weekend programs."
- "... We must also invest in training and education to prepare incumbent jobholders with skills to meet the rigors of the new economic environment and provide them access to the broad knowledge and concrete tools offered by apprenticeships, internships, and postsecondary education."

- "… We need to fully fund joint labor-management apprenticeship programs and reinvigorate our industrial crafts programs to train the next generation of skilled American craft workers."
- "… We recognize the special value and importance of our Historically Black Colleges and Universities and other minority serving institutions in meeting the needs of our increasingly diverse society and will work to ensure their viability and growth."
- "… We will make college affordable for all Americans by creating a new American Opportunity Tax Credit to ensure that the first $4,000 of a college education is completely free for most Americans. In exchange for the credit, students will be expected to perform community service."
- "… We will continue to support programs, especially the Pell Grant program, which open the doors of college opportunity to low-income Americans."
- "… We will enable families to apply for financial aid simply by checking a box on their tax."

The Democrats place a major focus on education, especially when it comes to helping the underprivileged.

Republicans strongly value public education too and have several objectives in common with the Democrats; but, as you will see, they take a different approach to furthering education in America.

The Republicans have stated a goal of "world class in every zip code." Here is what they believe in more detail:

Some Republican Party Platform Statements

- "… Education Means a More Competitive America – Education is a parental right, a state and local responsibility, and a national strategic interest. Maintaining America's preeminence requires a world-class system of education, with high standards, in which all students can reach their potential."
- "… Education is essential to competitiveness, but it is more than just training for the work force of the future. It is through education that we ensure the transmission of a culture, a set of values we hold in common."
- "… All children should have access to an excellent education that empowers them to secure their own freedom and contribute to the betterment of our society."
- "… We reaffirm the principles that have been the foundation of the nation's educational progress toward that goal: accountability for student academic achievement; periodic testing on the fundamentals of learning, especially math and reading, history and geography; transparency, so parents and the general

public know which schools best serve their students; and flexibility and freedom to innovate so schools and districts can best meet the needs of their students."

- "... We advocate policies and methods that are proven and effective: building on the basics, especially phonics; ending social promotion; merit pay for good teachers; classroom discipline; parental involvement; and strong leadership by principals."
- "... We ... support parental options, including home schooling, and local innovations such as schools or classes for boys only or for girls only and alternative and innovative school schedules."
- "... We support state efforts to build coordination between elementary and secondary education and higher education such as K-16 councils and dual credit programs."
- "... To ensure that all students will have access to the mainstream of American life, we support the English First approach and oppose divisive programs that limit students' future potential."
- "... All students must be literate in English, our common language, to participate in the promise of America."
- "... We support family literacy, which improves the literacy, language, and life skills of both parents and children along with the continued improvement of early childhood programs, such as Head Start, from low-income families."
- "... We reaffirm our support for the childcare tax credit that helps parents choose the care best for their family."
- "... School districts must have the authority to recruit, reward, and retain the best and brightest teachers, and principals must have the authority to select and assign teachers without regard to collective bargaining agreements. Because qualified teachers are often not available through traditional routes, we support local efforts to create an adjunct teacher corps of experts from higher education, business, and the military to fill in when needed."
- "... Teachers must be protected against frivolous litigation and should be able to take reasonable actions to maintain discipline and order in the classroom."
- "... We encourage the private-public partnerships and mentoring that can make classroom time more meaningful to students by integrating it with learning beyond school walls. These efforts are crucial to lowering the drop-out rate and helping at-risk students realize their potential. We encourage state efforts to ensure that personnel who interact with children pass thorough background checks and are held to the highest standards of conduct in STEM subjects: science, technology, engineering, and math."
- "... Parents should be able to decide the learning environment that is best for their child. We support choice in education for all families, especially those with children trapped in dangerous and failing schools, whether through charter schools, vouchers, or tax credits for attending faith-based or other nonpublic schools, or the option of home schooling."

- "… We will energetically assert the right of students to engage in voluntary prayer in schools and to have equal access to school facilities for religious purposes."
- "… We renew our call for replacing 'family planning' programs for teens with increased funding for abstinence education, which teaches abstinence until marriage as the responsible and expected standard of behavior as the best way to prevent out-of-wedlock pregnancies and sexually transmitted diseases."
- "… We oppose school-based clinics that provide referrals, counseling, and related services for abortion and contraception. Schools should not ask children to answer offensive or intrusive personal nonacademic questionnaires without parental consent."
- "Although the Constitution assigns the federal government no role in local education, Washington's authority over the nation's schools has increased dramatically. In less than a decade, annual federal funding has shot up 41 percent to almost $25 billion, while the regulatory burden on state and local governments has risen by about 6.7 million hours – and added $141 million in costs – during that time. We call for a review of Department of Education programs and administration to identify and eliminate ineffective programs, to respect the role of states, and to better meet state needs."
- "… To get our schools back to the basics of learning, we support initiatives to block-grant more Department of Education funding to the states, with requirements for state-level standards, assessments, and public reporting to ensure transparency."
- "… The overall financial aid system [of higher education], with its daunting forms and confused rationales, is nothing less than Byzantine. It must be simplified. We call for a presidential commission to undertake that task and to review the role of government regulations and policies in the tuition spiral."
- "… We affirm our support for the public-private partnership that now offers students and their families a vibrant marketplace in selecting their student loan provider."

Observationally, Republicans acknowledge the significance of various educational aspects, but specifics on proposed changes are sometimes perceived as limited. A key emphasis within the party centers on advocating for parental rights and local control over education, especially regarding curriculum content related to sex, gender, and culture, focusing on the age-appropriateness of materials and ensuring parental involvement and awareness. Additionally, Republican education policies broadly support school choice, highlight the importance of STEM education, and include various initiatives to enhance educational outcomes. This blend of priorities reflects a multifaceted approach to education reform that balances concerns over specific curriculum content with broader goals for systemic improvement. The debate over voucher programs primarily centers on whether it is constitutional to fund religious education with public tax money, raising concerns about the separation of church and state. Critics argue that this practice may violate the Establishment Clause of the First Amendment of the United States. It is worth noting that the Constitution did not formalize federal involvement in education, leaving it primarily within the purview of state and local authorities. However, education, as mentioned above, benefits from significant federal funding of approximately $25 billion annually. While some of this expenditure is directed toward achieving specific policy goals and priorities set by politicians, it also serves various essential purposes, including improving educational equity and addressing critical challenges within the education system.

Ideological Perspectives on Censorship

Originally, schools operated without federal oversight, with minimal involvement from state legislators, emphasizing local control over education funding, primarily through local property taxes. Despite this, both federal and state governments have intervened, with federal involvement notably increasing in the 20th century through establishing the Department of Education in 1979 and enacting various education laws. While the Founding Fathers recognized the value of education, the Constitution lacked a comprehensive framework for funding education, leaving its development and management primarily to state and local levels. Initially, restricting sexually-graphic books in schools appeared justifiable for child protection, aligning with "protecting the welfare and safety of all citizens," yet a potential contradiction emerged when similar arguments were applied to justify gun restrictions for public safety.

Is there a Constitutional Contradiction?[95]

The comparison between banning books and banning guns involves two different areas of the U.S. Constitution: the First Amendment, which protects freedom of speech (including books and written materials), and the Second Amendment, which protects the right to keep and bear arms. The perceived contradiction arises from different legal interpretations and societal values placed on these rights:

1. First Amendment – Freedom of Speech: This includes the right to read, disseminate, and access information. However, this right is not absolute. Courts have allowed certain limitations, especially in school environments, where the content must be appropriate for minors and support educational goals. Banning books in schools is often justified on these grounds, although it can be legally contested if seen as overly broad or unjustified censorship.

2. Second Amendment – Right to Bear Arms: This is also subject to interpretation and limitations. The U.S. Supreme Court has recognized that this right is not unlimited and can be subject to specific regulations. However, the extent and nature of permissible gun control measures are hotly debated. Some argue for more stringent controls for public safety, while others see such controls as infringements on constitutional rights.

The apparent contradiction arises from the varying legal standards and societal considerations applied to rights, with courts frequently weighing the balance between individual rights and public welfare in both cases, taking into account the nature of the proper historical context and prevailing societal attitudes, with these issues subject to evolution based on new legal precedents, societal changes, and shifts in the political landscape.

The two parties have radically different ideas when it comes to controlling the educational environment.

Democratic Positions on Censorship in Education

- **Emphasis on inclusive and diverse curricula**: A wide range of perspectives should be taught, including those related to race, gender, sexual orientation, and other social issues. They often argue that exposing students to a variety of viewpoints fosters critical thinking and a more informed citizenry.
- **Protection of academic freedom**: This principle allows educators to teach and research without undue interference or censorship. They may oppose efforts to restrict teachers' ability to address certain topics in the classroom.
- **Opposition to censorship of LGBTQ+ content**: They argue that such content is essential for promoting understanding, tolerance, and inclusivity.
- **Concerns about misinformation and disinformation**: May advocate for measures to promote media literacy and critical thinking skills among students.
- **Local control and community input**: Support the idea that decisions about school curricula should be made at the local level with input from educators, parents, and community members. They may be wary of top-down mandates or censorship efforts that limit local control.
- **First Amendment rights**: Like Republicans, Democrats also value First Amendment rights, including free speech, and may be cautious about policies that infringe upon these rights in schools.

Republican View on Censorship in Education

- **Concerns about political bias**: Perceive there is political bias and ideological censorship in educational institutions, particularly in higher education. They argue that schools and universities should provide a more balanced and diverse range of viewpoints.
- **Opposition to censorship of conservative ideas**: Argue that conservative voices and viewpoints are marginalized or suppressed in academic settings, and they advocate for the protection of free speech and intellectual diversity on campuses.
- **Concerns about curriculum content**: This relates to issues such as critical race theory, gender identity education, and sex education. They may advocate for more oversight or parental involvement in curriculum decisions.
- **Support for First Amendment rights**: Emphasize the importance of First Amendment rights, including free speech and religious freedom, and are critical of policies or actions in schools that they believe infringe upon these rights.

- **Parental control and transparency**: Support giving parents greater control over their children's education and curriculum choices. They may advocate for increased transparency and parental involvement in school policies and decisions.

Concerns about school curriculums have evolved into fears that the education system is being politicized to mold the minds of our youth to support one or other of the parties when they grow up. This struggle for control potentially contradicts our fundamental rights of freedom of speech and expression, as well as the separation of church and state, and hinders students' ability to learn to think independently. Are the parties so concerned that their children would grow up to only think the way they are taught? There may be a constitutional contradiction between defending parental rights for greater control over their children's education and curriculum choices, yet taking these rights away when it comes to gender issues.

The tension between maintaining academic freedom and ensuring a balanced, inclusive curriculum is at the forefront of these debates. The nation's approach to education is likely to continue to shape not only the minds of students but also the contours of our political discourse and societal norms. Finding common ground amid these complex issues remains a significant task for local government that requires thoughtful dialogue, collaboration, and a steadfast commitment to a well-rounded education system that prepares students for an ever-changing world. It is more a matter of timing not morals, because any student who lives in our "online society" is exposed to all sides of every issue well before parents realize it.

Proposal: Encourage greater involvement by citizens in local school boards to help ensure that political and religious bias does not invade the classroom and the focus remains on critical thinking skills, basic knowledge, and the open-mindedness needed to succeed in this world.

Project HeadStart

Public education serves as a potent equalizer in our society and is cherished by Americans. As stated above, it should be enshrined as an inherent, inalienable right.

Early education is a foundational right and must be accessible to all children. Project Head Start, initiated by the U.S. Department of Health in 1964 under President Lyndon Johnson, aimed to support children from low-income families with education, health, nutrition, and parental involvement. This commendable program should continue. It is funded through grants directly to local public and private non-profit and for-profit agencies which provide these services in their communities. By going directly to providers, the program is economically efficient as it avoids a layer of state bureaucracy. This might seem to run counter to the intent of the Constitution of relegating to states that which are not defined duties of the federal government. However, the federal government justifies its involvement in education, as well as health and social services, under the General Welfare Clause of the Constitution (Article I, Section 8), which allows Congress to provide for the common defense and general welfare of the United States. The program has grown from **904,140** participants in 2013 to **985,153** in 2022.[46]

When public education begins, typically around age four or five, children from impoverished and disadvantaged backgrounds often find themselves at a substantial disadvantage. Their parents may not be well educated or lack childcare, transportation, and money for school fees, books, proper nutrition, and materials. For these children to have a fair chance, their education must start even earlier, ideally by age two. Without this early start, they may perpetually lag more privileged students, who benefit from educated parents' involvement in their education, stable home environments, proper nutrition, wider opportunities to learn, and overall well-being.

> **Proposal: Project Head Start should be revitalized to enhance its effectiveness and expand its use. Encourage parents to enroll their infants and toddlers in Early Head Start, which serves children from birth to age three. This program precedes the main Head Start program for children aged three to five. Both provide early childhood education, health services, and family support.**

Art in Secondary Schools

The study of art in secondary schools has often been the subject of political debate but is crucial for many reasons. Firstly, it fosters creativity, encouraging students to express themselves in imaginative ways, which is a valuable skill that can be transferred across various fields, including science, technology, and business. It also enhances cultural and historical awareness, giving students insights into diverse histories and ways of expressing creativity. Critical thinking skills are honed through analyzing and interpreting art, which can be applied to numerous situations. Artistic pursuits improve communication skills, as creating and discussing art helps students articulate their thoughts and emotions. Art further develops emotional intelligence, fostering empathy and aiding mental health. The physical act of creating art enhances fine motor skills and hand-eye coordination.

Moreover, art teaches perseverance and focus, as it often requires patience and attention to detail. Completing art projects instills a sense of accomplishment and boosts confidence, which is vital for personal growth. For those interested in creative careers, art education provides a solid foundation in the skills and knowledge needed. It ensures a balanced approach to learning, complementing analytical subjects and fostering a holistic educational experience. And with the advent of Artificial Intelligence in creating images, images, and sounds, gaining proficiency in these tools may be critical for future careers. Overall, art education is integral in developing well-rounded, creative, and empathetic individuals equipped with a broad range of essential life skills.

> **Proposal: We need to support the arts in schools and in public life, as it says we must in the Constitution.**

Recap - Education

2023-2024 Positions on Education		
Area of Concern	**Democrats**	**Republicans**
Education	Emphasize increased federal funding for public schools, support for early childhood education, affordable college and student loan debt relief, and policies promoting educational equity and inclusivity.	Focus on school choice including charter schools and vouchers, local control over education policies, limited federal intervention, and reforms to higher education financing to reduce dependency on student loans.

7. Energy and Environmental Stewardship

The role of energy in every nation's economy is crucial, whether they are producers or consumers. Energy's close relationship with the environment is also undeniable. Many processes used to create energy lead to carbon emissions, which are widely regarded as a primary contributor to global warming – a concern of global magnitude. However, discerning the truth when it comes to energy use and the environmental impact of carbon emissions is challenging. The powerful oil and coal industries often resist competition from alternative energy sources and oppose additional costs linked to carbon emissions. There are claims that these energy producers and their supporters, including certain political groups, contribute to public confusion and delay necessary actions. They have disputed scientific evidence and observable environmental changes, such as the reduction in polar ice fields, melting glaciers, and rising temperatures and water levels. From a perspective that favors scientific evidence over unsubstantiated claims, the rapid depletion of Earth's finite oil reserves appears unsustainable for the world's long-term survival. The question arises: Why should we exhaust our limited oil supply hastily?

Energy

On the surface, the Republicans seem in favor of Big Oil and the Democrats are for alternative energy sources and reduction of oil use. However, their positions are more elaborate than this simplistic view.

Democrats' Views on Energy

- "Energy is important to the economy, to national security, and to the health of our planet."
- "The energy threat we face today may be less immediate than threats from dictators, but it is as real and as dangerous. The dangers are eclipsed only by the opportunities that would come with change. We know that the jobs of the 21st Century will be created in developing new energy solutions. The question is whether these jobs will be created in America, or abroad. We should use government procurement policies to incentivize domestic production of clean and renewable energy."
- "We commit to fast-track investment of billions of dollars over the next ten years to establish a green energy sector that will create up to five million jobs."

- "We'll create an energy-focused youth job program to give disadvantaged youth job skills for this emerging industry."
- "We will call on businesses, government, and the American people to make America 50 percent more energy efficient by 2030, because we know that the most energy efficient economy will also gain the competitive edge for new manufacturing and jobs that stay here at home."
- "We will help pay for all of it by dedicating a portion of the revenues generated by an economy-wide cap and trade program (see below) – a step that will also dramatically reduce our greenhouse gas emissions and jumpstart billions in private capital investment in a new energy economy."
- "We'll dramatically increase the fuel efficiency of automobiles, and we'll help auto manufacturers and parts suppliers convert to build the cars and trucks of the future and their key components in the United States. And we will help workers learn the skills they need to compete in the green economy. We are committed to getting at least 25 percent of our electricity from renewable sources by 2025."
- "We will create new federal-local partnerships to scale the success and deployment of new energy solutions, install a smarter grid, build more efficient buildings, and use the power of federal and military purchasing programs to jumpstart promising new markets and technologies."
- "We'll invest in advanced biofuels like cellulosic ethanol which will provide American-grown fuel and help free us from the tyranny of oil. We will use innovative measures to dramatically improve the energy efficiency of buildings."
- "To lower the price of gasoline, we will crack down on speculators who are driving up prices beyond the natural market rate."
- "We will help those who are hit hardest by high energy prices by increasing funding for low-income heating assistance and weatherization programs, and by providing energy assistance to help middle-class families."
- "We will make it a top priority to reduce oil consumption by at least 35 percent, or ten million barrels per day, by 2030. This will more than offset the amount of oil we are expected to import from OPEC nations in 2030."

The Republicans have said that "energy costs are spiraling upward, food prices continue to rise, and as a result, our entire economy suffers." Of course, recent inflation has impacted all prices, including food and gasoline. **Many older Americans can remember 1950 when gasoline (leaded) was $0.27 per gallon. Of course, adjusted for inflation, that is equivalent to $3.32 today. Surprisingly: the average price of gas on February 16, 2024, is $3.31**[79].

The price of a barrel of oil (using Illinois Sweet – one of the industry standards) has risen from $53.79 per barrel in 1974 to $69.70 as of February 2023 when adjusted for inflation. That is a 29% increase over 49 years. This increase of 0.6% per year has been more than offset by the greater efficiency of our oil-using products (like how many miles the cars of today get per gallon compared to the 1970s). Our consumption of oil is also up, having increased from 16.7 million barrels per day (MBPD) in 1974 to 20.6 MBPD in February 2023, which is a 23% increase, mainly due to population increases.

Of course, on a short-term basis, oil prices fluctuate wildly at times; but over the long-term it does not appear to be spiraling out of control.[129]

It is interesting to note that the United States exports more in finished oil products (gasoline, diesel fuel) than it imports. Here is a breakdown:[129-02]

US Oil Imports and Exports

- The U.S. produces 10 million barrels of crude oil per day.
- The U.S. consumes 8 million barrels of crude oil per day.
- The U.S. refines 12 million barrels of crude oil per day.
- The U.S. exports 4 million barrels of refined products per day.

The point of this reality check on U.S. energy production is that gas prices are determined by business decisions rather than political ones. And we produce more oil than we consume, so foreign sourced oil is an economic decision, not a necessity.

Republicans' Views on Energy

- "This winter, families will spend for heat what they could have saved for college, and small businesses will spend for fuel what could have covered employee health insurance."

- "The ongoing transfer of Americans' wealth to OPEC – roughly $700 billion a year – helps underwrite terrorists' operations and creates little incentive for repressive regimes to accept democracy, whether in the Middle East or Latin America."

- "It didn't have to be this way, and it must not stay this way. Our nation must have a robust energy supply because energy drives prosperity and increases opportunity for every American. We reject the idea that America cannot overcome its energy challenges."

- "Together we can build a future around domestic energy sources that are diverse, reliable, and cleaner. We can strengthen our national security, create a pathway to growing prosperity, and preserve our environment."

- "Increasing our production of American-made energy and reducing our excessive reliance on foreign oil will:

  - bring down the high cost of gasoline and diesel fuel;
  - create more jobs for American workers; and
  - enhance our national security.

- "In the long run, American production should move to zero-emission sources, and our nation's fossil fuel resources are the bridge to that emissions-free future."

- "We simply must draw more American oil from American soil. We support accelerated exploration, drilling, and development in America, from new oilfields off the nation's coasts to onshore fields such as those in Montana, North Dakota, and Alaska. The Green River Basin in Colorado, Utah, and Wyoming offers recoverable shale oil that is ready for development, and most of it is on federal lands."

- "To deliver that energy to American consumers, we will expand our refining capacity. Because of environmental extremism and regulatory blockades in Washington, not a single new refinery has been built in this country in 30 years. We will encourage refinery construction and modernization and, with sensitivity to environmental concerns, an expedited permitting process."

- "Any legislation to increase domestic exploration, drilling, and production must minimize any protracted legal challenges that could unreasonably delay or even preclude actual production. We oppose any efforts that would permanently block access to the coastal plain of the Arctic National Wildlife Refuge."

- "Nuclear energy is the most reliable zero-carbon emissions source of energy that we have."

- "Republicans believe we should pursue dramatic increases in the use of all forms of safe, affordable, reliable – and clean – nuclear power."

- "As new plants are constructed using the highest safety and operation standards, the nation's industrial and manufacturing base will be rejuvenated. The labor force will expand, with nearly 15,000 high quality jobs created for every new nuclear plant built."

- "Alternate power sources must enter the mainstream. The technology behind solar energy has improved significantly in recent years, and the commercial development of wind power promises major benefits both in costs and in environmental protection. Republicans support these and other alternative energy sources, including geothermal and hydropower, and anticipate technological developments that will increase their economic viability. We therefore advocate a long-term energy tax credit equally applicable to all renewable power sources.

- "We support measures to modernize the nation's electricity grid to provide American consumers and businesses with more affordable, reliable power."

- "America's most affordable and abundant energy resource and the source of most of our electricity remains a strategic national resource that must play a major role in energy independence. We look to innovative technology to transform America's coal supplies into clean fuels capable of powering motor vehicles and aircraft. We support coal-to-liquid and gasification initiatives, just as we support investment in the development and deployment of carbon capture and storage technologies, which can reduce emissions." [They say the Democrats are against expanded use of coal fired power plants.]

- "Natural gas is plentiful in North America, but we can extract more and do a better job of distributing it nationwide to cook our food, heat our homes, and serve as a growing option as a transportation fuel. Both independently and in cooperation with alternative fuels, natural gas will be an essential part of any long-term energy solution."

- "We embrace the open energy cooperation and trading relationship with our neighbors Canada and Mexico, including proven oil reserves and vast, untapped Canadian hydroelectric generation."

- "Conservation through greater efficiency – We can construct better and smarter buildings, use smarter thermostats and transmission grids, increase recycling, and make energy-efficient consumer purchases. Wireless communications, for example, can increase telecommuting options and cut back on business travel."

- "New Technologies for Cars and Other Vehicles We must continue to develop alternative fuels, such as biofuels, especially cellulosic ethanol, and hasten their technological advances to next-generation production."

- "As America develops energy technology for the 21st century, policy makers must consider the burden that rising food prices and energy costs create for the poor and developing nations around the world. Because alternative fuels are useless if vehicles cannot use them, we must move quickly to flexible fuel vehicles; we cannot expect necessary investments in alternative fuels if this flexibility does not become standard. We must also produce more vehicles that operate on electricity and natural gas, both to reduce demand for oil and to cut CO_2 emissions. Given that fully 97 percent of our current transportation vehicles rely on oil, we will aggressively support technological advances to reduce our petroleum dependence."

You cannot talk about energy without talking about energy independence and the environment, as extracting energy from our multitude of potential sources has varying impacts on our air, water, global climates, and land.

Energy Independence

Energy independence hinges on developing efficient, innovative technologies. Meanwhile, conserving our domestic oil and gas resources is vital for long-term needs. Reducing energy consumption will also help extend the lifespan of global reserves. Despite claims of larger-than-expected oil reserves, prudent usage remains essential. Maintaining a robust manufacturing capacity, encompassing plants, skills, and production capabilities, will be crucial for defense.

We should continue to increase our strategic stockpiles of critical resources, including the expected needs of the manufacturing we should be bringing back to America.

> **Proposal: We should stockpile enough oil, munitions, and other critical raw materials to fight two global wars at the same time if necessary.**

> **Proposal: We need to find the underlying cause of oil supply shortages and fluctuating prices. Speculators can contribute to fluctuations in the price per barrel of oil and price per gallon of fuel oil and gasoline, irrespective of actual supply and demand dynamics.**

> **Proposal: We must establish an independent panel of experts to assess the severity of carbon pollution and validate the reality of Global Warming, ensuring unbiased dissemination and widespread promotion of their findings without political influence or industry bias.**

Global Warming

The environment goes hand in hand with our energy policies. We could do more with domestic energy if we ignore its environmental impact. However, we have a beautiful country whose beauty is also an asset. Global Warming is about the potential devastation of overheating the planet - wildfires, floods, rising sea levels, famine, and more.

Democrats' Views on Global Warming

- "We must end the tyranny of oil in our time. This immediate danger is eclipsed only by the longer-term threat from climate change, which will lead to devastating weather patterns, terrible storms, drought, conflict, and famine. That means people [will be] competing for food and water in the next fifty years in the very places that have known horrific violence in the last fifty: Africa, the Middle East, and South Asia. That could also mean destructive storms on our shores, and the disappearance of our coastline. We understand that climate change is not just an economic issue or an environmental concern – this is a national security crisis."
- "Without dramatic changes, rising sea levels will flood coastal regions around the world. Warmer temperatures and declining rainfall will reduce crop yields, increasing conflict, famine, disease, and poverty. By 2050, famine could displace more than 250 million people worldwide. That means increased instability in some of the most volatile parts of the world."

Democrats' Proposals

- "We will invest in efficient and clean technologies at home while using our assistance policies and export promotions to help developing countries preserve biodiversity, curb deforestation, and leapfrog the carbon-energy-intensive stage of development."
- "We will reach out to the leaders of the biggest carbon emitting nations and ask them to join a new Global Energy Forum that will lay the foundation for the next generation of climate protocols. China has replaced America as the world's largest emitter of greenhouse gases. Clean energy development must be a central focus in our relationships with major countries in Europe and Asia. We need a global response to climate change that includes binding and enforceable commitments to reducing emissions, especially for those that pollute the most: the United States, China, India, the European Union, and Russia."
- "We will implement a market-based cap and trade system (see below) to reduce carbon emissions by the amount scientists say is necessary to avoid catastrophic change and we will set interim targets along the way to ensure that we meet our goal. We will invest in advanced energy technologies, to build the clean energy economy and create millions of new, good 'Green Collar' American jobs. Because the environment is a truly global concern, the United States must be a leader in combating climate change around the world, including exporting climate-friendly technologies to developing countries."

- "We will use innovative measures to dramatically improve the energy efficiency of buildings, including establishing a grant program for early adopters and providing incentives for energy conservation."
- "We will encourage local initiatives, sustainable communities, personal responsibility, and environmental stewardship and education nationwide."

From their last platform statements, the Republicans believe in the need for "continuing our stewardship over the environment." The Republicans quote President Theodore Roosevelt, who said, "The conservation of natural resources is the fundamental problem. Unless we solve that problem, it will avail us little to solve all others."[129-03]

Republican Platform Statements (2016-2022)

- **Access**: "Whether through family vacations, hunting or fishing trips, backpacking excursions, or weekend hikes, Americans of all backgrounds share a commitment to protecting the environment and the opportunities it offers. In addition, the public should have access to public lands for recreational activities such as hunting, hiking, and fishing."
- **Private Control**: "In caring for the land and water, private ownership has been the best guarantee of conscientious stewardship, while the world's worst instances of environmental degradation have occurred under governmental control. By the same token, it is no accident that the most economically advanced countries also have the strongest environmental protections."
- **Cleaner Air and Water**: "Our national progress toward cleaner air and water has been a major accomplishment of the American people. By balancing environmental goals with economic growth and job creation, our diverse economy has made possible the investment needed to safeguard natural resources, protect endangered species, and create healthier living conditions. State and local initiatives to clean up contaminated sites – brown fields – have exceeded efforts directed by Washington. That progress can continue if grounded in sound science, long-term planning, and a multiuse approach to resources."
- **Protect Private Property Rights**: "Government at all levels should protect private property rights by cooperating with landowners' efforts and providing incentives to protect fragile environments, endangered species, and maintain the natural beauty of America. … Future expansion of our National Park system, as well as designation of National Wilderness areas or Historic Districts, should be undertaken only with the active participation and consent of relevant state and local governments and private property owners."
- **Global Warming**: "The U.S should take steps to reduce carbon emissions. The same human economic activity that has brought freedom and opportunity to billions has also increased the amount of carbon in the atmosphere. While the scope and long-term consequences of this are the subject of ongoing scientific research, common sense dictates that the United States should take measured and reasonable steps today to reduce any impact on the environment. Those steps, if consistent with our global competitiveness will also be good for our national security, our energy independence, and our economy. Any policies should be global in nature, based on sound science and technology, and should not harm the economy."
- **Climate Change**: "The Solution: Technology and the Market – As part of a global climate change strategy, Republicans support technology-driven, market-based solutions that will decrease emissions, reduce excess greenhouse gasses

in the atmosphere, increase energy efficiency, mitigate the impact of climate change where it occurs, and maximize any ancillary benefits climate change might offer for the economy."

- **Reduce Emissions**: "To reduce emissions in the short run, we will rely upon the power of new technologies, as discussed above, especially zero-emission energy sources such as nuclear and other alternate power sources. ... We must unleash the power of scientific knowhow and competitive markets."

- **International Cooperation**: "Because the issue of climate change is global, it must become a truly global concern as well. All developed and developing economies, particularly India and China, can make significant contributions in dealing with the matter. It would be unrealistic and counterproductive to expect the U.S. to carry burdens which are more appropriately shared by all."

- **Cash Incentives**: "Using Cash Rewards to Encourage Innovation – Because [we] believe solutions to the risk of global climate change will be found in the ingenuity of the American people, we propose a Climate Prize for scientists who solve the challenges of climate change. Honoraria of many millions of dollars would be a small price for technological developments that eliminate our need for gas-powered cars or abate atmospheric carbon."

- **Avoid growth limitations**: "Doing No Harm – [We] caution against the doomsday climate change scenarios peddled by the aficionados of centralized command-and-control government. We can – and should – address the risk of climate change based on sound science without succumbing to the no-growth radicalism that treats climate questions as dogma rather than as situations to be managed responsibly."

- **No changes to our way of life**: "A robust economy will be essential to dealing with the risk of climate change, and we will insist on reasonable policies that do not force Americans to sacrifice their way of life or trim their hopes and dreams for their children. This perspective serves not only the people of the United States but also the world's poorest peoples, who would suffer terribly if climate change is severe – just as they would if the world economy itself were to be crippled. We must not allow either outcome."

Plus, more recently, the Republicans published an action plan:

2022 House Policy Blueprint: "Commitment to America"

The blueprint includes the following proposals about the environment and global climate change:

- **Boost domestic oil and gas production**: The blueprint calls for increased drilling on federal lands and waters, as well as streamlined permitting for oil and gas projects.
- **Build more climate-friendly energy sources**: The blueprint supports the development of nuclear power, hydropower, and renewable energy sources such as solar and wind.
- **Change environmental permission system to make construction easier**: The blueprint calls for streamlining the environmental review process for infrastructure projects.
- **Secure supply chains so other countries – notably China – cannot dominate them**: The blueprint calls for reducing reliance on China for critical minerals and other materials used in clean energy technologies.
- **Plant trees to pull more carbon from the atmosphere**: The blueprint supports planting trees and other vegetation to help offset carbon emissions.

The "Commitment to America" policy blueprint reflects a growing recognition among some Republicans that climate change is a real and serious problem. However, it also reflects the Republican Party's continued support for fossil fuels and its opposition to government regulation of the energy sector.

Republicans prioritize finding ways to reduce carbon emissions while ensuring that such efforts do not compromise our global competitive position or our way of life. They aim to strike a balance that considers the potentially uncertain environmental consequences of these actions.

Population growth amplifies global warming by increasing the demand for energy and food, leading to higher emissions of greenhouse gases as societies expand and consume more natural resources. The world population has increased by 75,000,000 in 2023 to reach a total of 8,000,000,000 in 2024.[89-02]

> **Proposal: With unfettered growth, the world will run out of food, fuel, and potable water. This is not a question of *if* but *when*. The world needs to set a limit on its population to a level the world can sustain. If the world cannot control its growth, rapid consumption of all critical resources and eventual widespread starvation is inevitable. America can choose to be either selfish or generous in the short-term and the long-term. We should not wait to address this issue. The world's resources are finite and will not support an infinite number of residents. Oil, natural gas, rare minerals, helium, and other resources are not renewable. We need to develop a "Forever Plan" identifying now what will need to be done to preserve the world's resources and to sustain life forever. This plan will radically affect economic growth by removing the component driven by population increases.**

As of the end of 2023, the world's proven oil reserves were estimated to be 1.755 trillion barrels.[79-01] It's important to note that "proven" refers to the quantity of oil resources that are known and recoverable under current economic and operational conditions. At the current rate of world consumption, this amount will last 47.3 years. Of course, this estimate is subject to change for several reasons. Firstly, discoveries can increase the total known reserves. Technological advancements in extraction methods can make previously inaccessible reserves available. Economic factors, such as fluctuations in oil prices, significantly influence the feasibility of extracting certain reserves. Geopolitical factors are also pivotal; political shifts and policy decisions in oil-rich countries can alter the reported size of their reserves. And global efforts towards sustainability and reducing carbon emissions are increasingly impacting decisions related to the exploration and exploitation of oil reserves, with a growing emphasis on transitioning to cleaner energy sources. On the other side of the ledger, the increase in energy consumption to improve standards of living in developing countries and the exponential growth of the world's population will consume more oil in the years ahead. **The point being that our supply of oil is not unlimited**.

> **Proposal: The U.S. should leave as much oil in the ground as possible because it is a depletable resource, and the day will come when the supply of oil around the world will run out. We will need our reserves to continue life as we know it.**

Cap and Trade, Carbon Emissions, and Manufacturing

"Cap and trade" is an environmental policy mechanism designed to reduce pollution through a market-based approach. It works by setting a "cap" on the emissions allowed from certain pollutants, like carbon dioxide. This cap is typically lowered over time, aiming to reduce overall pollution levels progressively. Under this system, emission allowances are distributed to companies, either through auctions or based on historical emissions. Companies can "trade" these allowances, creating a market incentive for reducing emissions. Companies that reduce their emissions below their allowance can sell their excess to others, incentivizing lower emissions overall. As the cap is gradually lowered, the scheme encourages innovation in clean technologies and practices, steering efforts towards a more sustainable future. This approach addresses immediate environmental concerns and contributes to the broader goal of combating climate change.

Climate change, characterized by the rise in global temperatures due to greenhouse gases, presents a formidable challenge to the world's ecosystems, economies, and societies. How this challenge is overcome is the subject of much debate.

While cap and trade is seen by many as a vital tool in curbing emissions and combating climate change, it's essential to consider the spectrum of viewpoints on this issue. Conservative perspectives often emphasize the potential economic drawbacks, such as the risk of increased operational costs for businesses and potential job losses. They advocate for a more balanced approach that weighs the economic impact against environmental benefits. While aimed at lessening climate change effects, some question whether these policies are an effective or fair way of tackling this global issue.

Passenger vehicles in the United States significantly contribute to the country's carbon dioxide (CO2) emissions. As of April 2023, on average, a typical passenger vehicle emits about 4.6 metric tons of carbon dioxide annually. This figure is based on the average gasoline vehicle having a fuel economy of approximately 22.0 miles per gallon and covering around 11,500 miles per year. Each gallon of gasoline burned creates about 8,887 grams of CO2. However, the total emissions can vary depending on the vehicle's fuel type, fuel economy, and the miles driven.[77]

Airline travel is more efficient than car travel when comparing per-person fuel consumption. A long-range flight on an airplane that is 75% full can achieve approximately 52 miles per gallon per person. In contrast, a car with only one occupant averages about 20 miles per gallon. Adjusting for the average car occupancy of 1.67 persons, the per-person mileage improves to 33.4 miles per gallon. This comparison indicates that, on a per-person basis, cars consume more fuel than airplanes.[79-02,181-10]

The United States is the second-largest emitter of greenhouse gases (GHGs), contributing about 15% to global emissions. China is the largest, at 26%.[79-03,04] The Intergovernmental Panel on Climate Change (IPCC) has warned of severe consequences if global warming exceeds 1.5°C above pre-industrial levels. In response, the U.S. has committed to reducing its GHG emissions by 50-52% by 2030 and achieving net-zero by 2050. However, the nation faces substantial economic damages from climate change by 2050, projected to cost annually $100 billion from extreme weather events, $50 billion from loss of agricultural productivity, another $50 billion from rising sea levels, and $20 billion from negative health impacts.

Cap and trade emerges as a crucial policy as studies indicate that it can lower emissions at a reduced cost compared to direct regulations. A 2021 study by Columbia University's Center on Global Energy Policy suggests that such a system in the U.S. could lead to a 26% reduction in GHG emissions by 2030, create 2.4 million jobs, and add $1.8 trillion to the economy.[78] Beyond these economic benefits, cap and trade is said to encourage investment in clean energy, spur innovation, and offer significant public health and environmental advantages.

Nonetheless, its implementation faces hurdles, including political opposition, concerns about its impact on low-income communities, and whether the scheme can be designed to work effectively in practice. Given the high costs of inaction on climate change, the urgency and significance of implementing a cap-and-trade system in the U.S. seems evident. Further research is required to detail such a system's specific economic costs and benefits.

> **Proposal: Firstly, it is essential to establish a realistic timeline for transitioning away from gasoline and diesel-fueled vehicles. By analyzing current trends in alternative energy vehicle development and infrastructure expansion, achievable targets can be set for this transition. A practical suggestion could be to ban the sale of new gasoline-powered cars by 2030. This target allows adequate time for manufacturers to adjust, alternative energy infrastructure to expand, and consumers to adopt new technologies. Such a goal, while ambitious, aligns with global efforts to reduce carbon emissions and encourages the development of sustainable transportation solutions.**

Carbon Emissions, and Manufacturing

America's current trade deficit is primarily attributed to the relocation of labor and pollution-intensive manufacturing jobs to countries with lower labor costs, such as Mexico, China, Vietnam, India, and Thailand. This is particularly challenging to address without a reciprocal demand for American goods and services. Although China imports some American products like Coca-Cola, McDonald's food items, and selected Ford vehicles, the traffic in trade is far greater in the opposite direction. Furthermore, China's growing capabilities in producing computer chips and software, traditionally strong U.S. exports, is exacerbating the trade imbalance. Recently, in response, the U.S. has begun building chip manufacturing facilities. The situation is further complicated by intellectual property rights issues, with frequent instances of unauthorized replication of American music, videos, movies, and other creative content by Chinese entities. This complex web of economic interactions presents significant challenges in rebalancing trade.

> **Proposal: We need to encourage the return of manufacturing and other jobs to the U.S. through advanced automation, robotics (where Japan currently leads), and innovation. Protecting our intellectual property through rapid innovation is crucial. We should consider re-introducing critical domestic manufacturing sectors such as steel production, stop the sale of U.S. Steel to a Japanese company, and increase our capacity for computerized machine tooling, to ensure self-sufficiency in a significant military conflict.**

The piracy of U.S. companies' intellectual property (IP) is a real concern, significantly impacting their financial stability, innovation potential, and global competitiveness. The top three countries for IP piracy are China, Russia, and India. In these countries, the logistics of legally enforcing IP rights is challenging, leading to widespread unauthorized reproduction and distribution of U.S. products. This problem results in considerable economic losses for American businesses and dampens their incentive to invest in new research and development. Furthermore, the issue strains trade relations and poses risks to consumers who may unknowingly purchase substandard or unsafe pirated products.

> **Proposal: We need to take a tougher stand on protecting U.S. companies' intellectual property.**

Party Positions on Cap and Trade

The Democratic Party supports cap and trade as a critical element of their environmental policy, viewing it as an effective market-based strategy to combat climate change. This aligns with the party's commitment to environmental protection, incentivizing companies to reduce greenhouse gas emissions through economic mechanisms. Democrats value cap and trade for its flexibility, allowing the market to identify the most cost-effective methods for emission reduction. Moreover, they see it as a vital tool for the United States to demonstrate global leadership in addressing climate challenges. To avoid such policies unfairly impacting low-income communities, they advocate for measures that offset potential economic drawbacks.

The Republican Party is concerned about cap and trade's potential economic impact, including higher energy costs and job losses in specific industries. Republicans instead favor alternative environmental approaches, such as direct technological innovation or voluntary industry measures, advocating for minimal government intervention in the market. There is also notable skepticism within the party about the effectiveness of cap and trade in significantly reducing global greenhouse gas emissions, especially without parallel efforts from other major emitting countries and international cooperation on climate policies.

Reducing Eyesores and Pollution

The Highway Beautification Act, championed by Lady Bird Johnson in 1965, aimed to control outdoor advertising and preserve the natural beauty along America's highways. Despite its ambitious intentions, the act has faced challenges in effectively regulating billboards. Poor enforcement, overly flexible guidelines, and amendments that protect billboards have increased the number along our highways (estimated to be 450,000, up 50% from 1965) and the size and increased illumination of billboards, especially in rural and unzoned areas. Today, there are significantly more billboards on federal highways than when the act was first implemented, highlighting the need for continued efforts and policy reforms to realize Lady Bird Johnson's vision of highway beautification.

> **Proposal: The number of billboards should be limited and reflect the commerce of the area (i.e., more allowance in tourist destinations such as Orlando, Gatlinburg, Branson, etc.).**

Light pollution, a consequence of industrial civilization and urban development, has grown significantly over the past century, obscuring our view of the night sky and disrupting ecosystems. The effects of light pollution extend beyond merely hindering our ability to observe the stars; it also has profound implications for wildlife, particularly nocturnal species, by altering natural behaviors, migration patterns, and even predator-prey dynamics. Moreover, the excessive use of artificial lighting contributes to energy wastage and carbon footprint.

> **Proposal: Cut energy usage and light pollution by reducing the number of lights on at night and have them shine downward and only when motion is detected so we can again see the stars in urban areas.**

In large urban areas, the dual challenges of noise and air pollution significantly affect the quality of life and environmental health. Addressing these issues is crucial for creating more livable, sustainable urban spaces.

> **Proposal: Noise and air pollution need to be further reduced in large urban areas. Hybrid/electric cars should be mandated as soon as possible, especially in urban areas.**

Plastic litter is a significant concern due to its non-biodegradable nature and its tendency to break down into microplastics, which can infiltrate food chains.

> **Proposal: Litter still needs to be reduced – the world is not an ashtray for smokers or a trashcan for gum chewers. Perhaps, the U.S. can take a leaf out of Singapore's book and have tougher laws and stricter enforcement – though not have such draconian punishments as caning. Plastic grocery bags MUST be outlawed and plastic needs to be made biodegradable or eliminated from packaging. Microplastics must be removed from our food and water sources, quickly.**

Recap - Energy and the Environment

2023-2024 Positions on Energy and the Environment		
Area of Concern	**Democrats**	**Republicans**
Energy and Energy Independence	Support transitioning to renewable and clean energy sources, like solar and wind, to achieve energy independence and address climate change. Emphasize reducing fossil fuel reliance, creating green jobs, and investing in sustainable energy infrastructure for economic growth. Advocate for international cooperation and agreements to tackle global climate challenges.	Emphasize energy independence with a diverse mix of fossil fuels and renewables. They prefer less regulation, endorsing market-driven strategies for energy efficiency and independence. The party supports expanding domestic energy production, including drilling and mining, for economic growth and national security while aiming to balance environmental concerns with resource utilization.
Global Warming and Climate Change	Prioritize climate change mitigation and environmental protection by reducing greenhouse gas emissions and supporting international efforts like the Paris Climate Agreement. Advocate for a transition to renewable energy and away from fossil fuels, protecting natural habitats and wildlife and ensuring clean air and water. And emphasizes environmental justice, focusing on the impact of climate change and pollution on marginalized communities.	Focus on balancing economic growth with conservation, favoring deregulation and market-driven solutions. Emphasize energy independence, including fossil fuel use, while often questioning the extent of human impact on climate change. Prioritize natural resource management and conservation, emphasizing technological innovation to meet environmental goals.

| Cap and Trade | Support cap and trade as a market-based strategy to reduce greenhouse gas emissions and combat climate change. This approach aligns with their broader commitment to environmental protection, offering a flexible mechanism that allows the market to identify the most efficient ways to reduce emissions. They see cap and trade as a way to achieve emissions targets without overly stringent regulations, so long as such policies do not disproportionately affect low-income communities. | Skeptical of cap and trade, viewing it as potentially harmful to economic growth and job creation. Argue that such market-based regulatory mechanisms can increase energy costs for businesses and consumers. Favor less government intervention in the market and promote alternative approaches to environmental issues, such as technological innovation or voluntary industry standards. For balancing environmental concerns with economic considerations. |

8. Foreign Relations, Trade, Multilateralism, Security

Our relationships with foreign powers, whether in relation to international air travel, trade, warfare, peace initiatives, or military affairs, shape the political landscape of the United States. Our political parties have different visions of the nation's role on the global stage.

America's Responsibility to the World

What does America owe the rest of the world? Our innovations have helped every country in the world. We have defended others when needed. It is true that we had a head start in terms of our natural resources, which led to lifestyles, freedoms, and wealth per capita of which the rest of the world could only dream. But we also innovated to make the most of these advantages, whether that was in scientific research, space exploration, or technology. That is how we created our wealth.

There are two contrasting viewpoints about America's role in supporting the global community. liberals advocate for using American resources to reduce global poverty and create more equitable living standards worldwide. This perspective is driven by a sense of moral obligation and the belief that wealthier nations have a duty to assist those less fortunate.

Conversely, conservatives caution against providing resources to the rest of the world, arguing that such actions might lead to the depletion of said resources, potentially compromising national interests. They emphasize prioritizing America's needs first, concerned that without careful management efforts to elevate global living standards could exacerbate worldwide resource scarcity and economic instability.

This issue requires a multifaceted and well-planned strategy. First, we need to explore various ways to better conserve our natural resources. For example, cutting back on domestic transportation can help save energy, reduce greenhouse gas emissions, and decrease wear on roads and bridges. Second, we need to balance safeguarding America's resources and interests with our moral duty of providing international humanitarian aid. This approach understands the need for both global responsibility and national self-care. It also considers how international aid can support broader geopolitical goals like global stability and forming economic/trade partnerships with other countries.

Should America Isolate Itself?

While isolationism may sound attractive and resonate with political rhetoric, its practical implementation often falls short of its theoretical appeal. Isolationism, defined as the policy or practice of remaining apart from the affairs or interests of other countries, particularly in political matters, has perceived benefits but carries numerous drawbacks and consequences.

Isolationism Pros and Cons

Pros

1. **Preservation of Sovereignty**: Isolationism can help preserve a nation's sovereignty by avoiding entanglements in foreign affairs or alliances that may compromise its independence or autonomy. It allows a nation to prioritize its own interests and decisions without external interference.
2. **Avoidance of Foreign Conflicts**: By staying out of international conflicts or wars, isolationist countries can save lives and resources that would otherwise be expended in military engagements. This approach reduces the risk of casualties and the financial burden of maintaining a large military presence abroad.
3. **Focus on Domestic Priorities**: Isolationism allows a nation to focus its resources, attention, and efforts on addressing domestic issues such as economic development, infrastructure improvement, social welfare, and education. By prioritizing internal stability and prosperity, isolationist policies aim to strengthen the nation from within.
4. **Reduced Dependency on Foreign Entities**: Isolationism can reduce a nation's dependency on foreign trade, resources, or alliances. By limiting engagement with other countries, a nation may seek to become more self-sufficient in terms of economic production, energy resources, and national security.
5. **Avoidance of Cultural Homogenization**: Isolationism may help preserve a nation's unique cultural identity, traditions, and values by limiting exposure to external influences. This approach can promote cultural diversity and safeguard traditional practices from being overshadowed or diluted by global trends.
6. **Protectionism and Economic Security**: Isolationist policies can include protectionist measures such as tariffs, quotas, or subsidies to shield domestic industries from foreign competition. While controversial, such measures aim to protect jobs, industries, and economic stability within the nation.
7. **Budgetary Savings**: By reducing or eliminating foreign aid expenditures, isolationist policies can lead to immediate cost savings for the government. These savings can be redirected towards domestic priorities such as infrastructure development, education, healthcare, or tax cuts.

Cons

1. **Economic Impact**: Isolationism can lead to reduced international trade and investment opportunities. By limiting engagement with other countries, a nation may miss out on potential economic benefits derived from trade partnerships and foreign investments.

2. **Political Isolation**: Isolationist policies can strain diplomatic relations with other nations, leading to increased tension and potential conflicts. Lack of engagement in international forums and agreements may also diminish a country's influence and ability to address global challenges collaboratively.

3. **Technological and Cultural Stagnation**: Isolationism can impede the flow of ideas, innovations, and cultural exchange. Restricting interactions with other countries may limit access to new technologies, advancements, and diverse perspectives, hindering progress and development.

4. **National Security Risks**: Isolationism may weaken alliances and cooperative defense mechanisms, leaving a nation more vulnerable to security threats. By isolating itself from international security arrangements, a country could find itself less prepared to respond to emerging security challenges and threats.

5. **Humanitarian Concerns**: Isolationism may hinder efforts to address global humanitarian crises and promote human rights internationally. By withdrawing from global engagements, a nation may neglect its moral responsibility to support vulnerable populations and uphold humanitarian principles.

6. **Erosion of Soft Power**: Isolationism can diminish a nation's soft power, which is its ability to influence others through cultural, ideological, and diplomatic means. By withdrawing from international dialogue and cooperation, a country may lose credibility and influence in shaping global norms and perceptions.

Successful diplomacy demands skilled leadership encompassing communication, negotiation, cultural competence, analytical thinking, emotional intelligence, flexibility, networking, conflict resolution, knowledge of diplomatic protocol, and language proficiency. Presidents like Franklin D. Roosevelt and George H. W. Bush exemplify such adeptness, with Roosevelt's leadership during World War II and pivotal role in shaping the United Nations, and Bush's handling of the Cold War's end, German reunification, and the Gulf War coalition-building effort showcasing their prowess.

Foreign Relations with Muslim Countries

Enhancing our foreign relations with Muslim countries should be a strategic initiative for the U.S. A multifaceted and culturally sensitive approach would include engaging in regular diplomatic dialogue, fostering economic partnerships, and emphasizing mutual respect for cultural and religious values. Initiating educational and cultural exchanges can bridge gaps in understanding and respect. Collaboratively addressing global challenges like climate change, public health, and regional conflicts, including the Palestinian-Israeli issue, is crucial. Combating Islamophobia, supporting human rights and democratic values, and employing effective public diplomacy, using the media constructively to change attitudes, are vital.

> **Proposal: We need an equivalent to the Geneva Convention to define our long-term relationship with the global Muslim community. Creating such a memorandum of understanding might help bring an end to our ongoing battle with extreme factions or at least put the radicals under pressure from many moderates.**

Foreign Relations and Aid

Democrats believe our country has a responsibility to ensure global security, saying, "To renew American leadership in the world, we will rebuild the alliances, partnerships, and institutions necessary to confront common threats and enhance common security. Needed reform of these alliances and institutions will not come by bullying other countries to ratify American demands. It will come when we convince other governments and peoples that they too have a stake in effective partnerships. It is only leadership if others join America in working toward our common security."

The Democrats include in their platform "support of Africa's democratic development, strengthening Africa's democratic development and respect for human rights, while encouraging political and economic reforms that result in improved transparency and accountability, and recommit [the U.S.] to an Alliance of the Americas."

The TV show *West Wing* once presented an appealing doctrine: "We will defend freedom from tyranny everywhere." While America is making efforts in this direction, it needs to be more comprehensive and all-encompassing.

The Republicans position on foreign relations is as follows: "The international promotion of human rights reflects our heritage, our values, and our national interest. Societies that enjoy political and economic freedom and the rule of law are not given to aggression or fanaticism.

They become our natural allies. Republican leadership has made religious liberty a central element of U.S. foreign policy. Asserting religious freedom should be a priority in all America's international dealings. We salute the work of the U.S. Commission on International Religious Freedom who urges special training in religious liberty issues for all U.S. diplomatic personnel. To be successful international leaders, we must uphold international law, including the laws of war, and update them [and defend them] when necessary. Our moral standing requires that we respect what are American principles of justice. In any war of ideas, our values will triumph."

Republican Positions on Foreign Relations

- A thorough reform of [the state departments] structure to ensure that promotions and appointments are based on performance in supporting the nation's agenda.
- Waging a much more effective battle in the war of ideas through foreign media communications (e.g., Radio Free Europe).
- The establishment of an Inter-Agency Task Force on Human Trafficking, reporting directly to the president, and increased diplomatic efforts with foreign governments that have been negligent toward this evil.
- The UN must reform its "scandal-ridden and corrupt management and become more accountable and transparent in its operations and expenses," including:
  - The UN "must never serve as a substitute for principled American leadership"; and
  - The UN should be encouraged to authorize the acceptance and participation of Israel in all matters.
- The ideological campaign against Vatican participation in UN conferences and other activities should be opposed.
- Any effort by the UN to address global social problems must respect the fundamental institutions of marriage and family.
- Any organizations involved in abortion should not be funded.
- The U.S. should not accept the jurisdiction of the International Criminal Court over Americans (especially servicemen and officials).

Republicans also say, "Including the world's poor in an expanding circle of development is part and parcel of the Republican approach to world trade through open markets and fair competition. It must also be a top priority of our foreign policy." This initiative exemplifies a strategy that both parties might support, with Republicans favoring "open markets and fair competition" to assist the world's poor, while the Democrats typically adopt a more direct approach.

The Republicans have also stated their commitment to assisting foreign countries in reaching high-impact goals. These include fostering the rule of law through democratic governance, improving literacy and learning, and building the foundations for economic development – namely clean water, more efficient agricultural practices, and microcredit funding for small enterprises. They also prioritize maternal and child health, especially safer child birthing and nutrition, in countries affected by epidemics of HIV/AIDS, malaria, and tuberculosis. Furthermore, they advocate for the development of a foreign assistance strategy that serves the national interest. Specifically, this involves a review and improvement of the Foreign Assistance Act of 1961 to align foreign assistance policies, operations, budgets, and statutory authorities.

These do not seem to be typical Republican principles and might raise skepticism were it not for the fact that, according to the Center for Global Development, aid to Africa increased from $1 billion to $4.2 billion under President George W. Bush's administration.

Foreign Trade

Democrats believe that foreign trade should strengthen the American economy and create more American jobs, while also laying a foundation for democratic, equitable, and sustainable growth around the world.

Democrat Stances on Foreign Trade

- "Trade has been a cornerstone of our growth and global development, but we will not be able to sustain this growth if it favors the few rather than the many."
- "We must build on the wealth that open markets have created and share its benefits more equitably."
- "We must also show leadership at the World Trade Organization to improve transparency and accountability and to ensure it acts effectively to stop countries from continuing unfair government subsidies to foreign exporters and non-tariff barriers on U.S. exports."
- "We will not negotiate bilateral trade agreements that stop the government from protecting the environment, food safety, or the health of its citizens; give greater rights to foreign investors than to U.S. investors; require the privatization of our vital public services; or prevent developing country governments from adopting humanitarian licensing policies to improve access to life-saving medications."
- "We will work with Canada and Mexico to amend the North American Free Trade Agreement so that it works better for all three North American countries. We will work together with other countries to achieve a successful completion of the Doha Round Agreement that would increase U.S. exports, support good jobs in America,

protect worker rights and the environment, benefit our businesses and our farms, strengthen the rules-based multilateral system, and advance development of the world's poorest countries."

- "Just as important, we will invest in a world-class infrastructure, skilled workforce, and cutting-edge technology so that we can compete successfully on high-value-added products, not sweatshop wages and conditions."

- "We will end tax breaks for companies that ship American jobs overseas and provide incentives for companies that keep and maintain good jobs here in the United States."

The Republicans want greater international trade, "aggressively advanced on a truly level playing field," which they believe will mean more American jobs, higher wages, and a better standard of living. They also feel it is also "a matter of national security and an instrument to promote democracy and civil society in developing nations."

Republican Stances on Foreign Trade

- "With 95 percent of the world's customers outside our borders, we need to be at the table when trade rules are written to make sure that free trade is indeed a two-way street. We encourage multilateral, regional, and bilateral agreements to reduce trade barriers that limit market access for U.S. products, commodities, and services."

- "We will contest any restrictions upon our farm products within the World Trade Organization (WTO) and will work to make the WTO's decision-making process more receptive to the arguments of American producers."

- "We pledge stronger action to protect intellectual property rights against pirating and will aggressively oppose the direct and indirect subsidies by which some governments tilt the world playing field against American producers. To protect American consumers, we call for greater vigilance and more resources to guard against the importation of tainted food, poisonous products, and dangerous toys. Additionally, we recognize the need to support our growth in trade through appropriate development and support of our ports in order to ensure safe, efficient and timely handling of all goods."

War, Peace, and Military Strength

In the past, the Democrats' focus was on ending the war in Iraq and then the war in Afghanistan. Now, the Democrats, along with the mixed-party Congress, are concentrating on new global challenges, such as unrest in Ukraine and the Middle East, climate change, cybersecurity threats from China, Russia, North Korea, and others, and emerging geopolitical tensions. Their long-term objective is reinforcing American leadership worldwide by advocating for strong diplomatic relations, sustainable development, and technological innovation. Acknowledging the evolving nature of modern threats, they emphasize the need for a versatile and technologically-advanced military capable of responding to conventional and unconventional threats. This approach focuses on cyber defense and the importance of alliances and partnerships to tackle issues that span national borders, such as pandemics and international terrorism.

They also say: "We will not hesitate to use force to protect the American people or our vital interests whenever we are attacked or imminently threatened. But we will use our armed forces wisely, with others when we can, unilaterally when we must. We believe we must also be willing to consider using military force in circumstances beyond self-defense to provide for the common security that underpins global stability – to support friends, participate in stability and reconstruction operations, or confront mass atrocities. But when we do use force in situations other than self-defense, we should make every effort to garner the clear support and participation of others."

Both parties would agree that our military has done an excellent job creating "outposts" round the world to position our fighting capabilities close to where they might be needed. However, as threats in the Middle East, Asia (China and North Korea), and Africa grow, we need to put America more on a defensive "war footing."

> **Proposal: We need to conduct a detailed inventory of our military hardware to establish whether we rely on China to produce any parts and ensure that we have the means for producing those items in America.**

> **Proposal: We should increase our capacity to rapidly transport men, equipment, and supplies for military purposes if we are going to continue to be the defender of democracy, especially in those parts of the world from which we source our critical resources. We should dramatically increase our robotic warfare capabilities on land, air, and sea. We should increase our ability to defend our shores – to avoid any repeat of instances such as a Russian submarine patrolling off our coast in August 2009.[181-11]**

> **Proposal: We should develop sensors of biological and chemical agents upwind from our prevailing air currents (the westerlies off the west coast). We are vulnerable to attack via the disbursal of debilitating agents into the airstream that passes across America.**

> **Proposal: We must expand our development of robotic military machines including robot soldiers. We must development the ability to remove dangerous weapons in space.**

Democrats have spoken about increasing the size of the military and rebuilding our armed forces to meet the "full spectrum needs of the new century."

Democratic Positions on the Military

- "We must build up our special operations forces, civil affairs, information operations, engineers, foreign area officers, and other units and capabilities that remain in chronic short supply; invest in foreign language training, cultural awareness, human intelligence, and other needed counter-insurgency and stabilization skill sets; and create a specialized military advisor corps, which will enable us to better build up local allies' capacities to take on mutual threats."
- "We will develop Civilian Capacity to Promote Global Stability and Improve Emergency Response. We will build the capacity of U.S. civilian agencies to deploy personnel and area experts where they are needed, so that we no longer must ask our men and women in uniform to perform non-military functions. The creation of a volunteer Civilian Assistance Corps of skilled experts (e.g., doctors, lawyers, engineers, city planners, agriculture specialists, police, etc.) who are pre-trained and willing to aid in emergencies will involve more Americans in public service and provide our nation with a pool of talent to assist America in times of need at home and abroad. We will work with private industry, the research community, and our citizens, to build a trustworthy and accountable cyber-infrastructure that is resilient, protects America's competitive advantage, and advances our national and homeland security."

Republicans believe "peace is attained through strength – an enduring peace, based on freedom and the will to defend it and that that goal still requires the unity of Americans beyond differences of party and conflicts of personality – giving way to a common goal of security for our country and safety for our people."

The Republicans pledge to "all who have played a role in defending our homeland that we will support their continued vigilance and assure they have the authority and resources they need to protect the nation." The waging of war – and the achieving of peace, they say, "should never be micromanaged in a party platform, or on the floor of the Senate and House of Representatives for that matter."

But the Constitution calls for Congress to authorize war, which they have not been doing. The last time Congress declared war was in 1941; yet, since then we have fought "major conflicts" in Korea, Vietnam, Panama, Kuwait, Iraq, Afghanistan, been involved in small skirmishes that would fall into the definition of war, and played supporting roles in other conflicts (e.g., Ukraine). Congress seems to adhere to the *Merriam-Webster Dictionary* definition of war as "a state of usually open and declared armed hostile conflict between states or nations." They must need the whole country to be in conflict or wait until another country declares war on us.

> **Proposal: If our armed forces, or our allies, come under fire, we should formally declare it as a war and offer them our total and unwavering support rather than providing limited assistance incrementally.**

The Republican stance on the military underscores a dedication to bolstering defense capabilities, promoting veteran support initiatives, and advocating for robust national security strategies, embodying a commitment to strength, resilience, and strategic leadership on the global stage.

Republican Positions on the Military

- "In dealing with present conflicts and future crises, our next president must preserve all options. It would be presumptuous to specify them in advance and foolhardy to rule out any action deemed necessary for our security."
- "We acknowledge and appreciate the significant contributions of all of America's First Responders, who keep us safe and secure and who are ever ready to come to our aid. The security of our country is now everyone's responsibility, from the Department of Homeland Security to state and local first responders, private businesses, and individual families. The fact that eighty percent of our critical infrastructure is in private hands highlights the need for public-private partnerships to safeguard it, especially in the energy industry. Along with unrelenting vigilance to prevent bioterrorism and other WMD-related attacks, we must regularly exercise our ability to quickly respond if one were to occur."
- "We must be able to thwart cyber-attacks that could cripple our economy, monitor terrorist activities while respecting Americans' civil liberties, and

> protect against military and industrial espionage and sabotage. All this requires experienced leadership."
>
> - "We must develop and deploy both national and theater missile defenses to protect the American homeland, our people, our Armed Forces abroad, and our allies. Effective, layered missile defenses are critical to guard against the unpredictable actions of rogue regimes and outlaw states, reduce the possibility of strategic blackmail, and avoid the disastrous consequences of an accidental or unauthorized launch by a foreign power."

A large part of our taxes goes towards protecting our country and interests around the world. The political differences between Republicans and Democrats on foreign relations, trade, and the military are marked and significant, which creates a tug-of-war against our domestic needs when it comes to funding.

Republicans often emphasize a strong military posture, prioritizing national security and defense spending, and favor aggressive foreign policies. They are also known for supporting free trade but focusing on policies prioritizing American economic interests. Democrats, on the other hand, advocate for diplomatic and multilateral approaches in foreign relations, emphasizing alliances and international cooperation. They support fair trade policies that include environmental and labor standards. They typically focus on strategic and efficient defense spending and prioritize veteran care. These distinctions reflect the broader ideological perspectives of each party, shaping their approach to global challenges and international engagement.

Recap – Foreign Relations

2023-2024 Positions on Foreign Relations, Trade, Multilateralism, and Security		
Area of Concern	**Democrats**	**Republicans**
Foreign Relations, Trade, Multilateralism, and Security	Advocate strengthening international alliances, promoting fair trade policies focusing on human rights and environmental standards, advocating for cooperative multilateral approaches to global issues, and maintaining a balanced approach to national security.	Emphasize assertive foreign relations, prioritize American economic interests in trade policies, tend to favor unilateral actions over multilateralism, and advocate for a robust national defense and security posture.

9. Government Regulations

In examining the political differences between Democrats and Republicans regarding government regulations, we encounter a significant ideological divide that defines much of the American political discourse. Democrats advocate for more robust regulatory frameworks, seeing them as crucial for safeguarding public welfare, protecting the environment, addressing societal challenges, promoting fairness in various sectors, and ensuring fair economic practices. Republicans, on the other hand, tend to favor less government intervention, arguing that overregulation can hinder economic growth and encroach upon personal freedoms. This examination offers a deeper understanding of how each party views the role and scope of government regulation across various sectors, including industry, finance, social issues, and environmental protection.

Examples of Democratic Views on Government Regulations

- **Economic and Business Regulations**: Democrats support stricter regulations on businesses to ensure fair competition, consumer protection, and ethical practices. They often advocate for regulations that address income inequality, such as minimum wage laws and worker protection standards. Democrats also tend to favor regulatory measures aimed at curbing Wall Street excesses, as seen in their support for the Dodd-Frank Act following the 2008 financial crisis.
- **Environmental Regulations**: They support measures aimed at combating climate change, reducing pollution, and preserving natural resources. Policies such as the Clean Air Act and the Paris Climate Agreement often receive strong support from Democratic lawmakers.
- **Healthcare Regulations:** They support regulations to expand access, control costs, and ensure quality. The Affordable Care Act (ACA), which aimed to increase health insurance coverage and regulate the insurance industry, is a key example.
- **Technology and Privacy Regulations**: They support regulations that ensure net neutrality and protect online consumer privacy and data security. They argue for the need to regulate tech giants to prevent monopolistic practices and protect user rights.

Republicans, on the other hand, favor reducing government regulations they see as burdensome or overly restrictive. They may argue that excessive regulations can stifle economic growth and innovation.

Examples of Republican Views on Government Regulations

- **Economic and Business Regulations**: Republicans typically argue for deregulation in the business sector, believing that reducing government oversight fosters a more favorable business climate, encourages entrepreneurship, and stimulates economic growth. They often seek to roll back regulations perceived as burdensome for businesses, like certain provisions of the Dodd-Frank Act, arguing that these regulations can be overly restrictive and hinder economic expansion.
- **Environmental Regulations**: They advocate for more balanced environmental regulations, prioritizing economic considerations alongside environmental protection. They often argue that some environmental regulations can be too costly for businesses and may negatively impact economic growth. Republicans may support deregulatory actions, such as withdrawing from the Paris Climate Agreement, based on economic arguments.
- **Healthcare Regulations**: They push for less government intervention in healthcare, advocating for market-based solutions and competition to drive down costs and improve quality. They have consistently sought to repeal or modify the Affordable Care Act (ACA), arguing that it imposes too many regulations on the healthcare industry and limits consumer choice.
- **Technology and Privacy Regulations**: They emphasize the importance of a free and open Internet, free from government control. They typically argue against stringent regulations on Internet service providers and tech companies, citing concerns about the impact on innovation and free-market competition.

Democrats and Republicans hold divergent views on government regulation. Democrats advocate for robust regulations across sectors such as the economy, environment, and healthcare, which are vital for ensuring fairness, protecting public welfare, and preserving environmental health. Conversely, Republicans prioritize free-market principles and minimal government intervention, advocating deregulation to spur economic growth, encourage innovation, and uphold individual freedoms. These differing stances encapsulate each party's core beliefs, with Democrats prioritizing the government's role in societal welfare and Republicans emphasizing market efficiency and personal liberties.

Consumer Protection

The government's involvement in consumer protection in the United States has evolved significantly over time, reflecting growing recognition of the need to safeguard consumers against unfair, deceptive, or harmful business practices. In the early 20th century, the U.S. government began to take more active steps in consumer protection, starting with legislation like the Pure Food and Drug Act of 1906 and the Federal Trade Commission Act of 1914, which established the Federal Trade Commission (FTC) to prevent unfair business practices. Another landmark was the establishment of the Consumer Product Safety Commission (CPSC) in 1972, responsible for protecting the public from unreasonable risks of injury or death associated with consumer products. Yet another significant milestone was the creation of the Consumer Financial Protection Bureau (CFPB) in 2010, following the financial crisis of 2007-2008, to oversee financial products and services, especially regarding mortgages, credit cards, and student loans. These agencies and laws represent the government's ongoing commitment to protecting consumers' rights and ensuring fair and safe market practices.

Democrats favor increased government intervention and regulation, advocating for robust laws and oversight to protect consumers from unfair or harmful business practices. They often support strong regulatory bodies like the CFPB and endorse legislation to enhance consumer rights and safety. Republicans, on the other hand, tend to prioritize free-market principles and are more cautious about government intervention. They often argue that excessive regulation can stifle innovation and competition and advocate for a more balanced approach where the market is crucial in ensuring consumer protection, with minimal but effective government oversight.

> **Proposal: Enhanced enforcement is vital to safeguard the public from fraud and con artists. Prioritizing perpetrators operating across state lines as federal targets is crucial. States should allocate more resources to investigation and enforcement efforts, while stricter penalties are needed to deter fraudulent activities.**

> **Proposal: Phone companies should be mandated to monitor and investigate high-volume usage actively and reported spam numbers. Collaboration with Apple and Google to share information on blocked and spam calls is crucial. Calls flagged by consumers as 'delete and report junk' should incur a chargeback to the caller, aiming to identify, penalize, and prosecute privacy violators and disruptors.**

Minimum Wage

The minimum wage is a subject of considerable debate between Democratic and Republican lawmakers. Democrats advocate for increasing the minimum wage, arguing that it ensures financial security for workers, reduces poverty, and helps narrow the income inequality gap. They believe a higher minimum wage stimulates the economy by increasing consumer spending. On the other hand, Republicans often express concerns about the potential negative impacts of a higher minimum wage. They argue that it could lead to job losses, especially among smaller businesses that might find it harder to sustain the increased wages compared to larger corporations. Republicans also caution that a raised minimum wage could result in higher prices for consumers as businesses pass on the extra costs.

However, there seems to be a legitimate concern when the existing minimum wage is insufficient for basic living expenses, such as being unable to afford a decent apartment because rents have gone up. This situation indicates an economic imbalance, suggesting an adjustment to the minimum wage might be appropriate. The economy is dynamic and not all costs go up in tandem with each other.

A $15 per hour minimum wage has yet to be widely adopted across the United States at time of writing. While the movement has gained significant momentum, and some states and cities have done so, most states still operate with lower minimum wage levels. The federal minimum wage remains below $15 per hour, at $7.25, reflecting a nationwide divide in policy adoption.[97]

> **Proposal: Index the minimum wage to the average rent for a two-bedroom condominium divided by 32%, which is a reasonable ratio of rent to total income, and which will ensure that the pay earned by two minimum wage earners remains in line with the cost of living. This approach can be tailored to local areas.**

Recap - Government Regulations

2023-2024 Positions on Government Regulation		
Area of Concern	**Democrats**	**Republicans**
Government Regulation	Emphasize the need for robust regulatory frameworks to ensure consumer protection, environmental sustainability, and fair economic practices.	Focus on minimizing government intervention to encourage economic growth, individual freedoms, and market-driven solutions.
Consumer Protection	Advocate for strong government regulations and oversight to protect consumers, emphasizing the importance of robust laws and agencies to safeguard against unfair and harmful business practices.	Favor minimal government intervention in consumer protection, emphasizing free-market solutions and the belief that too much regulation can hinder business innovation and competition.
Minimum Wage	Support raising the federal minimum wage to $15 an hour, seeing it as crucial for reducing income inequality and ensuring a living wage for all workers. They argue that this increase would help workers sustain themselves and their families, boost consumer spending, and stimulate economic growth.	Oppose increases in the federal minimum wage, arguing that it can lead to job losses and hurt small businesses. They advocate for a market-driven approach, suggesting that wage decisions are best made by businesses and industries based on market conditions and regional cost-of-living differences.

10. Gun Control – Second Amendment

The Constitution provides for citizens to own guns – that means they can carry them, use them to protect themselves and other lawful purposes, but did not explicitly state that citizens could use them to overthrow our government if it takes on too much power, although some argue that this is implied. The founding principle of gun ownership was upheld by the Supreme Court in June 2008 when they ruled that the right to bear arms is an individual right as well as a collective right.[165] The Supreme Court has said that efforts to chisel away at this right are improper according to the original intentions.

Some Americans believe that the Second Amendment is about protecting the right to hunt game. That is only one consideration and not the most important. Guns are not only useful for hunting and self-defense, but they are also a massive deterrent to invasion by a foreign power.

Author's Personal Experience

While checking out of a game lodge in Tanzania, a young man at the counter curiously asked if all Americans owned guns. I recalled overhearing him earlier, mentioning to a friend that he was a staunch Communist. His question seemed meant to probe the feasibility of a Communist takeover in America. I informed him that not only do many Americans own guns, but some even have machine guns. I immediately saw his face drop as he realized the magnitude of the challenge of capturing America. This served as a stark reminder to me that widespread gun ownership can function as a significant deterrent against invasion.

However, the recent increase in gun violence within the United States necessitates a serious reevaluation of the motivations behind gun ownership. While hunting rights remain a crucial aspect of life in rural communities, they may not constitute the primary justification for the Second Amendment's protection of gun ownership, particularly within urban areas. **In any event, Americans must stop shooting Americans!**

It is imperative for American citizens to recognize that gun ownership comes with immense responsibility and that resorting to violence against fellow citizens other than in self-defense is unacceptable and contradicts the fundamental principles of a just and peaceful society.

Republicans advocate for broad Second Amendment rights, opposing most forms of gun control as infringements on individual freedoms. Democrats tend to support more stringent gun control measures, including background checks and restrictions on certain types of firearms, viewing these measures as necessary for reducing gun violence and improving public safety.

Given the consistent upholding by the Supreme Court of the constitutional right to bear arms, substantial changes to gun laws that restrict access to guns are unlikely, but limitations related to safety may still be considered. Recently, nine states have enacted successful bans on "assault rifles" and high-capacity magazines, with these bans being upheld by the U.S. Supreme Court. Restrictions on "ghost guns," guns assembled with mail-order parts and without serial numbers, are still under review by the federal courts, as are the use of "bump stocks," additions to semi-automatic rifles allowing them to shoot hundreds of rounds per minute.

The Supreme Court recognizes that the right to bear arms is not absolute and can be subject to certain limitations. In cases concerning bans on assault rifles and high-capacity magazines, it may consider whether these restrictions are reasonable and in line with public safety concerns. This approach reflects an effort to reconcile the constitutional right to bear arms with the state's responsibility to protect its citizens, and decisions can vary based on the specifics of each case.

Proposals:

1. **Just as one needs to learn how to drive a car and be licensed to demonstrate an understanding of its operation, ability to handle it safely, and awareness of its inherent danger, every gun buyer should be required to learn how to use a gun and understand gun safety.**
2. **We should find ways to assess gun owners' understanding of gun safety, which may help to prevent accidents that result from improper storage of firearms (which should be secured) and ammunition (which should be kept separate from guns).**
3. **We also need to find more effective ways to prevent those with mental health problems from owning guns, for their own safety (so they do not have easy access to a gun for committing suicide, for example) and for the safety of others.**

Mass Shootings

The recurring tragedy of mass shootings has become an alarming and all too familiar feature of contemporary society. These horrific events, characterized by the indiscriminate targeting of innocent individuals in public spaces, have ignited passionate debates about gun control, mental health, and the role of government in preventing such atrocities. Mass shootings not only shatter lives and communities but also raise profound questions about the complex intersection of individual rights, public safety, and the need for effective policies to prevent future acts of mass violence.[122]

Researchers and law enforcement have identified some common traits among individuals who have carried out mass shootings.

Mass Shooting Common Factors and Motivations[122]

1. **Mental Health Issues**: Some mass shooters have a history of mental health problems or psychiatric disorders. They may believe that violence is a solution to their perceived problems or struggles.

2. **Perceived Injustice or Grievance**: In some cases, individuals who commit mass shootings feel wronged, oppressed, or marginalized in some way. They may believe that their violent actions are a way to seek revenge or rectify what they perceive as injustices against them.

3. **Desire for Notoriety**: Some mass shooters seek attention and notoriety through their actions. They may be influenced by previous high-profile shootings and aspire to achieve a similar level of infamy.

4. **Ideological or Extremist Beliefs**: In certain cases, individuals are motivated by extremist political, religious, or racial ideologies. These beliefs can drive them to commit acts of violence as a means of advancing their agendas.

5. **Social Isolation and Alienation**: Feelings of loneliness, social isolation, and alienation from others can contribute to some individuals turning to violence to gain a sense of power, control, or belonging.

6. **Access to Firearms**: The availability of guns can make it easier for individuals with violent intentions to carry out their plans.

7. **Copycat Behavior**: Some mass shooters seek to emulate or exceed the actions of previous perpetrators they have read about in the media or online.

8. **Personal Crisis**: Relationship problems, job loss, financial difficulties, or other life stressors can contribute to individuals resorting to violence.

9. **Lack of Effective Intervention**: In some cases, individuals who exhibit warning signs of violence may not receive adequate mental healthcare or intervention, causing their grievances or mental health issues to escalate.

These contributing factors enforce the argument that the death penalty may not be an effective deterrent. Such crimes often stem from mental illness, extremist ideologies, or personal grievances, where the fear of punishment may not be a significant deterrent.

It is crucial to emphasize that identifying and addressing the complex motivations behind mass shootings is an ongoing challenge for federal and state law enforcement, mental health professionals, and society. It requires a national debate on gun control.

In December 2023, the Biden administration introduced the "Safer States Initiative," aimed at combating gun violence at the state level. Vice President Kamala Harris announced this initiative, which includes two new executive actions. The first action provides states with model legislation for the safe storage of guns and holds individuals legally accountable for injuries caused by unsecured weapons. The second action offers a model for reporting lost and stolen firearms to assist law enforcement. These measures are in response to a series of mass shootings and aim to encourage state-level policy changes, especially in the context of congressional inaction and court rulings protective of gun possession rights.[10-01]

Republican leaders and presidential hopefuls, particularly those attending the National Rifle Association's April 2023 convention, consistently affirm their support for gun rights. They argue that gun availability is not the issue, rather it is to do with other issues like the mental health of the perpetrator or a lack of safety at schools. Florida governor Ron DeSantis, for instance, supported compulsory institutionalization for individuals with mental health challenges, reflecting the Republican focus on mental health in addressing gun violence. This perspective opposes stricter gun laws, believing they would be ineffective and compromise our constitutional rights. Instead, Republicans propose improving mental health services and bureaucratic processes related to gun purchases. They believe violence at schools can be prevented through increased armed security and robust safety protocols.[10-02]

Mental Health Services

Reestablishing mental health facilities for people who might be at risk of committing gun violence has pluses and minuses. On the positive side, such community facilities provide access to comprehensive mental healthcare, allow for early intervention, and provide a safe environment for those at risk. However, there are significant concerns, including the potential for stigmatization of patients, high costs of establishment and maintenance, risks of long-term institutionalization, variable quality of care, and ethical dilemmas associated with involuntary treatment. Avoiding these drawbacks is crucial if such facilities are to be reestablished.

Proposals:

1. **Prioritize early detection of and intervention in mental health issues, particularly among young people. This involves training educators, parents, and community members to recognize warning signs and providing resources for early intervention, such as a way for teachers to refer a student to mandatory counseling.**
2. **Integrate mental health services into community settings, such as schools, workplaces, and healthcare facilities. This makes mental healthcare more accessible and reduces the stigma associated with seeking help.**
3. **Consider the expansion of mental health facilities and programs to destigmatize treatment.**

Recap – Gun Control

2023-2024 Positions on Gun Control		
Area of Concern	**Democrats**	**Republicans**
Gun Control	Advocate for stricter gun control measures, including comprehensive background checks, banning assault weapons, and closing gun show loopholes to reduce gun violence and enhance public safety.	Oppose stricter gun control measures. They advocate for responsible gun ownership, focusing on mental health issues and enforcing existing laws rather than creating new regulations.
Mental Health Services	Emphasize the need for comprehensive access to mental healthcare, including increased funding for mental health programs and the integration of mental health services into primary healthcare and community settings.	Focus on reinforcing mental health infrastructure, emphasizing early intervention and treatment, and supporting policies to prevent mental illness from escalating into violence, including gun-related incidents.

11. Healthcare and Wellness

Health Coverage

This is another subject of debate that vividly encapsulates the ideological gap between Democrats and Republicans, with each advocating distinct visions for the nation's healthcare system. Democrats emphasize universal coverage and push for broader government involvement in regulating and subsidizing healthcare to ensure accessibility and affordability for all. On the other hand, Republicans advocate for a market-driven approach, emphasizing individual choice, private sector solutions, and minimal government intervention, arguing that these elements are crucial to improving quality and driving down costs. This encapsulates the differing priorities and philosophies of the two parties when it comes to governance and social welfare.

Democrats have been working to reform and extend healthcare. They view it as a fundamental right and advocate for policies that expand coverage, control costs, and improve the quality of care. This stance includes support for programs like the Affordable Care Act, which aims to extend health insurance to the uninsured and regulate the insurance market. Their view is rooted in the belief that proactive government policies are essential in addressing the needs of all citizens, reducing disparities, and navigating the complexities of the healthcare system.

Democratic Positions on Healthcare

- "Ensuring quality, affordable health care for every single American is essential to children's education, workers' productivity and businesses' competitiveness … providing it would end cost-shifting from the uninsured, promote prevention and wellness, stop insurance discrimination, help eliminate health care disparities, and achieve savings through competition, choice, innovation, and higher quality care."
- "Families and individuals should have the option of keeping the coverage they have or choosing from a wide array of health insurance plans, including many private health insurance options and a public plan. Coverage should be made affordable for all Americans with subsidies provided through tax credits and other means."
- "Health care should be a shared responsibility between employers, workers, insurers, providers and government."
- "Health insurance plans should accept all applicants and be prohibited from charging different prices based on pre-existing conditions."
- "No one should have to worry about losing health coverage if they change or lose their job."

> - "An Emphasis on Prevention and Wellness. All Americans should be empowered to promote wellness and have access to preventive services to impede the development of costly chronic conditions, such as obesity, diabetes, heart disease, and hypertension. Chronic-care and behavioral health management should be assured for all Americans who require care coordination."
> - We need aggressive efforts to cut costs and eliminate waste from our health system … including driving adoption of state-of-the-art health information technology systems, privacy-protected electronic medical records, reimbursement incentives, and an independent organization that reviews drugs, devices, and procedures to ensure that people get the right care at the right time."
> - "We should increase competition in the insurance and drug markets; remove some of the cost burden of catastrophic illness from employers and their employees; and lower drug costs by allowing Medicare to negotiate for lower prices, permitting importation of safe medicines from other developed countries, creating a generic pathway for biologic drugs, and increasing use of generics in public programs."

They also support a strong healthcare workforce, the elimination of disparities in healthcare, and a strong partnership with states, local governments, tribes, and territories and oppose Republican Party's attempts to undermine a woman's ability to make her own life choices and obtain reproductive healthcare, including birth control. They say they will "end health insurance discrimination against contraception and provide compassionate care to rape victims" and will never "put ideology above women's health."

In sum, the Democrats are committed to expanding access, ensuring affordability, and upholding healthcare as a fundamental right for all citizens. Through policies like the Affordable Care Act and proposals for further expansions of government-supported healthcare, Democrats aim to create a more inclusive and equitable healthcare system. Their focus on government intervention and regulation reflects a belief in the state's vital role in providing healthcare security, addressing systemic inequities, and safeguarding public health. This perspective underscores a broader vision of a society where healthcare is not a privilege but a guaranteed service for every individual, irrespective of economic or social status.

On the other hand, the Republican Party's philosophy embodies market-driven solutions and limited government intervention. Republicans advocate for a healthcare system where personal choice, competition, and private-sector innovation are vital to enhancing quality and reducing costs. They emphasize the importance of individual responsibility and the freedom to choose healthcare providers and insurance plans. Critical of extensive government mandates and regulations, such as those seen in the Affordable Care Act, Republicans propose alternatives focused on deregulation, tax incentives, and health savings accounts to promote efficiency and consumer-driven care. This section delves into the Republican vision for healthcare, dissecting their policy proposals, ideological underpinnings, and the intended outcomes of their approach to healthcare reform in the United States.

The Republicans' slogan is, "Health Care Reform: Putting Patients First."

They say: "Americans have the best doctors, the best hospitals, the most innovative medical technology, and the best scientists in the world. Our challenge and opportunity are to build around them the best health care system. Republicans believe the key to real reform is to give control of the health care system to patients and their healthcare providers, not bureaucrats in government or business."

They believe American families and businesses are "dissatisfied with the current state of health care" for several reasons, outlined below:

Republicans' List of American Dissatisfactions

- Most Americans work longer and harder to pay for healthcare.
- Dedicated health care providers are changing careers to avoid litigation.
- The need to hold onto health insurance is driving family decisions about where to live and work.
- Many new parents worry about the loss of coverage if they choose to stay at home with their children.
- The need – and the bills – for long-term care are challenging families and government alike.
- American businesses are becoming less competitive in the global marketplace because of insurance costs.
- Some federal programs with no benefit to patients have grown exponentially, adding layers of bureaucracy between patients and their care.

They go on to say:

- "It is not enough to offer only increased access to a system that costs too much and does not work for millions of Americans. The Republican goal is more ambitious: Better health care for lower cost."
- "The first rule of public policy is the same as with medicine: Do no harm."
- "Republicans support the private practice of medicine and oppose socialized medicine in the form of a government-run universal health care system."

Republican Pledges to Reform Healthcare

- "We will protect citizens against any and all risky restructuring efforts that would complicate or ration health care."
- "We will encourage health promotion and disease prevention."
- "We will facilitate cooperation, not confrontation, among patients, providers, payers, and all stakeholders in the health care system."
- "We will not put government between patients and their health care providers."
- "We will not put the system on a path that empowers Washington bureaucrats at the expense of patients."
- "We will not raise taxes instead of reducing health care costs."
- "We will not replace the current system with the staggering inefficiency, maddening irrationality, and uncontrollable costs of a government monopoly."
- "We must make insurance more affordable and more secure and give employees the option of owning coverage that is not tied to their job."
- "The current tax system discriminates against individuals who do not receive health care from their employers, gives more generous health tax benefits to upper income employees, and fails to provide every American with the ability to purchase an affordable health care plan."
- "[We] propose to correct inequities in the current tax code that drive up the number of uninsured and to level the playing field so that individuals who choose a health insurance plan in the individual market face no tax penalty. All Americans should receive the same tax benefit as those who are insured through work, whether through a tax credit or other means."
- "Because the family is our basic unit of society, we fully support parental rights to consent to medical treatment for their children including mental health treatment, drug treatment, alcohol treatment, and treatment involving pregnancy, contraceptives and abortion."

Republicans say they will also advance a variety of targeted reforms to "improve the quality of care, lower costs, and help Americans – men, women, and children – live longer and healthier lives."

Republican Targeted Reforms

- "To reduce the incidence of diabetes, cancer, heart disease, and stroke, we call for a national grassroots campaign against obesity, especially among children. We call for continuation of efforts to decrease use of tobacco, especially among the young."
- "Closing the health care information gap."
- "Protect good health care providers from frivolous lawsuits."
- "Modernize long-term care options for all."
- "Encourage primary care as a specialty."
- "Fund medical research." (I'd suggest that this may exclude stem cell research).
- "Taxpayer-funded medical research must be based on sound science."
- "No health care professional – doctor, nurse, or pharmacist – or organization should ever be required to perform, provide for, or refer for a health care service against their conscience for any reason. This is especially true of the religious organizations which deliver a major portion of America's health care, a service rooted in the charity of faith communities."
- "Reduce Medicare costs – Medicare patients must be free to add their own funds, if they choose, to any government benefits, to be assured of unrationed care."
- "Our Medicaid obligations will consume $5 trillion over the next ten years. Medicaid now accounts for 20-25 percent of state budgets and threatens to overwhelm state governments for the indefinite future. We can do better while spending less. The first step is to give Medicaid recipients more health care options. Several states have allowed beneficiaries to buy regular health insurance with their Medicaid dollars. This removes the Medicaid 'stamp' from people's foreheads, provides beneficiaries with better access to doctors, and saves taxpayers' money. We must ensure that taxpayer money is focused on caring for U.S. citizens and other individuals in our country legally."
- "Building a Health Care System for Future Emergencies – To protect the American people from the threats we face in the century ahead, we must develop and stockpile medicines and vaccines so we can deliver them where urgently needed. Our health care infrastructure must have the surge capacity to handle large numbers of patients in times of crisis, whether it is a repeat of Hurricane Katrina, a flu pandemic, or a bioterrorism attack on multiple cities. Republicans will ensure that this infrastructure, including the needed communications capacity, is tightly integrated into our homeland security needs."

The U.S. healthcare system continues to have many challenges, some longstanding and others emerging. Insurance companies still exert significant control, often affecting patient access to necessary treatments. The high cost of drugs remains a concern, with issues around safety and side effects, including extreme cases where drugs prescribed for non-life-threatening conditions list death as a potential side effect. The use of emergency rooms for routine care continues, reflecting broader issues of access and efficiency in healthcare delivery.

Healthcare spending is at an all-time high, with out-of-pocket expenses burdening patients, particularly impacting Hispanic and other similar communities. Staffing shortages, exacerbated by the COVID-19 pandemic, have led to burnout among healthcare workers, underlining the need for better support and working conditions.

Amidst these challenges, the potential of artificial intelligence (AI) in healthcare looms large. AI promises to revolutionize diagnostics, offering faster and more accurate analyses, which could lead to improved treatment plans and patient outcomes. This technological advancement represents hope for a more efficient and effective healthcare system.

The Democratic Party is committed to lowering prescription drug prices by empowering Medicare to negotiate these prices. They also focus on eliminating surprise medical billing and improving access to mental health and substance abuse treatments. Addressing disparities in healthcare, expanding long-term care services, and supporting reproductive health rights are also crucial aspects of their healthcare agenda.[102,103]

The Republican Party emphasize patient control and quality in healthcare, advocating for the repeal of the Affordable Care Act (Obamacare). They focus on modernizing and securing the financial footing of Medicare and Medicaid, proposing reforms such as a premium-support model for Medicare and block grants for Medicaid to encourage state-level innovation. They also highlight the need for cost-saving competition among providers and protections against fraud and abuse in Medicare.[103]

> **Proposal: Encourage physical fitness in children much more than we do now. American obesity is a growing problem (pun intended) for the country as a whole**

In summary, the Republican vision for healthcare is centered on the ideals of free-market competition, personal responsibility, and minimal government involvement. Advocating for policies that enhance individual choice and private sector innovation, Republicans propose a healthcare framework where market dynamics are crucial in driving efficiency and reducing costs. Their approach, characterized by opposition to extensive government mandates and support for deregulation and consumer-driven solutions, reflects a fundamental belief in the power of market forces and individual autonomy in shaping a sustainable and effective healthcare system.

Euthanasia

While the Democratic Party does not have a formal national policy on euthanasia, there is broad support among Democrats for medically-assisted dying. This is evidenced by the fact that most states that have enacted aid-in-dying laws, including Oregon, Washington, Vermont, California, Colorado, Washington, D.C., Hawaii, Maine, New Jersey, and New Mexico, traditionally favor the Democrats. These laws empower individuals to have control over their end-of-life decisions in accordance with their values and beliefs.[104,105]

Public surveys, including a 2020 Gallup poll, indicate strong support for physician-assisted dying among Democrats, with 85% agreeing that physicians should be able to assist in terminal patients' deaths.[106] This support, however, has not translated into universal enactment of aid-in-dying legislation, partly due to opposition from religious groups and political polarization.

It is important to note that the support for euthanasia and physician-assisted dying within the Democratic Party is framed within the context of personal autonomy, compassion for the suffering, and ensuring that terminally ill patients can make informed decisions about their end-of-life care. The party's inclination is towards policies that support assisted suicide, with safeguards to ensure patients fully understand their choice and that there is no chance of survival from their illness.[104,105] Of course, a person's religion may take precedence over any legislation.

The Republican Party does not have a unified national policy on euthanasia. Historically, Republicans have tended to oppose euthanasia and physician-assisted suicide, often citing moral, ethical, and religious reasons. This opposition is rooted in their belief in the sanctity of life and a preference for palliative care options that do not hasten death.

In states where legislation on medically-assisted dying has been proposed or passed, Republican lawmakers have often been among the most vocal opponents. Their arguments frequently center around concerns about the potential for abuse, the sanctity of life, and the role of medical professionals in end-of-life care.

It is important to note that within the Republican Party, individual lawmakers and constituents might hold different opinions based on their personal beliefs, religious convictions, and interpretations of individual rights and medical ethics.

Recap – Healthcare and Wellness

2023-2024 Positions on Healthcare and Wellness		
Area of Concern	**Democrats**	**Republicans**
Health Coverage	Focus on expanding access to affordable healthcare for all, strengthening the Affordable Care Act, and moving towards more comprehensive coverage options, including public health insurance options.	Emphasize reducing government involvement, advocating for market-based solutions and revising or repealing elements of the Affordable Care Act to enhance individual choice and cost efficiency.
Euthanasia	Generally, support the right to choose assisted dying in terminal cases, emphasizing the importance of individual autonomy and compassionate end-of-life care while ensuring strict legal safeguards and ethical guidelines.	Oppose assisted dying, prioritizing the sanctity of life and ethical concerns, and often advocate for palliative care alternatives and strict enforcement of laws against physician-assisted suicide.

12. Citizenship, Immigration, and Enforcement

Immigration is a major issue for Americans, most of whom are descendants of immigrants – all except Native Americans, of course, and some believe they came across a land bridge from Asia. The issue is the "legality" of how immigrants have entered or are entering our country. Of course, entry into the country was not restricted until around 1882, when a law passed by President Chester A. Arthur only restricted lunatics, paupers, and criminals – and then Congress amended it to add Chinese for 10 years, later making the restriction permanent.[121] Every ancestor of Americans that arrived before that date arrived in the same manner as every "illegal alien" who arrived in the U.S. this year. They just showed up at one of our entry ports and were let through or snuck through where we do not have entry points.

Hiroshi Motomura, University of North Carolina law professor and nationally recognized expert on citizenship and immigration, has identified three approaches America has taken to the legal status of immigrants (considering only legal immigrants) in his book *Americans in Waiting: The Lost Story of Immigration and Citizenship in the United States*.

1. The first [approach], dominant in the 19th century, treated immigrants as in transition – that is, as prospective citizens. As soon as people declared their intention to become citizens, and before the five-year wait was over, they received multiple low-cost benefits, including eligibility for free homesteads (in the Homestead Act of 1869), and in many states the right to vote. The goal was to make America attractive so large numbers of farmers and skilled craftsmen would settle new lands.
2. By the 1880s, a second approach took over, treating newcomers as "immigrants by contract." An implicit deal existed whereby immigrants who were literate and could earn their own living were permitted in restricted numbers (except for Asians). Once in the United States, they would have limited legal rights, but were not allowed to vote until they became citizens and would not be eligible for the New Deal government benefits available in the 1930s.
3. The third more recent policy is "immigration by affiliation," Motomura argues, whereby the treatment in part depends on how deeply rooted people have become in America. An immigrant who applies for citizenship as soon as permitted, has a long history of working in the United States, and has significant family ties (such as American-born children), is more deeply affiliated and can expect better treatment.[120]

The contemporary debate on immigration in the United States reflects a complex interplay of historical, legal, and ethical considerations. On the one hand, the United States, a nation primarily built by immigrants, should maintain an inclusive and welcoming stance towards new arrivals, recognizing their contributions to the societal fabric. However, this prompts discussion around the importance of lawful entry and adherence to established immigration processes and raises concerns over national security and resource allocation. This debate also touches on the sensitive issue of birthright citizenship and the rights of children born in the U.S. to non-citizen parents.

Both parties grapple with these challenges, seeking a balance between upholding the nation's legacy as a land of opportunity and ensuring the integrity and sustainability of its immigration system. The current discourse is not just about the adequacy of existing laws but also about defining what it means to be American, whether through birth, lineage, or legally pledging allegiance to the country. As a democracy, the United States continually evolves its policies.

Citizenship

Most Americans are unfamiliar with the rules around what constitutes citizenship. We all know that if you are born in America to American parents, you are automatically a citizen. Many people believe that citizenship in America gives them certain rights over those who are in America but not born here.

Birthright citizenship, a principle stating that any child born in the U.S. automatically becomes a citizen, subject to certain exceptions, is hotly debated. A Republican candidate has claimed the right to modify this practice through executive order because it is not explicitly detailed in the Constitution. This stance challenges the precedent established by the Supreme Court's 1898 decision in United States v. Wong Kim Ark, which is considered "settled law" and affirms birthright citizenship for most children born on U.S. soil, regardless of their parents' citizenship status.

Here are the official rules for American citizenship.

In the tables below, a U.S. citizen is someone who has full citizenship rights in the United States. These include the right to vote, the right to live and work in the U.S., and the right to receive assistance from U.S. embassies and consulates while abroad. U.S. citizens can be either born in the United States, born abroad to U.S. citizen parents, or become naturalized citizens after meeting certain requirements. A U.S. national includes all U.S. citizens and certain individuals who are not citizens but owe their allegiance to the United States. The most common examples of U.S. nationals who are not citizens are people born in American Samoa or certain former citizens of the Trust Territory of the Pacific Islands. U.S. nationals who are not citizens have most of the rights of U.S. citizens, including the right to enter and live in the United States. However, they cannot vote in federal elections and are not eligible for specific government jobs.

Paths to Citizenship – The Official Rules

Birth within the United States

The Supreme Court has never explicitly ruled on whether children born in the United States to illegal immigrant parents are entitled to birthright citizenship via the 14th Amendment, although it has generally been assumed that they are. A birth certificate issued by a U.S. state or territorial government is evidence of citizenship and is usually accepted as proof of citizenship.

In the case of United States v. Wong Kim Ark, 169 U.S. 649 (1898), the Supreme Court ruled that a person becomes a citizen of the United States at the time of birth, by virtue of the first clause of the 14th amendment of the Constitution, if that person:

• is born in the United States;

• has parents that are subjects of a foreign power, but not in any diplomatic or official capacity of that foreign power;

• has parents that have permanent domicile and residence in the United States; or

• has parents that are in the United States for business.

Through Birth Abroad to Two United States Citizens

A child is automatically granted citizenship in the following cases:

1. Both parents were U.S. citizens at the time of the child's birth.

2. At least one parent lived in the United States prior to the child's birth.

INA 301(c) and INA 301(a) (3) state, "and one of whom has had a residence." The FAM (Foreign Affairs Manual) states "no amount of time specified."

A person's record of birth abroad, if registered with a U.S. consulate or embassy, is proof of citizenship. They may also apply for a passport or a Certificate of Citizenship to have their citizenship recognized.

Through Birth Abroad to One United States Citizen

A person born on or after November 14, 1986, is a U.S. citizen if all the following are true:

1. One of the person's parents was a U.S. citizen when the person in question was born.

2. The citizen parent lived at least five years in the United States before the child's birth.

3. A minimum of two of these five years in the United States were after the citizen parent's 14th birthday.

INA 301(g) makes additional provisions to satisfy the physical-presence requirements for periods citizens spent abroad in "honorable service in the Armed Forces of the United States, or periods of employment with the United States Government or with an international organization." Additionally, citizens who spent time living abroad as the "dependent unmarried son or daughter and a member of the household of a person" in any of the previously mentioned organizations can also be counted.

A person's record of birth abroad, if registered with a U.S. consulate or embassy, is proof of citizenship. Such a person may also apply for a passport or a Certificate of Citizenship to have a record of citizenship. Such documentation is often useful to prove citizenship in lieu of the availability of an American birth certificate.

Different rules apply for persons born abroad to one U.S. citizen before November 14, 1986. United States law on this subject changed multiple times throughout the 20th century, and the law is applicable as it existed at the time of the individual's birth.

Rules for American Citizenship

1. **Title 8 of the U.S. Code, Section 1401 defines the following as people who are "citizens of the United States at birth":**
   - Anyone born inside the United States or territories subject to the jurisdiction of.
   - Any Indian or Eskimo born in the United States, provided being a citizen of the U.S. does not impair the person's status as a citizen of the tribe.
   - Anyone born outside the United States, both of whose parents are citizens of the U.S., as long as one parent has lived in the U.S.
   - Anyone born outside the United States, if one parent is a citizen and lived in the U.S. for at least one year and the other parent is a U.S. national.
   - Anyone born in a U.S. possession, if one parent is a citizen and lived in the U.S. for at least one year.
   - Anyone found in the U.S. under the age of five, whose parentage cannot be determined, as long as proof of non-citizenship is not provided by age 21.
   - Anyone born outside the United States, if one parent is an alien and as long as the other parent is a citizen of the U.S. who lived in the U.S. for at least five years (with military and diplomatic service included in this time).
   - A final, historical condition: a person born before 5/24/1934 of an alien father and a U.S. citizen mother who has lived in the U.S.

2. **Those not covered by Title 8 Section 1401**
   - **Derivative Citizenship**: In some cases, individuals may acquire U.S. citizenship through their parents or grandparents, even if they were not born within the United States. This is often referred to as derivative citizenship, and it has specific requirements and conditions outlined in the Immigration and Nationality Act (INA) of 1952.
   - **Naturalization**: People who do not acquire citizenship at birth and do not have a direct claim under Section 1401 may become U.S. citizens through the naturalization process. Naturalization involves fulfilling certain residency requirements, demonstrating good moral character, passing English and civics tests, and taking the Oath of Allegiance.
   - **Special Provisions**: There are special provisions and exceptions in the INA that apply to specific groups, such as members of the U.S. armed forces, adopted children of U.S. citizens, and certain international adoptees.
   - **Marriage to a U.S. Citizen**: In some cases, individuals who marry U.S. citizens may be eligible to apply for citizenship after meeting certain residency and other requirements.

Naturalization

When does a person who lives in a country but was not born there become a citizen? This question is addressed in a variety of ways across different countries. Can a person become a citizen simply by asking for citizenship or by taking a test? Under which conditions should a person be allowed to become a citizen? How much importance is placed on how a person came to be in the country?

Citizens by birth normally have full privileges. On the other hand, naturalized citizens, depending on the country to which they emigrated, may or may not be allowed full privileges. They may or may not be permitted to run for office (or certain offices), hold certain government jobs, or vote. These rights may change through marriage to a national. Some countries will grant citizenship if the person is willing to make a large capital investment in the country with long-lasting benefits.[39] A recent concept is "earned right" – to become a citizen by fulfilling certain obligations, such as contributing one's money, time or labor.[40]

Limitations placed on naturalized citizens may affect their ability to:

- Hold high public office: To do so, in the United States, requires meeting specific constitutional eligibility criteria around age and residency; the president must be a "natural-born citizen." This requirement, however, does not imply that where you were born is directly linked to your loyalty to the country. The assumption that non-native-born individuals might inherently have divided loyalties is subjective and not a legal or universally acknowledged standard in U.S. governance. Those wishing to be employed in the public sector, particularly in sensitive roles within national security or intelligence agencies, must undergo stringent background checks and security clearances assessing various factors, including potential foreign ties. These checks are comprehensive and do not solely focus on the individual's place of birth; naturalized citizens who meet the security requirements may hold sensitive positions in the government. For most public jobs in the U.S., the primary requirement is legal citizenship or residency status, ensuring the individual's legal right to work in the country, rather than their place of birth.
- Vote: The right to vote has two dimensions:
  - Who can vote? In the U.S. it was any citizen aged 21 and above until 1971, when the legal age for voting was lowered to 18 in recognition of the age of our soldiers with the ratification of the 26th Amendment to the U.S. Constitution.
  - On what are they permitted to vote? Typical subjects for voting are initiatives, referendums, and elections. In America, naturalized citizens are NOT permitted to vote on federal initiatives (i.e., federal laws) and, in most cases, citizens do not vote directly on state laws. Even amendments to the Constitution are not voted on

by individual citizens, only by state representatives. This is common for democracies.

Below are some questions to ponder.

How do we determine who is an "official" American? One approach could be to issue certified Americans with identification cards. Alternatively, we could respect individual privacy and manage this through government service approval processes, such as when claiming entitlements like social security.

When should a person who lives in America, contributes to its development, swears to defend it, works, and pays taxes – and has done so for an extended period – be afforded some or all the protections of the Constitution?

When can an illegal entrant to America be permitted to remain and apply for citizenship, if ever? Is it enough if they have been registered for five years, contributed to society, paid taxes, raised a family, and sworn allegiance?

Our definition of who can claim to be an American is not absolute; it has changed over time and may need further evolution in the future.

All Americans are born equal – equal to everyone else in the world, not just equal to others born in America. Everyone living in America, citizens or not, is born with certain inalienable rights. Our Declaration of Independence says so:

Rights of Citizens and Residents

"We hold these truths to be self-evident, that all men are created equal, that they are endowed by their Creator with certain unalienable Rights, that among these are Life, Liberty and the pursuit of Happiness. … That to secure these rights, Governments are instituted among Men, deriving their just powers from the consent of the governed."

Hopefully, one day, citizens worldwide will enjoy the same inalienable rights and opportunities as Americans do, including access to education, employment, voting, and all the other freedoms Americans cherish. In the meantime, America must uphold and defend the rights afforded by its democracy while welcoming others to join us whenever possible.

> **Proposal: Clearer standards should be developed to specify which new laws and which legal changes must be voted on by state citizens and more of the proposed laws should require state citizen approvals than are required now.**

Illegal Aliens

Illegal immigration remains an ongoing, complex issue in America without a straightforward solution. Given the vastness of our borders, extensive coastlines, and the openness of our society, curtailing illegal immigration without compromising personal privacy or security presents significant challenges.

It might seem hypocritical to refuse contemporary immigrants the same opportunities that were once available to earlier generations, many of whom are the ancestors of current citizens. This stance questions the fairness of those who arrived earlier or were born to families with deep American roots having a more legitimate claim to residency and citizenship than recent arrivals. It challenges us to consider the evolving nature of immigration and whether the principles that guided past policies should still hold true in a changing global context. This argument invites a reexamination of what it means to be an American and whether the rights and privileges associated with this identity should be equally accessible to all who seek them, regardless of their origin or date of arrival.

> **Proposal: One approach to gaining better control over this problem may involve issuing a government "non-surveillable," block-chain controlled identity (ID) card, complete with a person's photograph and contact information securely stored in a government database accessible only to authorized public officials and, with the given individual's permission, employers. Procedures would be needed for those whose identity is not confirmed. It may be time for all citizens to endorse the idea of a national ID card. The government already knows who most of us are, where we live, and where we work through social security and Medicare, state driver's licenses, passports, TSA, Medicaid, and other databases. This proposal should be advanced in a non-partisan way if it is going to work. The ID must be identity-theft-proof.**

A national identity e-card may be seen by some as an unacceptable intrusion into their lives. Although logically you should only be concerned if you are doing something illegal. However, there could be the potential for abuse of power by law enforcement authorities, including depending on how the country addresses the illegal immigrants already residing in the country.

Immigration

As a nation that values self-determination, the United States faces complex decisions about its immigration policies. Those with voting rights, representing the American populace, indirectly influence these policies through democratic processes. While established paths to citizenship exist, there is ongoing debate about whether these rules adequately or appropriately address current challenges.

It is reasonable to assert that, given America's size and global standing, structured immigration rules are necessary. However, managing these rules requires a careful balance between maintaining national security and upholding America's long-standing tradition of welcoming immigrants.

Concerns about unregulated immigration include compromising national security, with the potential for criminal elements or security threats to enter the country. It is crucial to address these concerns with evidence-based policies that accurately assess and mitigate risks without unfairly stigmatizing entire groups of immigrants.

Most immigrants are motivated by the pursuit of a better life. While many arrive with limited resources, immigrants, particularly the younger generation, have the potential to contribute a wide and diverse range of benefits to our society, including through paying taxes that help to fund social security and other public programs, a point to remember in discussions about the long-term sustainability of immigration policies.

Democratic Views

The Democrats believe that we need comprehensive immigration reform, not just piecemeal efforts:[129-05]

Democratic Views on Immigration Policy

- "We must work together to pass immigration reform in a way that unites this country, not in a way that divides us by playing on our worst instincts and fears. We are committed to pursuing tough, practical, and humane immigration reform in the first year of the next administration."

- "We cannot continue to allow people to enter the United States undetected, undocumented, and unchecked. The American people are a welcoming and generous people, but those who enter our country's borders illegally, and those who employ them, disrespect the rule of the law. We need to secure our borders, and support additional personnel, infrastructure, and technology on the border and at our ports of entry. We need additional Customs and Border Protection agents equipped with better technology and real-time intelligence. We need to dismantle human smuggling organizations, combating the crime associated with this trade. We also need to do more to promote economic development in migrant-sending nations, to reduce incentives to come to the United States illegally. And we need to crack down on employers who hire undocumented immigrants."

- "We realize that employers need a method to verify whether their employees are legally eligible to work in the United States, and we will ensure that our system is accurate, fair to legal workers, safeguards people's privacy, and cannot be used to discriminate against workers."

- "We should fix the dysfunctional immigration bureaucracy that hampers family reunification, the cornerstone of our immigration policy for years. Given the importance of both keeping families together and supporting American businesses, we will increase the number of immigration visas for family members of people living here and for immigrants who meet the demand for jobs that employers cannot fill, as long as appropriate labor market protections and standards are in place."

- "For the millions living here illegally but otherwise playing by the rules, we must require them to come out of the shadows and get right with the law. We support a system that requires undocumented immigrants who are in good standing to pay a fine, pay taxes, learn English, and go to the back of the line for the opportunity to become citizens. They are our neighbors, and we can help them become full tax-paying, law-abiding, productive members of society."

Republican Views

Republicans believe we need greater border security, saying: "Immigration policy is a national security issue, for which we have one test: Does it serve the national interest? By that standard, Republicans know America can have a strong immigration system without sacrificing the rule of law."[124-126]

Republican Views on Immigration Policy

"Enforcing the rule of law at the border and throughout the nation, we simply must be able to track who is entering and leaving our country."

"Our determination to uphold the rule of law begins with more effective enforcement, giving our agents the tools and resources they need to protect our sovereignty, completing the border fence quickly and securing the borders, and employing complementary strategies to secure our ports of entry. Experience shows that enforcement of existing laws is effective in reducing and reversing illegal immigration."

"Our commitment to the rule of law means smarter enforcement at the workplace, against illegal workers and lawbreaking employers alike, along with those who practice identity theft and traffic in fraudulent documents. That means that the E-Verify system – which is an Internet-based system that verifies the employment authorization and identity of employees – must be reauthorized. A phased in requirement that employers use the E-Verify system must be enacted."

"The rule of law means guaranteeing to law enforcement the tools and coordination to deport criminal aliens without delay – and correcting court decisions that have made deportation so difficult."

"It means enforcing the law against those who overstay their visas, rather than letting millions flout the generosity that gave them temporary entry."

"It means imposing maximum penalties on those who smuggle illegal aliens into the U.S., both for their lawbreaking and for their cruel exploitation. It means requiring cooperation among federal, state, and local law enforcement and real consequences, including the denial of federal funds, for self-described sanctuary cities, which stand in open defiance of the federal and state statutes that expressly prohibit such sanctuary policies, and which endanger the lives of U.S. citizens."

"It does not mean driver's licenses for illegal aliens, nor does it mean that states should be allowed to flout the federal law barring them from giving in-state tuition rates to illegal aliens, nor does it mean that illegal aliens should receive social security benefits, or other public benefits, except as provided by federal law."

"We oppose amnesty. The rule of law suffers if government policies encourage or reward illegal activity. The American people's rejection of en masse legalizations is especially appropriate given the past failures of the federal government to enforce the law."

"Embracing Immigrant Communities – Today's immigrants are walking in the steps of most other Americans' ancestors, seeking the American dream, and contributing culturally and economically to our nation. We celebrate the industry and love of liberty of these fellow Americans."

"Both government and the private sector must do more to foster legally present immigrants' integration into American life to advance respect for the rule of law and a common American identity. It is a national disgrace that the first experience most new Americans have is with a dysfunctional immigration bureaucracy defined by delay and confusion; we will no longer tolerate those failures."

"In our multiethnic nation, everyone – immigrants and native-born alike – must embrace our core values of liberty, equality, meritocracy, and respect for human dignity and the rights of women."

"One sign of our unity is our English language. For newcomers, it has always been the fastest route to prosperity in America. English empowers. We support English as the official language in our nation, while welcoming the ethnic diversity in the United States and the territories, including language. Immigrants should be encouraged to learn English. English is the accepted language of business, commerce, and legal proceedings, and it is essential as a unifying cultural force. It is also important, as part of cultural integration, that our schools provide better education in U.S. history and civics for all children, thereby fostering a commitment to our national motto, E Pluribus Unum."

"We are grateful to the thousands of new immigrants, many of them not yet citizens, who are serving in the Armed Forces. Their patriotism is inspiring; it should remind the institutions of civil society of the need to embrace newcomers, assist their journey to full citizenship, and help their communities avoid patterns of isolation."

• "Welcoming Refugees – Our country continues to accept refugees from troubled lands all over the world. In some cases, these are people who stood with America in dangerous times, and they have first call on our hospitality. We oppose, however, the granting of refugee status based on lifestyle or other non-political factors."

Proposal: As a country, we need to decide what rights non-citizens enjoy when on America's soil. Visitors should be protected as far as their inalienable rights, including being protected from discrimination, supported by the rule of law (U.S. law), and given basic emergency healthcare if needed.

Proposal: We should have a national referendum on the rules defining naturalization, and those, if any, that should be applied to "illegal" immigrants who have been living and working in America for an extended time. We should consider a constitutional amendment to clearly define the rules of citizenship, particularly regarding individuals with foreign-born parents. This amendment would differentiate between immigrants and those merely visiting America for leisure or work. There may come a time when everyone will be considered a citizen of the world.

Proposal: We need to stand against economic growth by immigration – a million legal immigrants per year will have a demonstrable impact on our population growth. According to the Center for Immigration Studies, 1,052,415 immigrants were given permanent residence in the financial year ending in 2007. Of those, 689,820 were family-sponsored; 162,176 were employment based; 136,125 were refugees or asylees [sic]; and 64,294 were from other categories.[184] Notice that 162,176 jobs were filled by people with green cards. Similar figures for 2022 indicate that the rate of immigration is continuing in the range of 1.1 million to 1.2 million per year.[211] Projections are that if immigration continues at the rate of 1.3 million growing to 2 million per year until 2050, the U.S. population will be 439 million, versus what would have been 345 million.[185] Clearly, absorption of the large quantities of immigrants will put stress on jobs, housing, food production, prices, water supplies, and government services. Hopefully, they will find gainful employment and help to grow our economy. Also, figures only include the legal people. Net Illegal immigration may add as much as another million or more people per year.

Recap – Citizenship, Immigration, and Enforcement

2023-2024 Positions on Citizenship, Immigration, and Enforcement		
Area of Concern	**Democrats**[129-06]	**Republicans**[129-07,08,09]
Citizenship, Immigration, and Enforcement	Advocate for comprehensive immigration reform, prioritizing family reunification, a pathway to citizenship for undocumented immigrants, and humane treatment of asylum seekers and refugees.	Emphasize strong border security, strict enforcement of existing laws, and prioritize legal immigration. They oppose paths to citizenship for undocumented immigrants and support measures against sanctuary cities.

13. Individual Freedoms

Historically, Republicans and Democrats have always had different views on individual freedoms. The Republican Party, born out of an anti-slavery platform in the 19th century, initially focused on civil rights and individual liberties, championing freedom from government overreach. This perspective was heavily influenced by classical liberal principles of economic freedom, property rights, and limited government intervention.

In contrast, the Democratic Party, with its early 19th-century origins and ties to agrarian interests, initially held more conservative views on social issues, including a resistance to civil rights reforms. However, during the 20th century, the Democrats underwent a significant ideological shift, especially with the New Deal era and the civil rights movement. They began advocating for expanded civil liberties, social freedoms, and a more interventionist government role in ensuring equal rights and protections, particularly for marginalized groups.

This historical journey underlines how both parties have evolved, sometimes switching stances on crucial issues. Republicans, while maintaining their advocacy for economic freedom and limited government, have increasingly emphasized individual rights in areas like gun ownership and religious expression. Democrats, meanwhile, have become the standard-bearers for progressive social policies, advocating for broader civil liberties and government involvement in securing these rights. The parties' evolving histories are reflected in their current platforms.

Balanced Framework of Rights and Responsibilities in the U.S. Constitution

The U.S. Constitution establishes a framework that protects individual rights while defining the powers of different levels of government. It does not explicitly specify a hierarchical order of rights and responsibilities, starting with individual rights and descending through family, religion, and government at local, state, and federal levels. Instead, it focuses on balance and interplay among these entities.

Individual rights, especially as outlined in the Bill of Rights and subsequent amendments, are a cornerstone of the Constitution. These rights are fundamental to the American legal system and include freedom of speech, religion, and due process. However, these rights exist within a broader context of shared power and responsibility.

While not detailed in the Constitution, the family is recognized in law and legal precedents as a fundamental unit with certain protections, particularly concerning privacy and child-rearing. Religion is explicitly mentioned in the First Amendment, which prohibits the establishment of a state religion while protecting the free exercise of religion, allowing individuals and religious communities to practice freely. Religions play a significant role in imparting moral values, which helps in guiding citizens' behavior.

Local governments, extensions of state governments, handle many aspects of daily governance and are the closest to the citizens. State governments have powers reserved for them, especially those not delegated to the federal government, as per the 10th Amendment. The federal government has specific enumerated powers, and its role is particularly pronounced in matters that affect the nation as a whole.

Decisions are made at different levels based on the nature of the issue and the appropriate jurisdiction as defined, or not, by the Constitution and our laws. The judiciary, particularly the Supreme Court, plays a crucial role in interpreting the Constitution and resolving conflicts among these various entities and levels of government.

This system is designed not as a strict hierarchy but as a dynamic and flexible framework, ensuring that a diverse range of interests and perspectives are represented and balanced within the governance structure of the United States. It underscores the importance of a balanced approach where individual rights, societal needs, and government powers are continuously navigated and adjusted.

Individual Responsibility

The Democratic Party emphasizes the importance of personal responsibility in conjunction with societal support systems. They advocate for individuals to actively participate in their communities and make responsible choices, especially when it comes to healthcare, education, and employment. However, Democrats also stress the role of government in providing opportunities and safety nets to enable individuals to fulfill their responsibilities. This includes access to affordable healthcare, quality education, and economic opportunities, ensuring individuals have the tools and resources necessary to succeed. The party often highlights the interconnectedness of individual actions and societal welfare, advocating for policies encouraging personal responsibility and addressing systemic challenges that may impede it.

Personal responsibility is a core principle of the Republican Party. They strongly advocate for individual accountability in various aspects of life, including financial independence, employment, and lifestyle choices. Republicans believe that individuals should take responsibility for their actions and decisions and that government intervention should be minimal. This perspective extends to areas like healthcare, where they support market-based solutions and personal choice, and education, where they often advocate for school choice and parents being responsible for their children's education. The party also underscores the importance of hard work and self-reliance, arguing that individuals should strive to be self-sufficient and not overly dependent on government assistance. This viewpoint reflects a broader belief in limited government and that personal freedom and responsibility are key to a prosperous and thriving society.

How "Free" Should We Be?

As a society, there is a notable inconsistency in upholding the principle of liberty or true freedom of choice for individuals. Within a framework respecting absolute personal autonomy, an individual would have the unequivocal right to make decisions about their own life, including the decision to end it. This would mean legalizing euthanasia (under strict guidelines to ensure it is an informed and voluntary choice).

Under such a framework, decisions on personal safety matters, such as the use of motorcycle helmets, should rest with the individual. Of course, not wearing a helmet, given the statistics, is foolish. In the United States, according to the National Highway Traffic Safety Administration (NHTSA) in 2021, motorcyclists are about 2,400% more likely than people in passenger cars to die in a traffic crash per vehicle mile traveled.[136] Of 100 motorcycle accidents where the rider died, 37 would have been saved if wearing a helmet and 67 of 100 would have avoided brain injuries.[137]

However, the issue becomes more complex when it comes to seat belts. Seat belts reduce the risk of death by 45% and cut the risk of serious injury by 50% among drivers and front-seat passengers. In crashes, people not wearing seat belts are 3,000% more likely to be ejected from a vehicle, which significantly increases the likelihood of fatal outcomes or severe injuries. And yet, one in seven drivers still do not buckle up.[138] Choosing to wear a seat belt impacts more than just the individual; it affects overall vehicle safety. In accidents, an unbelted driver can lose control, while unbelted backseat passengers risk being thrown forward, potentially injuring others. Moreover, drivers are responsible for ensuring all passengers, especially children, are secured with seat belts. This practice transcends personal choice, emphasizing a commitment to all occupants' collective safety and well-being.

This perspective aligns with the broader belief that personal freedom should be balanced with public safety and the rights of others. A child should have the right to protection from physical or mental harm caused by parental or guardian neglect. Therefore, while advocating for individual freedoms, it is crucial to recognize the boundaries set by the potential impact on others.

Having personal choice suggests that the government should not interfere in an individual's health decisions, such as a woman having an abortion. The tricky element here comes in determining at which point fertilized cells become a person. Doctors cut our tumors, moles, and warts all the time. These are living cells but not living persons. In certain religious interpretations, the fetus is regarded as a separate individual. And a fetus, in that view, can begin as early as conception. From this perspective, the abortion decision is not solely about personal liberty, as it involves the rights of another potential person.

This leads us on to a broader principle that personal liberty should be exercised if it does not harm or impede the peace and safety of others. In the case of abortion, this principle becomes complex, as it involves balancing the rights and liberties of the woman with the perceived rights of the fetus. Thus, the debate over abortion encompasses not only the right to personal choice but also the interpretation of when and how the rights of others, in this case, the fetus, come into play. This complexity is at the heart of the ongoing debate, reflecting the challenge of aligning personal liberty with ethical and moral considerations.

The Democratic Party champions liberty and freedom of choice, advocating for policies that empower individuals in critical aspects of their lives. They staunchly support reproductive rights, asserting a woman's autonomy over her healthcare decisions, including access to abortion and contraception. The party is vocal about LGBTQ+ rights, advocating for marriage equality, anti-discrimination measures, and comprehensive healthcare access.

The Republican Party emphasizes the principles of individual liberty and personal responsibility, advocating for policies reinforcing these ideals. In terms of social issues, Republicans traditionally uphold conservative family values, advocating against abortion and emphasizing the importance of religious freedom. The party generally supports limited government intervention in the economy and personal lives, promoting free-market principles and lower taxation to foster economic growth and innovation.

> **Proposal: A fundamental principle should be that an individual's behavior, if it does not physically or mentally harm others, should not be restricted by law. This implies that individuals should have the freedom to engage in potentially risky activities, such as not wearing a motorcycle helmet. It is true, however, that society may bear the costs of such freedoms, for example, in the form of medical bills and long-term care resulting from a motorcycle accident. This societal cost can be viewed as a trade-off for greater overall freedom and fewer restrictive laws. Nevertheless, it's crucial that the freedoms of adults should not result in harm or pain inflicted upon others especially children.**

Voting Rights

The Voting Law

Initially, the U.S. Constitution didn't define voter eligibility, leaving it to states. Article I, Sections 2 and 4, and Article II, Section 1, allowed states to set voting qualifications and election processes, creating diverse and restrictive practices, often limiting voting to white male property owners. Later amendments – the 15th, 19th, 24th, and 26th – explicitly expanded and protected voting rights across race, gender, and age.

Voting Rights Amendments

- 15th Amendment (1870): Prohibits the denial of the right to vote based on race, color, or previous condition of servitude. This amendment was crucial in ensuring African Americans, particularly former slaves, had the right to vote.
- 19th Amendment (1920): Grants women the right to vote, a landmark change in extending suffrage to half the population.
- 24th Amendment (1964): Eliminates poll taxes in federal elections. Poll taxes had been used in some states to prevent low-income individuals, particularly African Americans, from voting.
- 26th Amendment (1971): Lowers the voting age from 21 to 18, a response to arguments that those old enough to be drafted for military service should also have the right to vote.

These amendments collectively expanded the franchise and addressed various forms of discrimination and barriers to voting.

Party Positions on Voting

The Democratic Party in the U.S. strongly supports expansive voting rights and works to eliminate voting barriers. They advocate for accessible voting methods like automatic registration, early voting, and mail-in ballots and oppose voter ID laws, arguing that these disproportionately affect minorities, older adults, and low-income groups. Fighting against voter suppression and gerrymandering, they seek fair representation in elections. The party also wishes to restore voting rights to ex-inmates, accommodate disabled and non-English speaking voters, ensure shorter voting lines, and improve voting materials while opposing unfair voter roll purges, all to ensure inclusive participation in democracy.

The Republican Party focuses on ensuring election integrity and preventing voter fraud. Central to this stance is their advocacy for stricter voting regulations, including implementing voter ID laws. The party contends that such laws are essential to maintain the integrity of elections by ensuring that only eligible voters participate, thereby preventing potential voting irregularities and fraud. This emphasis on secure voting systems is further reflected in their support for measures like regularly updating voter rolls to remove ineligible voters and requiring identification for voting and voter registration.

Republicans express caution regarding automatic voter registration, mail-in voting, and extended early voting periods, viewing these practices as susceptible to abuses that could compromise election integrity. In line with this perspective, many in the party champion more stringent verification processes and support restricting voting for individuals with felony convictions.

Regarding campaign finance, the Republican Party often endorses the Citizens United v. FEC decision, viewing it as a matter of free speech and opposing extensive government regulation of political spending. Overall, the Republican perspective on voting rights and election reforms is anchored in a commitment to secure and fair elections, focusing on measures they believe are necessary to prevent fraud and uphold the electoral process's integrity.

Following the 2020 election, the Republican Party has increasingly favored more restrictive voting policies, as evidenced by a trend in Republican-led state legislatures to limit voting methods such as mail voting, which white and nonwhite voters extensively used during the pandemic. Some argue that the motivation behind this is that such methods are used more commonly by voters supporting the Democrats, which in fact they are. In a survey conducted in October 2020, Pew Research found that 49% of Democrats preferred voting by mail compared to 23% of Republicans.[139-01] Additionally, there has been a push for strict photo ID requirements and a notable shift toward removing individuals from voter registration lists if they have not recently voted or confirmed their registration.

Despite these trends, there remains bipartisan support for specific policies, such as requiring electronic voting machines to produce paper ballots and ensuring a minimum of two weeks for early, in-person voting before election day. Furthermore, Republicans have raised concerns about the voting challenges faced by active military personnel and have opposed measures like the wholesale restoration of voting rights to convicted felons and expedited naturalization procedures. They argue that such measures could distort the electoral process.

Republicans strongly support the right of states to require official government-issued photo identification for voting. They advocate for rigorous measures to prevent ballot tampering, emphasizing the role of the Department of Justice in safeguarding the integrity of elections. This commitment extends to supporting state and local election officials in maintaining the integrity of the voting process, especially in the areas of voter registration and absentee ballots, to prevent voter fraud and abuse. This approach reflects a deep concern for election security and a desire to uphold strict standards in the voting process.[139]

The disagreement between parties on basic constitutional rights highlights the need for an impartial judiciary, especially the Supreme Court, to interpret and uphold these rights.

Direct Voting as a Process

There are those who echo the wishes of some of our Founding Fathers that we move away from party politics towards directly electing public officials and voting on new laws.

Direct Voting Options

In a direct voting system, citizens typically participate in decision-making through referendums, plebiscites, or initiatives. Here's a brief explanation of each:

1. **Referendum**: This is a direct vote in which an entire electorate votes on a particular proposal. This approach can lead to adopting a new law, changing an existing law, or deciding on a specific governmental policy.
2. **Plebiscite**: Like a referendum, a plebiscite is a method of direct democracy that gauges public opinion on a specific issue. The critical difference is that plebiscites are often non-binding, meaning the results are used as a guide rather than a mandate.
3. **Initiative**: This process allows citizens to propose or initiate a statute or constitutional amendment. Initiatives may be direct or indirect. With a direct initiative, a measure is put directly to a vote after enough signatures are collected. With an indirect initiative, the proposal is first submitted to the legislature, which can approve it or submit it to the voters for a decision.

Direct voting carries several advantages and disadvantages. Benefits include enhanced democratic participation, leading to greater civic engagement; reduced political polarization, as decisions focus more on issues than party allegiances; and increased accountability of officials directly elected by the populace. On the flip side, there are challenges with feasibility and practicality, the potential to overwhelm voters with information, and a risk that minority rights could be overshadowed. This shift would require a significant overhaul of the current democratic system.

> **Proposal: Investment should be made so that we can vote on every issue securely from the comfort of our home over the Internet or from our cell phones. Ensuring that our vote will be counted and remain unaltered – with an audit trail for each vote making recounts unnecessary. It could also include the opportunity for voters themselves to correct any mistakes in their vote up to a given deadline. The outcome would not be revealed until reaching a specific deadline for everyone in that state.**

Redistricting

Vice President Elbridge Gerry signed a bill in 1812 that redistricted the state to benefit his Democratic-Republican Party, leading to the creation of a district resembling a salamander, hence the term "gerrymander." This practice has been used by both major political parties in the United States to manipulate electoral boundaries to gain partisan advantage, often resulting in oddly shaped districts designed to increase or decrease the electoral strength of particular demographic groups. Over the years, gerrymandering has become increasingly sophisticated, especially with the advent of computer technology, enabling precise control over redistricting to influence election outcomes.

The Supreme Court's stance has been that while partisan gerrymandering may be incompatible with democratic principles, it is not necessarily a constitutional violation, leaving most decisions about gerrymandering to state legislatures and courts. This finding means that while gerrymandering is often viewed as a form of political maneuvering that can undermine fair representation, it is not universally deemed illegal unless it violates specific constitutional principles, such as racial discrimination.

There are a range of perspectives within the Republican Party on this issue, with some members advocating for independent commissions while others support maintaining legislative control over the process. This diversity in opinion reflects the party's view on electoral matters more broadly, where the balance between ensuring fair representation and maintaining political advantage is often debated. In terms of restoring voting rights to felons, Republicans generally favor more stringent conditions. The party typically argues that these rights should be reinstated only after specific criteria beyond just serving a sentence are met, reflecting a cautious approach to re-enfranchisement. Overall, the Republican perspective on redistricting and voting rights tends to emphasize stricter controls and conditions, aligning with their broader focus on election integrity and voter fraud prevention.

The Democratic Party advocates for fair, transparent redistricting to ensure equitable representation, opposing gerrymandering, particularly when it benefits Republicans at minorities' expense. A key part of their stance is supporting independent or bipartisan commissions for redistricting to reduce political bias. They emphasize protecting minority voting rights in line with the Voting Rights Act and advocate for getting the public involved in redistricting, ensuring district lines reflect community interests. Democrats actively promote fair representation and legally challenge perceived unfair Republican-led gerrymandering. Although approaches within the party vary, and the party faces accusations of gerrymandering itself, their overall goal is equitable, less partisan redistricting.

> **Proposal: Gerrymandering must end. The boundaries of territories that vote for candidates need to be defined by geography, not politics. A bi-partisan-approved mathematical algorithm that functions the same across all the states should be able to determine fair districts.**

Election Security

The Democratic Party's stance on election security emphasizes integrity, accessibility, and transparency in the electoral process. They advocate for strong measures against cybersecurity threats and foreign interference, supporting federal funding for state and local governments to upgrade election infrastructure and enhance security protocols. Democrats also focus on voter protection policies to combat voter suppression and ensure equal access to the ballot box for all eligible voters. They call for greater transparency and oversight in election administration, advocating for paper ballot backups and post-election audits to verify election results' accuracy and integrity. Democrats prioritize the security of the voting process, advocating for measures against foreign interference and supporting the use of paper ballots for reliable audits.

Additionally, many Democrats back the movement to grant statehood to Washington, D.C., which would provide its residents with full congressional representation. The party's commitment to these reforms reflects its overarching goal to uphold and strengthen the democratic process, ensuring every eligible citizen can exercise their right to vote without undue barriers.

Republicans advocate for stricter voter identification laws and tighter controls on mail-in and absentee voting to prevent potential fraud. While recognizing the need to protect election infrastructure from external threats, they favor a state-led approach over federal intervention, reflecting their preference for decentralized governance. The party supports regular updates and audits of voting systems to ensure security, emphasizing states' autonomy in conducting elections and balancing traditional practices with modern security challenges.

The Republican Party opposes granting statehood to Washington, D.C., primarily because the Constitution established the nation's capital as a separate entity not belonging to any state. Republicans often argue that granting statehood to D.C. would require a constitutional amendment. Furthermore, there is a political dimension to this opposition: Washington D.C. is an electoral stronghold for the Democrats and granting it statehood would likely lead to more Democrats in Congress, potentially altering the balance of power. Republicans frequently propose alternative solutions, such as retroceding most of D.C. to Maryland, like how parts of D.C. were returned to Virginia in the 19th century. This opposition is consistent with the party's focus on maintaining current political structures and balances.

Freedom of Speech

The Democratic Party's views on freedom of speech are often intertwined with broader social issues, such as combating hate speech, addressing misinformation, and ensuring a safe and inclusive environment for diverse voices. Democrats advocate for regulations and policies that balance freedom of speech with protections against harmful or discriminatory rhetoric, particularly on social media and public platforms. This stance reflects their broader commitment to social justice, including rights related to healthcare access, climate change action, racial equality, and LGBTQ+ rights. These issues are at the forefront of the Democratic agenda, emphasizing the role of government in safeguarding these rights and providing equitable resources and opportunities for all citizens.

Contrastingly, the Republican Party emphasize fewer restrictions and a staunch defense against perceived censorship, especially regarding conservative viewpoints. Republicans often oppose what they see as excessive political correctness and advocate for absolute free speech rights, even if such speech may be controversial or offensive to some. They focus on rights associated with gun ownership, religious freedoms, and limiting government intervention in economic activities. These stances reflect a broader conservative philosophy prioritizing individual liberties, personal responsibility, and minimal government oversight, highlighting the fundamental ideological differences between the two parties regarding individual freedoms and rights. Their positions are closely tied to their expectations of individual responsibility.

Republicans advocate for safeguarding the American flag, a symbol of national unity, by proposing legislation against its desecration. They view this as honoring and respecting those who served under the flag. However, enforcing such a law raises a free speech debate. The principle of free speech in America encompasses the right to protest, including flag burning, even though it may be controversial or offensive to some, including veterans. While a potent symbol, the flag represents freedoms, including the right to free speech. Instances of flag burning, even internationally, inadvertently affirm this core American value. The Supreme

Court has ruled in Texas v. Johnson (1989) that burning the American flag is protected as symbolic speech under the First Amendment.[139-02]

So, in summary, both parties are in favor of freedom of speech, but one with certain limits, such as hate speech, and the other nearly without limits, subject to personal responsibility. This distinction underscores a fundamental difference in how each party views the balance between protecting free expression and addressing its potential harms in society.

Freedom of the Press

It's essential to understand the foundational role of freedom of the press in a democratic society. This freedom is a cornerstone for ensuring transparency, accountability, and the right of citizens to be informed, highlighting the complex interplay between governance, media autonomy, and public interest. The Democratic Party's strong support of a free and independent press emphasizes its role in holding power accountable and fostering informed public discourse. While valuing these freedoms, Democrats also express concerns about the spread of misinformation and hate speech, particularly on digital platforms, and advocate for responsible measures to address these issues. Additionally, the party champions net neutrality to ensure open and equal access to information online and promotes diversity and inclusivity in media representation to enrich public dialogue with varied perspectives. This stance reflects a balance between protecting fundamental freedoms and addressing the complexities of modern information dissemination.

The Republican Party strongly values freedom of the press, viewing it as a fundamental right crucial to American democracy. Republicans typically advocate for minimal government interference in public expression and media matters.

The party position says they are committed to protecting the right to freely express diverse opinions, including conservative views, by the media, safeguarding it from censorship or backlash.

Republicans also frequently express concerns about media bias and the importance of having a press that fairly represents different political viewpoints. While supporting open discourse, the party often highlights the need for responsible speech and the challenges posed by misinformation. The Republican approach to these freedoms underscores a strong commitment to upholding traditional values of free expression and an open press while advocating for fairness and balance in media representation.

Fourth Amendment (FISA, Search and Seizure, Privacy)

Privacy is not explicitly listed as a constitutional right. The interpretation of the Fourth Amendment of the Constitution by the Supreme Court over the years has established a legal framework that recognizes privacy as a protected right under the Constitution in various contexts.

This amendment is essential to the Bill of Rights, mandating that law enforcement obtain a warrant, supported by probable cause, to conduct searches and seizures of individuals, their homes, and personal property. It significantly influences police conduct and the protection of individual privacy rights.

The issues surrounding the Foreign Intelligence Surveillance Act (FISA) have become increasingly contentious, particularly with the enactment of the USA PATRIOT Act in 2001 and its subsequent renewals and amendments. Before the PATRIOT Act, FISA courts mainly focused on surveillance warrants against suspected foreign spies within the United States. However, the PATRIOT Act broadened the scope of the FISA courts, allowing more extensive surveillance powers for counterterrorism and reducing the legal threshold required for obtaining warrants. This expansion sparked debates over privacy rights and concerns about potential overreach and unwarranted surveillance of U.S. citizens.

Amid these changes in surveillance laws, the National Security Agency (NSA) has emerged as a central figure in the discussion of privacy and surveillance.

The NSA is a crucial U.S. government agency tasked with monitoring, collecting, and analyzing information from across the globe for foreign and domestic intelligence and counterintelligence purposes. Its primary roles The scope includes signals intelligence (SIGINT) activities, enhancing the security of government communications through information assurance, strengthening cybersecurity measures, supporting military and government functions, and engaging in advanced research in cryptography and cryptanalysis. All these efforts are conducted within stringent legal and policy frameworks to protect national security while upholding civil liberties. The NSA's capabilities in intercepting Internet communications, highlighted by Edward Snowden's revelations in 2013, demonstrate the far-reaching impact of these legal changes. Under the USA PATRIOT Act, government surveillance powers were enhanced, including the ability to request library records and monitor telephone calls with a lowered threshold for wiretapping by intelligence agencies. While domestic surveillance typically requires legal justification, such as a warrant, there have been ongoing debates about the legality and extent of these practices.

In recent years, both Democratic and Republican lawmakers have raised issues regarding the transparency and accountability of the FISA courts. Democrats typically emphasize stronger privacy protections and oversight against government surveillance overreach, while

Republicans have a greater focus on national security when addressing privacy concerns, reflecting differing priorities in the approach to NSA and FISA-related policies. Critics argue that the secretive nature of these courts, where decisions are made without public scrutiny and often without representation for the surveillance targets, poses a significant challenge to civil liberties. Furthermore, the renewal of key provisions of the PATRIOT Act has been a flashpoint in political debates, with demands for greater transparency in the FISA warrant process, stricter standards for evidence, and better oversight to prevent abuses. Proponents of the current system emphasize the need to balance civil liberties with national security imperatives. This ongoing debate reflects the broader tensions in American politics over balancing national security and individual privacy rights in the post-9/11 era.

Role of Secrecy

Secrecy is essential in government for national security, diplomatic negotiations, competitive bidding processes, and protecting classified information. Americans want to believe that our government retains more military capability than it publicly reveals (like the A-bomb that ended WWII in the pacific. However, as recently as 2010 and 2013, Edward Snowden, Chelsea Manning, or Julian Assange have been accused of releasing to the public classified information without authorization.

Yet, in politics, where transparency and open discourse are fundamental to democracy, it should be minimized. Excessive secrecy can undermine public trust and accountability and obstruct informed decision-making. This point is evident in examples like the recent Supreme Court ethics issues, Watergate, the Iran-Contra Affair, challenges with the Freedom of Information Act (i.e., delays and excessive fees), and timeliness and safeguards surrounding FISA warrants.

Conversely, promoting openness in politics enhances public engagement, fosters robust debates, and ensures accountability of elected officials. While certain situations require confidentiality, maintaining a transparent, participatory political system is crucial for upholding democracy's core values.

Transparency is particularly crucial when it comes to politics. Citizens have a fundamental right to be informed about their elected representatives' decisions, policies, and actions. An open government promotes accountability, ensuring that public officials act in the best interests of their constituents. For instance, citizens should have access to information about legislative processes, budget allocations, and policymaking. This access empowers them to engage in meaningful discourse, hold leaders accountable, and make informed decisions during elections.

Furthermore, transparency should extend to campaign financing and political contributions. Voters deserve to know who is funding political campaigns and to what degree, as this knowledge can shed light on potential conflicts of interest and undue influence within the political arena. Transparency in campaign financing plays a vital role in preserving the integrity of the democratic process.

In summary, while it is natural for government to keep some actions hidden, it is equally essential for citizens to be well informed about the inner workings of their government. This delicate balance between secrecy and transparency is necessary for a healthy, strong, and vibrant democracy. Secrecy should be limited to areas involved in our national security and in competitive bidding processes.

Proposals: While the specifics can vary, here are some general actions and areas of improvement that could enhance open government laws:

1. **Strengthen Freedom of Information Act (FOIA) Enforcement:** This will ensure that government agencies respond to requests promptly and transparently. Penalties for noncompliance should be more substantial to deter uncooperative behavior.
2. **Expand Scope of FOIA:** Consider expanding the scope of FOIA to cover more government entities, including contractors and subcontractors that perform government functions, to prevent the outsourcing of public responsibilities to evade transparency requirements.
3. **Streamline FOIA Processing:** Invest in technology and resources to expedite FOIA processing and reduce backlog, making it easier for the public to access government information.
4. **Mandatory Transparency Reporting:** Require government agencies to report on their transparency efforts, including the number of FOIA requests received, fulfilled, and denied, as well as the reasons for denials. This information should be readily accessible to the public.
5. **Strengthen Whistleblower Protections:** Strengthen protections for government whistleblowers to encourage reporting of misconduct or wrongdoing without fear of retaliation.
6. **Campaign Finance Reform:** Implement comprehensive reforms to increase transparency in political contributions and reduce the influence of money in politics. This expansion may include stricter disclosure requirements and limitations on campaign spending.
7. **Accessible and Open Data:** Promote the availability of government data in open, machine-readable formats to encourage innovation and public use of government information.
8. **Public Engagement:** Enhance mechanisms for public engagement in policymaking processes, such as soliciting public input on proposed regulations and initiatives and ensuring that public meetings and hearings are accessible.
9. **Protection of Journalists and Press Freedom:** Strengthen legal protections for journalists and safeguard press freedom to ensure investigative journalism can continue to hold the government to account.

Fifth and Sixth Amendments (Rights of the Accused)

The Fifth Amendment ensures protection against self-incrimination and double jeopardy, and the Sixth Amendment ensures a fair and speedy trial, the right to counsel, and the right to confront witnesses.

The Republican Party has often positioned itself as the party of law and order, a stance that became particularly prominent during the late 1960s and early 1970s. This positioning was partly in response to civil unrest and a perceived rise in crime. As a result, Republican administrations and lawmakers have frequently advocated for policies that emphasize strict law enforcement, tougher sentencing, and a more aggressive approach to crime.

However, it's important to note that not all Republicans uniformly support such measures, and there has been a growing movement within the party advocating for. a more balanced approach to that also considers the rights of the accused and addresses issues like prison overcrowding and the high cost of maintaining the criminal justice system.

On the other hand, Democrats have focused on reforming the criminal justice system, including ensuring the accused has the right to a fair trial and protection against self-incrimination. They have traditionally been more focused on expanding civil liberties and rights of the accused, advocating for reducing mandatory minimum sentences, promoting rehabilitation over incarceration, and addressing systemic racial disparities in the criminal justice system.

Property Rights

Property ownership is a fundamental right, yet it must align with society's needs and bear in mind the intrinsic role of government. Individuals should be free to use their property as they wish, provided it does not diminish the value of neighboring properties, pose a hazard to neighbors, or disrupt their peace and quiet. While a necessary tool, eminent domain should not be exploited for the commercial gains of individuals or companies; they should purchase land for economically justified uses. The use of eminent domain in redeveloping areas affected by urban blight is a delicate matter. It may be justified, provided it does not unreasonably displace resident property owners against their will. The collaboration between a private developer and the government, where eminent domain is employed to acquire land for development, is often part of a public-private partnership (PPP). In such arrangements, the government may use its eminent domain authority to obtain the land. Subsequently, the private developer typically enters into a lease or agreement with the government to build a structure or develop the property. This approach integrates public objectives with private sector participation.

However, PPPs also pose risks, such as a lack of transparency leading to potential favoritism and corruption. Conflicts of interest can skew decisions toward private benefits over public welfare. The higher the stakes when it comes to contract awards, the greater the potential for bribery and corruption. Inadequate regulatory oversight might result in mismanagement and unfairness. And collusion in bidding can compromise fair competition and project quality. There must be stringent oversight and transparent, robust legal frameworks to mitigate these risks.

The Democratic Party seeks to balance individual ownership with the broader interests of the community and environment. They support the prudent use of eminent domain, primarily for public benefit projects like infrastructure, while opposing its use for private commercial gain. Environmental protection is a key priority, often leading to support for regulations that may restrict certain uses of private property to safeguard public health and the environment. In urban areas, Democrats focus on policies promoting affordable housing and equitable development, balancing these goals with individual property rights. This position includes land use and zoning regulations aimed at managing urban development sustainably. The party advocates for measures to prevent foreclosure and provide housing crisis assistance for small property owners. In rural areas, preserving agricultural land and supporting farmers' rights is emphasized, along with environmental considerations. Overall, the Democrats want to harmonize the rights of individual property owners with the needs of the larger community and environmental sustainability.

The Republican Party strongly emphasize individual ownership and freedom, advocating for minimal government intervention. Republicans champion the right of property owners to use their land as they see fit, advocating against what they perceive as overreaching regulations, particularly those related to environmental protection, which they argue can impede economic development and infringe on individual rights. The party typically opposes the expansive use of eminent domain, primarily when it benefits private entities at the expense of individual property owners. In rural areas, Republicans strongly support the rights of farmers and landowners, often opposing regulations that restrict agricultural practices. They advocate for free-market solutions and private property rights in urban development, arguing that these lead to more efficient and equitable development. The party also focuses on protecting property owners from excessive taxation and foreclosure, promoting policies that bolster economic freedom and stability. This approach underscores a fundamental belief in the sanctity of private property and the role of individual liberty in fostering a prosperous and free society.

Eighth Amendment (Cruel and Unusual Punishment)

The Eighth Amendment prohibits the federal government from imposing excessive bail, excessive fines, and cruel and unusual punishment.

The Democratic Party's stance is grounded in a commitment to human rights and criminal justice reform. Many Democrats advocate against the death penalty, viewing it as inconsistent and prone to errors, potentially leading to irreversible injustices. They call for reforms in sentencing laws, particularly opposing mandatory minimum sentences for non-violent crimes and advocating for more judicial discretion. Improving prison conditions is another focus, as well as ensuring humane treatment, adequate healthcare, and mental health services for inmates. In juvenile justice, the party emphasizes rehabilitation and education over harsh punishments. Democrats also support bail reform, critiquing the current system's disproportionate impact on low-income individuals and advocating for alternatives that do not punish poverty. Additionally, they oppose excessive fines and fees, especially those that entrap people in cycles of debt and incarceration for minor offenses. Overall, their approach to the Eighth Amendment reflects a broader vision for a fairer, more equitable justice system.

The Republican Party tends to emphasize law and order, with a focus on supporting the rights of victims and ensuring public safety. Many Republicans support the death penalty as a deterrent to serious crimes and as a just punishment for the most heinous offenses, arguing for its fair and careful application. The party often advocates for strict sentencing laws, including mandatory minimums, to deter crime and ensure consistent punishment. While recognizing the need for humane conditions in prisons, Republicans typically prioritize the security and order of these institutions. In juvenile justice, there is a general emphasis on accountability and the prevention of re-offending, with a preference for strict punishments for serious juvenile crimes. The party is cautious about major reforms to the bail system, balancing the accused's rights with the community safety. Republicans support enforcing fines and fees while recognizing the need for fairness. Overall, the Republican approach to the Eighth Amendment aligns with a broader philosophy of upholding law and order, emphasizing the protection of society and the rights of victims.

Reparation

Individual freedoms, a cornerstone of democratic societies, often highlight the necessity for justice and equality, leading to the current discussions on reparations to address and amend historical inequities and infringements upon these freedoms.

Reparations, aimed at compensating African Americans for the enduring impacts of slavery and racial discrimination, is a thorny issue. Proponents believe reparations are necessary to redress historical injustices, rectify economic disparities, and foster national reconciliation. Many Democrats align with this perspective, viewing reparations as a vital component in addressing racial inequality. In contrast, most Republicans oppose the concept, citing concerns over practicality and fairness. They question the feasibility of redressing past wrongs and argue for focusing on current opportunities for all. The debate encapsulates broader discussions about historical accountability and the paths to achieving racial justice in modern America.

Some might argue that the North freed the enslaved people and ended slavery, so why should they pay reparation for the harm that the South did? This argument is rooted in historical and geographical perspectives. It suggests that regions or groups that did not directly engage in or benefit from the institution of slavery and who paid a substantial price to end it should not be held financially responsible for its consequences. This viewpoint raises questions about collective responsibility, historical accountability, and the scope of moral obligation in addressing the legacies of past injustices. It reflects the complexity of assigning responsibility for historical events and their long-term effects across different regions and generations.

The implementation of reparations for African Americans could set a precedent that might prompt similar claims from other groups, such as Native Americans, who have also faced historical injustices. This adds another layer of complexity to the reparations debate. What about the persecution of the Irish in New England during the 1800s? What about the stoning of Catholics in the early 1900s in Massachusetts?

Recap – Individual Freedoms

2023-2024 Positions on Individual Freedoms		
Area of Concern	**Democrats**	**Republicans**
Individual Responsibility	Emphasize individual responsibility in the context of social solidarity and community support, advocating for policies that balance personal accountability with collective welfare and equitable access to resources.	Emphasize individual responsibility as a cornerstone value, advocating for self-reliance, minimal reliance on government assistance, and personal accountability in economic and social matters.
Individual Freedoms	Advocate for individual freedoms, emphasizing the protection and expansion of civil liberties, personal privacy, and equal rights for all citizens.	Prioritize individual freedoms, with a focus on limited government intervention, personal responsibility, and the preservation of constitutional rights such as free speech and gun ownership.
Voting Rights	Advocate for expanding voting access and inclusivity, supporting measures like early voting, mail-in ballots, and opposing strict voter ID laws to ensure broader voter participation and accessibility.	Support stricter voting regulations, such as voter ID laws and limitations on mail-in voting, citing concerns about voter fraud and the integrity of the electoral process.
Freedom of Speech	Advocate for freedom of speech, with certain regulations to combat hate speech and misinformation, and to ensure a safe and inclusive environment for diverse voices.	Support a broad interpretation of freedom of speech with minimal restrictions, opposing perceived censorship and advocating for the right to express even controversial or offensive viewpoints.

Freedom of the Press	Champion freedom of the press as a fundamental pillar of democracy, advocating for transparency, the protection of journalistic rights, and the importance of a free and independent media in holding power accountable.	Support freedom of the press, viewing it as essential to democracy, but often expresses concerns about media bias and advocate for a more balanced and fair portrayal of news and events.
Role of Secrecy in Government	Advocate for limited government secrecy, prioritizing transparency and accountability in national and international affairs.	Support a degree of government secrecy necessary for national security and strategic governance.
Fourth, Fifth, and Sixth Amendments	Support strong protections, advocating for robust privacy rights against unreasonable searches, the right to due process, and fair and speedy trials to ensure justice and civil liberties for all individuals.	Emphasize the importance of individual rights against governmental overreach, the sanctity of due process, and the necessity of a fair legal system to maintain law and order.
Property Rights	Advocate for a balanced approach that considers public welfare and environmental protection and supports regulations that manage property use in the interest of the broader community.	Support property rights, emphasizing individual ownership and control, and advocate for fewer government regulations and restrictions on property use to uphold personal liberty and economic freedom.
Eighth Amendment – Rights of the Accused	Advocate for reforms in the criminal justice system to protect the rights of the accused, emphasizing fair trials, humane treatment, and addressing systemic inequalities.	Emphasize law and order in the criminal justice system, focusing on victims' rights and public safety, while also upholding the fundamental legal rights of the accused.

Cruel and Unusual Punishment	Typically oppose the death penalty and advocate for the humane treatment of prisoners, viewing certain punitive practices as cruel and unusual.	More supportive of the death penalty and tend to have a stricter interpretation of what constitutes cruel and unusual punishment, often prioritizing public safety and criminal justice efficiency.
Reparation	Its progressive members support exploring reparations for historical injustices such as slavery to address systemic inequalities and the long-term impact of discrimination.	Oppose reparations for historical injustices like slavery, often arguing that such measures are divisive, impractical to implement fairly, and not the responsibility of current generations.

14. Judiciary

The American judiciary, central to our democracy, has become a focal point for the distinct ideologies of the main parties. Democrats typically push for a progressive interpretation of the Constitution, supporting judges who promote civil liberties and modern societal values. Conversely, Republicans favor a conservative, originalist interpretation, endorsing judges who strictly adhere to the Constitution's original text. This philosophical divide heavily influences the selection and confirmation of judges, especially Supreme Court justices, thus shaping American legal precedents.

The Supreme Court's political leanings became more evident during President Franklin D. Roosevelt's New Deal era in the 1930s. Appointments and rulings often mirror the ideological leanings of the current president and Senate, a trend heightened by recent political polarization. This politicization significantly impacts law and society, affecting crucial issues like reproductive rights, voting regulations, and gun control. The conservative majority's originalist approach impacts high-profile cases and the broader interpretation of the Constitution.

The mid-20th century saw an intensification of the political battle over the judiciary. As the Supreme Court's role in shaping social policy grew, particularly in areas like civil rights and free speech, its composition became a critical political concern. Lifetime appointments for justices further raise the stakes, making each nomination a long-term investment in a party's vision of the law. As a result, judicial appointments, particularly to the Supreme Court, have become central to political strategy, allowing each party to shape the judiciary according to its ideological preferences, a trend with ongoing significant influence on American politics and law. The mid-20th century witnessed several landmark Supreme Court rulings that radically changed American society and law, with their impact persisting into the 21st century.

Profound Supreme Court Rulings in Recent Years

- **Brown v. Board of Education (1954)**: This decision declared that state laws establishing separate public schools for black and white students were unconstitutional, overturning the "separate but equal" doctrine of Plessy v. Ferguson. It marked a crucial step in the civil rights movement, leading to the desegregation of schools.
- **Miranda v. Arizona (1966)**: This ruling established "Miranda rights" for detained criminal suspects, including the right to remain silent and the right to an attorney. This decision significantly transformed police interrogation practices and reinforced the rights of the accused.
- **Loving v. Virginia (1967)**: This decision struck down state laws banning interracial marriage in the United States, ending all race-based legal restrictions on marriage and advancing civil rights.
- **Roe v. Wade (1973, Overturned in the Dobbs v. Jackson Women's Health Organization Case, June 24, 2022)**: This landmark decision legalized abortion nationwide, ruling that the Constitution protects a pregnant woman's liberty to choose to have an abortion without excessive government restriction. It was a pivotal moment in the reproductive rights movement. It was overturned after the addition of three justices appointed by President Donald Trump: Neil Gorsuch in 2017, Brett Kavanaugh in 2018, and Amy Coney Barrett in 2020.

The cases above tended to align with principles favored by the Democrats until the overturing of Roe v. Wade, which was clearly a Republican political objective. In the Dobbs v. Jackson decision, which overturned Roe v. Wade, the Supreme Court of the United States did not make a judgment on the morality of abortion. Instead, it ruled that the Constitution does not confer a right to abortion, effectively returning the authority to regulate abortion to individual states. This decision meant that states could set their abortion policies, leading to a varied set of laws across the country, from strict restrictions to protection of abortion rights. The court's ruling focused on constitutional interpretation only. But actions have consequences, which unfortunately have created confusion and reports of hardship on some women. Women in states with strict abortion bans or severe restrictions face significant challenges in accessing abortion services. They need to travel long distances to states with more permissive laws, navigate complex legal requirements, or confront financial and logistical barriers. Critics claim that these difficulties can disproportionately affect women from lower socioeconomic backgrounds, those without easy access to transportation or healthcare, and young or vulnerable populations.

The overturning of Roe v. Wade and the transfer of abortion regulation to state control has led to a patchwork of laws across the United States and significant disparities in access to abortion services based on geographic location. This shift has also sparked legal battles and increased political polarization around the issue of reproductive rights. (See later section on the Abortion issue.)

Composition of the Supreme Court

Following the nomination and subsequent congressional confirmation between 2017 and 2020 of three new justices with conservative leanings, concerns have been raised about the politicization of the selection process for the Supreme Court. These appointments, made during a Republican presidency, contributed to a shift in the court's ideological balance. This change was a significant factor in the Dobbs v. Jackson case, which led to the overturning of Roe v. Wade.

The History of the Supreme Court Composition

1789: The Judiciary Act established the court with six justices.

1801: The Judiciary Act of 1801 reduced the number to five, to take effect upon the next vacancy. However, this act was quickly repealed by the Judiciary Act of 1802 before any reduction took place, and the number returned to six.

1807: The number of justices was increased to seven under the Jefferson administration to accommodate the expansion of the nation.

1837: During Andrew Jackson's presidency, the number was raised to nine to reflect the growing number of federal judicial circuits.

1863: During the Civil War, the number rose to 10 under the Lincoln administration, again to align with the number of circuits.

1866: Post-Civil War, Congress passed the Judicial Circuits Act, which reduced the number to seven, to prevent President Andrew Johnson from making any appointments. This reduction was to occur as seats became vacant.

1869: The Judiciary Act of 1869, signed by President Ulysses S. Grant, set the number of justices at nine, where it has remained ever since.

Note: There are 13 Judicial Circuits today.

Based on its composition of appointees, historically, the Supreme Court has had leanings toward the conservative or liberal ends of the political spectrum.

The History of the Court's Political Leanings

Early Years (1789–1860s): Initially, the court's decisions were less ideologically driven and more focused on establishing its role and jurisdiction. However, even in this period, there were justices with federalist or Jeffersonian-Republican leanings, reflecting the politics of the time.

Post-Civil War to Early 20th Century: During this period, the court often had a conservative tilt, favoring business interests and states' rights. This period included the controversial "Lochner era," where the court often struck down laws seen as infringing on economic freedom.

The New Deal Era (1930s): President Franklin D. Roosevelt's New Deal policies initially faced resistance from a conservative court. Frustrated, Roosevelt proposed the "court-packing" plan to add more justices. While this plan failed, the court soon became more receptive to New Deal legislation, partly due to changes in its composition.

Mid-20th Century: This era saw the court take a more liberal turn, especially under Chief Justice Earl Warren (1953–1969). His court was known for landmark decisions that expanded civil rights, civil liberties, judicial power, and federal power.

Late 20th Century to Early 21st Century: The court's composition began to shift towards a more conservative stance with appointments by the presidencies of Richard Nixon, Ronald Reagan, and the Bushes. This period saw decisions reflecting conservative views on issues like abortion, affirmative action, and campaign finance.

Current Trends: The court has been perceived as leaning conservative, especially following recent conservative appointments. However, the court's decisions sometimes defy simple conservative/liberal categorizations, with justices occasionally making decisions that do not align strictly with the perceived ideology of their appointing president.

The other issue, which we reviewed earlier, is the possibility of establishing term limits for justices or providing for a method for replacing them when they have health or age-related cognitive issues. In September 2023, a bill was introduced to Congress called the Supreme Court Tenure Establishment and Retirement Modernization (TERM) Act, which proposes establishing 18-year term limits for Supreme Court justices. This act would also require justices who have completed their active service term to assume senior status while preserving life tenure and their ability to continue holding office and receiving compensation. Similar legislation was introduced in the U.S. Senate by Democrat senators Cory Booker, Sheldon Whitehouse, Richard Blumenthal, Brian Schatz, and Mazie Hirono. The TERM Act suggests that a new justice would be appointed every two years, aligning with this 18-year term structure. The debate around these bills has been highly partisan, with Democrats primarily supporting the reforms and Republicans opposing them.

These legislative efforts aim to restore balance, legitimacy, and fairness to the Supreme Court.

Recap - Judiciary

2023-2024 Positions on the Judiciary		
Area of Concern	**Democrats**	**Republicans**
Judiciary	Generally, support a progressive judiciary that interprets the Constitution in the context of modern societal values and places emphasis on advancing civil rights, social justice, and protecting individual liberties.	Favor a conservative judiciary that adheres to an originalist and textualist interpretation of the Constitution, emphasizing limited government, individual rights, and traditional values.
Supreme Court Ethics, Particularly in Relation to the Supreme Court Ethics, Recusal, and Transparency Act of 2022	Emphasize the need for stronger ethical standards and transparency, advocating for legislation to ensure accountability and integrity within the judiciary.	Largely critical, viewing such reforms as unnecessary and possibly an act of political intimidation or personal attack on specific justices.

15. Military

Common Defense

In America, the executive branch of our government runs the military. This includes the right to hire mercenaries, even for international wars, and to deploy state National Guard units. These rights may surprise some people. The National Guard reports to the state governor, their commander-in-chief, and has the purpose of defending against foreign invasion in their territory, quelling domestic violence, and assisting with natural disasters.

According to the U.S. Constitution (Article 1, Section 8, Clause 15), the president can deploy a state's National Guard for three specific purposes: executing federal laws, suppressing insurrections, and repelling invasions. This authority is part of a broader legal framework that outlines the president's role as commander-in-chief. Domestically, the National Guard typically operates under state governors' command (under Title 32 of the U.S. Code), with possible federal funding, primarily for state emergencies or local support. In contrast, under Title 10, the National Guard can be federalized, integrating into the regular U.S. Armed Forces for a variety of missions, including overseas deployments, as seen in Vietnam and other conflicts. The president's discretion in deploying the National Guard, whether domestically or internationally, is subject to congressional oversight. This power allows the president to use the National Guard for national defense, international peacekeeping, or other military operations, aligning with U.S. foreign and defense policy objectives. Factors influencing these deployment decisions include national security needs, international obligations, and strategic military considerations.

> **Proposal: States should not be permitted to use their National Guard for political purposes. National Guard soldiers should be trained at the same level as federal soldiers. The breadth of state militias across 50 states also serves as a deterrent to foreign armed invasion.**

While the combat mission in Iraq officially ended in 2021, the U.S. maintains a presence of about 2,400 military advisers and trainers, in Iraq and 800 in Syria as of December 2023. This information underscores the ongoing involvement of private contractors in U.S. military operations abroad.

Using these private entities has raised questions about the implications for U.S. foreign policy and military strategy. It's noted that these private contractors, including many foreign nationals, have been involved in various capacities, sometimes in ways that are not transparent to the public or fully accountable. This has led to concerns about the spread of highly skilled mercenaries worldwide, particularly as these individuals and groups can offer their services to the highest bidder, potentially causing instability in vulnerable regions.

> **Proposal: The extensive use of mercenaries should be abolished because it puts too much of our government's power in the hands of independent individuals, often outside of our organized military structure, and sometimes even outside the control of government representatives such as the CIA.**

Nuclear Weapons

Nuclear weapons have no place in a civilized world; but, as long as they exist anywhere in the world, we need to sustain superior capabilities. It is part of our nature as Americans that we believe our capabilities in war must exceed those of our potential enemies.

> **Proposal: The world must move toward verifiable elimination of nuclear weapons everywhere. And the world must agree that they do not belong in space. We also should adhere to the Geneva Convention if our opponents are also adhering to it.**

Volunteerism

Volunteering can be a powerful way for society to develop and people to grow, particularly young adults. It fosters a sense of community, empathy, and responsibility, offering invaluable lessons in selflessness and civic duty. The idea of young people dedicating a portion of their time to service has been a topic of discussion since at least 1960, yet it still needs to be implemented at a legislative level. Such a program would benefit society at large and enrich the volunteers' lives, providing them with unique experiences and a deeper understanding of the world around them. I would expect that the military, as one of the options, would be a beneficiary of such a program.

> **Proposal: Encourage individuals aged 18 to 25 to volunteer for societal benefits for two years. Service opportunities should extend beyond humanitarian missions or military roles to encompass aiding underserved American communities. By diversifying service options, this proposal aims to engage a range of interests and passions, maximizing the positive impact on both volunteers and the communities they serve.**

Recap - Military

2023-2024 Positions on the Military		
Area of Concern	**Democrats**	**Republicans**
Common Defense and Volunteerism	Emphasize strong common defense, encourage volunteerism for community betterment.	Advocate for a robust common defense, value volunteerism as a cornerstone of community strength.

16. Internet Security and Privacy

Above we described how the Fourth Amendment's protection against "unreasonable searches and seizures" has been interpreted as guaranteeing a certain level of privacy for individuals, their homes, and their personal belongings. The Supreme Court has also found privacy implications in other amendments, such as the First Amendment's freedom of association, the Third Amendment's prohibition against quartering soldiers in private homes, the Fifth Amendment's protection against self-incrimination, and the 14th Amendment's concept of personal liberty and restrictions on state action.

The Democratic and Republican parties have distinct and contrasting positions on digital privacy, leading to debates over government surveillance and personal data protection.

Democrats typically advocate for robust privacy laws to safeguard individual data, supporting regulations that limit the collection and use of personal information by corporations and government entities. They tend to favor policies that protect consumers and citizens in the digital age, emphasizing the need for transparency and consent in data practices.

On the other hand, Republicans prioritize national security and economic interests. They often advocate for less regulation of businesses, including in areas related to data privacy, emphasizing the importance of free enterprise and innovation.

The Internet

Both parties agree that the Internet is a crucial platform for political communication. Historically, the Democratic Party has been adept at harnessing the Internet for information dissemination and fundraising. They have effectively used tools like email lists for campaign fundraising and built a robust online infrastructure to promote their viewpoints, rally support, and counter opposing narratives.

Lee Atwater, a notable Republican strategist in the late 1980s, emphasized the need for the Republican Party to utilize the Internet fully. He foresaw the Internet's potential as a powerful political tool, comparable to the impact of newspapers and other media in shaping public opinion. Atwater cautioned that without embracing the Internet, the Republican Party risked being misrepresented and losing its influence. He likened the strategic use of the Internet to historical instances of the media shaping public opinion, such as German propaganda in the 1930s, though this comparison is contentious.[171]

Since the late 1980s, the Republican Party has caught up with and, in some respects, surpassed the Democrats, particularly in their engagement on alternative social media platforms. In recent years, concerned about perceived censorship and bias on mainstream platforms like

X, formerly known as Twitter, and Meta, formerly known as Facebook, conservatives have shifted towards using the likes of Parler, Gab, and Rumble. Republican politicians, influencers, and their supporters have increasingly utilized these alternative platforms to disseminate their messages, organize events, and engage with their base. They have provided Republicans with a more unfiltered and direct line of communication to their audience. In this way, they have built a solid and engaged community online, which has been particularly effective for grassroots mobilization and spreading their political messages. Both parties now recognize the pivotal roles played by the Internet and social media in disseminating messages, influencing public opinion, and mobilizing support. Both parties continue to adapt and refine their digital strategies.

While digital communications are critical in modern politics, it is also essential to balance the openness and accessibility of the Internet with the maintenance of legal and ethical standards.

> **Proposal: All utilities to homes, governments, and businesses should be installed underground and critical power grids protected from electromagnetic magnetic pulse attacks. The Department of Homeland Security has been given direction by Executive Order 13865 to establish resilience and security standards for U.S. critical infrastructure as a national priority. This endeavor needs to be accelerated.**

Internet Rules

In its early days, e-commerce resembled the Wild West, where anything went and no "sheriffs" were involved. Much money was stolen from innocent people during this period, akin to stagecoaches being held up and robbed. This situation still goes on but is gradually changing. The need remains for even further transformation.

The U.S. government's approach to regulating e-commerce aims to balance economic growth with consumer protection and the challenges of digital transactions. Consumer protection is a priority, enforced through laws like the Federal Trade Commission Act, which mandate truthful advertising and clear disclosure of terms.

Data privacy regulations like the California Consumer Privacy Act ensure the security of consumer data and require consent for its collection and sharing. The landscape of online sales tax collection has evolved post the Supreme Court's decision in South Dakota v. Wayfair, Inc., impacting out-of-state e-commerce businesses. Payment security is ensured through compliance with the PCI Security Standards Council's Data Security Standard (DSS), governing the secure processing, storage, and transmission of credit and debit card transactions.

Intellectual property rights combat counterfeit goods and piracy, while antitrust laws promote fair competition in e-commerce. The Americans with Disabilities Act mandates website accessibility for individuals with disabilities, and international trade laws govern cross-border transactions. This regulatory environment adapts to the evolving digital landscape, focusing on safely harnessing the power of artificial intelligence.

Democrats support comprehensive data protection policies like the California Consumer Privacy Act and advocate for stronger antitrust actions against dominant tech companies to safeguard consumer rights and promote fair competition. In contrast, Republicans prioritize a business-friendly regulatory environment, supporting more lenient data privacy standards to foster innovation. They oppose expansive antitrust measures, arguing they could hinder entrepreneurial growth and technological advancement.

However, those actions do not go far enough.

Proposal for New Internet Rules:

1. **If a user asks a company to reveal all the information they have on that person, they should be compelled to do so within 14 days.**
2. **If a user replies "STOP" to a text or unsubscribes from an email, the sending organization cannot sell, give, or transfer that phone number to any other entity (applies to political fundraising as well.) Removal requests must be honored immediately.**
3. **Protect Net Neutrality: Maintain a level playing field for all online services and content providers. This protects smaller businesses from being pushed out by big businesses buying greater access over smaller users.**
4. **Outlaw noreply@domain emails. People should be able to reply to any email they receive.**
5. **Every website that charges a fee for services must allow for contacting "support" or "customer service" by live chat or email to accommodate the hearing impaired, with chat responses within two minutes and email responses within 24 hours on weekdays, or 36 hours on weekends.**
6. **All sites that have subscribers (or auto-renewal arrangements) must give 30-days' notice to subscribers before auto-renewal and provide a hot link to immediately cancel that subscription or renewal.**
7. **All sites that charge a fee must supply a live link to discuss changes to services or request immediate refunds.**
8. **All sites charging a periodic subscription fee (e.g., monthly) must allow for immediate cancellation at least once per month. All sites charging an annual fee must allow early cancellation with a pro rata refund for the period unused. No "fee forfeiting" allowed.**
9. **When a response to a text is, "Report junk and delete" that should be sent to the network provider so that the sender can be suspended or blocked.**

Cybersecurity

In our increasingly digital and interconnected world, national, economic, and personal cybersecurity has emerged as a critical area of concern. It is essential to understand the different positions of the two major parties.

The Democratic Party's have a proactive and comprehensive approach, emphasizing the need for robust protections against cyber threats while also wishing to safeguard individual privacy and civil liberties. Democrats typically prioritize investment in cybersecurity infrastructure, advocating for increased funding and resources for government agencies and public sector entities to defend against cyberattacks. They also support strengthening partnerships between the public and private sectors to enhance information sharing and collaboration in addressing cyber threats. Additionally, the party often emphasizes the importance of international cooperation in combating global cybercrime and cyberterrorism, advocating for diplomatic efforts and multinational agreements. This aligns with their broader focus on technological innovation and digital inclusivity, reflecting a belief in the potential of technology to improve governance and public services, provided that robust cybersecurity measures are in place to protect data integrity and privacy.

The Republican Party take a strong national defense posture, highlighting the importance of protecting critical infrastructure and national security interests from cyber threats. Republicans typically advocate for a strategy that combines robust offensive and defensive capabilities, often supporting increased military and intelligence community involvement in cybersecurity. They tend to favor minimal government regulation on private sector cybersecurity practices, promoting a market-driven approach that encourages businesses to develop their own cybersecurity solutions. This perspective aligns with the Republican emphasis on individual responsibility and private-sector innovation in addressing complex challenges. The party also often stresses the importance of personal privacy and the protection of individual rights in the context of government surveillance and data collection efforts. Additionally, Republicans may focus on deterring and retaliating against state-sponsored cyberattacks, reflecting a broader emphasis on national sovereignty and security in the digital domain.

> **Proposal: We should do more to shore up our Internet to protect it from cyberattacks, as well as physical attacks. We might consider building out new infrastructure that is independent of the current networks, using new end-to-end encryption that is unbreakable by quantum computers.**

Freedom of Information Act

The Freedom of Information Act (FOIA) promotes government transparency by allowing public access to federal agency records. However, the effectiveness of the FOIA process is often questioned. Common challenges include requests being initially rejected for lack of specificity and requiring more detailed information. Additionally, requesters frequently encounter fees for copying documents, with no guaranteed cap on the cost unless they set a limit, which can lead to selective provision of information.

While some individuals successfully obtain the information they seek, many find the FOIA process cumbersome and inefficient, often receiving large volumes of irrelevant information or being discouraged by the quotation of oppressive fees. This can lead to a perception that the process is obstructive or designed to discourage persistent inquiries.

Some have suggested eliminating FOIA and automatically releasing all government information after a fixed period, like 15 or 20 years, with few exceptions. This approach, akin to a "sunset" clause for confidentiality, could potentially streamline access to historical government information. Long waits can be frustrating, especially when information is urgently needed. Here are some suggestions:

Proposed FOIA Improvements[169-01]

- **Streamlined Request Submission:** Simplify the FOIA request process by creating a standardized, user-friendly online submission platform across all federal agencies. This would reduce initial rejections due to lack of specificity.
- **Transparent Fee Structure:** Implement a clear, standardized fee structure for all agencies, including a cap on copying and processing fees, with a waiver or reduced fees for educational, journalistic, and non-profit requesters to ensure that cost is not a barrier to accessing information.
- **Enhanced Agency Training:** Provide comprehensive training to FOIA officers across all agencies, focusing on efficient information retrieval and customer service. This training should emphasize the importance of assisting requesters in refining their requests and understanding the process.
- **Digitalization of Records:** Accelerate the digitalization of government records for easier access and processing. Prioritize frequently requested documents and categories of information.
- **Proactive Disclosure:** Agencies should proactively disclose commonly requested information and regularly update publicly accessible databases. This approach reduces the number of individual requests needed and frees up resources to handle more complex inquiries.
- **Clear Timeline and Tracking:** Establish and enforce a clear timeline for processing FOIA requests, with regular updates provided to the requester. Introduce a tracking system, allowing requesters to check the status of their requests online.
- **Independent Review and Appeals Process:** Create an independent body to review complaints regarding FOIA processing and disputes. This body would offer an alternative to the often lengthy and costly legal appeals process.
- **Periodic Review and Sunset Clause:** Implement a periodic review of classified information with an established "sunset clause" for automatic declassification, subject to national security exceptions. This approach would increase the volume of accessible information over time.
- **Feedback Mechanism:** Establish a feedback mechanism for requesters to report on their experience with the FOIA process and use this feedback for continuous improvement of the system.

Recap - Internet Security and Privacy

2023-2024 Positions on Internet Security and Privacy		
Area of Concern	**Democrats**	**Republicans**
Internet Security and Privacy	Advocate for personal data protection, cybersecurity, and data safeguarding regulations. They prioritize international cooperation against cyber threats and election integrity protection. Democrats also support FBI wiretaps with court approval and have varying views on surveillance controls. Their focus is on ensuring eligible voter participation and robust cybersecurity against foreign cyberattacks on election infrastructure.	Favor FBI wiretaps with court approval and acknowledge internal divisions on surveillance controls. They prioritize election integrity and cybersecurity against foreign interference, often emphasizing state and local government roles in securing election infrastructure.
Freedom of Information Act (FOIA)	Advocate for transparency and accountability in government, a strong FOIA and in 2024. See the Citizen's Guide to the Freedom of Information Act (FOIA) at https://sgp.fas.org/foia/citizen.pdf.	Supports the principles of the Freedom of Information Act (FOIA) as part of its broader commitment to government transparency and accountability, advocating for reforms that enhance efficiency in processing FOIA requests while balancing national security and privacy concerns. Supported creating the Citizen's Guide to the Freedom of Information Act (FOIA).

17. Racial and Ethnic Equity

Our society grapples with the complexities of addressing historic disparities and promoting inclusivity. While both main political parties acknowledge the significance of racial and ethnic equity, their approaches, priorities, and proposed solutions diverge significantly.

The Democratic Party has long championed racial and ethnic equity. Democrats emphasize the need for comprehensive policy reforms to address systemic racism and promote inclusivity across all aspects of American life. They advocate for measures such as criminal justice reform, voting rights protection, and investment in education and healthcare in historically marginalized communities. They recognize the importance of diversity and representation in government and private sectors. Their approach is grounded in the belief that proactive government intervention and support is needed to ensure equal opportunities and rights for all Americans, regardless of their racial or ethnic background.

The Republican Party takes a different approach. Republicans tend to emphasize individual liberties, limited government intervention, and a colorblind approach to policymaking. They argue that policies should be race-neutral and that emphasizing racial or ethnic distinctions can lead to reverse discrimination. Republicans advocate for free-market solutions, tax cuts, and deregulation as means to promote economic opportunity and prosperity for all, believing that a strong economy benefits everyone, regardless of their racial or ethnic background. They often express concerns about the potential pitfalls of affirmative action and prefer merit-based approaches to address disparities. However, it is important to note the diverse opinions within the parties on these issues, and individual politicians may hold varying positions.

Recap - Racial and Ethnic Equity

2023-2024 Positions on Racial and Ethnic Equity		
Area of Concern	**Democrats**	**Republicans**
Racial and Ethnic Equity	Advocate for policies promoting racial and ethnic equity, aiming to address systemic inequalities and ensure equal opportunities for all individuals regardless of their racial or ethnic background.	Emphasize equal treatment and opportunity for all, focusing on individual merit and advocating against policies they perceive as promoting racial or ethnic preferences.

18. The Rule of Law

The rule of law, a fundamental principle in our society, is the bedrock for democratic governance, justice, and order. It embodies the concept that laws should govern a nation rather than arbitrary decisions by individual government officials. This principle ensures that all citizens, institutions, and entities, public and private, including the state itself, are accountable to publicly promulgated, equally enforced, and independently adjudicated laws. It is essential for democracy and the protection of human rights, assuring fairness in the treatment of citizens and holding society together through the consistent application of laws.

Laws – which define the rules of the state and associated penalties for violations – are, in civilized countries, endorsed by society through a governing body. The rule of law dictates that these laws, not governmental functionaries, should govern people's behavior. This position contrasts with undemocratic nations or those without respect for human rights, where dictators can create their own rules, a situation prevalent in several modern totalitarian governments.

Due process, an integral element of the rule of law, mandates that "the government must respect all the legal rights that are owed to a person according to the law of the land." This stance includes adherence to precedent-setting case law, following the guidance of past legal rulings. The rule of law safeguards against arbitrary governance, implying consistency in law application and ensuring that laws are reasonable and "just."[67]

This concept dates to Ancient Greek philosophers like Plato and Aristotle around 350 BC. Plato emphasized the supremacy of law over the government, stating, "Where the law is subject to some other authority and has none of its own, the collapse of the state ... is not far off; but if law is the master of the government and the government is its slave, then the situation is full of promise ..."[67] Aristotle also supported the rule of law, advocating that "law should govern" and those in power should be "servants of the laws."[67] This ideal was further embodied in the Magna Carta in 1215 AD, which subjected English sovereigns and magistrates to the law.[67]

In the United States, the notion that no one is above the law was pivotal during its founding. Thomas Paine, in 1776, expressed in *Common Sense*, "In America, the law is king ... in free countries, the law ought to be king; and there ought to be no other."[69] John Adams, in 1780, sought to establish "a government of laws and not of men" in the Massachusetts Constitution.[70] Thus, the rule of law does not guarantee democracy but is crucial for its existence and the defense of human rights.

The Democratic Party is steadfast in its commitment to upholding democratic principles, ensuring fairness and equality in applying laws, and safeguarding the independence of the judiciary. Democrats emphasize the importance of transparency and accountability in government, advocating for checks and balances to prevent abuse of power and to ensure that government actions are subject to legal scrutiny. They focus on protecting civil liberties and human rights, ensuring that laws are applied equally to all individuals, regardless of their status or background. They have a strong stance against discrimination and support reforms that address systemic injustices in the legal system. Additionally, Democrats typically stress the role of an independent judiciary in interpreting and enforcing laws, viewing this as crucial for maintaining a healthy democracy and upholding the rule of law.

The Republican Party emphasize strict adherence to the Constitution and a strong respect for the traditional legal framework. Republicans advocate for a literal and originalist interpretation of the Constitution, underscoring the importance of limited government intervention and the sovereignty of law as fundamental to maintaining order and protecting individual freedoms. They often stress the need for law enforcement and judicial systems to operate without political bias, ensuring that laws are enforced consistently and impartially. They focus on upholding public safety and property rights, with a strong stance against crime and support for stringent law-and-order policies. Furthermore, Republicans commonly advocate for judicial restraint, favoring judges who interpret the law rather than make it, thereby preserving the separation of powers and preventing judicial overreach. This approach reflects their broader commitment to maintaining stability, individual liberties, and the integrity of the legal system.

Understanding how the political parties envision the application of law and justice is essential for voters to understand if they are to support and defend a just, orderly, and free society. The recent politicization of the justice system raises concerns about its impartiality, which has the potential to weaken the rule of law and undermine the democratic process. Compromising the rule of law in this way can diminish public trust in the justice system and, consequently, in the democratic institutions it underpins. Legal scholars and political analysts often emphasize the importance of maintaining a nonpartisan and independent judiciary in upholding democratic principles. This highlights the need for vigilance and continuous evaluation to ensure the justice system remains an unbiased arbiter of law, thereby supporting a healthy democratic society.

Recap – The Rule of Law

2023-2024 Positions on The Rule of Law		
Area of Concern	**Democrats**	**Republicans**
The Rule of Law	Prioritize the rule of law through a commitment to fairness, equality, government transparency, and protecting civil liberties while advocating for judicial independence and reforms to address systemic injustices in the legal system.	Advocate for a strict, originalist interpretation of the Constitution, emphasizing limited government, judicial restraint, and consistent, impartial law enforcement to maintain order and protect individual freedoms.

19. Size of Government

The size and scope of government is a fundamental topic in American politics that draws sharply contrasting views from the Democratic and Republican parties. This debate centers around the extent of government involvement in the economy, social issues, and the daily lives of citizens, with each party advocating for a vision that reflects its core principles and ideologies.

The Democratic Party advocates for a more expansive role of government in society, perceiving it as a vital instrument for addressing social and economic inequalities, enhancing public services, and providing a safety net for all citizens. Democrats support increased government intervention in healthcare, education, and environmental protection, believing such involvement leads to more equitable outcomes and improves the general welfare of the public. This stance is rooted in the belief that government action can effectively tackle a wide range of societal challenges, from poverty and healthcare access to climate change. As a result, Democrats often favor policies involving government regulation and oversight, increased public spending in critical areas, and progressive taxation to fund these initiatives. This reflects a broader commitment to leveraging the mechanisms of government to promote social justice, economic fairness, and collective well-being.

The Republican Party typically advocates for a smaller, less intrusive government, emphasizing the importance of individual liberty, personal responsibility, and free-market principles. Republicans argue for reduced government intervention in the economy, favoring lower taxes, deregulation, and limited government spending to promote economic growth and individual freedom. This stance is rooted in the belief that a smaller government fosters a more efficient and competitive economic environment, encouraging innovation and entrepreneurship. In social policy, Republicans often support a reduced role for the federal government, advocating for state and local control over issues like education and healthcare. They argue that such decentralization allows for more tailored and effective governance, closer to the needs of the people. This perspective reflects a broader commitment to limited government as a key to preserving personal freedoms and ensuring efficient use of resources.

> **Proposal: The government should focus in the coming years on reducing costs by automating jobs that artificial intelligence can eliminate (e.g. tax auditing, data entry, customer service, and financial tracking). Consider creating a Cabinet Secretary for Technology and Artificial Intelligence.**

Recap - the Size of Government

2023-2024 Positions on the Size of Government		
Area of Concern	**Democrats**	**Republicans**
Size of Government	Advocate for a larger governmental role in society to address social and economic inequalities, provide essential services, and promote collective well-being through regulation, public spending, and progressive taxation.	Favor a smaller government with limited intervention in the economy and social issues, emphasizing individual freedom, free-market principles, and decentralization to promote efficiency, innovation, and economic growth.

20. Social Issues and Human Rights

Political party involvement in social issues and human rights is vital to maintaining a responsive and representative democracy, as it ensures diverse viewpoints and solutions are considered in pursuing a just and equitable society.

Role of the Family

The common belief in America is that the family household serves as a vital cornerstone for instilling moral values and appropriate behavior in children, a role considered of utmost importance to the structure and health of society. Through nurturing and guidance, families play a pivotal role in raising individuals who are responsible, well-adjusted, and capable of making positive contributions to their communities. This enduring role of the family holds even as societal trends evolve, notably in how and when families are formed. The contemporary trend of marrying later or opting not to marry at all is a multifaceted phenomenon that, while altering the traditional timeline of family formation, does not inherently undermine the importance of parenting.

This trend stems from individuals prioritizing career and educational goals, reflecting a broader societal emphasis on personal and financial readiness before embarking on parenthood, to ensure a secure environment for their future children. Moreover, social norms have evolved so there is now less pressure to marry early, a greater variety of family structures, and acknowledgment that effective parenting can occur outside the conventional marital framework. Interestingly, a knock-on effect of this delay in marriage is new parents being older, who often bring greater emotional maturity and resources to the role. However, it's important to note that they may also be less fertile, prompting some to explore alternative paths to parenthood. This trend reflects a modern view where personal fulfillment and self-actualization are vital precursors to starting a family, leading to a more deliberate approach to parenting that prioritizes the quality of the familial environment over the traditional marital timeline. In any event, the family unit is important.

The increase in remote work opportunities has presented a unique benefit in cases of divorce or separation, especially when it concerns families with children. This shift has notably lessened the need for the non-custodial parent to relocate geographically, allowing for continued close involvement in their child's life despite the physical separation from the custodial parent. This can help mitigate some of the challenges associated with family break-ups, maintaining a level of stability and the presence of both parents in the child's upbringing by facilitating more consistent and effective shared custody arrangements. This development supports the argument for government initiatives to promote and support remote working opportunities.

The Democrats recognize that "caring for family members and managing a household is real and valuable work." Their approach to families is to strengthen the support of children, especially their health and education, and to focus on jobs as one means of helping fathers remain with their families. They plan to provide transitional training to get jobs, remove tax penalties on married families, and expand maternity and paternity leave.

The Republicans recognize that children are our most precious resource. In the past, they called for a constitutional amendment: "… that fully protects marriage as a union of a man and a woman, so that judges cannot make other arrangements equivalent to it. In the absence of a national amendment, we support the right of the people of the various states to affirm traditional marriage through state initiatives." Many Republicans still feel this should be the standard. The current Republican position on same-sex marriage is divided, with the official platform opposing it but a growing number of members and leaders accepting or supporting it.

They say the "two-parent family still provides the best environment of stability, discipline, responsibility, and character." They take credit for passing the Defense of Marriage Act, affirming the right of states not to recognize same-sex "marriages" licensed in other states.

Democrats advocate for policies that support diverse family structures and work-life balance, emphasizing the importance of accessible childcare, inclusive parental leave, and flexible work arrangements. They often advocate for government-supported childcare programs and enhanced parental leave policies to accommodate all types of families. They also focus on education and community programs emphasizing child development and nurturing. Democrats are likely to support measures that ensure all parents, regardless of their family structure, have the resources and opportunities to provide a nurturing environment for their children. This perspective aligns with the party's broader goals of social equity and support for working families.

Some argue that marriage as an institution should not fall under the purview of government but rather religious entities. Given the increasingly temporary nature of the marriage contract in modern times, questions arise about the continued relevance and necessity of the institution itself.

Republicans typically emphasize the role of the family as a critical societal unit and may support policies that encourage traditional family structures while also recognizing the changing dynamics of modern family life. They often advocate for solutions that involve less government intervention, favoring market-driven childcare options and flexible work policies that encourage businesses to accommodate the needs of working parents. Republicans might support initiatives that promote parental choice in childcare and education, emphasizing the importance of family autonomy in these decisions.

> **Proposal: The government should advocate for working from home to support stronger families, which makes sense as more and more work is being done online. However, with the advent of artificial intelligence, more and more work is being automated, which may reduce work in general as well as work from home opportunities. AI may also create new kinds of jobs that can be performed at home.**

LGBTQ Rights

The issue of LGBTQ+ rights starkly illustrate the fundamental differences in viewpoints between the Democrats and Republicans. Each party's ideological foundations deeply influence their respective progressive and conservative stances, which guide their respective policies and attitudes toward the LGBTQ+ community.

Within both parties, the range of opinions on LGBTQ+ issues contribute to the complexity of the political discourse in this area, making it a significant aspect of understanding American political dynamics.

The Democrats support broader LGBTQ+ rights, advocating for policies like same-sex marriage, anti-discrimination laws covering sexual orientation and gender identity, and the protection of transgender rights. Their stance extends to opposing conversion therapy, promoting LGBTQ+ history in education, and advocating for greater LGBTQ+ representation in government. This approach is part of a wider commitment to civil rights and social justice, viewing LGBTQ+ rights as crucial in the battle against discrimination and for equality.

The Republican Party's position on LGBTQ+ rights has been more varied and complex, with a range of views within the party. Traditionally, many Republicans have taken conservative stances, often opposing measures such as same-sex marriage and the expansion of anti-discrimination protections to include sexual orientation and gender identity. This conservative perspective is often rooted in traditional values, religious beliefs, and a preference for limited government intervention in personal matters. However, there is a growing segment within the party that advocates for or accepts LGBTQ+ rights, reflecting a shift in societal attitudes. These members support policies like same-sex marriage and anti-discrimination laws. The party's stance is not monolithic and continues to evolve, with debates and differing views among its members regarding the extent and nature of support for LGBTQ+ issues.

Traditional Gender roles

As with the issues above, the debate over traditional gender roles is a prominent and often polarizing issue in American politics, with the Democratic and Republican parties offering distinct perspectives that reflect their underlying ideologies. This discourse addressing the evolving nature of gender roles in society encompasses a range of topics, from family dynamics to professional opportunities.

The Democratic Party advocates for a more progressive and fluid understanding of gender roles, challenging traditional norms and stereotypes. They support for policies that promote gender equality in the workplace, such as equal pay, parental leave, and the representation of women in leadership positions. Democrats also tend to support social and educational initiatives that encourage the breaking down of traditional gender barriers, aiming to create an inclusive environment where individuals are free to express their identities and pursue roles regardless of gender. The party's approach is often driven by a broader commitment to social justice and the belief that gender should not limit an individual's opportunities or societal roles.

The Republican Party again tend to be more conservative, often upholding and valuing conventional views of gender in family and societal structures. They believe in the importance of traditional family values and roles, where gender-specific roles are seen as beneficial and stabilizing factors in society. Republicans may be less supportive of policies that significantly alter traditional gender dynamics, preferring to maintain established norms. While there is a spectrum of views within the party, with some members advocating for more modern approaches to gender roles, the predominant stance emphasizes the preservation of traditional gender roles.

Abortion

The issue of abortion stands as one of the most divisive and emotionally charged topics in American political discourse, with the Democratic and Republican parties holding starkly contrasting views which reflect the broader ideological differences between the parties. Understanding these positions is essential for grasping the complexities of the abortion debate in the United States, which touches on ethical, moral, religious, and legal questions surrounding issues of women's rights and personal autonomy.

One argument for banning abortion is that some women use it as their means of "birth control." This is a complex topic, often entangled in personal, cultural, and political debates. Research indicates that most women seeking abortions do not use it as their primary method of birth control, with many reporting having used some form of contraception that either failed or was used incorrectly.[20-28]

The reasons behind seeking an abortion are diverse, encompassing factors like contraceptive failure, lack of access to effective birth control, financial constraints, health concerns, and socio-economic challenges. Additionally, inadequate access to contraception and comprehensive sex education are significant contributors to unintended pregnancies, subsequently leading to abortions. Medical and public health professionals do not view abortion as a substitute for regular contraception, considering the physical, emotional, and financial implications of the procedure. Regular contraception is more accessible, less invasive, and less costly compared to abortion. Policy approaches aimed at reducing the number of abortions often emphasize the importance of increasing access to contraception, enhancing sex education, and providing better support for women both during and after pregnancy. Overall, while abortion may occasionally be the only method of birth control used, evidence suggests it is not commonly employed as the primary method.

The Democratic Party strongly supports abortion rights, framing it as a fundamental aspect of women's reproductive rights and healthcare. Democrats advocate for the right of women to make decisions about their bodies, including the choice to have an abortion. This stance is rooted in a belief in personal autonomy and the separation of church and state. The party typically opposes legislation that seeks to restrict access to abortion, arguing that such restrictions disproportionately affect disadvantaged groups and undermine women's health and rights. They emphasize the importance of safe, legal, and accessible abortion services as part of comprehensive healthcare.

The Republican Party holds a pro-life stance, opposing abortion except in certain circumstances, such as rape, incest, or danger to the mother's life, where some party members allow for exceptions. This position is often grounded in religious and moral beliefs that life begins at conception, and, therefore, abortion is viewed as morally wrong.

While the Republican Party officially opposes abortion, internal conflict simmers. Conservative base voters see opposition as a core value, while moderates and pragmatists push for softer stances or strategize electoral appeal. The party grapples with balancing priorities, navigating shifting public opinion, and deciding whether to prioritize legislation, cultural change, or both in their pursuit of an anti-abortion future. In short, the Republican stance on abortion is far from monolithic, reflecting the complexity of the issue and the party itself. Republican official positions support legislation that restricts access to abortion, including measures such as mandatory waiting periods, parental consent laws for minors, and outright bans, either at any stage or after a certain point in pregnancy.

As of the end of 2023, 17 states, all of which are Republican-controlled, have near-total bans on abortion (with only exceptions for rape, incest, or danger to the mother's life): Alabama, Arkansas, Idaho, Indiana, Kentucky, Louisiana, Mississippi (no exceptions), Missouri, Oklahoma, South Carolina, North Dakota (no exceptions), South Dakota (no exceptions), Tennessee (no exceptions except for affirmative defense), Texas (no exceptions), West Virginia, Florida (banned after six weeks), and Nebraska (banned after six weeks).[20-28]

The party's approach reflects a broader focus on traditional family values and the protection of unborn life, with an emphasis on alternatives to abortion, such as adoption or foster care.

Abortion is a difficult topic to address, especially when it comes to the government's involvement. On the one hand, there is debate over whether the government should define when life begins or defend life; and, on the other, whether it should allow individuals to make personal decisions about their lives.

This perspective raises questions about the balance between the government's duty to defend life, liberty, and the pursuit of happiness, as outlined in the Constitution, and its potential interference in the personal decisions of citizens. The Founding Fathers' writings suggest a preference for minimal government interference in individual actions, adding another layer to this debate.

In the argument of when life begins, two choices are discussed: at conception or at the point of viability. The point of viability can range from the earliest week where a premature birth can survive in vitro to when fully born. The earliest "miracle" birth survived from week 21, but 23 weeks is usually the earliest possible survival age, with only a 17% survival rate.[20-29]

Establishing when life begins is a complex and multifaceted issue encompassing ethical, moral, and scientific considerations, each contributing to differing viewpoints on the legal recognition and protection of life at various stages of development. The complexity arises from the challenge of reconciling these diverse perspectives within legal frameworks, making it a contentious topic in both public discourse and legal circles. For instance, considering whether the murder of a pregnant woman the day after conception should be treated as a double homicide is a nuanced debate. Similarly, the issue of late-term abortion is contentious and raises ethical and legal questions.

Balancing the individual rights of the mother, the potential rights of the father, and those of the fetus needs careful consideration. Someone prioritizing individual rights may advocate for the primacy of the parent's choice until the fetus reaches viability. At this stage, the fetus is often considered to have rights that merit government protection. Before viability, the mother's rights typically take precedence. The role and rights of the father in this context remain a subject of ongoing debate, especially concerning his responsibilities post-birth.

The definition of life extends beyond merely living cells, as evidenced by the routine removal of tumors, warts, and appendices. The key issue is sustainability – whether cells can sustain themselves outside the body. By this logic, life begins when cells become self-sustaining. The argument that a fetus's cells may become self-sustaining in the future parallels the notion that an unfertilized egg could potentially develop into a fetus.

Religious beliefs about the "soul" further complicate this debate. If it occurs, the timing of the soul's entry into a living being is speculative and varies across beliefs. Some of certain faiths might hypothesize that a soul is acquired months after birth or even at a specific age. A more scientific approach to defining the beginning of life could be the ability to breathe independently, with or without assistance, thereby surviving detached from the mother.

The debate on whether the government should intervene in determining when life begins involves moral, religious, and constitutional considerations. The decision is complex due to varying moral beliefs across different religions and among those without religious affiliations, suggesting that government involvement might be inappropriate. However, contrasting this view is the argument for governmental intervention based on the 14th Amendment, which some interpret as extending protection to life at all developmental stages, including the unborn. However, the U.S. Supreme Court has not definitively affirmed this interpretation, particularly concerning the unborn.

In Roe v. Wade (1973), the Supreme Court recognized the right to privacy under the Due Process Clause of the 14th Amendment, extending it to a woman's decision to have an abortion. This right was to be balanced against the state's interests, namely in regulating abortions to protect women's health and the potentiality of human life, allowing for state regulation in certain stages of pregnancy.

However, on June 24, 2022, Roe v. Wade was overturned based on the court's interpretation that the Constitution does not explicitly guarantee the right to abortion, indicating that this issue should be decided by individual states rather than at the federal level. This resulted in a patchwork of inconsistent state laws. This decision underscores the evolving legal landscape around abortion rights, reflecting varying interpretations of constitutional principles, especially concerning the right to privacy and its application in the context of abortion rights.

Abortion is a deeply personal decision made by some expecting mothers, who have to consider potential challenges like bringing children into a life of neglect or poverty, complex issues like the sanctity of life, and alternative solutions like going through with the birth and giving up their baby for adoption.

Proposals to Encourage Consensus

1. Achieving national peace and unity depends on a balanced abortion policy anchored in broad consensus. The sooner this can be achieved, the better. Congressional action is essential to guide the nation toward this agreement, addressing the need for interstate consistency. While it may not fulfill every individual's expectation, pursuing a solution that garners wide acceptance is vital for mitigating this divisive national issue, easing shared anxieties, and restoring societal harmony.

2. Balancing individual needs with societal concerns requires setting reasonable limitations, especially for "medical necessity." Respecting the judgment of medical professionals suggests that a national standard for such limitations might be preferable, reducing the need for state-by-state variations and potentially giving states a more limited role in these decisions. The government should remain impartial on personal rights, neither advocating for nor obstructing access. While religious groups have the right to set their internal guidelines and practices according to their beliefs, extending these rules to affect non-members through public policy or law, especially in public institutions, can conflict with the constitutional principles of religious freedom and the separation of church and state. Safe and regulated procedures are crucial to avoiding the horrors of the past.

3. Birth control and emergency contraception should be widely available to help reduce unwanted pregnancies and thereby lower abortion rates.

4. While complex, abortion should be a matter of individual choice, taking into consideration the potential impact of another life.

5. Using abortion as a primary contraception method should be widely discouraged, and counseling for those undergoing multiple abortions should be available.

6. Health insurance companies should be banned from denying coverage for abortions. While pregnancy prevention is possible, denying coverage could disproportionately affect low-income women. Fairness, though not a legal right, is an essential ethical consideration in policymaking, reflecting principles embedded in our Constitution.

Religious Freedom

Religious freedom, a cornerstone of American democracy, intertwines with various aspects of national life, including education, law, and public policy, reflecting the diverse religious landscape of the United States. Understanding the distinct approaches of each party is crucial for grasping this issue's impact on American society and politics.

The Democratic Party typically has a broad interpretation of religious freedom, advocating for the separation of church and state as a fundamental principle. This approach ensures that government does not favor or discriminate against any religion, promoting a pluralistic society where all faiths are respected. Democrats often focus on protecting the rights of minority religions and non-religious individuals, and they are cautious about legislation or policies that might allow for religious-based discrimination under the guise of religious freedom. Their stance reflects a commitment to inclusivity and protecting individual rights in a diverse society.

The Republican Party often interprets religious freedom as protecting the rights of individuals and institutions to act in accordance with their religious beliefs, even in public or commercial settings. This includes supporting the rights of businesses and individuals to make decisions based on their faith and advocating for the presence of religious values in public life, such as in education and government. Republicans are more likely to support legislation that they believe defends these freedoms, even if others see such measures as discriminatory. Their perspective is grounded in a view of religious freedom as a fundamental right that should not be infringed upon by government intervention.

Religion in Government

Democrats say: "We honor the central place of faith in our lives. Like our Founders, we believe that our nation, our communities, and our lives are made vastly stronger and richer by faith and the countless acts of justice and mercy it inspires. We believe that change comes not from the top-down, but from the bottom-up, and that few are closer to the people than our churches, synagogues, temples, and mosques."

Democrats also say they believe in faith-based service organizations. They add "… there is no conflict between supporting faith-based institutions and respecting our Constitution. We will ensure that public funds are not used to proselytize or discriminate."

Republicans believe that: "… our Constitution guarantees the free exercise of religion and forbids any religious test for public office, and it likewise prohibits the establishment of a state-sponsored creed." And they believe: "The public display of the Ten Commandments does not violate the U.S. Constitution and accurately reflects the Judeo-Christian heritage of our country." They also: "... affirm every citizen's right to apply religious values to public policy and the right of faith-based organizations to participate fully in public programs without renouncing their beliefs, removing religious objects or symbols, or becoming subject to government-imposed hiring practices."

Concerns have been raised about how some Republican policies may allow religion to influence government proceedings. Critics argue that this could challenge the constitutional principle of separation of church and state. They suggest that religious organizations seek to influence government decisions without being subject to governmental control, which also might contradict the Constitution's intentions. This perspective underscores the tension between religious freedom and governmental neutrality in the United States.

The religious landscape in the United States has undergone notable changes, especially in recent years. Data from the Pew Research Center indicates that most American adults (55%) seldom or never attend religious services, while only 36% report attending at least once a week . Public Religion Research Institute (PRRI), an American nonprofit, nonpartisan research organization, highlights a continued decline in church attendance, noting a drop in weekly attendance from 19% in 2019 to 16% in 2023, a trend observed across various religious denominations.[20-21] Despite this, those who remain active in their religious communities tend to be highly satisfied with their congregations, with more than 80% expressing optimism about their church's future. This satisfaction spans across Christian denominations.[20-21]

The pandemic has also played a role in these longer-term trends of decreasing religious participation over the past two decades. Gallup reports that U.S. church attendance remains lower than pre-pandemic levels, with an average of 30% attending services from 2020 onwards, compared to 34% between 2016 and 2019.[20-22]

There is a rich, complex, and diverse range of religious beliefs and practices across the world that offer solace, unity, and moral guidance to many. However, it is essential to recognize that religious differences have historically been a source of conflict and strife. The Arab-Israeli conflict exemplifies the intricate interplay of religious and geopolitical tensions. Further, in various parts of the world, including some Muslim-majority regions, there have been notable cases of religious intolerance and hostility towards other faiths like Hinduism, Sikhism, and Buddhism. Nothing creates fear and hostility more than ignorance and distrust. Additionally, intra-religious conflicts, such as those between Shia and Sunni Muslims, have deep historical roots and add another layer of complexity.

These long-standing conflicts, however, should not overshadow the positive intent of many religions to uphold peace, show compassion, provide moral instruction, and encourage cooperation. Any negative impact that a religion may have is not a reflection of all adherents or communities within that faith.

Understanding and addressing the root causes of religious conflicts is essential for fostering healthy international relationships and moving toward global peace and harmony. This requires an awareness of the diverse beliefs within religions, the historical background of any tensions, and the role of religion in the wider socio-political context. The fact that religious leaders and their religious tenets govern many countries should reinforce the importance of America maintaining a separation between religion and state, as enshrined in some constitutional frameworks. This separation helps to prevent religious conflicts from influencing governmental decisions and ensures the equal treatment of all citizens, regardless of their faith.

The official scriptures of Christianity and Islam – the Bible and the Quran, respectively – have played significant roles in shaping belief systems and worldviews for billions of people. However, it is essential to recognize that interpretations of these texts can vary widely and can be sources of misinformation or conflict.

In the case of the Bible, some interpretations conflict with specific scientific theories like evolution. However, many religious individuals and scholars have found ways to reconcile their faith with science by viewing religious texts as allegorical or metaphorical rather than literal. Various religious denominations and religious scientists fully embrace scientific principles and see no inherent contradiction between their faith and scientific understanding.

Regarding the Quran, it is crucial to emphasize that interpretations of its teachings vary widely. While some verses have been interpreted in a way that appears to promote violence, prominent scholars emphasize that those positions were given in a historical context that no longer exists, and numerous passages emphasize peace, compassion, and justice. Most Muslims, 75% to 80% according to Pew Research, reject extremist interpretations and actively work for peace and interfaith dialogue.[20-27] There are about two billion Muslims and 2.3 billion Christians in the world.

Does the Quran Say to Kill Non-believers?

There are various interpretations of Quranic directives about non-believers, often depending on the context of revelation and broader Islamic principles. The Quran does contain verses that discuss the relationship between Muslims and non-believers. However, it is essential to understand these verses in their historical context. Many of these verses were revealed during times of conflict and were specific to situations of war and aggression. They are not blanket directives for all times and situations. For instance, the Quran instructs Muslims to treat non-Muslims courteously in a spirit of kindness and generosity, given that they are not hostile towards Muslims (Quran 60:8-9).[20-24]

Islam, generally recognized as a religion of peace, does not teach hatred against anyone. The Quran teaches Muslims to be compassionate to all "mankind," regardless of creed or religion. Muslims are allowed to have non-Muslim friends, and the motto of the Ahmadiyya Muslim Community, "love for all, hatred for none," is grounded in Islamic teachings.[20-25]

Prophet Muhammad demonstrated tolerance and kindness towards non-Muslims, interacting amicably, visiting the sick, exchanging gifts, and conducting business with them. He also showed respect towards Christian delegations and other religious groups, setting an example his companions emulated.[20-26]

It is crucial to note that Islamic teachings emphasize justice, compassion, and mercy. The actions and sayings of the Prophet Muhammad, as well as the teachings of the Quran, have been interpreted and practiced in various ways throughout Islamic history. However, the fundamental message of Islam is about peace, respect, and understanding among people of all faiths.

There is no head of the Islam religion. Islamic leadership is decentralized mainly and diffused, varying significantly across different regions, sects, and communities. Within the Muslim community (Ummah), it typically takes the form of local religious leaders, scholars, and clerics, known as imams or sheikhs, who lead prayers, offer guidance, and provide religious education. Their influence and authority are generally confined to their local communities or specific groups.

Additionally, the Sunni and Shia branches of Islam, the two main sects within the religion, have different approaches to religious authority:

- Sunni Islam: This sect does not have a formal clergy system. Religious scholars, known as 'ulama, play an influential role in interpreting Islamic teachings and law. Imams in Sunni Islam primarily lead prayers and do not have a hierarchical structure akin to that of a global leader.
- Shia Islam: Shia Muslims have a more structured clerical hierarchy. Senior religious leaders, known as ayatollahs, have significant religious authority, especially in countries with large Shia populations like Iran. The concept of "Marja' al-Taqlid" (Source of Emulation) is important in Shia Islam, where followers emulate a senior cleric's religious interpretations and rulings.

It is essential to recognize that religion, like any complex human phenomenon, can have positive and negative aspects. While it can be misused to justify violence and intolerance, it also serves as a source of moral guidance, community, and charitable efforts for countless individuals and organizations. Therefore, religion must be considered a multifaceted and nuanced aspect of human culture, capable of promoting good and being misused for harmful purposes. How individuals interpret and practice their faith varies greatly and is influenced by cultural, historical, and personal factors.

If the world had no religions, there should be less conflict, but it may necessitate teaching or regulating morality through laws or philosophy. There could be concerns about the loss of cultural identity and meaning or purpose. Similarly, a world dominated by a single religion might experience decreased conflict, greater uniformity, and centralized religious authority, but it could also limit freedom of belief and expression and lead to a decline in cultural diversity. Imagine if the Islam, Jewish, Christian and the other religions combined their doctrines into a single one. One world religion might follow and perhaps peace might ensue. As previously discussed, cultural diversity will diminish over time as the global spread of ideas, cultural convergence, technological expansion, and evolving values impact our societies.

Role of God, Morals, and Religious Freedom

Laws should not be biased towards the beliefs of any specific religion or group of religions at the expense of the freedoms of other religions or non-religious citizens. Laws, in their nature, represent certain moral points of view. Laws based on specific morals may be reasonable as long as those morals are not shaped by the agenda of any organized religion and are universally relevant and widely accepted by all citizens.

In the opinion of our Founding Fathers, organized religion has no place in influencing the creation or interpretation of laws – laws must be based on unbiased reasoned judgment of people with no personal or organizational agenda. Jefferson wrote a letter to the Danbury Baptist Association in 1802 to answer a letter from them written in October 1801.

Jefferson's Letter to the Danbury Baptist Association in 1802

(Bold for emphasis)

To messers Nehemiah Dodge, Ephraim Robbins, & Stephen S. Nelson a committee of the Danbury Baptist association in the state of Connecticut.

Gentlemen,

The affectionate sentiments of esteem & approbation which you are so good as to express towards me, on behalf of the Danbury Baptist association, give me the highest satisfaction. my duties dictate a faithful & zealous pursuit of the interests of my constituents, and in proportion as they are persuaded of my fidelity to those duties, the discharge of them becomes more & more pleasing.

Believing with you that religion is a matter which lies solely between man & his god, that he owes account to none other for his faith or his worship, that the legitimate powers of government reach actions only, and not opinions, I contemplate with sovereign reverence that act of the whole American people which declared that their legislature should make no law respecting an establishment of religion, or prohibiting the free exercise thereof, thus building a wall of separation between church and state. [Congress thus inhibited from acts respecting religion, and the Executive authorized only to execute their acts, I have refrained from presenting even occasional performances of devotion presented indeed legally where an Executive is the legal head of a national church, but subject here, as religious exercises only to the voluntary regulations and discipline of each respective sect.] Adhering to this expression of the supreme will of the nation in behalf of the rights of conscience, I shall see with sincere satisfaction the progress of those sentiments which tend to restore to man all his natural rights, convinced he has no natural right in opposition to his social duties.

I reciprocate your kind prayers for the protection and blessing of the common Father and creator of man, and tender you for yourselves and your religious association, assurances of my high respect & esteem.

(signed) Thomas Jefferson

Jan.1.1802.[181-09]

"Thomas Jefferson was a man of deep religious conviction – his conviction was that religion was a very personal matter, one which the government had no business getting involved in."[181-09]

The Democratic Party emphasizes the importance of religious freedom, endorsing the idea that every individual has the right to practice their faith freely without government interference. The party supports a pluralistic society where morals and values, influenced by diverse religious and secular beliefs, coexist and are respected. Democrats advocate for policies that protect the separation of church and state while ensuring that religious institutions and individuals can practice their faith. They also stress the importance of moral principles in shaping public policy, advocating for justice, equality, and compassion in a way that respects the diverse religious landscape of the United States. This stance includes supporting the rights of individuals to follow their moral and religious convictions in their personal lives while ensuring that such convictions do not infringe on the rights and freedoms of others.

The Republican Party firmly upholds the significance of religious freedom, viewing it as a cornerstone of American democracy. Republicans often emphasize the role of Judeo-Christian values in shaping the nation's moral and ethical foundations and advocate for policies that reflect these principles. The party champions the protection of religious expression in public life and opposes government actions that limit religious freedoms. Republicans support the rights of religious organizations and individuals to practice their beliefs without interference and advocate for the freedom of religious expression across all aspects of society, including in schools and public spaces. They also frequently stress the importance of traditional family values and morals, advocating for legislation and policies that protect them. Overall, the Republican position emphasizes a strong connection between the nation's prosperity and its adherence to religious and moral principles.

Cultural History

The approach to cultural history, especially in the context of contentious issues like Confederate symbolism, cultural revisionism, and renaming public places, sharply divides the Democratic and Republican parties in the United States. These issues are deeply interwoven with the nation's complex historical narrative, touching on the themes of race, heritage, and national identity.

Democrats advocate for a reevaluation and, often, revision of cultural history, including the removal of Confederate statues and the renaming of public spaces named after Confederate figures. This stance is rooted in a desire to confront and rectify historical injustices and to promote a more inclusive narrative that acknowledges the darker chapters of American history, such as slavery and racial discrimination. Democrats tend to view these acts of revisionism as necessary steps towards healing and progress, reflecting a broader commitment to social justice and equality.

Republicans, on the other hand, typically defend the preservation of traditional historical symbols, including Confederate monuments, viewing them as part of the nation's heritage and cultural history. They often oppose the renaming of public spaces and the removal of statues, arguing that these actions amount to erasing history. The Republican stance emphasizes the importance of maintaining historical continuity and learning from the past rather than revising it. This approach reflects a broader view that upholds traditional narratives and values, seeing them as foundational to the nation's identity and continuity.

In conclusion, the exploration of social issues and human rights in the context of American politics reveals deep ideological divides between the Democratic and Republican parties. These differences, reflecting contrasting interpretations of equality, liberty, and cultural values, significantly shape policy and societal discourse. Whether it is LGBTQ+ rights, gender identity, abortion, religious freedom, immigration, or cultural history, these topics are not just political but reflect the evolving dynamics of American society. Understanding these divergent perspectives offers key insights into the ongoing debate and struggle over the direction and nature of social change in the United States. The only way that Americans can become truly united is if the two parties can find common ground and compromise on some of their principles. Negotiation and compromise are the way to unity. Otherwise, our country will remain unsettled and its citizens at odds with each other.

Recap - *Social Issues and Human Rights*

2023-2024 Positions on Social Issues and Human Rights		
Area of Concern	**Democrats**	**Republicans**
LGBTQ+ Rights	Advocate for LGBTQ+ rights, supporting policies like same-sex marriage, anti-discrimination laws, and the protection of transgender rights, reflecting their commitment to equality and social justice.	Positions vary, with many members traditionally upholding conservative values and opposing measures like same-sex marriage and expansive anti-discrimination laws, though there is a growing acceptance of some LGBTQ+ rights within the party.
Sexual Orientation and Gender Identity	Support the rights and protections of individuals based on sexual orientation and gender identity, advocating for anti-discrimination laws and equal treatment, as part of their broader commitment to LGBTQ+ rights and inclusivity.	Demonstrate a cautious or opposing stance on issues related to sexual orientation and gender identity, favoring limited government intervention, and prioritizing religious freedom and personal liberties, though there is a growing diversity of opinions within the party.
Traditional Gender Roles	Promote a progressive and flexible view of gender roles, advocating for gender equality and challenging traditional norms to support diverse identities and opportunities in society.	Uphold more traditional views of gender, emphasizing conventional family values and roles, while showing cautiousness towards policies that significantly alter established gender dynamics.
Abortion	Staunchly support the right to abortion, viewing it as a crucial aspect of women's reproductive rights and healthcare, and advocate for maintaining legal access to abortion services.	Hold a pro-life stance, advocating for restrictions or outright bans on abortion, often based on moral and religious grounds, while emphasizing alternatives like adoption and support for traditional family values.

Religious Freedom	Champion a broad interpretation of religious freedom, emphasizing the separation of church and state to ensure equal respect for all faiths and protection against religious discrimination, while upholding the rights of both religious and non-religious individuals in a diverse society.	View religious freedom as the right of individuals and institutions to live and operate according to their religious beliefs, advocating for the integration of these values into public life and policy, and often supporting legislation that defends these rights, even in public or commercial spheres.
Religion in Government	Advocates for a clear separation of church and state, ensuring government neutrality towards religion while protecting individuals' freedom to practice their faith.	Supports a robust presence of religious values in government, advocating for policies that reflect Judeo-Christian principles while championing the freedom of religious expression.
Role of God, Morals, and Religious Freedom	Champions religious freedom and pluralism, advocating for the separation of church and state while ensuring policies reflect compassion and equality, respecting a diverse spectrum of religious and secular beliefs.	Emphasizes the integral role of Judeo-Christian values in America's foundation, advocating for religious freedom in public life and policies that uphold traditional morals and family values.

Cultural History	Advocate for a reevaluation of cultural history, supporting the removal of Confederate symbols and the renaming of spaces named after Confederate figures, as part of a broader effort to address historical injustices and promote a more inclusive and honest portrayal of American history.	Favor preserving traditional historical symbols, including Confederate monuments and spaces named after Confederate figures, advocating for the maintenance of established narratives which they view as integral to honoring the nation's heritage and learning from its history.

PART III: FUTURE GOVERNANCE

Chapter 9: Looking Ahead

Our Founding Fathers fought and worked hard to create a government for America that has been doing a respectable job at preventing power being concentrated in a single individual or group, as in a monarchy. And, it has allowed gradual and controlled turnover of power every four to eight years. That is remarkable in the world. However, we may have now come to a point in the evolution of our government that we have become a "duopoly," where the entire power of governing America is shared between the two major political parties; and, more specifically, their leaders, who dictate the party agendas. The parties have structured political donations so that most of the money goes to them. They control who can donate money and to whom. Within their respective party they control who gets the benefit of the vast party coffers for campaign funding and who gets the media attention to be elected or reelected.

In our political duopoly, the domination of two parties has led to limited voter choices and heightened polarization, often resulting in extreme positions. This system tends to overlook minority interests, as the focus shifts to appealing to a broader electorate. Innovation and new ideas may stagnate as the electoral system continues to favor established parties, making it challenging for new or smaller parties to emerge. Such a structure can reduce the accountability of these parties, as they face little competition, potentially leading to voter disenfranchisement, especially among those who do not align closely with either of the dominant parties.

The question is: Does this structure work for the American people anymore and will it work in our future?

Chapter 10: Recommendations

In a more serious vein, at the heart of the Constitution are the "rights and needs" of America's citizens. Rights are inalienable and do not change. However, our needs do. Given the state of our Congress and how it is failing to fulfil our needs, we may need to consider changing how we are represented.

In contemplating the dynamic nature of society and governance, it is essential to recognize the delicate balance between the inalienable rights enshrined in the U.S. Constitution and the evolving needs of the populace. The apparent inadequacy of Congress in addressing these changing needs raises questions about whether constitutional reform is necessary, particularly concerning the structure and function of Congress. A discerning approach is needed to differentiate between the timeless rights that must be upheld and specific provisions that may no longer be relevant in the modern context.

Central to this discussion is the Constitution's role in maintaining a balance of power, a fundamental aspect of governance. Convening a Constitutional Convention would represent a significant shift from traditional processes and may be needed to address these concerns.

> **Proposal: One possibility, as discussed earlier, is to change from a Congress-driven decision-making process to one where legal changes are enacted upon an 80% approval rate in a national vote, ensuring more direct democratic engagement.**
>
> **The approval rate needs to be higher than a simple majority in order to protect all classes of citizens. Congress and state legislatures would be involved in drafting the proposed legal changes, but the approval would be by popular vote (via a block-chain, secure voting system). This innovative proposal necessitates thoroughly considering the practical and legal challenges inherent in significantly altering the constitutional framework, particularly given the high threshold set for approval.**

This reflection underscores the importance of ongoing adaptation and reassessment in democratic governance to ensure it remains responsive and relevant to the citizenry's rights and needs.

Given that Congress is defined by our Constitution, then our Constitution may need to change. When we consider the state of our Constitution, we need to distinguish the rights that are inviolable and those which need to be updated. In doing so, we need to keep in mind the purpose of government, which is to maintain a balance of power.

> **Proposal: Call a Constitutional Convention to redraft the Constitution, but only if we use the above representation structure. The revision must be approved by 80% of citizens in a national vote, not by Congress and not ratified state by state. We need to ensure consistency across the country, which may come at the expense of maintaining differences between states. Besides, the Senate would maintain the states' perspectives when nationally-approved bills reach their desks.**

Absolutism, defined by an unwavering refusal to compromise, poses a grave threat to our democracy. Rigid intransigence on critical issues not only leads to stalemates but also hampers progress across various fronts. Recognizing that nothing in life is absolute is vital for the health of our democratic system. Change, whether for better or worse, is an inherent aspect of life and society.

Moreover, while some may view an absolute stance as a shrewd negotiating tactic, aiming to ensure any compromise swings in their direction, this approach often backfires. If the opposing party detects this tactic and responds by entrenching their position even more deeply, it results in a deadlock where neither party is willing to budge. This scenario, far from fostering productive negotiation, only exacerbates the divide and impedes the possibility of finding a middle ground.

Chapter 11. Summation

Giving the sheer volume of information above about the two major parties, a simple analogy might be helpful to sum things up:

An Analogy

Democrats are like idealistic teenagers, eager to try new things and who may care as much about their friends (allies) as their family. They often show less concern for costs than the benefits to them, their family, and friends, may approach religious practices with a lighter touch, and are driven by a belief that they can change the world. Their approach to problem-solving is often fueled by passion and urgency, reflecting the boundless energy and enthusiasm typical of youth.

Republicans, on the other hand, can be likened to these teenagers' more cautious and conservative parents. They fondly recall the "good old days" or reminisce about tougher times, and are vigilant about financial matters, often keeping a tight rein on expenditures. They may encourage regular religious attendance and strive, though not always successfully, to instill responsibility in the younger generation. They yearn for a return to the values and norms of their youth and place a high value on tradition and established methods.

This analogy, comparing Democrats to adventurous teenagers and Republicans to their more traditional parents, is meant to illustrate the distinct perspectives and values of the two parties in a non-derogatory way. Another was of looking at the two perspectives fundamentally is that Republicans are advocating for keeping control within the states while the Democrats are advocating for creating consistency across all the states.

Both Democrats and Republicans possess valid viewpoints, and it is crucial to acknowledge and respect the differences between them. Also, of course, not all Democrats think like other Democrats and not all Republicans think like their fellow Republicans. Our Founding Fathers understood that to address differing opinions effectively, the implementation of "checks and balances" among the three branches of government would be essential. While it's unlikely that this system will bring universal agreement on every issue, its proper functioning ensures ongoing progress and governance.

Regardless of our different views, we MUST nurture our democracy to keep it vibrant and dynamic while striving to reunite America into a cohesive and harmonious community of citizens. As citizens, we must protect our government's critical balance of power. So that, together, we can and will continue to do great things for everyone on this tiny blue planet.

Lastly, we have these realities we must always face:

1. There will always be people on the extremes who harm or help others, who obey or break the law, who are greedy or generous, and who either agree or disagree with our views.
2. Women will find a way to an abortion if that is their intent.
3. Jobs will always be important as they sustain people by giving them opportunities to use their energy and creativity, providing sustenance, self-worth and fulfillment.
4. As long as we live in a world with diverse governance, religions, and priorities, conflict and war will persist. Establishing a unified global government, a single religion, and a universal rule of law based on one Constitution will be a long time from now but would go a long way toward ending strife.
5. Humans are curious beings and will always have a thirst for knowledge, whether memorized through education or served up by artificial intelligence.
6. Taxes (and death). Benjamin Franklin famously wrote in a letter to Jean-Baptiste Leroy in 1789, "Our new Constitution is now established, everything seems to promise it will be durable; but, in this world, nothing is certain except death and taxes." Lifespans may be expanded but taxes will always be around.
7. A need for food, water, air, and transportation, unless quantum mechanics' entanglement negates the need.[191]
8. Addictions, people (and governments) that profit from them, and people who fall victim to them.
9. Someone in charge.
10. Sex and procreation.
11. Money or other means of exchange.
12. Liars and cheats in politics. ("Repeat a lie often enough and people will begin to believe it," attributed to Nazi Minister of Propaganda, Joesph Goebbels)
13. Dishonorable and honorable government representatives.
14. New issues to address and people willing to take on those challenges.

In the near future, advancements in Artificial Intelligence and robotics could lead to a decreased need for professions such as lawyers, medical diagnosticians, managers, and vehicle drivers, among others. This significant transformation has the potential to drastically reshape our economy. Change, you got to love it!

And, someday, there will no longer be:

1. Ethnicities
2. Multi-level governments
3. Multiple constitutions
4. Population growth (we will eventually run out of food, water, land, air)
5. Multiple religions
6. Disease
7. Wars
8. Crime

Then ask yourself these questions:

1. How do you want to be governed?
   a. By one person dictating to you (top-down)?
   b. By your local community dictating to you (bottom up)?
   c. By one party (like China)?
   d. By rule of law?
   e. By your own choice?
2. How do you want order maintained?
   a. By force?
   b. By your conscience?
   c. By consensus (i.e., rule of law)?
3. Would you prefer to have to ask for permission or have the freedom to give yourself permission?

   Your answers above are the choices you make when you vote or when you don't. Please vote!

THE END

THE CONSTITUTION OF THE UNITED STATES OF AMERICA

The following text is a transcription of the Constitution in its original form.

We the People of the United States, in Order to form a more perfect Union, establish Justice, ensure domestic Tranquility, provide for the common defence, promote the general Welfare, and secure the Blessings of Liberty to ourselves and our Posterity, do ordain and establish this Constitution for the United States of America.

Article I

Section. 1.

All legislative Powers herein granted shall be vested in a Congress of the United States, which shall consist of a Senate and House of Representatives.

Section. 2.

The House of Representatives shall be composed of Members chosen every second Year by the People of the several States, and the Electors in each State shall have the Qualifications requisite for Electors of the most numerous Branch of the State Legislature.

No Person shall be a Representative who shall not have attained to the Age of twenty-five Years and been seven Years a Citizen of the United States, and who shall not, when elected, be an Inhabitant of that State in which he shall be chosen.

Representatives and direct Taxes shall be apportioned among the several States which may be included within this Union, according to their respective Numbers, which shall be determined by adding to the whole Number of free Persons, including those bound to Service for a Term of Years, and excluding Indians not taxed, three fifths of all other Persons. The actual Enumeration shall be made within three Years after the first Meeting of the Congress of the United States, and within every subsequent Term of ten Years, in such Manner as they shall by Law direct. The Number of Representatives shall not exceed one for every thirty Thousand, but each State shall have at Least one Representative; and until such enumeration shall be made, the State of New Hampshire shall be entitled to chuse [sic] three, Massachusetts eight, Rhode-

Island and Providence Plantations one, Connecticut five, New-York six, New Jersey four, Pennsylvania eight, Delaware one, Maryland six, Virginia ten, North Carolina five, South Carolina five, and Georgia three.

When vacancies happen in the Representation from any State, the Executive Authority thereof shall issue Writs of Election to fill such Vacancies.

The House of Representatives shall chuse [sic] their Speaker and other Officers; and shall have the sole Power of Impeachment.

Section. 3.

The Senate of the United States shall be composed of two Senators from each State, chosen by the Legislature thereof for six Years; and each Senator shall have one Vote.

Immediately after they shall be assembled in Consequence of the first Election, they shall be divided as equally as may be into three Classes. The Seats of the Senators of the first Class shall be vacated at the Expiration of the second Year, of the second Class at the Expiration of the fourth Year, and of the third Class at the Expiration of the sixth Year, so that one third may be chosen every second Year; and if Vacancies happen by Resignation, or otherwise, during the Recess of the Legislature of any State, the Executive thereof may make temporary Appointments until the next Meeting of the Legislature, which shall then fill such Vacancies.

No Person shall be a Senator who shall not have attained to the Age of thirty Years and been nine Years a Citizen of the United States, and who shall not, when elected, be an Inhabitant of that State for which he shall be chosen.

The Vice President of the United States shall be President of the Senate, but shall have no Vote, unless they be equally divided.

The Senate shall chuse [sic] their other Officers, and also a President pro tempore, in the Absence of the Vice President, or when he shall exercise the Office of President of the United States.

The Senate shall have the sole Power to try all Impeachments. When sitting for that Purpose, they shall be on Oath or Affirmation. When the President of the United States is tried, the Chief Justice shall preside: And no Person shall be convicted without the Concurrence of two thirds of the Members present.

Judgment in Cases of Impeachment shall not extend further than to removal from Office, and disqualification to hold and enjoy any Office of honor, Trust or Profit under the United States:

but the Party convicted shall nevertheless be liable and subject to Indictment, Trial, Judgment and Punishment, according to Law.

Section. 4.

The Times, Places and Manner of holding Elections for Senators and Representatives, shall be prescribed in each State by the Legislature thereof; but the Congress may at any time by Law make or alter such Regulations, except as to the Places of chusing Senators.

The Congress shall assemble at least once in every Year, and such Meeting shall be on the first Monday in December, unless they shall by Law appoint a different Day.

Section. 5.

Each House shall be the Judge of the Elections, Returns and Qualifications of its own Members, and a Majority of each shall constitute a Quorum to do Business; but a smaller Number may adjourn from day to day, and may be authorized to compel the Attendance of absent Members, in such Manner, and under such Penalties as each House may provide.

Each House may determine the Rules of its Proceedings, punish its Members for disorderly Behaviour, and, with the Concurrence of two thirds, expel a Member.

Each House shall keep a Journal of its Proceedings, and from time to time publish the same, excepting such Parts as may in their Judgment require Secrecy; and the Yeas and Nays of the Members of either House on any question shall, at the Desire of one fifth of those Present, be entered on the Journal. Neither House, during the Session of Congress, shall, without the Consent of the other, adjourn for more than three days, nor to any other Place than that in which the two Houses shall be sitting.

Section. 6.

The Senators and Representatives shall receive a Compensation for their Services, to be ascertained by Law, and paid out of the Treasury of the United States. They shall in all Cases, except Treason, Felony and Breach of the Peace, be privileged from Arrest during their Attendance at the Session of their respective Houses, and in going to and returning from the same; and for any Speech or Debate in either House, they shall not be questioned in any other Place.

No Senator or Representative shall, during the Time for which he was elected, be appointed to any civil Office under the Authority of the United States, which shall have been created, or the

Emoluments whereof shall have been increased during such time; and no Person holding any Office under the United States, shall be a Member of either House during his Continuance in Office.

Section. 7.

All Bills for raising Revenue shall originate in the House of Representatives; but the Senate may propose or concur with Amendments as on other Bills.

Every Bill which shall have passed the House of Representatives and the Senate, shall, before it become a Law, be presented to the President of the United States: If he approve he shall sign it, but if not he shall return it, with his Objections to that House in which it shall have originated, who shall enter the Objections at large on their Journal, and proceed to reconsider it. If after such Reconsideration two thirds of that House shall agree to pass the Bill, it shall be sent, together with the Objections, to the other House, by which it shall likewise be reconsidered, and if approved by two thirds of that House, it shall become a Law. But in all such Cases the Votes of both Houses shall be determined by yeas and Nays, and the Names of the Persons voting for and against the Bill shall be entered on the Journal of each House respectively. If any Bill shall not be returned by the President within ten Days (Sundays excepted) after it shall have been presented to him, the Same shall be a Law, in like Manner as if he had signed it, unless the Congress by their Adjournment prevent its Return, in which Case it shall not be a Law.

Every Order, Resolution, or Vote to which the Concurrence of the Senate and House of Representatives may be necessary (except on a question of Adjournment) shall be presented to the President of the United States; and before the Same shall take Effect, shall be approved by him, or being disapproved by him, shall be repassed by two thirds of the Senate and House of Representatives, according to the Rules and Limitations prescribed in the Case of a Bill.

Section. 8.

The Congress shall have Power To lay and collect Taxes, Duties, Imposts and Excises, to pay the Debts and provide for the common Defence and general Welfare of the United States; but all Duties, Imposts and Excises shall be uniform throughout the United States.

To borrow Money on the credit of the United States.

To regulate Commerce with foreign Nations, and among the several States, and with the Indian Tribes.

To establish a uniform Rule of Naturalization, and uniform Laws on the subject of Bankruptcies throughout the United States.

To coin Money, regulate the Value thereof, and of foreign Coin, and fix the Standard of Weights and Measures.

To provide for the Punishment of counterfeiting the Securities and current Coin of the United States.

To establish Post Offices and post Roads.

To promote the Progress of Science and useful Arts, by securing for limited Times to Authors and Inventors the exclusive Right to their respective Writings and Discoveries.

To constitute Tribunals inferior to the supreme Court.

To define and punish Piracies and Felonies committed on the high Seas, and Offences against the Law of Nations.

To declare War, grant Letters of Marque and Reprisal, and make Rules concerning Captures on Land and Water.

To raise and support Armies, but no Appropriation of Money to that Use shall be for a longer Term than two Years.

To provide and maintain a Navy.

To make Rules for the Government and Regulation of the land and naval Forces.

To provide for calling forth the Militia to execute the Laws of the Union, suppress Insurrections and repel Invasions.

To provide for organizing, arming, and disciplining, the Militia, and for governing such Part of them as may be employed in the Service of the United States, reserving to the States respectively, the Appointment of the Officers, and the Authority of training the Militia according to the discipline prescribed by Congress.

To exercise exclusive Legislation in all Cases whatsoever, over such District (not exceeding ten Miles square) as may, by Cession of particular States, and the Acceptance of Congress, become the Seat of the Government of the United States, and to exercise like Authority over all Places purchased by the Consent of the Legislature of the State in which the Same shall be, for the Erection of Forts, Magazines, Arsenals, dock-Yards, and other needful Buildings;--And

To make all Laws which shall be necessary and proper for carrying into Execution the foregoing Powers, and all other Powers vested by this Constitution in the Government of the United States, or in any Department or Officer thereof.

Section. 9.

The Migration or Importation of such Persons as any of the States now existing shall think proper to admit, shall not be prohibited by the Congress prior to the Year one thousand eight hundred and eight, but a Tax or duty may be imposed on such Importation, not exceeding ten dollars for each Person.

The Privilege of the Writ of Habeas Corpus shall not be suspended, unless when in Cases of Rebellion or Invasion the public Safety may require it.

No Bill of Attainder or ex post facto Law shall be passed.

No Capitation, or other direct, Tax shall be laid, unless in Proportion to the Census or enumeration herein before directed to be taken.

No Tax or Duty shall be laid on Articles exported from any State.

No Preference shall be given by any Regulation of Commerce or Revenue to the Ports of one State over those of another; nor shall Vessels bound to, or from, one State, be obliged to enter, clear, or pay Duties in another.

No Money shall be drawn from the Treasury, but in Consequence of Appropriations made by Law; and a regular Statement and Account of the Receipts and Expenditures of all public Money shall be published from time to time.

No Title of Nobility shall be granted by the United States: And no Person holding any Office of Profit or Trust under them, shall, without the Consent of the Congress, accept of any present, Emolument, Office, or Title, of any kind whatever, from any King, Prince, or foreign State.

Section. 10.

No State shall enter into any Treaty, Alliance, or Confederation; grant Letters of Marque and Reprisal; coin Money; emit Bills of Credit; make any Thing but gold and silver Coin a Tender in Payment of Debts; pass any Bill of Attainder, ex post facto Law, or Law impairing the Obligation of Contracts, or grant any Title of Nobility.

No State shall, without the Consent of the Congress, lay any Imposts or Duties on Imports or Exports, except what may be absolutely necessary for executing it's inspection Laws: and the net Produce of all Duties and Imposts, laid by any State on Imports or Exports, shall be for the Use of the Treasury of the United States; and all such Laws shall be subject to the Revision and Control of the Congress.

No State shall, without the Consent of Congress, lay any Duty of Tonnage, keep Troops, or Ships of War in time of Peace, enter into any Agreement or Compact with another State, or with a foreign Power, or engage in War, unless actually invaded, or in such imminent Danger as will not admit of delay.

Article II

Section. 1.

The executive Power shall be vested in a President of the United States of America. He shall hold his Office during the Term of four Years, and, together with the Vice President, chosen for the same Term, be elected, as follows:

Each State shall appoint, in such Manner as the Legislature thereof may direct, a Number of Electors, equal to the whole Number of Senators and Representatives to which the State may be entitled in the Congress: but no Senator or Representative, or Person holding an Office of Trust or Profit under the United States, shall be appointed an Elector.

The Electors shall meet in their respective States, and vote by Ballot for two Persons, of whom one at least shall not be an Inhabitant of the same State with themselves. And they shall make a List of all the Persons voted for, and of the Number of Votes for each, which List they shall sign and certify, and transmit sealed to the Seat of the Government of the United States, directed to the President of the Senate. The President of the Senate shall, in the Presence of the Senate and House of Representatives, open all the Certificates, and the Votes shall then be counted. The Person having the greatest Number of Votes shall be the President, if such Number be a Majority of the whole Number of Electors appointed; and if there be more than one who have such Majority, and have an equal Number of Votes, then the House of Representatives shall immediately chuse [sic] by Ballot one of them for President; and if no Person have a Majority, then from the five highest on the List the said House shall in like Manner chuse [sic] the President. But in chusing the President, the Votes shall be taken by States, the Representation from each State having one Vote; A quorum for this purpose shall consist of a Member or Members from two thirds of the States, and a Majority of all the States shall be necessary to a Choice. In every Case, after the Choice of the President, the Person having the greatest Number of Votes of the Electors shall be the Vice President. But if there should remain two or more who have equal Votes, the Senate shall chuse [sic] from them by Ballot the Vice President.

The Congress may determine the Time of chusing the Electors, and the Day on which they shall give their Votes, which Day shall be the same throughout the United States.

No Person except a natural born Citizen, or a Citizen of the United States, at the time of the Adoption of this Constitution, shall be eligible to the Office of President; neither shall any Person be eligible to that Office who shall not have attained to the Age of thirty five Years, and been fourteen Years a Resident within the United States.

In Case of the Removal of the President from Office, or of his Death, Resignation, or Inability to discharge the Powers and Duties of the said Office, the Same shall devolve on the Vice President, and the Congress may by Law provide for the Case of Removal, Death, Resignation or Inability, both of the President and Vice President, declaring what Officer shall then act as President, and such Officer shall act accordingly, until the Disability be removed, or a President shall be elected.

The President shall, at stated Times, receive for his Services, a Compensation, which shall neither be increased nor diminished during the Period for which he shall have been elected, and he shall not receive within that Period any other Emolument from the United States, or any of them.

Before he enter on the Execution of his Office, he shall take the following Oath or Affirmation:--"I do solemnly swear (or affirm) that I will faithfully execute the Office of President of the United States, and will to the best of my Ability, preserve, protect and defend the Constitution of the United States."

Section. 2.

The President shall be Commander in Chief of the Army and Navy of the United States, and of the Militia of the several States, when called into the actual Service of the United States; he may require the Opinion, in writing, of the principal Officer in each of the executive Departments, upon any Subject relating to the Duties of their respective Offices, and he shall have Power to grant Reprieves and Pardons for Offences against the United States, except in Cases of Impeachment.

He shall have Power, by and with the Advice and Consent of the Senate, to make Treaties, provided two thirds of the Senators present concur; and he shall nominate, and by and with the Advice and Consent of the Senate, shall appoint Ambassadors, other public Ministers and Consuls, Judges of the Supreme Court, and all other Officers of the United States, whose

Appointments are not herein otherwise provided for, and which shall be established by Law: but the Congress may by Law vest the Appointment of such inferior Officers, as they think proper, in the President alone, in the Courts of Law, or in the Heads of Departments.

The President shall have Power to fill up all Vacancies that may happen during the Recess of the Senate, by granting Commissions which shall expire at the End of their next Session.

Section. 3.

He shall from time to time give to the Congress Information of the State of the Union, and recommend to their Consideration such Measures as he shall judge necessary and expedient; he may, on extraordinary Occasions, convene both Houses, or either of them, and in Case of Disagreement between them, with Respect to the Time of Adjournment, he may adjourn them to such Time as he shall think proper; he shall receive Ambassadors and other public Ministers; he shall take Care that the Laws be faithfully executed, and shall Commission all the Officers of the United States.

Section. 4.

The President, Vice President and all civil Officers of the United States, shall be removed from Office on Impeachment for, and Conviction of, Treason, Bribery, or other high Crimes and Misdemeanors.

Article III

Section. 1.

The judicial Power of the United States shall be vested in one supreme Court, and in such inferior Courts as the Congress may from time to time ordain and establish. The Judges, both of the supreme and inferior Courts, shall hold their Offices during good Behaviour, and shall, at stated Times, receive for their Services a Compensation, which shall not be diminished during their Continuance in Office.

Section. 2.

The judicial Power shall extend to all Cases, in Law and Equity, arising under this Constitution, the Laws of the United States, and Treaties made, or which shall be made, under their Authority;--to all Cases affecting Ambassadors, other public Ministers and Consuls;--to all Cases of admiralty and maritime Jurisdiction;--to Controversies to which the United States shall be a Party;--to Controversies between two or more States;-- between a State and Citizens of another State,--between Citizens of different States,--between Citizens of the same State claiming Lands under Grants of different States, and between a State, or the Citizens thereof, and foreign States, Citizens or Subjects.

In all Cases affecting Ambassadors, other public Ministers and Consuls, and those in which a State shall be Party, the supreme Court shall have original Jurisdiction. In all the other Cases before mentioned, the supreme Court shall have appellate Jurisdiction, both as to Law and Fact, with such Exceptions, and under such Regulations as the Congress shall make.

The Trial of all Crimes, except in Cases of Impeachment, shall be by Jury; and such Trial shall be held in the State where the said Crimes shall have been committed; but when not committed within any State, the Trial shall be at such Place or Places as the Congress may by Law have directed.

Section. 3.

Treason against the United States shall consist only in levying War against them, or in adhering to their Enemies, giving them Aid and Comfort. No Person shall be convicted of Treason unless on the Testimony of two Witnesses to the same overt Act, or on Confession in open Court.

The Congress shall have Power to declare the Punishment of Treason, but no Attainder of Treason shall work Corruption of Blood, or Forfeiture except during the Life of the Person attainted.

Article IV

Section. 1.

Full Faith and Credit shall be given in each State to the public Acts, Records, and judicial Proceedings of every other State. And the Congress may by general Laws prescribe the Manner in which such Acts, Records and Proceedings shall be proved, and the Effect thereof.

Section. 2.

The Citizens of each State shall be entitled to all Privileges and Immunities of Citizens in the several States.

A Person charged in any State with Treason, Felony, or other Crime, who shall flee from Justice, and be found in another State, shall on Demand of the executive Authority of the State from which he fled, be delivered up, to be removed to the State having Jurisdiction of the Crime.

No Person held to Service or Labour in one State, under the Laws thereof, escaping into another, shall, in Consequence of any Law or Regulation therein, be discharged from such Service or Labour, but shall be delivered up on Claim of the Party to whom such Service or Labour may be due.

Section. 3.

New States may be admitted by the Congress into this Union; but no new State shall be formed or erected within the Jurisdiction of any other State; nor any State be formed by the Junction of two or more States, or Parts of States, without the Consent of the Legislatures of the States concerned as well as of the Congress.

The Congress shall have Power to dispose of and make all needful Rules and Regulations respecting the Territory or other Property belonging to the United States; and nothing in this Constitution shall be so construed as to Prejudice any Claims of the United States, or of any particular State.

Section. 4.

The United States shall guarantee to every State in this Union a Republican Form of Government and shall protect each of them against Invasion; and on Application of the Legislature, or of the Executive (when the Legislature cannot be convened), against domestic Violence.

Article V

The Congress, whenever two thirds of both Houses shall deem it necessary, shall propose Amendments to this Constitution, or, on the Application of the Legislatures of two thirds of the several States, shall call a Convention for proposing Amendments, which, in either Case, shall be valid to all Intents and Purposes, as Part of this Constitution, when ratified by the Legislatures of three fourths of the several States, or by Conventions in three fourths thereof, as the one or the other Mode of Ratification may be proposed by the Congress; Provided that no Amendment which may be made prior to the Year One thousand eight hundred and eight shall in any Manner affect the first and fourth Clauses in the Ninth Section of the first Article; and that no State, without its Consent, shall be deprived of its equal Suffrage in the Senate.

Article VI

All Debts contracted and Engagements entered into, before the Adoption of this Constitution, shall be as valid against the United States under this Constitution, as under the Confederation.

This Constitution, and the Laws of the United States which shall be made in Pursuance thereof; and all Treaties made, or which shall be made, under the Authority of the United States, shall be the supreme Law of the Land; and the Judges in every State shall be bound thereby, any Thing in the Constitution or Laws of any State to the Contrary notwithstanding.

The Senators and Representatives before mentioned, and the Members of the several State Legislatures, and all executive and judicial Officers, both of the United States and of the several States, shall be bound by Oath or Affirmation, to support this Constitution; but no religious Test shall ever be required as a Qualification to any Office or public Trust under the United States.

Article VII

The Ratification of the Conventions of nine States, shall be sufficient for the Establishment of this Constitution between the States so ratifying the Same.

Amendments

US Archives on the Bill of Rights:[190]

During the debates on the adoption of the Constitution, its opponents repeatedly charged that the Constitution as drafted would open the way to tyranny by the central government. Fresh in their minds was the memory of the British violation of civil rights before and during the Revolution. They demanded a "bill of rights" that would spell out the immunities of individual citizens. Several state conventions in their formal ratification of the Constitution asked for such amendments; others ratified the Constitution with the understanding that the amendments would be offered.

On September 25, 1789, the First Congress of the United States therefore proposed to the state legislatures 12 amendments to the Constitution that met arguments most frequently advanced against it. The first two proposed amendments, which concerned the number of constituents for each Representative and the compensation of Congressmen, were not ratified. Articles 3 to 12, however, ratified by three-fourths of the state legislatures, constitute the first 10 amendments of the Constitution, known as the Bill of Rights.

1st Amendment (1791): Guarantees the right to the freedoms of speech, press, and religion. Protects the right to petition the government.

2nd Amendment (1791): Guarantees the people's right to own and bear arms for their defense.

3rd Amendment (1791): Citizens cannot be forced to quarter soldiers during times of peace.

4th Amendment (1791): Citizens cannot be forced to subject themselves to seizure and search without a search warrant and probable cause.

5th Amendment (1791): Prohibits abuse of governmental authority in legal procedures. Establishes rules for indictment by eminent domain and grand jury. Guarantees the due process rights. Protects citizens from self-incrimination and double jeopardy.

6th Amendment (1791): Guarantees fair and speedy jury trial and the rights to know the accusation, the accuser, and to find counsel and witnesses.

7th Amendment (1791): Reserves individuals' rights to jury trial depending on the civil case, and cases already examined by not be re-opened by another court.

8th Amendment (1791): Forbids exorbitant bails and fines and punishment that is unusual or cruel.

9th Amendment (1791): Reserves the rights of citizens which are not specifically mentioned by the U.S. Constitution.

10th Amendment (1791): Reserves powers that are not given to the U.S. government under the Constitution, nor prohibited to a State of the U.S., to the people and the States.

11th Amendment (1795): State sovereign immunity. States are protected from suits by citizens living in another state or foreigners that do not reside within the state borders. Ratified: Feb. 7, 1795

12th Amendment (1804): Modifies and clarifies the procedure for electing vice-presidents and presidents.

13th Amendment (1865): Except as punishment for criminal offense, forbids forced-slavery and involuntary servitude.

14th Amendment (1868): Details Equal Protection Clause, Due Process Clause, Citizenship Clause, and clauses dealing with the Confederacy and its officials.

15th Amendment (1870): Reserves citizens the suffrage rights regardless of their race, color, or previous slave status.

16th Amendment (1913): Reserves the U.S. government the right to tax income.

17th Amendment (1913): Establishes popular voting as the process under which senators are elected.

18th Amendment (1919): Denies the sale and consumption of alcohol.

19th Amendment (1920): Reserves women's suffrage rights.

20th Amendment (1933): Also known as the "lame duck amendment," establishes date of term starts for Congress (January 3) & the President (January 20).

21st Amendment (1933): Details the repeal of the Eighteenth Amendment. State laws over alcohol are to remain.

22nd Amendment (1951): Limit the terms that an individual can be elected as president (at most two terms). Individuals who have served over two years of someone else's term may not be elected more than once.

23rd Amendment (1961): Reserves the right of citizens residing in the District of Columbia to vote for their own Electors for presidential elections.

24th Amendment (1964): Citizens cannot be denied the suffrage rights for not paying a poll tax or any other taxes.

25th Amendment (1967): Establishes the procedures for a successor of a President.

26th Amendment (1971): Reserves the right for citizens 18 and older to vote.

27th Amendment (1992): Denies any laws that vary the salaries of Congress members until the beginning of the next terms of office for Representatives.

REFERENCES

01. https://www.census.gov/popclock/?intcmp=home_pop. Accessed Dec. 31, 2023.

01-01. The University of Chicago, Harris School of Public Policy. "The Overlooked Power of Moderate Voters in the Era of Polarization." New research led by Professor Anthony Fowler makes an empirical case for renewed attention to the middle of the political spectrum. 14 February 2022, by Mike Pilarz, harris.uchicago.edu/news-events/news/overlooked-power-moderate-voters-era-polarization.

01-02. "The Politics Watcher. "Congress: Finding the Middle Ground: Understanding Moderate Political Views." The Politics Watcher, published on Friday, June 16, 2023, at 8:22 PM EST, thepoliticswatcher.com/pages/articles/congress/2023/6/17/finding-middle-ground-understanding-moderate-political-views.

01-03. Gallup. "U.S. Political Ideology Steady; Conservatives, Moderates Tie." POLITICS, 17 Jan. 2022, BY LYDIA SAAD, news.gallup.com/poll/388988/political-ideology-steady-conservatives-moderates-tie.aspx.

01-04. "Google." Google Search, "350 Years: The History of the Jews in America." Submitted by Suzanne Sobczak. Copyright © 2005, Weaver Family Foundation. www.WeaverFoundation.org. Page 1 of 9. Available at: https://www.boulderjcc.org/clientuploads/Lesson%20Plans/1JewishHistoryandCulture_6-8.pdf.

01-05. WeChronicle. 'How Colonialism Created a Rigid Social Hierarchy in America.' WeChronicle, 2023, https://wechronicle.com/colonial-america/examining-the-impact-of-colonial-social-hierarchies-on-american-class-structure/.

02. Jeffersonian Cyclopedia. http://etext.virginia.edu/toc/modeng/public/JefCycl.html.

02-a. Washington Edition, vol. II, p. 252.

02-b. Washington Edition, vol. I, p. 36; Ford Edition, vol. I, p. 49.

02-c. Note in Destutt Tracy's Political Economy. Washington Edition, vol. VI, p. 573. 1816.

03. The Adams-Jefferson Letters, Edited by Lester J. Cappon, Volumes I and II, Published for The Institute of Early American History and Culture at Williamsburg, Virginia by The University of North Caroline Press, Chapel Hill, printed by Van Ress Press, New York, NY 1959

04. Thomas Jefferson to A. Coray, 1823, The Writings of Thomas Jefferson, Memorial Edition (Lipscomb and Bergh, editors), 20 Vols., Washington, D.C., 1903-04. 15:488 (http://etext.virginia.edu/jefferson/quotations/jeff1000.htm)

05. Thomas Jefferson to Samuel Kercheval, 1816. ME 15: (http://etext.virginia.edu/jefferson/quotations/jeff1000.htm)

06. OpenAI. "ChatGPT." October 2023.

10. "Criminal Law of Singapore." Wikipedia, Wikimedia Foundation, August 2023.

10-01. Ward, Myah. "White House Announces New State-Based Gun Violence Initiative." POLITICO, 13 Dec. 2023, www.politico.com/news/2023/12/13/white-house-gun-violence-00131473.

10-02. Leonard, Kimberly. "The Politics of Mass Shootings in the Gunshine State." POLITICO, 27 Oct. 2023, www.politico.com/newsletters/florida-playbook/2023/10/27/the-politics-of-mass-shootings-in-the-gunshine-state-00123930.

11. Naegeli, Phyllis. "The History of Political Parties in the United States." EdHelper, August 2023. http://www.edhelper.com/ReadingComprehension_34_26.html. Page 4.

12. "Sunday Morning." CBS, 18 Oct. 2009.

13. " UNAFEI. August 2023. http://www.unafei.or.jp/english/pdf/PDF_rms/no56/56-12.pdf.

14. "Lobbying." Wikipedia, Wikimedia Foundation, August 2023. http://en.wikipedia.org/wiki/Lobbying.

15. The Washington Post. 21 June 2005, http://www.washingtonpost.com/wp-dyn/content/article/2005/06/21/AR2005062101632.html.

16. "Federal Employment Statistics." U.S. Office of Personnel Management, August 2023. http://www.opm.gov/feddata/HistoricalTables/TotalGovernmentSince1962.asp.

17. Garrett, Thomas A., and Russell M. Rhine. "On the Size and Growth of Government." Federal Reserve Bank of St. Louis Review, Jan./Feb. 2006, http://research.stlouisfed.org/publications/review/06/01/GarrettRhine.pdf.

18. "Article 11 of the Treaty of Tripoli." Ratified by the U.S. Senate. The treaty was ratified by the U.S. Senate and is considered a historical document affirming the secular nature of the United States government.

19-01. Jefferson, Thomas. "The Writings of Thomas Jefferson." Edited by Andrew A. Lipscomb and Albert Ellery Bergh, vol. 16, 1907, p. 113.

19-02. Madison, James. "A Memorial and Remonstrance Against Religious Assessments." 1785. Madison and other members of the Virginia General Assembly wrote this document. It argued against a bill that would have established a state church in Virginia. The document contains a passage that is similar to this quote:

"Who does not see that the same authority which can establish Christianity, in exclusion of all other Religions, may establish with the same ease any particular sect of Christians, in exclusion of all other Sects? That the same authority which can force a citizen to contribute three pence only of his property for the support of any one establishment may force him hereafter to contribute three pounds. And that in time the same authority which can force him to pay three pounds, may force him to pay whole hundreds, or thousands?"

19-03. Paine, Thomas. "The Age of Reason; Being an Investigation of True and Fabulous Theology." 1794.

21. "Roman Law." Wikipedia, Wikimedia Foundation, August 2023. http://en.wikipedia.org/wiki/Roman_Law.

22. Kelly, Kevin. "The New Socialism." Wikipedia, Wikimedia Foundation, Aug. 2023, en.wikipedia.org/wiki/The_New_Socialism, p. 23.

23. Dahl, Robert A., and Seymour Martin Lipset. Who Governs? August 2023, p. 29.https://en.wikipedia.org/wiki/Who_Governs%3F.

24. Naegeli, Phyllis. "The History of Political Parties in the United States." EdHelper, August 2023. http://www.edhelper.com/ReadingComprehension_34_26.html.

25. Münsterberg, Hugo. American Traits from the Point of View of a German. Houghton Mifflin, 1901. 240 pgs. http://www.questia.com/read/54118835.

26. "Natural Justice." Wikipedia, Wikimedia Foundation, October 2023. http://en.wikipedia.org/wiki/Natural_justice.

27. Wikipedia contributors. "Social Contract - John Locke's Second Treatise of Government (1689)." Wikipedia, The Free Encyclopedia, Oct. 2023, en.wikipedia.org/wiki/Social_contract#John_Locke.27s_Second_Treatise_of_Government_.281689.29.

28. New World Encyclopedia contributors. "Socrates." New World Encyclopedia, Sept. 2023, www.newworldencyclopedia.org/entry/Socrates.

29. Wikipedia contributors. "Direct Democracy." Wikipedia, The Free Encyclopedia, Sept. 2023, en.wikipedia.org/wiki/Direct_democracy.

29-01. OpenAI. ChatGPT Version 3.5. 2023. Accessed Sept. 2023, openai.com/chatgpt.

30. Wikipedia contributors. "Socialism." Wikipedia, The Free Encyclopedia, Sept. 2023, en.wikipedia.org/wiki/Socialism.

30-01. "Democratization." Britannica, Encyclopædia Britannica, Inc., www.britannica.com/topic/democratization.

31. Taylor, Bayard. A Visit to China in the Year 1853. G.P. Putnam, 1860, p. 448.

32. "Democracy." Wikipedia, Wikimedia Foundation, Sept. 2023, en.wikipedia.org/wiki/Democracy.

33. "Pluralism (Political Philosophy)." Wikipedia, Wikimedia Foundation, Sept. 2023, en.wikipedia.org/wiki/Pluralism_(political_philosophy).

34. "Right to Petition." Wikipedia, Wikimedia Foundation, 1 Feb. 2010, en.wikipedia.org/wiki/Right_to_petition.

34-02. "Founding Fathers." Memoria Press, 1 Feb. 2010, www.memoriapress.com/articles/founding-fathers.html. Accessed Sept. 2023.

35. "Civil and Political Rights." Wikipedia, Wikimedia Foundation, Sept. 2023, en.wikipedia.org/wiki/Civil_and_political_rights.

36. "Democracy." Wikipedia, Wikimedia Foundation, Sept. 2023, en.wikipedia.org/wiki/Democracy.

37. "Individualism." Wikipedia, Wikimedia Foundation, Sept. 2023, en.wikipedia.org/wiki/Individualism.

38. "Separation of Powers." Wikipedia, Wikimedia Foundation, Sept. 2023, en.wikipedia.org/wiki/Separation_of_powers.

39. Global Citizen Solutions. "The Sixteen Best Citizenship by Investment Programs in 2024." Global Citizen Solutions, 26 Jan. 2024, www.globalcitizensolutions.com/best-citizenship-by-investment-programs/.

39-01. "Origin of Communism and Marxism." The 7th Fire, Sept. 2023, www.the7thfire.com/new_world_order/final_warning/origin_of_communism_and_marxism.htm.

39-02. Marx, Karl. "Critique of the Gotha Program." Marxists Internet Archive, 1 Feb. 2010, www.marxists.org/archive/marx/works/1875/gotha/index.htm.

39-03. Acton, Lord. Letter to Bishop Mandell Creighton. 1887.

39-04. Oxford Reference Dictionary, 2023, https://www.oxfordreference.com/display/10.1093/oi/authority.20110803100349558. Accessed Dec. 2023.

39-05. OpenAI. "ChatGPT." Dec. 2023.

39-06. "Why the US and EU are at odds over tech regulation." New Statesman. 25 February 2021. https://www.newstatesman.com/science-tech/2021/02/why-us-and-eu-are-odds-over-tech-regulation.

39-07. Skroejer, Morten, and Nicole Lawler. "Can the US and EU Rein in Big Tech with Diverging Approaches?" Atlantic Council, 20 Jan. 2022, www.atlanticcouncil.org.

39-08. Lawless, J. "The Right to Protest Is Under Threat in Britain, Undermining a Pillar of Democracy." AP World News, 26 Dec. 2023. and

"Managing Borders and Migration: Earned Citizenship." UK Border Agency, Sept. 2023, www.ukba.homeoffice.gov.uk/managingborders/managingmigration/earned-citizenship/.

39-09. von Thun, Max. "After Years of Leading the Charge Against Big Tech Dominance, is the EU Falling Behind?" TechPolicy.Press, 1 Mar. 2023, techpolicy.press/after-years-of-leading-the-charge-against-big-tech-dominance-is-the-eu-falling-behind/.

39-10. Whitener, M. "The Future of Antitrust: Ideology, Alternative Facts, and the Rule of Law." Georgetown University, n.d., https://georgetown.app.box.com/s/qocakyltho8s3xz2p87otbi973ucz87a.[39-12]

39-11. Sisco, J. "Here's How Biden May Cement His Antitrust Legacy in 2024." Politico, 30 Dec. 2023, www.politico.com/news/2023/12/30/heres-how-biden-may-cement-his-antitrust-legacy-in-2024-00132756.39-12. Werden, G. J., and Froeb, L. M. "Don't Panic: A Guide to Claims of Increasing Concentration." Antitrust, vol. 74, Fall 2018.

39-13. Neuro, Benzinga. "Former Microsoft CEO Steve Ballmer To Pocket $1B Annually In Dividends." Benzinga, 26 Dec. 2023, www.msn.com/en-us/money/other/former-microsoft-ceo-steve-ballmer-t.

39-14. "Alexis de Tocqueville on the Tyranny of the Majority." Edsitement, National Endowment for the Humanities, 2023, https://edsitement.neh.gov/curricula/alexis-de-tocqueville-tyranny-majority.

39-15. Camia, Catalina. "More than 300 Republicans Ask Supreme Court to Back Gay Marriage." UsaToday, ONPOLITICS, 6 Mar. 2015, www.usatoday.com/story/news/politics/onpolitics/2015/03/06/gay-marriage-supreme-court-republicans/81556582/.

39-16. "Whatever Happened To Equality Of Opportunity?" Hoover Institution. Accessed 16 June 2023. Hoover Institution.

40-02. "Founding Fathers." Memoria Press, Feb. 1, 2010. http://www.memoriapress.com/articles/founding-fathers.html.

41 "Whig Party (United States)." Wikipedia, Wikimedia Foundation. Sep. 2023. en.wikipedia.org/wiki/Whig_Party_(United_States).

41-01. "Democratic-Republican Party." Wikipedia, Wikimedia Foundation, [September 2023]. http://en.wikipedia.org/wiki/Democratic-Republican_Party.

42. "Whig Party (United States)." Wikipedia, Wikimedia Foundation, [September 2023]. http://en.wikipedia.org/wiki/Whig_Party_(United_States).

43. Jefferson, Thomas. "Thomas Jefferson's First Inaugural Address." Wikisource, [September 2023]. http://en.wikisource.org/wiki/Thomas_Jefferson's_First_Inaugural_Address.

44. "Capitalism." Wikipedia, Wikimedia Foundation, [September. 2023], en.wikipedia.org/wiki/Capitalism.

45. OpenAI. "ChatGPT." [September 2023].

46. Bard query. [September 2023].

47. Federal Bureau of Investigation. "Uniform Crime Reporting [United States], 1930-2022." ICPSR, 23 Nov. 2023. https://doi.org/10.3886/ICPSR03666.v1 and United States Department of Justice. Federal Bureau of Investigation. "Uniform Crime Reports [United States], 1930-1959." Inter-university Consortium for Political and Social Research [distributor], 19 Jun. 2003. https://doi.org/10.3886/ICPSR03666.v1.

48. Pew Research Center. "The Changing Face of Congress in 8 Charts: Race, Ethnicity, Gender, Generation, Immigrant Status, Education and More." 19 Feb. 2019. Retrieved on 26 Nov. 2023, from https://thelawmakers.org/find-representatives.

49. "Which is Cheaper: Execution or Life in Prison Without Parole?" HG.org Legal Articles. [September 2023]. https://www.hg.org/legal-articles/which-is-cheaper-execution-or-life-in-prison-without-parole-31614.

50. York, Erica. "Summary of the Latest Federal Income Tax Data, 2020 Update." Tax Foundation, 25 Feb. 2020, https://taxfoundation.org/data/all/federal/summary-of-the-latest-federal-income-tax-data-2020-update/.

51. Madison, James. "Federalist Paper #10." The Federalist Papers.

52. Wikipedia contributors. "John Emerich Edward Dalberg-Acton." Wikipedia, The Free Encyclopedia. Wikipedia, The Free Encyclopedia, [September 2023]. http://en.wikipedia.org/wiki/John_Emerich_Edward_Dalberg-Acton.

53. "Crime: Total Crimes Per Capita." NationMaster. [September 2023]. http://www.nationmaster.com/graph/cri_tot_cri_percap-crime-total-crimes-per-capita.

54. "Proceedings and Debates of the 111th Congress, Second Session." Congressional Record, vol. 156, pt. 15, U.S. Government Publishing Office, 2010, p. 10169.

55. Boesky, Ivan F. "Greed is all right, by the way." Speech, Haas School of Business, University of California, Berkeley, 1986.The exact wording of the statement is disputed, but it is generally agreed that Boesky expressed a positive view of greed and its role in the economy.

56. BARD. [September 2023]

57. "National Debt by Year Compared to GDP and Major Events." The Balance Money. [September 2023]. https://www.thebalancemoney.com/national-debt-by-year-compared-to-gdp-and-major-events-3306287.

58. Idea 1: Stricter Regulation of High-Frequency Trading (HFT)

Hendershott, T., Kissell, R., & Menkveld, A. J. "High-frequency trading and market microstructure." Journal of Financial Economics, vol. 100, no. 2, 2011, pp. 405-429.

Menkveld, A. J. "The high-frequency trading paradox." Journal of Financial Markets, vol. 16, no. 1, 2013, pp. 1-5.

U.S. Securities and Exchange Commission. "The flash crash: A review of the Securities and Exchange Commission's findings and recommendations." 2014.

Idea 2: Enhanced Transparency in Derivatives Trading

Financial Stability Board. "The role of transparency in derivatives markets." 2011.

Bank for International Settlements. "Derivatives markets and financial stability." 2012.

International Organization of Securities Commissions. "Transparency in the over-the-counter derivatives market: A regulatory perspective." 2013.

Idea 3: Reforming the Credit Rating System

Financial Stability Board. "The credit rating agency conundrum." 2012.

U.S. House Committee on Financial Services. "Reforming the credit rating agencies." 2010.

European Commission. "Credit rating agencies: A new European framework." 2016.

Idea 4: Reinforcing the Separation Between Investment and Commercial Banking

Sanders, B. "The return of Glass-Steagall: Why we need to revive the separation of commercial and investment banking." The American Prospect, vol. 41, no. 2, 2010, pp. 32-37.

Stiglitz, J. E., & Wolf, M. "Glass-Steagall in the 21st century." Foreign Affairs, vol. 89, no. 3, 2010, pp. 135-147.

Volcker, P. A. "Restoring financial stability: Why we need to revive Glass-Steagall." Speech, Brookings Institution, Washington, DC, 2010.

59. Tax Policy Center. "What Are the Major Federal Excise Taxes, and How Much Money Do They Raise?" Urban Institute & Brookings Institution, https://www.taxpolicycenter.org/briefing-book/what-are-major-federal-excise-taxes-and-how-much-money-do-they-raise. Accessed 1/2/2023.

59-01. "Economic Research Service." U.S. Department of Agriculture, https://www.ers.usda.gov/topics/crops/sugar-and-sweeteners/. Accessed 1/2/2024.

59-02. Gibson, Suzanne A., et al. "Understanding the Link between Sugar and Cancer: An Examination of the Preclinical and Clinical Evidence." NIH Public Access Author Manuscript, National Institutes of Health, 4 Sept. 2016, ncbi.nlm.nih.gov/pmc/articles/PMC5546054/.

59-03. MD Anderson Cancer Center. "Does Sugar Cause Cancer?" MD Anderson Cancer Center, 2023, www.mdanderson.org/cancerwise/does-sugar-cause-cancer.h00-159354754.html.

59-04. Cancer Research UK. "Sugar and Cancer – What You Need to Know." Cancer News, Cancer Research UK, 15 Dec. 2023, www.cancerresearchuk.org/about-cancer/causes-of-cancer/diet-and-cancer/does-sugar-cause-cancer.

59-05. Cancer Council. "Does Sugar Cause Cancer?" Cancer Council Australia, 2023, cancercouncil.org.au/cancer-information/causes-and-prevention/diet-and-exercise/does-sugar-cause-cancer/.

59-06. Pandey, Ashutosh. "Airbus-Boeing WTO Dispute: What You Need to Know." DW, 13 Oct. 2020, www.dw.com/en/airbus-boeing-wto-dispute-what-you-need-to-know/a-49442616. Accessed 1/3/2024.

59-07. "Alcohol Tax Modernization: ABV Tax and other Drink Tax Reforms." Tax Foundation, Tax Foundation, taxfoundation.org/alcohol-tax-modernization/.

59-08. Arendt, Hannah. The Origins of Totalitarianism. Harcourt, Brace, Jovanovich, 1973.

59-09. U.S. Department of State. "Human Rights and Democracy." United States Department of State, www.state.gov. Accessed 9 Feb. 2024.

59-10. McCain Institute. "Advancing Freedom Promotes U.S. Interests." McCain Institute for International Leadership, www.mccaininstitute.org. Accessed 9 Feb. 2024.

59-11. Thomas, Virginia. "Solitude in a Social World." Psychology Today, Sussex Publishers, 30 Mar. 2022, www.psychologytoday.com/us/blog/solitude-in-a-social-world/202203/is-your-solitude-authentic.

59-12. Zhang, Jia Wei, and Thuy-Vy T. Nguyen. "Balance between Solitude and Socializing: Everyday Solitude Time Both Benefits and Harms Well-Being." Scientific Reports, vol. 11, no. 1, Dec. 2021, www.nature.com/articles/s41598-021-94858-0.

59-13. Centers for Disease Control and Prevention (CDC). "Health Topics - Tobacco." POLARIS, https://www.cdc.gov/policy/polaris/healthtopics/tobacco/index.html.

59-14. DiNardo, John, and Thomas Lemieux. "Alcohol, Marijuana, and American Youth: The Unintended Consequences of Government Regulation." Journal of Health Economics, vol. 20, no. 11, 2001, pp. 991-1010, https://www.nber.org/papers/w4212.

59-15. United States, Department of the Treasury. Alcohol and Tobacco Tax and Trade Bureau Congressional Budget Justification and Annual Performance Plan and Report FY 2023. "In FY 2021, TTB collected approximately $20.3 billion in excise taxes from the alcohol, tobacco, firearms, and ammunition industries." 2023, https://home.treasury.gov/system/files/266/14.-TTB-FY-2023-CJ.pdf.

59-16. "Key Elements of the U.S. Tax System." Tax Policy Center Briefing Book, Tax Policy Center, https://www.taxpolicycenter.org/briefing-book/what-are-major-federal-excise-taxes-and-how-much-money-do-they-raise.

59-17. Fiscal year 2022 deficit: "Joint Statement of Janet L. Yellen, Secretary of the Treasury, and Shalanda D. Young, Director of the Office of Management and Budget, on Budget Results for Fiscal Year 2022." U.S. Department of the Treasury, 21 Oct. 2022, www.home.treasury.gov/news/press-releases/jy0919.

59-18. Fiscal year 2021 deficit details: "Joint Statement by Secretary of the Treasury Janet L. Yellen and Acting Director of the Office of Management and Budget Shalanda D. Young on Budget Results for Fiscal Year 2021." U.S. Department of the Treasury, 22 Oct. 2021, www.home.treasury.gov/news/press-releases/jy0387.

59-19. Fiscal year 2022 budget deficit halving: Lawder, David. "U.S. 2022 Budget Deficit Halves to $1.375 Trillion Despite Student Loan Costs." Reuters, 21 Oct. 2022, www.reuters.com/article/us-usa-budget/u-s-2022-budget-deficit-halves-to-1-375-trillion-despite-student-loan-costs-idUSKBN2HG2L0.

59-20. 2023 deficit projection: "The 2023 Deficit Is Projected To Total $1.5 Trillion. Here's Why It Could Be Even Higher." Peter G. Peterson Foundation, 20 June 2023, www.pgpf.org/blog/2023/06/the-2023-deficit-is-projected-to-total-15-trillion-heres-why-it-could-be-even-higher.

59-21. Macrotrends. "U.S. Life Expectancy 1950-2024." https://www.macrotrends.net/countries/USA/united-states/life-expectancy#:~:text=Chart%20and%20table%20of%20U.S.,a%200.08%25%20increase%20from%202022.

59-22. Shmerling, Robert H., MD. "Why Life Expectancy in the US Is Falling: COVID-19 and Drug Overdoses Are the Biggest Contributors." Harvard Health Publishing, Harvard Medical School, 20 Oct. 2022, www.health.harvard.edu/blog/why-life-expectancy-in-the-us-is-falling-202210202835.

59-23. Democracy Index 2022: Stagnation, War and No Post-COVID Revival." Democracy Without Borders, 10 Feb. 2023.

59-24. "Authority in Religious Traditions." Encyclopedia.com, www.encyclopedia.com/religion/encyclopedias-almanacs-transcripts-and-maps/authority-religious-traditions.

59-25. Nieuwsma, Alexandra. "The American Nation-State, Cosmopolitanism, and Identity Politics in the Millennial Imagination." Providence, providencemag.com/2021/american-nation-state-cosmopolitanism-identity-politics-millennial-imagination

59-26. Funk, Josh. "Annual letter: Warren Buffett says to ignore Wall Street pundits." AP News, 24 Feb. 2024, apnews.com.

59-27. American Enterprise Institute - AEI. "2009 Tire Tariffs Cost US Consumers $926K per Job Saved and Led to the Loss of 3 Retail Jobs per Factory Job Saved." AEI, www.aei.org.

59-28. Amadeo, Kimberly. "Trump's Steel and Aluminum Tariffs." The Balance, 2020, www.thebalance.com.

59-29. Lumber Coalition. "U.S. Department of Commerce Issues Final Antidumping and Countervailing Duty Determinations on Canadian Softwood Lumber Imports." Lumber Coalition, 2017, www.lumbercoalition.org.

59-30. Federal Reserve History. "The Second Bank of the United States." Federal Reserve History, Federal Reserve Bank of San Francisco, www.federalreservehistory.org/essays/second_bank_of_the_united_states.

59-31. United States Inflation Rate, 1946-2021." MacroTrends, www.macrotrends.net/countries/USA/united-states/inflation-rate-cpi. Accessed 2 Mar. 2024.

61. Münsterberg, Hugo. American Traits from the Point of View of a German. Houghton Mifflin, 1901.

62. "American Traits from the Point of View of a German." Questia. [September 2023]. http://www.questia.com/read/54118835.

63. "Universal Declaration of Human Rights." United Nations, [September 2023]. http://www.un.org/en/documents/udhr/.

64. "Totalitarianism." Wikipedia, Wikimedia Foundation, [September 2023]. http://en.wikipedia.org/wiki/Totalitarianism.

65. "Marxism." Wikipedia, Wikimedia Foundation, [September 2023]. http://en.wikipedia.org/wiki/Marxism.

66. "Capitalism." Wikipedia, Wikimedia Foundation, [September 2023]. http://en.wikipedia.org/wiki/Capitalism.

67. "Rule of Law." Wikipedia, Wikimedia Foundation, [September 2023]. http://en.wikipedia.org/wiki/Rule_of_Law.

68. "Magna Carta." Wikipedia, Wikimedia Foundation, [September 2023]. http://en.wikipedia.org/wiki/Magna_Carta.

69. "Common Sense (Pamphlet)." Wikipedia, Wikimedia Foundation, [September 2023]. http://en.wikipedia.org/wiki/Common_Sense_(pamphlet).

69-01. "'Incompetent dumpster fire': Michigan GOP rocked by financial turmoil and infighting.", Curt Devine, Audrey Ash, Allison Gordon, Daniel Strauss, and Jason Carroll, CNN, https://www.cnn.com/2023/12/20/politics/michigan-gop-financial-turmoil-infighting-invs?cid=ios_app.

69-02. Note from Author. I wrote the paragraph during Obama's term, not Trump's.

69-03. Schoffstall, Joe. "427 Former Members of Congress Moved to Lobbying or Similar Work." Washington Free Beacon, 22 Sept. 2015, https://freebeacon.com/issues/427-former-members-of-congress-moved-to-lobbying-or-similar-work/.

69-04. Nadler, Judy, and Miriam Schulman. "Lobbying Ethics." Markkula Center for Applied Ethics, Santa Clara University, www.scu.edu/ethics/focus-areas/government-ethics/resources/lobbying-ethics/.

69-05. Hong, Ki. "Lobbying regulation: a global phenomenon." Reuters, 23 Oct. 2015, www.reuters.com/article/us-lobbying-regulation-idUSKCN0SH2L120151023. 2015, https://freebeacon.com/issues/427-former-members-of-congress-moved-to-lobbying-or-similar-work/.

69-07. American Bar Association. 'How Venezuela Lost the Rule of Law.' American Bar Association, [publication date if available], www.americanbar.org. Accessed [date you accessed the site].

69-08. General Social Survey, conducted by NORC at the University of Chicago in 2006. Results discussed in 'The General Social Survey' by Demo Memo, 29 May 2008, demomemo.blogspot.com/2008/05/.

69-09. https://gemini.google.com/app/25a99b1451db4661. Accessed 2/9/2024. Which listed the following as partial sources from which it compiled this list:

- The US Census Bureau's website, which provides statistics on population demographics and diversity: https://www.census.gov/topics/population.html.

- Pew Research Center reports on immigration and religious diversity: https://www.pewresearch.org/.

- "American Pragmatism" movement and its influence on US culture: https://www.philosophytalk.org/shows/american-pragmatism.

- The Global Entrepreneurship Monitor (GEM): https://www.gemconsortium.org/.

- Gallup offers polls on career aspirations and work ethic in the US: https://www.gallup.com/topic/employee-engagement.aspx.

- The "American Dream" concept and its historical context: https://www.bushcenter.org/catalyst/state-of-the-american-dream/churchwell-history-of-the-american-dream.

- Michael Novak's "The Spirit of Democratic Capitalism" exploring self-reliance in American culture: https://www.amazon.com/Spirit-Democratic-Capitalism-Michael-Novak/dp/0819178233.

- The Pew Research Center study on personal debt: https://www.pewresearch.org/.

- Giving USA: https://givingusa.org/.

- Volunteerism statistics from organizations like the Bureau of Labor Statistics: https://www.bls.gov/news.release/volun.toc.htm.

- Polls on patriotism conducted by institutions like Pew Research Center or Gallup.

- Historical studies on American national identity, like David Hackett Fischer's "Albion's Seed": https://www.amazon.com/Albions-Seed-British-Folkways-cultural-ebook/dp/B000SEKM9C.

- Pew Research Center's reports on religious demographics and trends in the US.

- Pew Research Center studies on technology adoption and internet usage in the US.

- Isaac Asimov's "Innovation and Opportunity": https://www.aboutamazon.com/news/innovation-at-amazon.

- Pew Research Center studies on political polarization and public opinion.

- Major news articles or reports analyzing the current political climate in the US.

- Milton's "Areopagitica": http://www.gutenberg.org/ebooks/608.

- Studies on debate culture and its place in American society.

69-10. U.S. Bureau of Labor Statistics. "All Employees, Federal [CES9091000001]." FRED, Federal Reserve Bank of St. Louis, 2 Feb. 2024, fred.stlouisfed.org/series/CES9091000001.

69-11. chatGPT v3.5, accessed 2/13/24. Response was: In 1960, the federal civilian and military personnel breakdown was: Federal civilian personnel: Approximately 2.2 million and Military personnel: Approximately 1.3 million. These numbers are approximate and may vary slightly depending on the specific source and methodology used for calculation.

69-12. "Sources: Statistical Abstract of the United States. U.S. Census Bureau, "Historical Statistics of the United States, Colonial Times to 1970. And:

U.S. Census Bureau. "Historical Population Estimates."

U.S. Census Bureau, www.census.gov/data/tables/time-series/demo/popest/pre-1980-national.html.

U.S. Bureau of Economic Analysis (BEA). "National Income and Product Accounts Tables."

U.S. Office of Management and Budget (OMB). "Budget of the United States Government: Historical Tables."

U.S. Department of Commerce, www.bea.gov/data/national/national-accounts.

U.S. Government Publishing Office, www.govinfo.gov/app/collection/budget/2023/.

69-13. Guzman, Gloria, and Melissa Kollar. Income in the United States: 2022. U.S. Census Bureau, Report Number P60-279, 12 Sept. 2023, www.census.gov/library/publications/2023/demo/p60-279.html.

69-14. Wong, Belle, J.D. "Average Salary By State In 2024." Forbes Advisor, Forbes, 23 Aug. 2023, www.forbes.com/advisor/business/average-salary-by-state/.

69-15. Statista Research Department. "U.S. Total Number of Lobbyists 2000-2022." Statista, 3 Nov. 2023, www.statista.com/statistics/257340/number-of-lobbyists-in-the-us/.

70. "John Adams." Wikiquote, Wikimedia Foundation, [September 2023]. http://en.wikiquote.org/wiki/John_Adams.

71. "U.S. Constitution." [Adapted from]. [September 2023]. http://www.usConstitution.net.

71-01. "Ten All-American Traits." New Strategist, 29 May 2008. http://www.newstrategist.com/store/index.cfm/feature/30_15/ten-all-american-traits.cfm.

71-02. "Poll: Gallup Evolution Survey." Pollster. [September 2023]. http://www.pollster.com/blogs/poll_gallup_evolution_survey.php.

72, Birnbaum, Jeffrey H. "The Road to Riches Is Called K Street, Lobbying Firms Hire More, Pay More, Charge More to Influence Government." The Washington Post, 22 June 2005. http://www.washingtonpost.com/wp-dyn/content/article/2005/06/21/AR2005062101632.html.

72-01 Author [Charles Patton] enhanced with added traits.

73. "Federal Election Campaign Act." Answers.com. [September 2023]. http://www.answers.com/topic/federal-election-campaign-act.

74. "Politics of Venezuela." Wikipedia, Wikimedia Foundation, [September 2023]. http://en.wikipedia.org/wiki/Politics_of_Venezuela.

75. "Spain–United States Relations." Wikipedia, Wikimedia Foundation, [September 2023]. http://en.wikipedia.org/wiki/Spain–United_States_relations.

76a. U.S. Energy Information Administration. "Annual Energy Outlook 2023." [September 2023]. https://www.eia.gov/outlooks/aeo/.

76b. International Energy Agency. "Oil 2023." [September 2023]. https://www.iea.org/reports/oil-2023.

76c. "World Energy Outlook 2022: Executive Summary." International Energy Agency. [September 2023]. https://www.iea.org/reports/world-energy-outlook-2022/executive-summary.

77. U.S. Environmental Protection Agency. "Greenhouse Gas Emissions from a Typical Passenger Vehicle." 2018. https://19january2021snapshot.epa.gov/greenvehicles/greenhouse-gas-emissions-typical-passenger-vehicle_.html.

78. Auffhammer, M., Park, J., and Stavins, R. N. "The Economic and Environmental Impacts of a Carbon Tax and Cap-and-Trade System in the United States." Columbia University Center on Global Energy Policy, July 2021.

79. US Retail Gas Price." YCharts, YCharts, Inc., Accessed 16 February 2024, https://ycharts.com/indicators/us_gas_price.

79-01. Xu, Conglin, and Laura Bell-Hammer. "Global Oil and Natural Gas Reserves Both Increase." Oil & Gas Journal, 4 Dec. 2023, www.ogj.com/general-interest/economics-markets/article/14302481/global-oil-and-natural-gas-reserves-both-increase.

79-02. "Average Vehicle Occupancy Remains Unchanged From 2009 to 2017." Department of Energy, U.S. Department of Energy, 30 July 2018, www.energy.gov/eere/vehicles/articles/fotw-1040-july-30-2018-average-vehicle-occupancy-remains-unchanged-2009-2017.

79-03. Friedrich, Johannes, et al. "This Interactive Chart Shows Changes in the World's Top 10 Emitters." World Resources Institute, 2 Mar. 2023, www.wri.org.

79-04. "Global Greenhouse Gas Emissions Data." U.S. Environmental Protection Agency, www.epa.gov.

79-05. "Executive Orders and the Supreme Court." JURIST - Legal News & Commentary, www.jurist.org/archives/feature/executive-orders-and-the-supreme-court.

79-06. "Executive Orders 101: What Are They and How Do Presidents Use Them?" National Constitution Center, 23 Jan. 2017, constitutioncenter.org/blog/executive-orders-101-what-are-they-and-how-do-presidents-use-them.

81. White House Office of Public Engagement. "The Open Government Initiative." 2009. https://www.whitehouse.gov/ope/.

82. Obama, Barack. "The Open Government Memorandum." 2009. https://obamawhitehouse.archives.gov/the-press-office/transparency-and-open-government.

83. Sunlight Foundation. "The Sunlight Foundation Open Government Principles." 2009. https://sunlightfoundation.com/.

84. Center for Responsive Politics. "The Center for Responsive Politics Open Government Principles." 2009. https://www.opensecrets.org/.

85. "The Freedom of Information Act." 1967. https://www.law.cornell.edu/uscode/text/5/552.

86. Government Accountability Office. "Government Accountability Office: Status of Federal Programs." 2019. https://www.gao.gov/.

87. National Academies of Sciences, Engineering, and Medicine. "Early Childhood Education and Care." 2017. https://nap.nationalacademies.org/.

88. Government Accountability Office. "Government Accountability Office: Workforce Development Programs." 2016. https://www.gao.gov/.

89. National Low Income Housing Coalition. "The Outlook for Fair Housing: Examining the Role of Federal Programs." 2015. https://nlihc.org/annual-housing-policy-conference.

89-01. Republican National Committee. "Republican Platform." 2008. https://www.presidency.ucsb.edu/documents/2008-republican-party-platform.

89-02 Schneider, M. (2023, December 28). World population up 75 million this year, standing at 8 billion on Jan. 1. AP World News. Retrieved from https://apnews.com/article/world-population-census-bureau-growth-b2a32ff77b9f3ae977c943014fe2b853.

89-03. "Most Expensive Ever: 2020 Election Cost $14.4 Billion." OpenSecrets, Center for Responsive Politics, https://www.opensecrets.org/news/2021/02/2020-cycle-cost-14p4-billion-doubling-2016.

91. "Progressivism." Wikipedia, Wikimedia Foundation, October 2023. http://en.wikipedia.org/wiki/Progressivism.

92. "Glenn Beck Show." Fox Television. 18 Jan. 2010.

93. "Progressivism." ProgressiveLiving.org. October 2023. http://www.progressiveliving.org/progressivism_1.htm.

94. "Contribution Limits." Federal Election Commission, October 2023. https://www.fec.gov/help-candidates-and-committees/candidate-taking-receipts/contribution-limits/.

95. OpenAI. "ChatGPT." October 2023.

96. Raw Story, "A 'prophetic' Alexander Hamilton note described Trump almost to a T", Matthew Chapman. *Raw Story*, November 3rd, 2023. Bias warning: Publication has been called Left-wing and Independent.

97. "Minimum Wage." U.S. Department of Labor, U.S. Department of Labor, www.dol.gov/agencies/whd/minimum-wage. Accessed 16 Feb. 2024.

98. McCann, Adam. "Average Credit Card Interest Rates." WalletHub, 26 Feb. 2024, wallethub.com/edu/cc/average-credit-card-interest-rate/50841. Fact checked by Alina Comoreanu.

101. "Historical Debt Outstanding." TreasuryDirect, http://www.treasurydirect.gov/govt/reports/pd/histdebt/histdebt.htm. and

"U.S. National Debt by Year." Infoplease, http://www.infoplease.com/ipa/A0104753.html. and

"Historical Statistics." U.S. Census Bureau, http://www.census.gov/compendia/statab/hist_stats.html.

102. Democratic National Committee. "Health Care." Democrats.org, 2023. https://democrats.org/where-we-stand/the-issues/health-care/.

103. Physicians for a National Health Program. "Republican and Democratic platforms on health care." 2023. https://pnhp.org/news/republican-and-democratic-platforms-on-health-care/.

104. "Why Democrats Should Become the Party of Medically Assisted Dying." Washington Monthly. February 12, 2022. https://www.washingtonmonthly.com/.

105. "Democrats platform and policy on Euthanasia." iSideWith. October 2023. https://www.isidewith.com/.

106. "Americans' Strong Support for Euthanasia Persists." Gallup, 2018. https://www.gallup.com/.

111. "Republican Platform 2008." The American Presidency Project. http://www.presidency.ucsb.edu/ws/index.php?pid=78545.

112. "Democratic Platform 2008." The American Presidency Project. http://www.presidency.ucsb.edu/ws/index.php?pid=78283.

113. "Constitution Party Platform 2008." Constitution Party. http://www.Constitutionparty.com/party_platform.php.

114. "Green Party Platform 2008." Green Party of the United States. http://green.gpus.org/platform/2000/2002summary.html.

115. "Libertarian Platform 2008." Libertarian Party. http://www.lp.org/platform.

116. "Origin of Public Education in the U.S." The Agonist. http://www.agonist.org/Learning-Center/education/originofpubliceducationintheus.html.

120. Wikipedia contributors. "Immigration to the United States." Wikipedia, The Free Encyclopedia. Wikipedia, The Free Encyclopedia, October 2023. http://en.wikipedia.org/wiki/Immigration_to_the_United_States. And Motomura, Hiroshi. Americans in Waiting: The Lost Story of Immigration and Citizenship in the United States. Oxford University Press, 2006.

121. The Presidents of The United States of America, Frank Freidel, White House Historical Association in cooperation with the National Geographic Society, 5026 New Executive Office Building, 726 Jackson Place, N.W., Washington, D.C. 20506, sixth edition, second printing, 1974.

122. chatGPT OpenAI. "ChatGPT." October 2023.

123. The White House. "Build Back Better: Investing in America." 2 Nov. 2023. https://www.whitehouse.gov/briefing-room/statements-releases/2021/10/28/president-biden-announces-the-build-back-better-framework/.

124. Heritage Foundation. "The Case for Private Sector Disaster Relief." Dec. 2017. https://heritage-foundation.org/donations/help-in-natural-disasters/.

125. Republican Party. "Republican Party Platform." https://prod-cdn-static.gop.com/docs/Resolution_Platform_2020.pdf.

126. The Heritage Foundation. "Commentary." 12 Dec. 2010.

127. Obama, Barack. "Remarks at Cooper Union in New York City." 27 Mar. 2008.

128. Clinton, Hillary. Speech at Georgetown University, 2009.

129. "Historical Oil Prices Chart." InflationData.com. October 2023. https://inflationdata.com/articles/inflation-adjusted-prices/historical-oil-prices-chart/.

129-02. "U.S. Petroleum Net Imports." U.S. Energy Information Administration. https://www.eia.gov/dnav/pet/hist/LeafHandler.ashx?n=pet&s=mttntus2&f=m. and

"Petroleum Products Net Imports." U.S. Energy Information Administration. https://www.eia.gov/dnav/pet/hist/LeafHandler.ashx?n=pet&s=mttntus2&f=m. and

"FAQ: How much petroleum does the United States import and export?" American Geosciences Institute. https://www.americangeosciences.org/critical-issues/faq/how-much-oil-does-us-export-and-import.

129-03. Republican National Committee. "2016 Republican Party Platform." Republican National Convention, Cleveland, OH, 18-21 July 2016.

129-04. "Social Security Trust Fund depletion date is 2034 without action." Financial Planning. October 2023. https://www.financial-planning.com. and

"Social Security's Financial Outlook: The 2023 Update in Perspective." Center for Retirement Research at Boston College, 2023. https://crr.bc.edu. and

"The Ratio of Workers to Social Security Beneficiaries Is at a Low and Projected to Decline Further." Peter G. Peterson Foundation. October 2023. https://www.pgpf.org.

129-05. Democratic National Committee. "Creating a 21st Century Immigration System." Democrats.org. October 2023 https://democrats.org/where-we-stand/the-issues/immigration-reform/.

129-06 Democratic Platform. "Where we stand on Immigration." Democrats.org. https://democrats.org/where-we-stand/the-issues/immigration-reform/

129-07. "Republicans and Democrats Have Different Top Priorities for U.S. Immigration Policy." Pew Research Center. October 2023. https://www.pewresearch.org/short-reads/2022/09/08/republicans-and-democrats-have-different-top-priorities-for-u-s-immigration-policy/.

129-08. "Republican and Democratic Party Platforms Reflect Parallel Universes on Immigration Policy." Migration Policy Institute. October 2023. https://www.migrationpolicy.org/article/republican-and-democratic-party-platforms-reflect-parallel-universes-immigration-policy.

129-09. "Republicans' Perspectives on Immigration." Politicsphere.com. October 2023. https://www.politicsphere.com/republicans-perspectives-on-immigration/.

131. Centers for Disease Control and Prevention (CDC). "Economic Facts about U.S. Tobacco Production and Use." 2020. https://www.cdc.gov/tobacco/data_statistics/fact_sheets/economics/econ_facts/index.htm.

132. Centers for Disease Control and Prevention. "Economic Facts about U.S. Tobacco Production and Use." 2020. Centers for Disease Control and Prevention, https://www.cdc.gov/tobacco/data_statistics/fact_sheets/economics/econ_facts/index.htm.

133. DiNardo, J., and Lemieux, T. "Alcohol, Marijuana, and American Youth: The Unintended Consequences of Government Regulation." Journal of Health Economics, vol. 20, no. 6, 2001, pp. 991-1010.

134. U.S. Department of the Treasury. "Alcohol and Tobacco Tax and Trade Bureau (TTB) Statistical Release." 2021. https://www.ttb.gov/statistics/stat-release.shtml.

135. Tax Foundation. "How High Are Marijuana Taxes in Your State?" 2021. https://taxfoundation.org/marijuana-taxes-state-2021/.

136. National Highway Traffic Safety Administration. Motorcycle Safety. 2023. https://www.nhtsa.gov/road-safety/motorcycles.

137. Liu, BC, et al. "Helmets for Preventing Injury in Motorcycle Riders." Cochrane Database of Systematic Reviews, 23 Jan. 2008, www.cochrane.org/CD004333/INJ_helmets-are-shown-to-reduce-motorcyclist-head-injury-and-death.

138. "Policy Impact: Seat Belts." Centers for Disease Control and Prevention, National Center for Injury Prevention and Control, 3 Jan. 2011, www.cdc.gov/motorvehiclesafety/seatbeltbrief/index.html.

139. "Pew Research Center." Republicans and Democrats Move Further Apart in Views of Voting Access, 22 Apr. 2021, www.pewresearch.org/politics/2021/04/22/republicans-and-democrats-move-further-apart-in-views-of-voting-access/. Accessed 7 Jan. 2

139-01: Pew Research Center. "Views on Voting by Mail." Pew Research Center, 13 Oct. 2020, www.pewresearch.org/politics/2020/10/13/views-on-voting-by-mail/.

139-02. Texas v. Johnson, 491 U.S. 397. Supreme Court of the United States. 21 June 1989.

161. "Death Penalty Representation." Death Penalty Information Center. October 2023. http://www.deathpenaltyinfo.org/death-penalty-representation.

162. "Capital Punishment." Wikipedia, Wikimedia Foundation. October 2023. http://en.wikipedia.org/wiki/Capital_punishment.

163. "About the Arguments." Death Penalty Curriculum for Teachers. October 2023. http://deathpenaltycurriculum.org/teacher/c/about/arguments/argument4b.htm.

163-02. Fox News. [October 2023].

164. Becker, [Author's First Name Unk]. "Antitrust Chronology." St. Olaf College. October 2023. http://www.stolaf.edu/people/becker/antitrust/by_date.html.

165. NPR. [October 2023].

166. Environmental Defense Fund. October 2023.

167. "Car Emissions Fact Sheet." Environmental Defense Fund. October 2023. http://www.edf.org/documents/2209_CarEmissionsFactSheet.pdf.

168. "Europe Charges Microsoft with Abuse." Network World. October 2023. http://www.networkworld.com/news/2009/011709-europe-charges-microsoft-with-abuse.html.

169-01. OpenAI. "ChatGPT." October 2023.

171. "Republican Issues and Suggestions." Republican Policies. http://republicanpolicies.com/.

Author Note: For the Jeffersonian Cyclopedia entries, since specific URLs for each entry are not provided, I will format them as references to a print source. See Jeffersonian Cyclopedia at http://etext.virginia.edu/etcbin/foleyx-browse?id=Taxation,%20Basis%20of.

172-02. Jefferson, Thomas. "Reply to Vermont Address." Washington ed., vol. 4, p. 418. Washington, 1801.

173-02. Jefferson, Thomas. "To F. Hopkinson." Washington ed., vol. 2, p. 586; Ford ed., vol. 5, p. 76. Paris, Mar. 1789.

174-02. TITLE: Preface to Tracy's Political Economy, EDITION: Washington ed. Vi, 570, PLACE: [none given], DATE: 1816

175-02. Jefferson, Thomas. "First Annual Message." Washington ed., vol. 8, p. 9; Ford ed., vol. 8, p. 119.

176-02. Jefferson, Thomas. "To Samuel Smith." Washington ed., vol. 7, p. 285; Ford ed., vol. 10, p. 252. Monticello, 1823.

177-02. Jefferson, Thomas. "To J. W. Eppes." Washington ed., vol. 6, p. 195; Ford ed., vol. 9, p. 395. Poplar Forest, Va., Sep. 1813.

178-02. Jefferson, Thomas. "Second Annual Message." Washington ed., vol. 8, p. 21; Ford ed., vol. 8, p. 187. Dec. 1802.EDITION: Ford ed., viii, 187, DATE: Dec. 1802

179. "Capitalism." Wikipedia, Wikimedia Foundation, October 2023. http://en.wikipedia.org/wiki/Capitalism.

180-02-b. Jefferson, Thomas. "Autobiography." Washington ed., vol. 1, p. 36; Ford ed., vol. 1, p. 49. 1821.

181. Gillet, [Author's First Name unk.]. CIRANO, [November 2023].

181-02. Jefferson, Thomas. "To John Adams." Washington ed., vol. 6, p. 224; Ford ed., vol. 9, p. 426. Monticello, 1813.

181-03. "Andrew Jackson." Wikipedia, Wikimedia Foundation, October 2023. http://en.wikipedia.org/wiki/Andrew_Jackson.

181-04. "End the Fed." The Foundation for Rational Economics and Education, Inc. (FREE), Grand Central Publishing, Hachette Book Group, 2009.

181-05. "Independent Treasury System." Wikipedia, Wikimedia Foundation, October 2023. http://en.wikipedia.org/wiki/Independent_Treasury_System.

181-06. "Calculate Carbon Footprint." The Carbon Company. October 2023. http://www.carboncompany.com/calculate-carbon-footprint.

181-07. "Passenger Vehicles in the United States." Wikipedia, Wikimedia Foundation, October 2023. http://en.wikipedia.org/wiki/Passenger_vehicles_in_the_United_States.

181-08. "What is the total number of lawyers in the US?" WikiAnswers. October 2023. http://wiki.answers.com/Q/What_is_the_total_number_of_lawyers_in_the_US.

181-09. "Jefferson's Wall of Separation Letter." U.S. Constitution Online. October 2023. http://www.usConstitution.net/jeffwall.html.

181-10. Google Answers. October 2023.

181-11. "Russian Submarines." CNN. [August 2009]. http://www.cnn.com/2009/US/08/05/russian.submarines/index.html.

182. Princeton Weekly Bulletin, [November 2023].

183. "Title of the Bill." GovTrack.us, [November 2023]. http://www.govtrack.us/congress/bill.xpd?bill=h110-984.

184. "Current Numbers." Center for Immigration Studies, [November 2023]. http://www.cis.org/CurrentNumbers.

185. "U.S. Immigration Policy Likely to Boost Population." YaleGlobal Online, [November 2023]. http://yaleglobal.yale.edu/content/us-immigration-policy-likely-boost-population.

186. Seabrook, Andrea. "2009 Was The Most Partisan Year Ever." NPR Radio News, 5:30 PM, 11 Jan. 2010.

190. Minnesota State University, Mankato founded in 1868, known then as Mankato Normal School. https://www.mnsu.edu/Constitution-day/the-Constitution/Constitutional-amendments-summary/.

191. Greene, Brian. "The Fabric of the Cosmos: Space, Time, and the Texture of Reality." New York: Vintage Books, 2004. Print.

20-21. Pew Research Center. "Attendance at Religious Services - Religion in America: U.S. Religious Data, Demographics and Statistics." 2023. Pew Research Center. https://www.pewresearch.org/.

20-22. Public Religion Research Institute. "The State of American Churches." 2023. PRRI. https://www.prri.org/.

20-23. Gallup. "U.S. Church Attendance Still Lower Than Pre-Pandemic." 2023. https://www.gallup.com/.

20-24. IslamReligion.com. "Rights of Non-Muslims in Islam (Part 1 of 13)." [n.d.]. https://www.islamreligion.com/articles/394/rights-of-non-muslims-in-islam-part-11/.

20-25. AlIslam.org. "Does Islam Teach Muslims to Hate Non-Believers?" [n.d.]. https://www.alislam.org/articles/does-islam-teach-muslims-to-hate-non-believers/.

20-26. IslamReligion.com. "Rights of Non-Muslims in Islam (Part 1 of 13)." [n.d.]. https://www.islamreligion.com/articles/394/rights-of-non-muslims-in-islam-part-11/.

20-27. Pew Research Center. "Muslim Publics Share Concerns about Extremist Groups." 10 Sep. 2013. https://www.pewresearch.org/global/2013/09/10/muslim-publics-share-concerns-about-extremist-groups/.

20-28. Guttmacher Institute. "About Half of U.S. Abortion Patients Report Using Contraception in the Month They Became Pregnant." Guttmacher Institute, 11 Jan. 2018, www.guttmacher.org/news-release/2018/about-half-us-abortion-patients-report-using-contraception-month-they-became.

20-29. Bradley, Sarah. "When can my baby survive outside the womb?" BabyCenter, 15 Sept. 2022, www.babycenter.com/health/premature-babies/fetal-viability-by-week-what-age-is-the-age-of-viability_40005764.

211. Department of Homeland Security. Legal Immigration and Adjustment of Status Report for FY 2022. Department of Homeland Security, 2022.

212. "Highway Beautification Act." Environmental Working Group, December 2023, https://www.ewg.org/research/highway-beautification-act.

INDEX

The Final End

www.ingramcontent.com/pod-product-compliance
Lightning Source LLC
Chambersburg PA
CBHW080401270326
41927CB00015B/3309